UNDERSTANDING EVERYDAY LIFE

INTERNATIONAL LIBRARY OF SOCIOLOGY
AND SOCIAL RECONSTRUCTION

Founded by Karl Mannheim
Editor W. J. H. Sprott

A catalogue of books available in the INTERNATIONAL LIBRARY OF
SOCIOLOGY AND SOCIAL RECONSTRUCTION and new books in
preparation for the Library will be found at the end of this volume

UNDERSTANDING EVERYDAY LIFE

Toward the reconstruction of sociological knowledge

Edited by
JACK D. DOUGLAS

LONDON
ROUTLEDGE & KEGAN PAUL

First published in Great Britain 1971
by Routledge & Kegan Paul Ltd
Broadway House, 68–74 Carter Lane
London EC4V 5EL
Printed in Great Britain by
Lowe & Brydone (Printers) Ltd., London

ISBN 0 7100 7066 7

Contents

Preface

We are all profoundly involved in everyday life and, because we human beings are necessarily social and thinking animals, we are all profoundly committed to understanding our everyday social lives. Our everyday, common-sense thinking includes an immense number of ideas about the human actors we encounter in our everyday lives. Our common-sense theories of motives, by which we try to explain and, thereby, anticipate and control what others will do, are an obvious example of how extensive and complex these theories are. There are literally hundreds, perhaps thousands, of possible "motives," and each possible motive must be commonsensically analyzed in the context of a number of basic motives and characteristics that are believed applicable to any motive — sincerity and insincerity, honesty and dishonesty, trustworthiness and untrustworthiness, and so on. In this sense, each man is necessarily his own sociologist; and *everyday sociology* is an extremely complex set of facts, ideas, theories, ideologies, and philosophies demanding expert knowledge of those who would practice it well.

It is an obvious question, then, whether there is any special purpose to be served by creating a *discipline* of sociological thought. Would not such a discipline be simply paralleling and competing with everyday sociologies? How would it differ, if at all, from literature or any of the many other forms of thought that are disciplined but firmly grounded in common-sense ideas about man and society? These are the kinds of questions that faced the social thinkers who created sociology as an independent discipline of social thought. The consideration of them in various forms took up a great deal of early "sociological" thought in the nineteenth century. By the end of the nineteenth century those who called themselves sociologists had found the answer that satisfied them and that was to become the basic answer of all of classical (or traditional) sociology. They had created sociology as a "science of society," to be cast in the mold of the classical natural sciences. It is this absolutist mold of classical science that was to remain dominant in sociology and the other social sciences long after it had been destroyed in the natural sciences by the revolutions wrought by relativity and quantum mechanics.

The "obvious" answer to these traditional sociologists was that sociology must be created and developed in exactly the same way they believed the natural sciences were: sociology must be independent of and in opposition to common-sense ideas about man and society. The ideas of common sense were continually derided as imprecise, misleading, unsuited for scientific use, and so on. As is well known, this is the way Durkheim (1954:41–42) began *Suicide*, probably the most famous work of classical, positivistic sociology:

> Since the word "suicide" recurs constantly in the course of conversation, it might be thought that its sense is universally known and that the definition is superfluous. Actually, the words of everyday language, like the concepts they express, are always susceptible of more than one meaning, and the scholar employing them in their accepted use without further definition would risk serious misunderstanding. Not only is their meaning so indefinite as to vary, from case to case, with the needs of argument, but, as the classification from which they derive is not analytic, but merely translates the confused impressions of the crowd, categories of very different sorts of fact are indistinctly combined under the same heading, or similar realities are differently named. So, if we follow common use, we risk distinguishing what should be combined, or combining what should be distinguished, thus mistaking the real afflnities of things, and accordingly misapprehending their nature. . . . But these natural affinities of entities cannot be made clear safely by such superficial examination as produces ordinary terminology; and so the scholar cannot take as the subject of his research roughly assembled groups of facts corresponding to words of common usage. He himself must establish the groups he wishes to study in order to give them the homogeneity and the specific meaning necessary for them to be susceptible of scientific treatment. Thus the botanist, speaking of flowers or fruits, the zoologist of fish or insects, employ these various terms in previously determined senses. . . .
>
> The essential thing is not to express with some precision what the average intelligence terms suicide, but to establish a category of objects permitting this classification, which are objectively established, that is, correspond to a definite aspect of things.

Sociology, then, was to be done outside of and in opposition to common sense and, thus, common-sense sociology. As Durkheim's statement suggests, if we follow "common use" in studying social phenomena, we will surely wind up "misapprehending their nature." But there is a definite flaw in this conception of sociology as a natural science:

Preface

as bodies, human beings may look like material stuff (in the same way rocks and planetary bodies do), but, as thinking bodies, humans are very unlike rocks and planetary bodies. The "forces" that move human beings, *as* humans beings rather than simply as physical bodies, are not gravitational forces or the forces of elementary particles. They are "meaningful stuff." They are internal ideas, feelings, motives. What Durkheim referred to as their nature is largely made up this meaningful stuff.

All human actions of any significance to sociology are meaningful actions. All significant orderings of human phenomena, which alone make any science of those phenomena possible, are the result of some kind of social meanings; and no significant scientific description, analysis, or explanation of those orderings is possible without some fundamental consideration of those social meanings. Although this may appear obvious, it took several centuries of misbegotten mechanistic social theories to convince those dedicated to the absolutist ideal of hard (natural) science (of treating man as an object) that what was commonsensically obvious was also true. By the time Durkheim and the many other founders of classical sociology began writing, the necessarily meaningful nature of all social phenomena was recognized, however vaguely and inconsistently. Geographic determinists, moon-phase theorists, and even gene type theorists have all slowly disappeared from the ranks of social scientists.

But what was a *real* scientist to do with this quintessential form of "subjective" stuff-meanings? It seemed obvious that a scientist would have to reject common-sense meanings, but what then? Durkheim and the other positivists found their solution in treating all social phenomena *as if* they were objects. That is, they looked for a way by which they could study and analyze social phenomena using the traditional methods of classical science (experimental controls, quantification, hypothesis testing, and so on). A way was found. They imposed their "scientific" presuppositions upon the realm of social phenomena, but in doing so they distorted the fundamental nature of human existence—they bootlegged common-sense meanings into their object-like data and theories and created an *as if* science of man.

As I have shown elsewhere (Douglas, 1967), Durkheim was forced by his whole argument to inadvertently rely on the common-sense meanings of each of his fundamental variables (intention, suicide, education, and so on) for the relations he believed existed between those variables and for his explanations of those relations. The man who derided the common-sense meanings of suicide based his book on the subject and his whole argument for classical sociology on the "official statistics" that have always been based on the common-sense meanings of suicide. The man who rejected intention as too subjective for any scientific consideration based his whole work on disembodied numbers (suicide rates) which may look object-like but are actually the outcome of necessarily commonsensical evaluations of the "intentions" of individuals by unseen coroners, police, priests, medical examiners, and other officials. The man who so confidently and arrogantly derided common sense became the captive of common sense. This might be seen as simply another joke played on the hapless creature of reason by the absurdities of reality were it not for the fact that generations of functionalists, structuralists, experimentalists, and other absolutists in the social sciences have followed the same path in creating the *as if* social sciences and were it not for the fact that these "experts" have increasingly used their scientific rhetoric to control our lives through their growing effect on government policies. There is no humor in the specter of technological tyranny.

Rather than imposing an *as if science* on our everyday lives, we must seek to understand everyday life. Rather than explicitly adopting the common-sense understandings of everyday life, or proposing to reject those understandings while covertly building our sociological understanding on them, we must begin all sociological understanding of human existence with an understanding of everyday life gained from a systematic and objective study of the common-sense meanings and actions of everyday life. We must always begin by studying these meaningful social phenomena on their own grounds, but, true to our goal of creating a science of man's existence, we must then seek an ever more general, trans-situational (objective) understanding of everyday life. This is the fundamental program of all phenomenological and existential sociologies.

The accelerating progress in the realization of this revolutionary program has begun to transform the sociological enterprise. This does not mean that we shall now sweep aside all other forms of sociology. All revolutions do produce rhetorical excess, but all revolutions also borrow far more from the ancient regimes than the revolutionaries care to admit. In sociology, as I have argued in Chapter 1, we shall long need certain forms of structural analyses of society that are not thoroughly based on more objective understandings of everyday life, for the simple reason that structural analyses are a practical necessity in a massive and complex society. Moreover, I believe that the calmer perspective of historical analysis will show that this intellectual revolution sought to replace absolutist perspectives on society that, although less true, were quite important in bringing us to this point of revolutionary change.

Preface

Still, the pressing necessity of rebuilding sociology as a scientific discipline is of paramount importance to those now engaged in the creative struggle. A rapidly growing proportion of sociologists has joined in the work of rebuilding the foundations of sociology. This book is intended both to clarify the basic aspects of this work and to contribute further to that work of rebuilding the science of society on a firm foundation.

The essays in this book are critical, theoretical, and empirical. Taken together, I believe they represent the best theory and research being done by those attempting to rebuild sociology. All of these essays share certain fundamental ideas about the scientific inadequacies of the conventional (absolutist) sociologies, and all of them share the fundamental ideas of phenomenological and existential sociology, though to varying degrees. But the reader will find some important differences in basic ideas and in strategies.

I have tried to lay the groundwork for an understanding of the basic issues, agreements, and disagreements in my general essay "Understanding Everyday Life" (Chapter 1). I have also tried to put this work into the general context of the many different kinds of phenomenological and existential sociology.

The other three essays in Part I also deal critically with the fundamental differences between the absolutist social sciences and the phenomenological social sciences, though each does so in a somewhat different way. John Heeren's essay, "Alfred Schutz and the Sociology of Common-Sense Knowledge" (Chapter 2), builds the groundwork for understanding the nature of the phenomenological analyses of common sense as used in everyday life. The essay by Thomas P. Wilson, "Conceptions of Interaction and Forms of Sociological Explanation" (Chapter 3), is one of the most systematic critical analyses of the traditional forms of sociological explanation. In "The Everyday World as a Phenomenon" (Chapter 4), Don Zimmerman and Melvin Pollner show exactly what the commitment to taking the theoretic stance toward everyday life (dealing with everyday life as a phenomenon) consists of and how it differs from the traditional use of everyday understandings as resource and result in sociological works.

The four essays in Part II provide a systematic analysis of the traditional and the phenomenological analyses of language and meaning. The essay by Lawrence Wieder, "On Meaning by Rule" (Chapter 5), and the essay by Aaron Cicourel, "The Acquisition of Social Structure: Toward a Developmental Sociology of Language and Meaning" (Chapter 6), deal with general theoretical issues. Roy Turner's essay, "Words, Utterances and Activities" (Chapter 7), and Matthew Speier's "The Everyday World of the Child" (Chapter 8) deal with more specific issues of theory in relation to their own concrete research on language use.

The two essays in Part III by Don Zimmerman (Chapter 9) and Peter Manning (Chapter 10) deal with some fundamental issues concerning the nature of rules and their use in organized activities. They show the fundamental inadequacies of the absolutist theory of the nature and uses of social rules in such organized activities.

Parts IV and V are concerned with important general questions about sociological theory. The three essays in Part IV by Norman Denzin, Don Zimmerman, and Lawrence Wieder attempt to clarify the fundamental differences and similarities between symbolic interactionism and ethnomethodology. The two essays in Part V by Alan Blum and Peter McHugh deal with the most general level of questions concerning the nature of sociological theory and truth.

Inevitably, many questions are merely touched upon and their solutions left programmatic. But I believe there is little doubt that the essays in this work make a very important contribution to the reconstruction of sociological knowledge, partly by providing answers to some fundamental questions they raise but even more by raising fundamental questions many sociologists have not thought of, questions we are convinced they will be working to answer for many decades to come.

Jack D. Douglas

PART ONE

Absolutist Sociologies and Phenomenological Sociologies

Understanding Everyday Life

All of sociology necessarily begins with the understanding of everyday life, and all of sociology is directed either to increasing our understanding of everyday life or, more practically, to improving our everyday lives. Yet, until quite recently, few sociologists realized that the understanding of everyday life must be the foundation of all sociological research and theory; and fewer still acted in accord with this crucial fact. The reasons for this were grounded in the complex web of background assumptions of the traditional sociological enterprise, which in turn were grounded in the background assumptions of classical science and of the official organizations of control in Western societies.

In recent years the rapidly growing research and analysis of everyday life have begun to transform the nature of the entire sociological enterprise. It is my primary purpose here to show why this transformation has been necessary and just what radical changes have, as a consequence, been made in the traditional sociological perspective on man and society.

Understanding Everyday Life as the Foundation of All Sociology

For several fundamental reasons, sociology, like all disciplines that purport to be theoretical and applied sciences of human action, necessarily begins and ends with the understanding of everyday life. Most important, even when sociologists have overtly opposed their work to the homilies of everyday common sense, they have covertly used common-sense understandings of everyday life to provide the fundamental data — the social meanings — of their research and theory, for the simple reason that there is no other way to "get at" the social meanings involved in social actions.

3

There was a time when many social scientists, including some who thought of themselves as sociologists, proposed to study and explain human actions entirely in terms of externally perceived events. But these halcyon days of the social mechanists are long since dead. Today there are few social scientists, other than the Skinnerians who have shown great wisdom in restricting their behavioristic research to the humble pigeon, who would try to describe or explain human actions without making some fundamental reference to what Collingwood called the inside, or the internal state, of the actor. The academic psychologists, still experiencing the nineteenth-century fears of the "unscientific subjectivism" of "mental states," have introduced various intervening variables, or organismic states, as a way of obliquely considering the internal states of the actor. But these psychologists' neo-mechanistic approach to the "internal states" has been so useless in explaining human social action that it has forced them to largely restrict their research and theories to the docile white rat, which has been purposefully bred to fit the theoretical presuppositions lying behind the maze. Sociologists, being unalterably stuck with human social actors, have felt forced to give ever greater consideration to the internal (symbolic) states of their actors. However much some sociologists today may be constrained in their thinking by the tatters and remnants of nineteenth-century positivism, there is no doubt that almost all of them agree that social actions are *meaningful* actions, that is, that they must be studied and explained in terms of their situations and their meanings to the actors themselves. The disputes over the kinds of meanings involved and the ways in which they are to be determined are fundamental, but there is now little dispute among sociologists over the proposition that social meanings are in some way the fundamental determinants of social actions.

A basic question for all sociologists becomes that of how these social meanings are to be determined: how are we to truthfully and reliably get at this fundamental data of all our sociological research and theory? The *only* truthful answer is that in some way we must rely upon our understandings of everyday life, gained through direct observations of that life and always involving the use of our own common-sense understandings derived from our direct involvements in it.

The only major source of disagreement with this proposition today comes from the dwindling ranks of those sociologists who are still committed to the Durkheimian (sociologistic) adage that the social must be explained socially. This adage has traditionally been interpreted as an attack on the supposed reductionism of social psychologists and, more recently, has been turned against those who argue for the primacy of understanding everyday life in *all* sociological theory. These arguments today are normally presented as defenses of macrosociology, structuralism, social systems analysis, comparative analysis, and the statistical-hypothetical analysis of social rates, all of which are often seen by their proponents as independent of, or even in opposition to, microsociology, situationalism, or reductionism.

All of these arguments against the basic proposition that *all* of the *science* of sociology *necessarily* begins with the understanding of everyday life share one simple but fundamental failure. They have all failed to follow their empirical evidence (or what they purport to be empirical evidence) back to its actual source. Whenever we do this, we find that there is only one source of empirical evidence for all of sociology (once we agree that social meanings are necessarily a form of evidence we are going to use in our theories). And that source is our understanding of everyday life. A brief examination of the original source of the major forms of empirical evidence used in the macroanalyses will easily demonstrate this.

1) Perhaps the oldest source of pseudoempirical evidence concerning social meanings used by the macroanalysts (and, unfortunately, by some systems analysts and behaviorists) is the presumed social omniscience of the analysts themselves. This is the evidence on social meanings that the analyst provides "from his own mind." (In this instance they are using what used to be pejoratively called armchair sociology.) That is, the analyst provides the social meanings he needs to construct or test his theory from his own mind, without any reference to concrete instances of empirical observations. But this implicit assumption of sociological omniscience, which I have analyzed more thoroughly in *American Social Order,*[1] is obviously contrary to the basic rules of positivistic science, so the macroanalysts who have used this source have always devised means of hiding the subjective source of such evidence. These means always involve constructing the appearance of empirical observation. A classical example was Durkheim's (1951) use of what Peristiany so rightly called *petitio princippi* to make his imputations of social meanings (such as the meanings of education to Jews) *appear to be* derived from some previous scientific observations of those meanings, whereas in fact any previous observations could only have been the sociologist's own common-sense experience of that realm of everyday life. (Durkheim's everyday experience with Jews and education would be a good example.)[2] Once we penetrate these rhetorically constructed

1. See especially Chapter 2.
2. Durkheim's uses of such devices as *petitio princippi* to impute social meanings to official social rates have been analyzed previously in Douglas (1967: especially 3–78).

B

appearances and recognize that the macroanalyst is really drawing on his own mind for the social meanings he is using to explain the actions of his social actors, it is easy to see that his own understanding of everyday life, derived from his common-sense experience, is the only source of his evidence on social meanings.

2) A third form of "evidence" commonly used by macroanalysts to provide the social meanings for their analyses is that of social rates, such as statistical rates of suicide, delinquency, and divorce. These social rates are commonly presented as derived independently of any understanding of everyday life and, in fact, are often used by the macroanalysts to "demonstrate the fallacies of common-sense understandings of everyday life." Durkheim's use of the "official social rates of suicide" is a classic example, but one could easily note many other works that share this approach.[3]

The social rates are taken by these macroanalysts to be products of the operation of the society as a whole. The rates are supposed to be the probabilistic outputs of the normal operation of the "social system," in a manner directly analogous to the way in which a closed system of gases produces a temperature reading on a thermometer. The social rate, then, is to be a direct representation of the state of the whole system at any given time. The macroanalyst, therefore, believes that he can use these rates to analyze the socially meaningful states of the whole system. But there are two fallacies in this argument.

First, the macroanalyst has been seduced by the appearance of "thing-like fact" given by numbers. As long as we merely take numbers at face value, as reproduced in official reports, they do indeed look like "hard facts" representing the overall workings of the social system; but it has never been good scientific practice to take any information at face value, and certainly not information constructed in secret by bureaucrats. (We can hardly imagine Galileo or Newton working with astronomical data published in the official records of court astrologers. In fact, it was in good part precisely because they were able to use the new evidence provided by Tycho Brahe and by the telescope, rather than the ancient evidence that had supported the heliocentric theories, that they developed their radically different theories.) Once we follow the "disembodied numbers" back to their sources to see how they were arrived at and what, therefore, they actually represent, we find that they are

---

3. I have examined the great mass of evidence available on the nature of social rates of "moral phenomena" in two works. See Douglas (1967: especially 163–234; 1971a: especially Chapters 3 and 4). The evidence now available concerning the real nature of "social rates" includes a number of important empirical studies. See especially Cicourel (1968). Also see the material reported from my study of coroners and medical examiners in Douglas (1971a: Chapters 3 and 4).

based on the most subjective of all possible forms of activity. This is especially true in the case of suicide statistics, which are the result of coroners' evaluations of the "intentions" of the actors involved,[4] but it is also true of all forms of moral statistics constructed by officials. We find, therefore, that the numbers that appear to be hard facts about the social system states are in fact based on officials' common-sense under-standings of everyday life. The macroanalyst has merely replaced his own common-sense understandings of everyday life with those of un-known officials.

Second, even if this were not the case, the macroanalyst could not validly infer the social meanings of such social rates without in some way making use of his, or someone's, understandings of everyday life. He would have nothing but numbers of events, which must themselves be defined in terms of understandings of everyday events if he is ever to relate his analyses to everyday events. The social meanings of those events would still have to be provided. When we look, for example, at how Durkheim provided those social meanings, we find that ad hoc procedures were used to arbitrarily apply common-sense understandings of everyday life to those social rates, though these common-sense under-standings were sometimes presented in the guise of theory.[5]

3) A third form of macroanalysis by which the sociologist often purports to avoid or supercede understandings of everyday life is found in surveys, especially the now omnipresent questionnaire survey. The survey, which involves the use of some random or stratified sampling of the whole society or social subgroup, is supposed to provide scientific data about the overall state of the system. But the case for surveys, especially questionnaire surveys, as a form of macrodata independent of understanding of everyday life is very weak. Though these under-standings are normally left quite implicit, unexamined, and com-monsensical, they are based in several ways on understandings of every-day life. First, as in the case of all other macroanalyses, the theoretical questions or hypotheses to which the surveys are directed are in fact derived from very old common-sense understandings of everyday life. Second, the basic idea of surveys developed from such common-sense questionings as those found in the work of public hygienists and report-

4. The evidence for this argument that coroners are making use of their common-sense understanding of everyday life to evaluate the "intentions" of actors before they will impute suicide as the cause of death has been presented in Douglas (1971a: Chapters 3 and 4).

5. I have previously analyzed the ways in which common-sense theories are commonly presented as abstract theories with no recognition of the origins of the "abstract theories" in the common-sense theories. See for example, the consideration of this in Douglas (1971a: Chapter 2).

ers doing interviews. Third, surveys presuppose an adequate common-sense understanding of everyday life that will enable the analyst to
competently interact with the members of the society to get valid (truthful) responses from them. More specifically, as Cicourel (1964) and
Churchill[6] have argued, questionnaire surveys assume a competent use
of the language, a vastly complex common-sense understanding of how
to ask questions, how to detect lying, how to interpret answers, and so
on. Fourth, the analysis of survey results through coding, factor
analysis, and so on, depends implicitly on the use of common-sense
understandings of everyday life to provide the real (underlying) meanings of the subjects' responses.

4) The fourth commonly used argument of the macroanalysts, the
argument that there exist *higher levels of order* in social phenomena, is
probably the most frequently used today and is certainly the most subtle.
This is the argument used by many comparative theorists and institutionalists to try to free themselves from the prior analysis of everyday life. They use this argument to justify their going directly to an
analysis of the society as a whole or the institutional groups as a whole,
rather than starting with an analysis of the lower-level orderings found in
everyday life and proceeding to an analysis of higher levels of social
ordering only when they have solved the problems of the lower levels.

There are two fundamental parts to this argument: (1) while it may in
fact be the case that all higher levels of orderings of social phenomena
are ultimately determined by lower levels of orderings, the higher levels
have their own interdependencies, so that they can be considered independent of the lower levels in this sense; and (2), at the least, it is
possible to study and analyze the higher levels independently of the
lower levels. Macroanalysts have often argued that there is an analogy
between ways in which natural scientists can study and analyze molecu-
lar interactions (higher levels of order) independently of atomic interactions (lower levels of order) and atomic interactions independently
of the interactions of subatomic particles (an even lower level of order).

The traditional form of this argument, contained in the adage that one
must study the social socially, committed the fallacy of social realism
found in Durkheim's early works, including the early editions of *Suicide,*[7] and go back to much earlier forms of social organicism, especially
to Rousseau's idea of collective conscience. The hypothesis of social

6. Lindsey Churchill has been doing extensive work on the nature of questionnaires
and questioning in our society and will publish a volume with The Russell Sage Foundation
on questioning in the near future. My own understanding of this work has largely been
gained through personal communication.
7. I have previously analyzed Durkheim's ideas about "social realism" in Douglas
(1967).

realism involves the fallacy of treating society *as if* it is somehow a separate level of existence, outside of the hearts and minds of live-and-breathing human beings; and constitutes the most extreme form of the *absolutist perspective on society*.[8] There are few comparativists or institutionalists today who would accept this social realism. Instead, most would agree with comparativists such as Levy (1952), who has argued that these theories are merely directed at different levels of analysis or generality and that the higher levels of order (or patterning) are *analytical* distinctions, not concrete distinctions, as the social realists believed. (Analogously, no natural scientist would argue that the molecules exist outside of and independently of their atomic and subatomic constituents, an argument that Lacombe (1926) long ago made against Durkheim's social realism.)

In this more sophisticated form of the argument, the macroanalysts who believe they can study and analyze whole societies or whole (institutional) groups independently of any understandings of everyday common-sense life are simply arguing that they can analyze the society or institutional group without having to make use of any understanding of everyday life. But, even if it made sense to argue that one could analyze the larger patterns of social life without first adequately understanding the smaller (everyday life) patterns, it still would not make sense to argue that one could validly and reliably determine what those larger patterns are without in some way making use of prior determinations of the nature of everyday communications in that society or group. This is true for the simple reason that *there is no way of getting at the social meanings from which one either implicitly or explicitly infers the larger patterns except through some form of communication with the members of that society or group; and, to be valid and reliable, any such communication with the members presupposes an understanding of their language, their uses of that language, their own understandings of what the people doing the observations are up to, and so on almost endlessly.* How, for example, could we possibly get valid and reliable determinations of the meanings of work or sex to the Japanese without understanding how to go about asking a Japanese person about work or sex in order to get "truthful" answers? But this is precisely the sort of thing

8. The "absolutist perspective on society" is the general phrase I have used to refer to the classical sociological perspective on society, which assumes that human actions are independent of the specific situations in which they occur, in the sense that they are determined by some factors outside of the situation and outside of the individual's committing the actions. The absolutist perspective, of course, goes back to the absolutist ideas about God's relation to man to be found in traditional Christianity. Absolutist ideas are also to be found in many different realms in Western thought, as, for example, in the ideas about absolutist governments analyzed by historians and political scientists for a very long time.

that constitutes part of what we have called understanding everyday life.[9]

In fact, then, the macroanalyst has found no escape from basing his analyses on some prior understanding of everyday life. That many of them have thought they had is probably due largely to their use of second-hand information, comparable to the social-rate analysts' dependence on information provided them by the official statisticians. They have often made use of information provided them by members of that society or by outsiders who have become "experts" on that society, largely through having lived in the society for years. It is these members of the society, or the experts who have become partial members, who have actually made use of common-sense understandings of everyday life in trying to provide information that those analyzing larger patterns of the society can use in their work. This in no way diminishes the dependence on understandings of everyday life, and it once again makes the sociologist dependent on information for which he cannot really determine the reliability and validity (unless he has some adequate study of everyday life that has provided him with the understanding he needs to make that determination of adequacy).

5) Those studies making use of historical data as their source for doing comparative analyses are a special case of number four above. All historical analyses are, of course, ultimately based on the primary source material, which consists entirely of member accounts. These accounts, like all member accounts, presuppose an adequate understanding of everyday life by the intended readers. Historical accounts, then, can be looked at as coded messages that can be adequately decoded only by one who already understands the code — the understandings of everyday life presumed by the coder.

While historical accounts are a special form of number four, they also pose a special problem that probably can never be solved. That is, because the messages presuppose an understanding of everyday life, while that very everyday life can never be adequately reached through any means other than those accounts themselves (or similar accounts that make the same presuppositions), it is clear that we can never reconstruct the exact meanings given to the messages by the original communicators. We can never know "how it really was" in another historical period because we can never know what the exact context of everyday life was. This is why most historians have come to recognize that we must always make use of our common-sense understandings,

9. The better comparative analysts, of course, have come increasingly to understand the importance of understanding everyday life in other societies for constructing valid sociological information about those societies. I have gained valuable insight into this from my discussions with Robert Cole.

gained from our everyday experience in our own time, to construct the meanings of historical accounts. This is why they have recognized that history must always remain much more inexact and less cumulative than those social disciplines that can make repeated (and, to some extent, controlled) forays into the realm of everyday life of the society they are studying. (It is only our belief that there is always something similar, something "human," about any form of everyday life that allows us to believe that historical analyses make sense at all. This belief in the highly transsituational possibilities of human meanings, which we shall analyze below, seems partially justified; but the problems are far more awesome than most historical analysts have realized, because they have not seen how much their analyses of the meanings of the primary source material are dependent on presumed understandings of everyday life.)

We see, then, that the macroanalysts have in fact always made either an implicit or an explicit use of common-sense understandings of everyday life in their analyses. Only one conclusion is justified; *Any scientific understanding of human action, at whatever level of ordering or generality, must begin with and be built upon an understanding of the everyday life of the members performing those actions.* (To fail to see this and to act in accord with it is to commit what we might call the *fallacy of abstractionism,* that is, the fallacy of believing that you can know in a more abstract form what you do not know in the particular form.)

This does not mean that we must stop all macroanalysis until we have a thorough scientific understanding of everyday life. After all, the real reason we are interested in macroanalysis in the first place is that it is of great practical importance to us as members of our society. It is only some form of analysis of general patterns and structures that enables us to know what is going on across the far reaches of our social world so that we can take practical steps to try to control our social world in a way that will enable us to achieve our goals in that world.[10] It is only some form of patterned or structural analysis of democracy, fascism, communism, and so on that allows us to make rational choices that can affect all of our everyday lives.[11] We must continue to do macroanalysis for very pressing practical reasons.

But this argument means that we must stop treating macroanalyses *as if* they were scientific arguments, that is, arguments based on carefully done, systematic observations of concrete phenomena. Above all, it means that we must stop treating such structural analyses as if they somehow constitute "*the* sociological imigination" and make use of

10. I have previously dealt with the practical importance of structural analyses. See, for example, "Freedom and Tyranny in a Technological Society" in Douglas (1970e), "Crime and Justice in American Society" in Douglas (1970c), and Douglas (1970b).

11. See "The Relevance of Sociology," in Douglas (1970a).

"hard data," while those who do systematic observations of everyday life and analyze from these observations the meanings of things to the members are treated *as if* they were "reductionists" making use of "soft data." The truth is the exact opposite. *The only valid and reliable (or hard, scientific) evidence concerning socially meaningful phenomena we can possibly have is that based ultimately on systematic observations and analyses of everyday life.* Anything else, certainly anything more abstract, can be valid and reliable only to the extent that it builds on the evidence provided by such studies of everyday life. (In a way, this is to say that the sociologists of everyday life found the social sciences on their heads and have turned them upright; they have finally begun the task of starting with first things first rather than *presupposing* adequate answers to all of the fundamental questions and going on from there.)

It must be the task of the macroanalysts to continually reorient and rebuild their studies, within the practical constraints posed by the pressing social problems facing us, on the understandings of everyday life provided by those who are doing these scientific studies of everyday life. To do anything less is not only to commit a fundamental fallacy or, even worse, to be intellectually dishonest, it is also to fail to make use of the only kinds of information that in the long run will make their ideas and theories truly practical. (As I have also argued (Douglas, 1970a), only a scientific knowledge of the realm of practical affairs, that is, everyday life, will ever allow us to know how to apply "knowledge" to that realm of practical affairs.)

At the same time, the analysts of everyday life must become increasingly concerned with the ways in which human beings construct order across their social situations, rather than concentrating so exclusively upon descriptions of single situations and upon analyses of actions bounded by a simple situation. To do less would be to fail to consider a crucial aspect of human reality and to doom the effort to practical irrelevance.[12]

Everyday Life As A Phenomenon: The Natural Stance And the Theoretic Stance

We see, then, that we have no choice in our point of departure. We must agree that social phenomena must be studied in some way as (subjectively) meaningful phenomena and that our common goal as sociologists is

12. I have previously tried (Douglas, 1971a) to synthesize a consideration of everyday life situations with transsituational orderings. I have also presented some of the argument concerning the need to synthesize the consideration of everyday situations with the consideration of the transsituational, or "structural," factors and have criticized the two extreme positions in Douglas (1970b).

to create a science of social actions. We then find that any scientific study of these phenomena necessarily begins with the systematic observation and analysis of everyday life, so this is where we necessarily begin. Finding the beginning, the fundamental questions to ask of nature, is always the most difficult thing for any science to accomplish. It has taken social scientists innumerable missteps, most of them inspired by simplistic analogies with the natural sciences, in the first century and half of their existence to find their proper beginning. Those of us who have recapitulated these mistakes in our own lives know the difficulties and the anguish of this search. And we know that we can never be certain that we have found a sure path to the knowledge we seek, but we feel that we have reached at least one clear and simple — fundamental — truth in all of our uncertainty. We have found our beginning in the analysis of everyday life. But where do we go from here? What is the best strategy for gaining an even better, a more scientific, understanding of everyday life?

The crucial questions we face in adopting a strategy for studying everyday life are what stance shall we adopt toward everyday life and what methods of analysis shall we use. The two questions are to some extent independent, but they also partially overlap because the stance or orientation we adopt toward everyday life from the beginning becomes an important determinant of our methods of analysis.

The first important point to note is that, instead of allowing our methods to determine our stance toward everyday life, we allow our stance to determine our methods. This is the opposite of the classical scientific approach to analyzing man. The classical approach was to assume that there is only one general set of criteria for scientific validity or truth and that it was embodied in the classical works of the natural sciences.

Thus the early social scientists adopted a conscious policy of studying man in the same way one would study any physical object. Having presupposed these methods, they adopted the stance most in accord with them. They adopted the absolutist perspective on man and society. That is, they viewed man as an object, causally determined (totally) by forces outside of his self. In accord with this perspective, they adopted an *absolutist (or objectivist) stance* toward everyday life.[13] They assumed that the phenomena of everyday life could and should be studied only in terms of clear and distinct (scientific) formal categories defined by them in advance of their studies. They assumed that these categories should be both independent of and in opposition to the common-sense

13. For the complete discussion of the absolutist stance toward everyday life, see Douglas (1971a: Chapter 2).

categories of men in everyday life. They assumed that all decisions about how one would decide that his results were true or false could and should be made in advance of studies of the everyday phenomena. And they assumed that the goal should be one of controlling the everyday phenomena in the way scientists seek to control the natural world. Sociologists will readily recognize the great similarity between these classical ideas and those stated so clearly in the "methodological ideals" of many of today's statistics and methods textbooks (Blalock's widely used text is a good example).[14] There is a direct historical lineage between these classical, "scientistic" ideas, which go back to the seventeenth century, and the methods of present-day positivistic sociologists, though these present-day methodologists normally think of themselves as modern and "working on the frontiers of sociological knowledge."[15] In general, the absolutist stance subsumed the everyday world under the methods of science and, in doing so, its users never realized that the everyday phenomena they observed were *scientified* phenomena. (The ultimate ideal, of course, has always been total experimental control. And, while only the academic psychologists have achieved this grand ideal with their carefully bred maze-rats and Skinner box pigeons, many sociologists, such as George Homans (1961), have extrapolated the beautifully simple theories derived from these mazes to all human action. If man cannot yet be put in the maze, at least we can assume that that is where he really belongs.)

The opposite extreme from the absolutist stance is the *natural stance*. The natural stance is that supposedly taken by men in everyday life, though whether or not they in fact take this stance is certainly an empirical question. It is the stance in which the everyday world is taken for granted as it is experienced in everyday life. It is that stance taken by the individual within the stream of everyday life. It is a stance that does not raise serious and persistent questions concerning the nature of the everyday experience but, instead, takes that experience as a fact. Husserl gave the idea its classical formulation:

   I find continually present and standing over against me the one spatio-temporal fact-world to which I myself belong, as do all other men

14. While the textbooks on statistics generally present an absolutist ideal of methods, they also commonly involve some recognition of the "practical constraints" of real research projects. Those statisticians who have themselves done a good deal of research, especially survey research, have been quite aware of the ways in which practical considerations come to determine the actual exercise of their activities as researchers. They are, therefore, recognizing that their research activities are grounded in everyday life, and the best of them have always accepted this fact. (I have gained a great deal of insight into this from my talks with Frederick Stephan.)

15. I have shown some of these relations between much earlier forms of social thought and contemporary forms of social thought in Douglas (1967).

found in it and related in the same way to it. This 'fact-world' as the word already tells us, I find *to be out there,* and also *take it just as it gives itself to me as something that exists out there.* All doubting and rejecting of the data of the natural world leaves standing the *general thesis of the natural stand-point.* 'The' world is as fact-world always there; at the most it is at odd points 'other' than I supposed, this or that under such names as 'illusion,' 'hallucination,' and the like, must be stuck *out of it,* so to speak; but the 'it' remains ever, in the sense of the general thesis, a world that has its being out there.[16]

The third general kind of stance toward the everyday world, as proposed by all phenomenologists since Husserl, is the *theoretic stance.*[17] To take the theoretic stance toward the everyday world is to stand back from, to reflect upon, to re-view the experience taken for granted in the natural stance. To take the theoretic stance is to treat the everyday world as a phenomenon, as Zimmerman and Pollner have put it (see Chapter 4 in this volume). At the most basic level, at its beginning, taking the theoretic stance involves what Husserl called the "phenomenological suspension" (or *epoché*). Natanson (1962: pp. 12-13.) has given what is probably the best general description of this phenomenological suspension:

> When I suspend or place in abeyance my common-sense belief in reality, I merely decide to make no use of the thesis which ordinarily guides our total cognitive and conative life; but this thesis is not to be understood as a proposition or a formulated article of faith. Rather, it is the unstated, utterly implicit theme of our common-sense relatedness to reality. . . .
>
> Phenomenological suspension or, to use Husserl's term, *epoché*, consists in making explicit to consciousness the thesis which unconsciously underlies every individual judgment made within ordinary life about reality. Suspension means first of all coming into awareness of the very meaning of the natural attitude itself. Negatively put, suspension of the General Thesis of the natural standpoint most certainly does not include or signify a denial of the reality of the external world or of the validity of our ordinary experience within it. Rather, as phenomenologist I place in phenomenological doubt (which is not psychological doubt) my traditional common-sense taking for granted of the very reality of the world within which things and events are noted and appraised. Suspension, then, involves a shift in modes of attention. The same reality I took for granted in typical fashion in naive attitude I now re-view in phenomenological attitude. The real world, everyday existence, etc., do not mysteriously vanish under *epoché*; they are merely seen in terms of a perspective hitherto unimagined and even unimaginable in common-sense terms. . . .

16. This quote is taken from Natanson (1962:34–44).

17. For a discussion of the relations and differences between the natural stance and the theoretical stance in sociology see Douglas (1971a: Chapter 3).

Epoché is the necessary condition to all other phenomenological procedures, for it guarantees the freedom of a starting point which refuses to remain within the metaphysical orientation of common-sense. And further, *epoché* is the clue to phenomenological method to the extent that it points to the kind of descriptive neutrality phenomenology encourages.

The commitment to the theoretic stance toward everyday experience is of crucial importance in determining the methods used to study everyday life and the further development of one's ideas about everyday life. The importance of the stance in these respects can be seen most clearly from an examination of the similarities and dissimilarities between sociology done from the theoretic standpoint and sociology done from the naturalistic standpoint.

The first fundamental methodological commitment of those phenomenological sociologists committed to taking the theoretic stance toward everyday life is to *study the phenomena of everyday life on their own terms, or to make use only of methods of observation and analysis that retain the integrity of the phenomena.* This means most simply that the phenomena to be studied must be the phenomena as experienced in everyday life, not phenomena created by (or strained through) experimental situations.[18] (The argument below that human actions are highly situational, and that human actors act in accord with their constructions of meanings for the concrete situations they face, will show further why experimentally induced acts cannot be taken as representative of everyday acts.) This is the basis of all phenomenological or existential methods.

The initial commitment to studying the phenomena on their own grounds separates all phenomenological or existential sociologies not only from the absolutist sociologies, such as structural-functionalism, but also from all of the behavioral perspectives on everyday life, which are best represented by some of the behavioral symbolic interactionists who mistakenly (?) see themselves as descended from George Herbert Mead.

Mead's works (1932, 1934, 1936), which have been among the most influential in American sociology in recent years, pose a problem for any analyst, for the simple reason that they incorporate a fundamental conflict in Mead's thought between social behaviorism and more phenomenologically oriented ideas. This problem is compounded and made very relevant to current sociological thought by the fact that this conflict has persisted in the work of many of the interactionist sociologists.

18. It is possible that we may eventually have a sufficiently detailed understanding of human action to be able to anticipate and thereby discount the effects of experimental situations on human actions. At that time we might find it worthwhile to make use of certain kinds of experimental situations to study human action. At the present time, however, experimental studies, such as small-group studies of human action, cannot be expected to have any bearing on human action outside of such experimental situations.

Maurice Natanson (1956), who is not only a phenomenologist but is also the person who wrote what is probably the best analysis of Mead's thought, has seen this very clearly and has proposed the most reasonable explanation of it:

> But both the unsystematic and fragmentary character of Mead's work and the related fact that his work has undergone the editing of his students and colleagues raise important questions. One such fundamental question is whether Mead is characterized as a "social behaviorist," for this is the tag that has been placed on him by most of his editors and followers (a notable exception is Professor Arthur E. Murphy, the editor of *The Philosophy of the Present*). A full and proper understanding of Mead's work depends on the answer to this question.
>
> My line of argument is that Mead is somewhat the captive of his interpreters and that this captivity is especially unfortunate, since a close reading of Mead's works reveals a wealth of insights that by far transcends even the broadest conception of behaviorism. The critique I will offer is intended to be an immanent criticism; it consists essentially in showing that there are fundamentally irreconcilable tendencies in Mead's position which create internal strains and ambiguities. Perhaps the major focus of these internal contradictions is the life-long difficulty Mead had in reconciling his early but deep-rooted behaviorism with the range of ideas he developed later which simply could not be handled within a behavioristic framework.

We must, then, make a basic distinction between the two parallel, but conflicting, strains of interactionist thought: *behavioral interactionism* and *phenomenological interactionism*. Both strains take everyday life as *the* fundamental human and sociological reality, but they then lead in opposite directions. While behavioral interactionism shares with phenomenological interactionism the commitment to take everyday life as *the* human reality rather than as some abstract structure created by the sociologist, behavioral interactionism immediately proceeds to impose ordering concepts and hypothetical forms of reasoning upon the everyday world, rather than seeking to describe and analyze the ordering concepts and forms of reason of the social actors.

Contemporary interactionists differ in the degree to which they emphasize one strain or the other, but almost without exception they have failed to see the conflicts between the two and, because of this, have often been tempted to use positivistic methods of observation and analysis, without seeing how this imposes a structure on everyday life that vitiates the other, more phenomenological, goals of their work. Some of the interactionists, especially Herbert Blumer,[19] have generally

---

19. Blumer's work has almost all been done from the phenomenological interactionist perspective, but some of his very recent works sound much more positivistic. The only question is how much this is an effect of the terminology used and how much of it is a change in the nature of his thought.

done phenomenological interactionism. Others, such as Howard Becker, have shown a tendency to move increasingly in the direction of phenomenological interactionism. (This is seen especially in Becker's (1963) movement from some of the behavioristic (causal) ideas of learning theory in his discussion of becoming a marijuana user to his more phenomenological ideas about the problems of labeling.) Others, such as Lofland (1969), shift back and forth between extreme positivism and Blumer's more phenomenological ideas.

The general problem of the interactionist tradition of thought and research in sociology is that its practitioners have rarely seen clearly and consistently the fundamental theoretical and methodological differences between a positivistic (absolutist) sociology and a phenomenological or existential sociology. As a result, their works are repeatedly vitiated by allowing positivistic methods and ideas to dominate and distort the phenomenological strain in Mead's own works. This is seen especially in their immediate and persistent concern with the "causation" of items of behavior (such as opiate addiction[20] and marijuana use[21]), the easy use of modified ideas of hypothesis testing and verification, the imposition of ideas of self-lodging on the social actors,[22] the immediate (and unexplicated) translation of everyday statements into abstract, theoretical statements (such as "defined as pleasurable"),[23] and so on.

Certainly the symbolic interactionists first discovered some important ideas about everyday life that have been borne out by more recent phenomenological investigations; and certainly the honor of first systematically taking everyday life (interaction) as the primary reality of man — and of sociology — will always be theirs. But there remains a great difference between taking everyday life as the primary reality (but partially studying this reality with conventional absolutist methods and ideas) and systematically studying it in such ways as to consistently retain the integrity of the phenomena. For this reason, in spite of certain important points of similarity between symbolic interactionism and ethnomethodology, there can be no genuine synthesis of the *two as a whole*, as was proposed recently by Norman Denzin (1969). Only the failure to see the basic commitment of Garfinkel's form of ethnomethodology to studying the phenomena on their own grounds, combined with a failure to see the strong behavioral strain in interactionism, would lead to this conclusion. (Zimmerman and Wieder's argument in Chapter 12 concerning the fundamental difference between the traditional, or structural, sociological analysis of "the problem of order" and Garfinkel's analysis

20. See especially Lindesmith (1947).
21. See Becker's (1963) discussion of marijuana use.
22. See the discussion of "self-lodging" in Denzin (1969:922–934).
23. Becker (1963) has explained marijuana use largely in terms of the social "definitions of it as pleasureable."

of "order" in terms of how the members go about presenting the features of order to each other are excellent examples of this.)

However, insofar as we interpret (or *re*interpret) Mead's symbolic interactionism as fundamentally phenomenological, we can argue that he and many of his successors have indeed retained the integrity of the phenomena and helped to provide the foundation for our studies of everyday life. This was the conclusion Natanson (1956:3-4) ultimately reached, and one which Denzin and others actually share:

> Moving within this style and outlook, my critique of Mead endeavors to illuminate its ultimate intent. It is my conviction that if it is once seen that Mead's position is not properly characterized as that of "social behaviorism," that, indeed, his theory of mind, of self, of society, of Act, of time, and of sociality is in all cases a transcension of the behavioristic framework, then Mead's status in the history of ideas comes into relief. As Mead moved in his development from such thinkers as James, Cooley, and Dewey, to philosophers like Bergson, Alexander, and Whitehead, so his thought is a movement from a problematic empiricism toward an idealistic and subjectivistic account of the nature of social reality. Implicit throughout my study is the attempt to show that almost all of the fundamental themes Mead explores bear amazing resemblance to the problems of phenomenological philosophizing in the tradition of Edmund Husserl. The greatest injustice that has been done to Mead, it seems to me, is that precisely these problems have been obscured in labeling Mead a "social behaviorist" and in treating his philosophy as simply another expression of pragmatism or naturalism.
>
> In conclusion, Mead's work may be characterized as a continual and persistent return to the phenomena of social reality in an effort to comprehend these phenomena and to describe them truly.

If we accept this interpretation of Mead's work, as I believe we should, we then find (phenomenological) interactionism to share with recent phenomenological sociologies both the commitment to the theoretic stance and the commitment to retain the integrity of the phenomena. But these two commitments sometimes do not go together in contemporary sociological thought, a fact that leads many sociologists to confuse the phenomenological studies and analyses of everyday life with other forms of analyses of everyday life. The commitment to *studying the phenomena on their own grounds* is by no means the exclusive property of those who take the theoretic (phenomenological) stance toward everyday life. It is shared equally by that kind of sociology Matza calls *naturalistic sociology* (or sociological naturalism). Naturalistic sociology, which goes back to the case studies of "immorality" in nineteenth-century Europe and to many studies done by the Chicago sociologists in the 1920's and later, also has the commitment to "remain true to the nature of the phenomenon under study or scrutiny." As Matza (1969:5) argues:

> So conceived, naturalism stands against all forms of philosophical general-

ization. Its loyalty is *to the world* with whatever measure of variety or universality happens to inhere in it. Naturalism does not and cannot commit itself to eternal preconceptions regarding the nature of phenomena. Consequently, it does not and cannot commit itself to any single preferred method for engaging and scrutinizing phenomena. It stands for observation or engagement of course for that is implicit in fidelity to the natural world. But naturalistic observation may also include experience and introspection, the methods traditionally associated with subjectivism.

But the commitment of phenomenological and existential sociology to taking the theoretic stance toward the everyday world leads to goals and methods that are basically different from those of naturalistic sociology. If one's only basic goal is to remain true to the phenomena, then there is no basic difference between one's goals and methods and those of the traditional humanistic perspective, which is certainly a disciplined form of thought but one that is thoroughly grounded in the natural stance of everyday life. Moreover, this continued grounding of naturalistic sociology in the natural stance of everyday life leads to a relative lack of concern with problems of objectivity. Matza has seen all of this very clearly. He concludes (1969:9):

> Naturalism has no other choice because its philosophical commitment is neither to objectivity nor subjectivity, neither to scientific method nor humanist sensibility. Its only commitment is fidelity to the phenomenon under consideration. Thus, in the study of man, there is no antagonism between naturalism and a repudiation of the objective view, not contradiction between naturalism and the humane methods of experience, reason, intuition, and empathy. Naturalism in the study of man is a disciplined and rigorous humanism.

It is this which turns naturalistic sociology back in the direction of traditional literature and largely restricts it to the kinds of experiences and generalizations (such as "appreciation," "diversity," and "complexity" in Matza's (1969) work) that are found in the common-sense (natural-stance) experience of the members themselves. Again, Matza (1969:9) himself has seen this as the (unfortunate) basis for at least a minimal form of common-sense generalization:

> But unfortunately, no philosophy can succeed in being anti-philosophical. A countertendency to abstract, classify, and generalize appeared partly because it was inevitable: the very act of writing or reporting commits the author to a *rendition* of the world, and a rendering is a sifting. Moreover, the naturalist could find in the world itself, especially among human subjects, a warrant for the countertendency: The human world itself was given to abstraction, generalization, and classification and thus it contained a measure of order and regularity.

By failing to make an initial commitment to the theoretic stance, all naturalistic sociologies, the most famous example of which is the work of Erving Goffman,[24] wind up largely restricting themselves to the description (or rendition, as Matza calls it) of experience and then treating that description as if it constituted the entirety of justifiable generalization (or theory). Even in their most serious forms, which Matza's certainly is, these naturalistic arguments have made the classical error of assuming it is possible to establish a presuppositionless understanding of everyday life, that is, an understanding that will somehow go beyond the common-sense understandings of the members in everyday life and yet will be founded entirely on that experience and will, therefore, be entirely comprehensible (or recapturable) by any member retaining the natural stance of that common sense. This idea of a presuppositionless understanding of everyday life is one that has continually perplexed the development of the understanding of everyday life. It is an idea that has even been inspired repeatedly by certain of Husserl's own statements about the phenomenological reduction, and it is an idea that has recently been given wide currency by the popularity of certain works by Alfred Schutz in which the *member test of validity* (by which a descriptive or interpretive account is considered true only if members accept it as plausible) is treated as a general principle rather than as a rule-of-thumb test that is normally very useful in doing field research.[25] (Some sociologists have also recently concluded that ethnomethodologists, such as Garfinkel, purport to provide presuppositionless analyses of everyday life because of their apparent "criticisms" of the conventional sociologists' natural-stance use of common sense as both resource and result in their analyses.[26] But this is a misunderstanding of what they are doing, as Zimmerman and Wieder point out in Chapter 12).

The whole idea of a presuppositionless understanding of everyday life has been repeatedly discredited by careful internal analyses of the arguments in favor of it. Husserl himself was well aware of the impossibility of a truly presuppositionless understanding or knowledge, as Marvin Farber (in Kockelmans, 1967:37–57) has argued so well:

> In the continuation of his description of the phenomenological method Husserl distinguished between ordinary presuppositions of a positive kind and that which is presupposed implicitly in all questioning and answering. The latter was held to exist necessarily, and to continue to exist, and was not acknowledged to be an assumption. It was regarded rather as the first thing to

24. That Goffman's work is a naturalistic sociology is not entirely apparent to the casual readers of his books. This is because many of his works are subsumed under the umbrella of structural analysis, but the structural aspects of the works really do not go beyond the first chapters. The rest is almost always highly naturalistic.

25. See Nicholson (1969).

26. For a discussion of the use of common sense as both "resource and result," see Chapter 4 in this volume.

be freely and expressly posited, and that "with a self-evidence which pre-
cedes all conceivable instances of self-evidence, and is contained implicitly in
them all."

Natanson has further clarified the whole issue in his argument that a
"presuppositionless philosophy does *not* mean a philosophy without
presuppositions; instead, what is involved is a philosophy which attends
phenomenologically to any commitment, however profound and primal,
which may be delineated in its own procedure. Presuppositions are
rendered explicit through phenomenological inspection and so neutral-
ized to whatever extent neutralization is possible in rational operations."[27] It is important to note, however, that no matter how far back
one goes in further reducing (or bracketing) one's phenomenological
"reductions," there inevitably comes a point at which one either accepts
total solipcism and the impossibility of "knowing" anything or grounds
his thought in some presupposed (commonsensical) experience.

The Phenomenological Reduction And Objectivity In The Science of Everyday Life

Accepting presuppositions as necessary, there obviously remains that
vast realm of common sense, of everyday experience that can be phenomenologically *bracketed*, that is, toward which one can take a theoretic
stance and reflect upon until the basic elements and relations of the
phenomenal experience are discovered. The question is, how far are we
going to "reduce" our everyday experience? How far back are we going
to go in seeking a clearer and more trustworthy understanding of our
everyday experience? This is not a great problem for the phenomenological philosopher, since he has started with the presupposition that he is
seeking ultimate truths about reality. He can continue to search until he
finds the ground level, if he so chooses; and, if he never finds it, many
philosophers will honor him all the more for carrying on the good search.
But the problem is different for anyone who purports to be engaged in a
scientific endeavor.

There may be some sociologists who would be content to keep reducing the everyday world in search of ultimate truths; and they might well
serve as an inspiration to the rest of us. But the existence of such
philosopher-sociologists is far more a figment of the anguished imaginations of some structuralists (a few of whom see the whole thing "as just
a bunch of philosophy," if not worse) than it is a fact. The sociologists of
everyday life see themselves as profoundly committed to a scientific
investigation of everyday life, as Husserl himself did; and this is cer-

27. See Natanson (1962: 34–44).

tainly not some kind of rhetorical commitment. Indeed, we have seen at the beginning of this chapter that it is precisely this sociology of every-day life that necessarily forms the foundation for every scientific study of human action. The question, then, is whether or not there are certain presuppositions to which this commitment to do a scientific investigation binds us.

The answer given by the positivistic scientist is that there are and that, in fact, we are committed to an experimental and quantitative (that is, absolutist) method and theory. The problem with this absolutist approach is that it confounds the tools of science, that is, the methods of investigation and the specific theories constructed, with the (essential) nature of science, so that any investigation or explanation that does not make use of these tools is seen as unscientific. But this confounding can be avoided if we recognize that there are certain, more fundamental, aspects of science about which we can all agree. These aspects seem to be (1) a commitment to discovering truths about the world as ex-perienced by human beings, (2) a commitment to grounding or testing any ideas proposed as truths in empirical observations of some kind *at some stage*, and (3) a commitment to accepting such tests as valid only when at some stage they can be made (publicly) shareable, that is, objective.

A great deal of argument has raged among sociologists and other social scientists over whether or not phenomenology "is really science," precisely because so many social scientists still think of science as necessarily positivistic, though this view and its attendant oper-ationalism, experimentalism, and quantification test of truth have long been discredited in the natural sciences by the revolutions produced by relativity, quantum mechanics, and the methods used to study elementa-ry particles. Confusion has been further compounded by the fact that various philosophers and historians of science, especially Popper and Kuhn (see especially Kuhn, 1962), have launched an increasingly thor-oughgoing phenomenological analysis of the nature of science that has contributed greatly to the accelerating "transvaluation" of science, by which the natural sciences themselves are seen (existentially) to be grounded in the common-sense experience of everyday life. This in-creasingly common view of science among scientists, philosophers, and historians has now gone so far as to seriously raise the ancient specter of solipcism. This development has been vividly depicted by Holton (1967:xxviii–xxix).

> From the beginning to the present day, science has been shaped and made
> meaningful not only by its specific, detailed findings but even more fundamen-
> tally by its thematic hypotheses. The reigning themata until about the
> mid-nineteenth century have been expressed perhaps most characteristically

by the mandala of a static, homocentric, hierarchically arranged cosmos, rendered in sharply delineated lines as in those of Copernicus' own hand-writing. It was a finite universe in time of space; a divine temple, God-given, God expressing, God-penetrated, knowable through a difficult process similar to that necessary for entering the state of Grace – by the works of the spirit and the hand. While not complete knowledge, it was as complete as the nature of things admits in this mortal life.

This representation was slowly supplanted by another, increasingly so in the last half of the nineteenth century. The universe became an unbounded, "restless" (to use the fortunate description of Max Born), weakly coupled ensemble of infinitely many separate individually sovereign parts and events. While evolving, it is continually interrupted by random discontinuities on the cosmological scale as well as on the submicroscopic scale. The clear lines of the earlier mandala have been replaced by undelineated, fuzzy smears, similar perhaps to the representation of distribution of electron clouds around atomic nuclei.

And now a significant number of our most thoughtful scholars seems to fear that a third mandala is rising to take precedence over both of these – the labyrinth with the empty center, where the investigator meets only his own shadow and his blackboard with his own chalk marks on it, his own solutions to his own puzzles.

It is this specter of solipcism, the fear that all possibility of shareable and demonstrable knowledge will be destroyed, that has led many serious social scientists to recoil from the fundamental idea that all social science knowledge in their field must be based on knowledge of everyday (common sense, subjective) life and that this knowledge can be gained only through methods devised for the purpose of retaining the integrity of the phenomena of everyday life. Many of them follow the argument and find they cannot refute it, but they recoil from the con-clusion and continue to insist upon the hopelessly discredited nine-teenth-century, positivistic "theory of verification." They become in-sincere "scientists" who construct *ad hoc theories* and act *as if* they were true, protecting them with the monopolistic controls available in some degree to all academic professions today.

While we may well condemn the choice of an insincere life, and even more of the unexamined life by those who will not even consider the argument, we must recognize the serious reasons for the fears that lead to that life, and we must deal with them directly and sincerely. Since few of even the best sociologists of everyday life have dealt with these issues, it is difficult to imagine how they might handle them. Some of them use traditional terminology and talk as if they were simply doing better what the traditional positivists were doing, yet no serious sociolo-gist of everyday life can possibly believe this, since the very basis of their work denies the fundamental assumptions of the positivistic method. In these cases positivistic insincerity is returned with existential insincerity, as each side struggles covertly for the prizes of respectability and power, which in our technological society often go to those who use the rhetoric of science most successfully.[28]

Once we recognize that all knowledge, certainly all knowledge of meaningful human phenomena, is ultimately grounded in our common-sense experience and, therefore, can never be totally examined and purged of "unrationalized" or practical elements and relations, then we must conclude that the foundation of all classical science, the *absolutist conception of objectivity*,[29] can never be achieved. This classical conception assumed that knowledge could be made objectlike (or thinglike, as Durkheim put it). It assumed that the knowing subject, the human mind, could devise means that could be externalized and used to eliminate all effects of that knowing mind on the knowledge gained. By the use of these procedures, which nineteenth-century scientists believed they had devised in their experimental procedures and their quantitative methods of measurement and analysis, the human mind was presumed capable of grasping the "thing in itself" and of locating these "noumena" within a pure realm of universal coordinates that would enable any knowing mind to grasp or know them independently of the concrete situations in which they were originally known or in which the knower grasped them at a particular time. Such knowledge was absolute, or what they called scientific, knowledge. It was absolutely objective.

Whether they thought of this absolute objectivity as an ideal or as an actuality matters little. It was this idea and all of the absolutist ideas associated with it that formed the basis of their whole theory of knowledge and justified the procedures that they used to obtain and test the truth of all empirical data. And it was these ideas that led to and justified the development of the positivistic ideas of sociological knowledge that were developed in the nineteenth century and have been passed down intact in sociology's present quantitative, experimental, functional and structural ideas.

In general, it was these ideas of absolutist science that led to the development of the absolutist perspective on society, which sought an absolute ("objective") knowledge of man completely independent of and in opposition to common sense by imposing experimental, quantitative, thing-like ideas on all "scientific" studies of man. It led first to the mechanistic social sciences. As these failed to provide any significant explanation and prediction of human events, they gave way to theories

28. I have previously discussed the importance of the rhetoric of science in the technological society in "The Rhetoric of Science and the Origins of Statistical Social Thought" in Tiryakian (1970).

29. See Douglas (1970a).

that increasingly gave consideration to "meaningful" (subjective) phenomena, but always within the absolutist mold that purported to transform
the subjective experience of social meanings into objective, externally
perceivable events. It was this ad hoc construction of evidence on the
social meanings, this treatment of objective (hard) measurements *as if*
they were independent of common-sense understandings of everyday
life, that turned much of sociology into an *as if* science.[30] It is this that
the sociology of everyday life seeks to transcend by taking the theoretic
stance toward everyday life.

But to recognize the necessity of rejecting classical objectivity does
not mean that we must or should relinquish our search for objective
knowledge. It simply means that we must modify our theory of knowledge and our conception of objectivity.

We begin our reconstruction of the meaning of scientific objectivity by
seeing that all human thought, at least that in an awakened state, is
intentional or purposeful. As Schutz, following Husserl and other phenomenologists, has argued so well, it is primarily intentions at any time
—our purposes at hand—that order human thought, that determine the
relevance of information and ideas about the world and ourselves. (John
Heeren in Chapter 2 has provided the best analysis of this intentional
theory of consciousness.) Information and ideas become conscious as we see them as useful to the attainment of our purposes at
hand. Human thought, then, is fundamentally oriented toward usefulness, toward doing things that have the effects we intend. This usefulness forms a fundamental part of the *ground* or foundation for all
thought, so that scientific knowledge itself must be seen as grounded in
its usefulness.[31] That this is not apparent to all of us today is due to the
fact that over the last several centuries the natural sciences (at least their
"theoretical" parts) have become increasingly independent of immediate
purposes; they have come to be seen by some of their practitioners as
"their own excuse for being." This idea of science for science's sake,
like art for art's sake or theory for theory's sake, is made possible by the
growing independence of modern man from the immediate demands of
nature. This idea is seen as desirable because our complex society finds
it useful to have disciplines concerned with the overall achievement of
long-run purposes. But these facts have merely led to the creation of
organized forms of intellectual activity that can be partially closed from
the rest of the world and in which the purposes at hand for the practitioners come to be the exercise of the intellectual activity itself. (The
grave danger is that as the discipline becomes more independent of

30. This is a point made very well by Cicourel (1964).
31. Again, see Douglas (1970a).

outside purposes it becomes more directed by the practical purpose, or the purpose at hand, of its own organization, which includes the monopolistic professional organization. In this sense the disciplines begin to feed on themselves and to become directed toward achieving their own purposes *against* the purposes of the outside world. This would appear to be a fundamental cause of the dangers of technological tyranny that we face today.)[32] This partial closing of modern scientific disciplines from the purposes at hand of the rest of society must not obscure the fact that ultimately scientific thought, like any other thought, is grounded in our purposes and, hence, in its usefulness to us. Scientific knowledge, then, must be seen as useful knowledge. Since it is grounded in our human purposes in the situations in which we find ourselves, it can never be fully independent of the properties of our minds or of our practical situations.

This practicality of human thought is what poses the "danger" of solipcism, or of total relativity of thought. But this danger can never be fully realized because equally fundamental aspects of the human mind and the human situation act in opposition to it. Indeed, it is because all of us in some way understand these other aspects, and take them so completely for granted as necessary aspects of our human situation, that we see solipcism as such a grave danger.

Most important, human beings cannot live without cooperating with other human beings, and human thought, which is essentially symbolic thought, cannot exist without a high degree of this cooperation from our earliest days. *All human knowledge is necessarily shared knowledge.* Moreover, since so many of our purposes in life are social, one of the most useful qualities of most knowledge is precisely that it can be shared. (Although this does not deny that each of us has personal "secrets," there is serious doubt that we can have "knowledge" of these secrets.) This, presumably, is the reason for the elaborate means developed in common-sense, practical thought for achieving this shareability of knowledge. This shareability of knowledge is so fundamental to doing practical thinking that it comes to be taken for granted for all "competent" or "ordinary" members of any social group. Indeed, the forms of knowledge most taken for granted in any group come to be seen as absolute — as independent of the knowing minds, as out there.

The fundamental goal of "objectivity" of knowledge is to make knowledge more useful. And the fundamental criterion, both common-sensical and scientific, by which this usefulness of knowledge is judged, the criterion assumed to make that usefulness certain, is the shareability

32. For the discussion of the dangers of technological tyranny see "Freedom and Tyranny in a Technological Society" in Douglas (1970e).

of knowledge. The shareability, or public nature, of knowledge, then, is the most basic "test" of its usefulness and its truth in both common sense and science (and usefulness and truth are overlapping conceptions).

The essential difference between common-sense practical thought and scientific thought is that scientific thought seeks to become (and purports to be) more useful than common sense by becoming more objective (or more shareable). This greater shareability of scientific knowledge is achieved primarily by progressively freeing the knowledge of concrete phenomena from the situation in which they are known. The mistake of the absolutist scientists was in seeing this "freeing" of knowledge from the situation as an absolute freeing and then acting *as if* they had achieved that goal. The examination of how science is done, as well as our rational consideration of the impossibility of ever totally rationalizing the infinite number of possible contingencies in any experimental situation, show us that this freeing is only relative (progressive). Moreover, this freeing is done not by making the knowledge objectlike or thinglike but by so examining the situation in which we do the knowing that we are able to (partially) specify the ways in which another observer would go about constructing the same kind of situation.[33] In the natural sciences this relative or partial freeing of knowledge from the situation is achieved by the use of experimental controls and designs. As we have seen, social scientists began their study and analysis of human action with the belief that they could achieve this freeing with the methods of the natural sciences. They failed to see that their approach imposed a structure on the phenomena that made it impossible for them to observe what they wanted to observe (the "truths" or "realities" of human action).

Most sociologists of everyday life rejected these distorting assumptions and the methods growing out of them, but in doing so tended to neglect all consideration of "objectivity." Most of their studies not only make no mention of the problems of objectivity but, more importantly, include no mention of the sociologist's field research methods. The field research methods of the various sociologies of everyday life have remained almost totally unexplicated and certainly untested by the repetition of the methods of observation to see if they yield comparable results. At the extreme, for example, we find the highly detailed accounts and subtle analyses of the social meanings of things to the members by Matza and Goffman with almost no explicit account of the methods involved and certainly no analysis of the "objectivity" of such

33. Some of these problems of reproducibility and objectivity are discussed in Douglas (1970a) and in "Observing Deviance" in Douglas (forthcoming).

methods. Since both of these researchers more or less explicitly retain the natural stance of common sense, we can assume that they are relying almost entirely on the taken-for-granted ideas of common sense about how one should rightly go about determining what people think and rendering accounts of that thinking. Matza and Goffman's research methods, then, are apparently more systematic forms of journalistic accounts. (Their accounts of patients' experiences and of the drug experience bear striking resemblances to the accounts of realistic journalism practiced by such authors as Norman Mailer.[34] As in the accounts of Mailer, there is no analysis of the question of how we can "really know," how other people are experiencing these things.) Again, some of the more positivistically oriented ethnomethodologists have often talked about their theoretical ideas as if they were directed at somehow determining the (indexical) meanings of things to the members involved by examining the external "features" of interaction settings, so they apparently feel justified in leaving all methodological questions unexplicated on the (indexical) assumption that recordings, films, and so on unproblematically provide one with "objective" evidence about those meanings. (The Wittgensteinian assumption that "meaning is its use" has also sometimes been invoked to justify the implicit assumption that observing the uses of statements somehow provides one with an externalized form of meaning.)[35] Such arguments, however, are obviously contrary to the fundamental ideas of indexicality (see the discussion of Garfinkel below) and to the actual practices of inferring meanings used by these sociologists. They are also contrary to all of the evidence we have that the meanings of the research situation, and of the social researcher himself, have a great effect on what human actors do in any nonsecret research setting.[36] Since the problems of objectivity are even more important for the social sciences than for the natural sciences, the failure to consider these questions is crucial.

As I have previously tried to show in some detail (Douglas, 1970a, forthcoming), there are four fundamental ways in which we must progressively free our research on everyday life from the situations in which we have made our observations: (1) We must provide systematic evidence concerning the properties of our research methods, especially of the situations in which we make our observations of everyday communications and communications in more formalized (interview) situations. In the past sociologists have generally taken the common-sense proce-

34. There is, of course, a growing form of literature, the naturalistic or journalistic novel, of which Norman Mailer's work is probably the best representative.

35. The different strategies of the different kinds of ethnomethodologists in dealing with meanings are dealt with below.

36. See "Observing Deviance" in Douglas (forthcoming).

dures for inferring social meanings so completely taken-for-granted that
they have restricted the discussions of their research methods to presentations of their experimental designs and methods of data analysis.
(Even the best reports on methods by field researchers, such as Whyte's
(1955:279–358) essay on his methods, provide us with little more than
glosses of the social properties of the situations in which their inferences
of social meanings took place.) Once again, our priorities must be in-
verted. (2) This information is of basic importance in making it possible
for us to carry out the crucial test of the situational freedom of research
findings—that is, *partial reproducibility*. We can reproduce the basic
properties of any research procedures to see if we get basically similar
results only if we know what those properties were. The importance of
specifying these properties of the research procedure is evident from the
conflicts that have arisen in the few attempts that have been made to
reproduce such findings. In anthropology the very different views of
Tepotzland produced by the research of Redfield and Lewis serves as an
excellent example. As I have previously argued (Douglas, forthcoming),
the sharply contrasting conclusions of Liebow and Clark about the
"quality of life" in American Negro slums gives us another and more
recent example of the great problem of getting such reproducibility in
our field research, but the problems can certainly never be solved if we
do not have the information on the methods used. (3) We must also
undertake systematic covert and overt field research studies of field
research methods to determine the reliability and validity of such methods. Most importantly, we must get at the effects of the different meanings of social research and particular social researchers held by different
groups and individuals in our society. Although this strategy does involve some ultimate indeterminancy, since we are making use of some of
the same methods to determine the truth of the findings of such methods,
this can be overcome by the use of more highly controlled and explicit
methods to study the field research methods and by consciously adopting a strategy of successive approximations toward better methods. (4)
We must become far more conscious and manipulative of the effects of
the involvements and organizations of the researchers on the findings.
This classical problem of involvement and objectivity, which I have
tried to deal with in some detail (Douglas, 1970a), has been dealt with in
important works by Becker, Gouldner, Tumin, and others in recent
years, but it has had all too little effect on the actual conduct of field
researchers.

   Establishing objectivity in social research is more problematic than it
is in research in the natural sciences for several reasons. First, the great
reliance of human beings on the taken-for-granted context of any communication to provide the complete meaning of the communication,

which forces us to rely very heavily on our common-sense under-standings of everyday communications (gained through our everyday experience) to infer the meanings of communications, means that much of the crucial determinant of what we are trying to "observe" will not be externally (hence, publicly) observable. Second, the crucial importance of the historical, biographical, and situationally developmental aspects of the contexts in determining the meanings of communications makes it impossible to do anything more than partially reproduce the basic as-pects of any field research.[37] (For example, it has frequently been pointed out that the general economic position of Americans had impor-tant consequences for the field research reported in *Street Corner Society* and in the Hawthorne studies. Since those conditions could certainly not be reproduced by any researcher, there would inevitably be some difference in findings.) Third, and very much compounding the other two, there is the relative inability of the researcher to control human events, except by putting the actors in a social situation that they themselves define as experimental and that, therefore, leads them to act in ways that are different from the ways they would act in their natural settings.

Hopefully, all of these problems can be progressively solved (although presumably there will always remain that irreducible dependence on common-sense understandings of everyday life) by our coming to know better what is fundamental in situations and what is incidental. As our knowledge grows, we can focus our attention more on increasing our objectivity about the fundamentals and worrying less about all of the other factors. (At the present time, given the great gaps in our objective understandings of everyday life, it is wisest to avoid the dangers of "premature" closures in our research that might exclude the fundamen-tal aspects. In view of this danger, and in view of the grave dangers of bias involved in advertently structuring the meanings of research situ-ations for the members that will continue to exist until we do have more objective understandings, some of us have purposefully adopted a strat-egy of *defocusing field research* in the initial stages of any research project.)[38]

Objectivity, the Theoretic Stance and the Scientific Strategies for Analyzing Everyday Life

We can see, then, that the commitment of the sociologists of everyday

37. The developmental and situational nature of human groups has always been under-stood commonsensically by the so-called panel of researchers doing conventional sociolog-ical research.

38. The strategy of defocusing field research has, for example, been the strategy I have used in my work on welfare workers with Rochelle Small and John Johnson.

life to seeking useful knowledge, which involves the commitment to make that knowledge transsituational ("objective"), has many fundamental implications for all of their work. Indeed, this commitment to transsituational knowledge leads us directly to a loosely defined, overall strategy for doing the sociology of everyday life. In general, this strategy, which is shared with most scientific endeavors, consists in concentrating much of one's efforts on those aspects of everyday life that promise to lend themselves best to the construction of such objective knowledge. The difficulty is that this rule-of-thumb strategy must be seen in the context of other rule-of-thumb strategies and must be problematically applied, hopefully with "wisdom," in concrete situations. This strategy is most complicated by our equally intense desire to find the fundamental aspects of everyday life that may someday be made objective knowledge but that must first be "intuited" by "creative insights" before that can happen, as we are told by our rule-of-thumb strategy concerning creativity. I believe it is the coexistence of these two partially conflicting goals in our research and theory that accounts for some important differences in the methods and theories used by the sociologists of everyday life.

There is an important, if not always clear, distinction in the phenomenological sociologies between those researchers and theorists who emphasize the external aspects of everyday interaction in a search for maximum objectivity and those who emphasize the meaningful (internal) aspects in a search for greater creative insight into what is leading to the external aspects. (In a way, of course, this recapitulates on a smaller scale the difference between positivistic and phenomenological sociologies. Recognizing this, however vaguely, has led a few so-called ethnomethodologists to actually consider themselves positivists, though this carries the difference within ethnomethodology to a ridiculous extreme.) In a general way, this distinction is found to be especially important in understanding the different strategies used by *linguistic phenomenological sociologists* and *situational phenomenological sociologists* (a distinction that is recapitulated within the specific phenomenological sociology of ethnomethodology in terms of the difference between *linguistic ethnomethodologists* and *situational ethnomethodologists*).

The linguistic phenomenological analysts of everyday life, who focus rather heavily on the concrete statements made by individuals, and who are most concerned with meticulous analyses of recorded conversations, are trying to maximize the objectivity (even demonstrability) of their findings by concentrating on what can be observed externally. These sociologists, such as Harvey Sacks,[39] David Sudnow, and their many

39. While Harvey Sacks and his many co-workers have written a great deal, some of which has long circulated in ditto form, little of this work has yet been published. Added to this problem of interpreting their ideas correctly is the problem created by the changes that

co-workers, are fundamentally different from the so-called psycholinguists and sociolinguists (who are positivists) because as phenomenological sociologists they are fundamentally concerned with the "meanings" of linguistic categories to the members of society in everyday life and, ultimately, with the implications of those meanings for the actions of the members. But these linguistic analysts of everyday life, especially the linguistic ethnomethodologists, have a strong tendency to agree with the Wittgensteinian edict that "language is its use," which leads them to try to get at "meanings" by analyzing the "uses" of language in everyday life. By concentrating on uses they tend to focus on what is often purported to be externally observable, hence most shareable (even recordable for all time). In early stages of their work some of them were actually tempted to think that they had solved the whole problem of meanings by making it all externally observable, in much the way the structural linguists believed they had, so that one would never have to ask whether or not what is spoken and done is in some way the result of some unseen phenomena "inside" the actors. In doing so they simply repeated the age-old mistake of the positivists. They failed at that time to see that the whole idea of use, of what constitutes a usage, really depends on some idea of what lies behind the externally observable events; "use" was a device for bootlegging the "social meanings" that they themselves could ultimately get at only by making use of unexplicated common-sense understandings of everyday life. It is probably for this reason that most of them abandoned that idea and began to study the situational "uses" of linguistic categories.

The situational phenomenological sociologists have been more consistently concerned with getting at the members' meanings and seeing how they are related to the members' (situational) actions. While these sociologists certainly are concerned with the analysis of everyday uses of language and see this as a fundamentally independent aspect of everyday life, they emphasize a more general and, hopefully, in the long run a more creative understanding of everyday life. They too are concerned with the objectivity of their findings but place less emphasis on this than on getting at the (what are sometimes called "deeper") situational meanings of things to the members. (There are even some sociologists of everyday life, especially Wieder and Cicourel (see Chapters 5 and 6 of this volume), who study language in everyday life more in this way than in the way of the linguistic ethnomethodologists. For them language tends much more to be seen in its more general context of all

---

have taken place in their ideas as their work has developed. Much of my own understanding of these ideas has necessarily come from numerous personal communications with most of the participants in the (erstwhile) underground movement of *California sociology*.

the "meaningful stuff" that goes on in everyday life, and language tends to be only one of their foci of concern, as can clearly be seen in the work of Cicourel,[40] Turner,[41] Speier,[42] Blum,[43] Jennings, and others.) But, as is the case with their linguistic colleagues, there is significant variation in the degree to which these situational analysts concentrate on questions of objectivity. At one extreme are the ethnomethodologists who use the idea of "members presenting features" much as their linguistically oriented colleagues use "social uses" to hang their analyses of situational meanings onto externally perceivable events. (Some of Garfinkel's work has this "externalizing" aspect, and this has probably been important in leading to his recent work with Sacks.)[44] At the other extreme are the more philosophical phenomenologists, such as Schutz[45] and Berger and Luckmann (1966), who make very sparing use of any careful observations of concrete situations and give very little consideration to problems of objectivity.

Disagreements over the best strategy are inevitable, since they are largely based on our own intuitive grasps of the situation facing us (what we would like to see as wisdom when we do it and guesswork when our opponents do it). Moreover, we will even find the same individual shifting between the two major goals of the scientific strategies for studying everyday life, so that his own strategies will vary and over time may appear inconsistent. What is important is to recognize what we are trying to do with these strategies, to recognize that objectivity and insight into the still nonobjectifiable understandings are both needed, and to try to achieve some balance between the two, at least over the whole enterprise if not in the work of each individual.

Given the early stage of the work, it seems inevitable that we shall have great problems in making our work objective and shall, consequently, have to make use of our own partially unexplicated common-sense understandings of everyday life. This means that we definitely must look at the whole idea of taking the theoretic stance toward everyday life as a strategy for progressive "reductions" of everyday life rather than as something that leads us immediately to seek *the* fundamental truths about everyday life. *We must consciously seek partial*

40. See Chapter 6 in this volume.
41. See Chapter 7 in this volume.
42. See Chapter 8 in this volume.
43. See Alan Blum, "The Meaning of Mental Illness," in Douglas (1970d).
44. This joint work of Garfinkel and Sacks appears in McKinney and Tiryakian (1970).
45. While the works of Alfred Schutz are certainly presented as being empirical statements about the everyday world, I think we should treat them as works of philosophy not works of social science, regardless of their great importance to the social sciences. Schutz, after all, made very little use of any systematic observations of everyday life independent of his own involvement in that everyday life.

(objective) truths that will be undone by further "reductions," or deeper analyses, of everyday life. This ancient scientific strategy, which Max Weber and others have seen as an essential part of science,[46] can be seen at work in many of our works on everyday life. In my own studies, for example, it has led to a conscious use of the largely unexplicated common-sense ideas about "meanings." As I argued (Douglas, 1967:235–246), I believe this common-sense idea is so fundamental and so problematic that it will probably be one of the last common-sense ideas that we ever understand objectively. For this reason, I have relied almost entirely on the common-sense understandings of my uses of the terms in specific contexts in my analyses of such things as the social meanings of suicide, the meanings of social "rules," and so on. This is obviously not because I do not see the problem of objectively determining the "meanings of meaning" to be important. As we do progressively solve the problem, I believe we shall clearly have to redo the analyses of such things as the social meanings of suicide and I believe that by doing so we shall move to a much greater useful knowledge of such phenomena. (I have, in fact, made what I hope is a first useful step in this progressive assault on the problem in my analysis of the complex and developmental relations between situational ideas and actions in Douglas (1971a: Chapter 5).)

Social Situations And Social Order

Just as the question of the situational and transsituational nature of "knowing" is fundamental to all questions of scientific objectivity, so is it fundamental to all of sociology. It is the recognition of the fundamental importance of the question of situationalism and transsituationalism that has most distinguished the phenomenological sociologies from the absolutist (structural) sociologies. And it is the differences in proposed solutions to this question that most distinguish one phenomenological sociology from another, especially the strictly phenomenological from the existential sociologies.

The situational nature of everyday life has been dealt with in the naturalistic sociologies and the phenomenological philosophies of everyday life primarily in terms of *physical situations of activities* and the *integrity of the situation.* The naturalistic sociologists, in keeping with their insistence on staying largely at the level of descriptive accounts of

46. This ancient strategy to which I refer is that of the changeability of science and the idea that progress is an essential part of this changeability. Science in this view is seen as an ever better approximation toward the "absolute truth." My own view and strategy, of course, is that while we can hope for progress through such reductions we will find each reduction more difficult than the previous one, so we can never approach this "absolute truth."

everyday experience, have placed great emphasis on the physical situating of everyday life. The earlier Chicago naturalistic sociologists made a basic distinction between primary (face-to-face) situations and secondary situations and saw the primary situations as basic to all social experience. Goffman (1963: 16, 21), probably the most important of the naturalistic sociologists, began with this position, developed various ideas about physical properties of situations that have important meanings for participants, such as front regions and back regions, and went on to develop an extensive description and (low level) analysis of face-to-face situations (or encounters) with a heavy emphasis on their physically situated nature:

> The factor emerges, then, that was much considered by Adam Smith, Charles Cooley, and G. H. Mead; namely the special mutuality of immediate social interaction. That is, when two persons are together, at least some of their world will be made up out of the fact (and consideration for the fact) than an adaptive line of action attempted by one will be either insightfully facilitated by the other or insightfully countered, or both, and that such a line of action must always be pursued in this intelligently helpful and hindering world. Individuals sympathetically take the attitutde of others persent, regardless of the end to which they put the information thus acquired. . . .
>
>   The term *situated* may be used to refer to any event occurring within the physical boundaries of a situation. Accordingly, the second person upon a scene transforms everything done by himself and by the one already there into situated activity, even though there may be no apparent change in the way the person already present continues with what he had been doing. The newcomer, if effect, transforms a solitary individual and himself into a gathering.

In general, Goffman's work is based on the "principle"[47] of the integrity of the situation, which maintains that any (face-to-face) situation is of importance in itself in determining (the meaning of) what goes on in the situation:

> The rule of behavior that seems to be common to all situations and exclusive to them is the *rule obliging participants to "fit in."* The words one applies to a child on his first trip to a restaurant presumably hold for everyone all the time: the individual must be "good" and not cause a scene or a disturbance; he must not attract undue attention to himself, either by thrusting himself on the assembled company or by attempting to withdraw too much from their presence. He must keep within the spirit or ethos of the situations; he must not be *de trop* or out of place. Occasions may even arise when the individual

---

47. The term principle in this context is not to be interpreted as "scientific law." Certainly the ideas are not that precise, formalized, or closed. Rather, I use the term principle to indicate that we are dealing with an idea that has very wide applicability and is of fundamental importance.

will be called upon to act as if he fitted into the situation when in fact he and some of the others present know this is not the case; out of regard for *harmony in the scene* he is required to compromise and endanger himself further by putting on an air of one who belongs when it can be shown that he doesn't (Goffman, 1963:11).

The philosophical phenomenologists have shared this idea of the integrity of the situation and have expressed it primarily in terms of what Schutz (1962) has called "the paramount reality of the *Lebenswelt*."[48]

The principle of the integrity of the situation is a specific form of the more general principle of the contextual determination of social events which has evolved in various ways in all of the phenomenological sociologies and which many of them, especially ethnomethodology as developed by Garfinkel (see below), have taken in some form to be *the* basic principle of phenomenological sociology. The basic idea of this principle is that concrete human events are always to some degree dependent on the situational context in which they occur and can be adequately explained only by taking into consideration that situational context. This idea would be no suprise to the sophisticated absolutist sociologists, who explicitly adopted the statistical or probabalistic method of analysis in order to eliminate—in an ad hoc fashion—all such contextual effects, or what they considered "individual differences." (Quetelet, for example, was very clear about this in his *Essai sur l'homme* of 1835.) Because of their implicit commitments to absolutist science and to determinism in human events, they believed one could have science only by excluding such concrete differences from the beginning. But once we make the commitment to retain, at least initially, the integrity of the phenomena, we have decided not to use such ad hoc procedures to eliminate from consideration the concrete differences in events. The dependence of these concrete events on their contexts is then easily recognized, since it is merely a formulation of the common-sense idea that all concrete events are in some ways unique in description, cause, and explanation.

The most important specific form of this general idea, however, is not only totally opposed to the conventional absolutist perspective on society, but much more unexpected. This is the principle of the *contextual determination of meaning,* the basic idea of which is that the context within which a given statement or action occurs is of fundamental importance in determining the meanings imputed to it by the members of society. This is the basic idea behind all phenomenological theories of meaning and is in complete opposition to the building-block theory of meaning to be found in all absolutist theories of society, lan-

48. The principle of the contextual determination of meanings has been dealt with in Douglas (1967: especially 242).

C

guage, etc. (which theory views the meanings of such things as independent of the contexts in which they occur and as coming in self-contained wholes (blocks) that can be put together (cemented) by accord with certain rules to produce the whole meanings imputed to any such concrete event).

There are at least two important kinds of contexts that determine meanings: (1) the *linguistic context* (which may or may not be independent of the second kind, and (2) the *practical (use) context*. Meanings are dependent on the linguistic context when they are (partially) determined for the members by other linguistic items or properties that occur in the same situation, such as the same text. They are dependent on the practical context when they are determined for the members by other nonlinguistic aspects of the situation in which they occur. The practical or use context consists primarily of such things as the time and place in which they occur and the knowledge that is taken for granted about the persons involved.

Some philosophers and linguists have long been aware of the many ways in which the occasion (context) of actual (practical) use determines the meanings of any word, statement, etc., for those giving or receiving the communication. Pierce proposed the term indexical to refer to the practical contextual determination of the meanings and Bar-Hillel (1954) presented the first thorough analysis of such indexical properties, or indexicality, of language.

The study and analysis of *indexicality* has since become the basic concern of those ethnomethologists who work with Garfinkel. Garfinkel (1967:11) himself has largely tied the definition of ethnomethodology to the study of the "awesome indexicality" of everyday actions and statements, and he has seen all conventional sociology by contract as concerned with trying to eliminate the indexical properties of everyday accounts.

> I use the term "ethnomethodology" to refer to the investigation of the rational properties of indexical expressions and other practical actions as contingent ongoing accomplishments of organized artful practices of everyday life. The papers of this volume treat that accomplishment as the phenomenon of interest. They seek to specify its problematic features, to recommend methods for its study, but above all to consider what we might learn definitely about it.

Any close reading of Garfinkel's statements about ethnomethodology makes it apparent that his goal is not simply that of studying the indexicality of everyday accounts. Rather, his more general concern is with the ways in which members go about showing each other, or presenting to each other, the "rational accountability" of their organized activities, but it is his contention that such "rational accountings" inevitably make use of indexical or reflexive ties between those accounts and the shared (organized) practical activities of the members involved in the communication to show that the accounts are in fact "rational."

In short, *recognizable* sense, or fact, or methodic character or impersonality, or objectivity of accounts are not independent of the socially organized occasion of their use. Their rational features consist of what members do with, what they "make of" the accounts in the socially organized actual occasions of their use. Members' accounts are reflexively and essentially tied for their rational *features* to the socially organized occasions of their use.

That tie established the central topic of our studies: the rational account-ability of practical actions as an ongoing, practical accomplishment. I want to specify the topic by reviewing three of its constituent, problematic phe-nomena. Wherever studies of practical action and practical reasoning are con-cerned, these consist of the following; (1) the unsatisfied programmatic dis-tinction between and substitutability of objective (context free) for indexical expressions: (2) the "uninteresting" essential reflexivity of accounts of prac-tical actions; and (3) the analyzability of actions-in-context as a practical accomplishment (Garfinkel, 1967:4).

Reflexivity, then, is seem as a necessary part of members' "rational accounting" for their activities, and it has thus far been the focus of the work of the situational ethnomethodologists who work with Garfinkel.

There can be little doubt now that the indexical, or taken-for-granted, properties of everyday communications are of fundamental importance in understanding everyday life and, thence, all human events. In addi-tion, any program for transforming the sociological enterprise from an absolutist discipline into one founded on objective understandings of everyday life will do well to begin with a thorough analysis of these contextual determinations of meanings, simply because the absolutist perspective is built largely on the assumption that such contextual fac-tors can be eliminated without destroying the possibility of scientifically explaining the natural phenomena.

But such a preponderant focus on contextual effects tends to distort the realities of everyday life. There are several fundamental reasons for believing this. First, it is almost certainly not the case that all account-ings, even rational accountings of practical activities, are "awesomely indexical." After all, absolutist (nonsituational or noncontextual) thought is not the creation of some mad scientist. *Absolutist thought is a funda-mental part of Western thought — of moral thought and rational thought.* It is the essential tension, never totally resolvable, between worldly (practical, contextual) thought and other-worldly (absolutist, noncontext-ual) thought that is so characteristic of Western thought[49] and that has always been clear to philosophers since Plato and Aristotle drew the

49. Crane Brinton has especially seen this tension between this-worldly thought and other-worldly thought as fundamental to Western thought in general.

battle lines between realism and nominalism. I have previously even *speculated* (Douglas, 1971a: Chapter 1) that this conflict is the necessary result of the symbolic nature of human thought and the necessary problems of existence we face. The absolutist strain of thought is still especially apparent in moral (rule) thought, in all arguments such as "It is a matter of principle," "I have no choice, "It is the will of God," and so on. But absolutist "rational" accounts are of awesome and growing importance in everyday American life today precisely because the classical (absolutist) forms of scientific thought are increasingly being imposed on all realms of everyday life. It is precisely this that forms the basis for the growing danger of *technological tyranny* in the scientific-technological society.[50]

Some of Garfinkel's work does in fact take important note of this absolutist scientific strain of thought in everyday, practical affairs. This is precisely true of the study of the Suicide Prevention Center (Garfinkel, 1967:11-18), which is one of those burgeoning forms of practical activity whose basic thrust is to make previously practical (coroner) work into scientific (medical examiner and psychological autopsy) investigation. This is also true of Garfinkel and Bittner's investigations of psychiatric records.[51] In each case, Garfinkel found a strong tendency within the members' activities toward doing away with their indexicality, even if this is, as Garfinkel so rightly sees it, an unsuccessful attempt. I believe that it leads the members to the creation of *as if* practices that are used to present a public image of scientific and professional rationality, even when they themselves recognize so clearly that their activities are necessarily very situationally determined. I believe it is this that led some of the coroners and medical examiners I studied (Douglas, 1971: Chapters 3 and 4) to be so "defensive," to apparently anticipate that I or other outsiders would use scientific standards to criticize their recognizedly practical work. Certainly they recognized the practical nature of their work, and would say that they could not see any way to make it "better," by which they seemed to mean more "scientific," but they recognized at the same time the "power," however rhetorical, of "scientific standards" in our society today. (I believe it is also a recognition of this that leads social workers we have been studying[52] to make a basic distinction between "what the agency says we are doing," which is based on ideas of therapy and professionalism, and "what we are really

50. For the discussion of the dangers of technological tyranny see "Freedom and Tyranny in a Technological Society" in Douglas (1970e).

51. See Garfinkel (1967: 186-207).

52. The study of social welfare workers is a research project I have been doing with Rochelle Small and John Johnson.

doing," which is often based on an explicit recognition that their work is all highly situationally determined.)

Garfinkel's own work and theory have probably focused so preponderantly on the contextual or situational effects both because of the radical difference between this and the traditional perspective on society and because of the highly routinized settings of his studies. His studies have been carried out primarily in social settings in which the activities have become rather highly organized and routinized, which are precisely those settings in which one will find that meanings have become the most taken for granted by members. The members do not have to verbalize their accounts very fully and they do not face many problems in providing justifiable accounts to other members because they have already been through most of the arguments about what should be done in the situations they face. To do studies of ongoing, highly organized activities is to do truncated analyses that are most apt to support findings of "awesome indexicality." If one were to study how members organize themselves, how they establish routines, and how they define and deal with "problems" and "new situations," he would find far less indexicality, though it would presumably still be there as the members bring the experience of the past shared situations to bear on the new experience. But the concentration on indexicality, especially in such highly organized settings, also leads to a minimal consideration of "how the members put it all together." That is the problem of social order.

As I have previously argued, the greatest problem we face is that of analyzing the complex relations and interdependencies that exist between the situational aspects of social meanings and those aspects that are largely independent of situations. And it is precisely an understanding of these interrelations that will enable us to deal effectively with the members' transsituational ordering of their social lives.

Bar-Hillel (1954:359) estimated that about 90 percent of everyday statements are indexical, but he also began his classic paper on indexicality by noting the varying degrees of (practical) indexicality in such statements.

Even very superficial investigation in the linguistic habits of users of ordinary language will reveal that there are strong variations in the degree of dependence of the reference of linguistic expressions on the pragmatic context of their production. Whereas, for instance, the sentence

(1) Ice floats on water

will be understood by almost every grown-up normal English-speaking person to refer to the same state of affairs (this statement needs, strictly speaking, some qualifications which however, in view of their generality, do not disturb the distinctions we are going to make), what the sentence

(2) It's raining

is intended to refer to will be fully grasped only by those people who know the place and the time of its production, and the identification of the intended reference of the sentence

(3) I am hungry

will require the knowledge of its producer and the time of its production. We must recognize that this variability in the degree of contextual determinations is normal in everyday life and of basic importance in determining the methods we must use to study such phenomena and the theories we should construct to deal with it. (For example, a recognition of this variability has great bearing on resolving the raging controversy over the use of questionnaires. Following our argument, we would expect that questions and answers that are less indexical would be more apt to yield reliable results. For example, one might well be able to get reliable estimates from questionnaire studies of "how many Americans drink orange juice each morning" or, less reliably because far more indexical, of "how many Americans now plan to vote for Mr. Nixon for President." But as the meanings of questions and answers become more dependent on the situations of use, we quickly approach the point at which questionnaire results are absurdly unreliable. This is why attitude studies, especially of racial attitudes, are notorious for having no reliable bearing on everyday actions.)[53]

Understanding the situational nature of human existence is crucial for developing any science of man. But an overconcentration on the contextual effects to the relative exclusion of trans-situational meanings leads, however inadvertently, to a failure to consider adequately the most crucial aspect of man, the symbol maker and user: his awesome capacity to transcend himself and his immediate situation, to bring a vast realm of previous experience to bear in constructing meanings and actions for his immediate situation, to coordinate (order) his immediate situations with those of many others beyond his immediate grasp, and to project himself into an as yet unrealized future.[54] As Schutz (1962:318) and many other phenomenologists have always argued:

> We have, however, to indicate that the face-to-face relationship character-ized so far is only one, although the most central, dimension of the social world. If we compare it with the world within my actual reach, we can also find dimensions in the social world comparable to the various forms of the world within my potential reach. There is the world of my contemporaries, with whom I am not biographically involved in a face-to-face relationship, but

53. In the long history of studies of racial attitudes it has normally been found that the expressed racial ideas and theories of individuals have no significant bearing on how the individuals behave in actual situations toward members of the various racial groups.

54. See Douglas (1971: Chapter 1).

with whom I have in common a sector of time which makes it possible for me to act upon them as they may act upon me within a communicative environment of mutual motivation. (In primitive societies in which the souls of the deceased are supposed to participate in the social life of the group, the dead are deemed to be contemporaries.) There is the world of my predecessors, upon whom I cannot act but whose past actions and their outcome are open to my interpretations and may influence my own actions; and there is the world of my successors of whom no experience is possible, but toward whom I may orient my actions in more or less empty anticipation. It is characteristic of all the dimensions of the social world other than the face-to-face relation that I cannot grasp my fellow-men as unique individuals but only experience their typical behavior, their typical pattern of motives and attitudes in increasing anonymity.

We cannot enter here into a detailed discussion of these various dimensions of the social world. But it is indispensable to keep the underlying problems in mind in order to analyze correctly certain issues connected with communication and the appresentational apperception of society.

The focus of the phenomenological philosophies and sociologies, however, has always been preponderantly on the situational aspects of everyday life. As a result, when they have not left the field entirely to the absolutist structualists they have either left the consideration of social order in a programmatic form or they have grafted structural ideas onto their situational analyses that largely deny the necessary freedom of individuals implicit in the whole idea of situationalness[55] and reinstate the "objectified" absolutized) tyranny of the structuralists. (This reinstatement of the absolutist structure is, unfortunately, all too clear in the Schutzian theory of common sense developed by Berger and Luckman (1966). This reinstatement is especially irrelevant in analyzing American society because this society is still so pluralistic that there cannot be the degree of "objectivation" of common sense demanded by their theory.) It is this search for a synthesis that partially differentiates the evolving *existential sociologies*[56] from the phenomenological sociologies that have built the foundation for understanding everyday life.

The fundamental challenge of the sociological endeavor today must be to develop (objective) useful knowledge of the complex gamut of everyday life, from unspoken exchanges of love to scientists' explicitly detailed search for transsituational knowledge, from mindless passions of angry mobs caught up in "the spirit of the moment" to systematic planning and construction of new societies—and a new world order in which pluralist differences are balanced against universal orderings. To

55. The situational nature of human activity makes it impossible to impose any total order on human life. The freedom to at least construct meanings for situations-at-hand is a necessary freedom.
56. See my discussion of this in Douglas (1971).

do this we must always begin with the members' understandings of their situations, but as we increase our understandings we must seek to transcend the members' understandings to create transsituational (objective) knowledge. Just as there is an essential tension between the situational and transsituational aspects of human existence, so is there an essential tension between the sociologist's new-found commitments to the integrity of the phenomena and to the theoretic stance. No doubt our objective knowledge will always remain partially grounded in the unexplicated situations of everyday use, but this is only to recognize that the scientific existence shares the ultimate absurdity of everyday life. If we can count on an ultimate similarity in all human existence resulting from the encounter of our common animal form with a common external world, then we do not face the necessity of accepting unresolvable conflicts in "objective" knowledge that could doom us to ultimate destruction. If we can create such transsituational knowledge quickly enough to prevent the tragedies that we unwittingly produce from the absurdities of our existence, then these absurdities should not prove at all uncomfortable. After all, they are most appropriate to the animal with a mind.

Alfred Schutz and the Sociology of Common-sense Knowledge

In a skeletal sense, the sociology of knowledge is concerned with the relationship between interests, broadly conceived, and "mental products," or knowledge. This is as true of Alfred Schutz as it is of such macrosociologists as Marx and Durkheim. This chapter is an analysis of Schutz's treatment of the interest-knowledge relation in the everyday world. Schutz's concern differs radically from that of earlier sociologists of knowledge in that they usually focused on particular, organized regions of social life, such as "the Chinese literati," "the intelligentsia," or "university." Even Durkheim, working in a different direction, ended his development with a study of the highly abstract Kantian categories. Schutz knew well that his approach diverged from the others; he directed more than a few critical remarks at "the so-called sociology of knowledge." In puzzling out the relation between interests and the everyday knowledge that structures our actions or interactions, Schutz has developed a sociology of common-sense knowledge that involves a complete reconstruction of the sociological framework, from its philosophical assumptions to suggestions for sociological investigations. In addition to presenting Schutz's scheme here, I will point out along the way how the work of later sociologists might be fitted into the Schutzian framework. A diagram illustrating certain aspects of the discussion has been included in this chapter.

To begin with, Schutz feels that in the common-sense world *interests* organize our constructs. Moreover, Schutz (1967:74) states that the very borderline between that which is taken for granted and that which

Process of Defining Situation – bringing relevant typifications, signs, symbols into play

Representation of group relations and other experiences (biography) in actor's consciousness

Choice of interest at hand

Situation defined

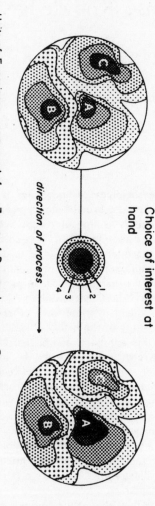

direction of process ⟶

Units of Experience – composed of typifications, signs, symbols, etc.

Unit A – Family
Unit B – Relations with legal system
Unit C – Religious experience
Unit D...Z (not represented) –
    Other relations and
    experiences

Zones of Decreasing Relevance

1. "primary relevance"
2. "secondary relevance" – means, conditions
3. "relatively irrelevant"
4. "absolutely irrelevant"

Process

Typifications of Unit A have become more relevant to problem at hand; Units B and C have become less relevant.

is problematic "depends on the pragmatic interest of the reflective glance which is directed upon it and thereby upon the particular Here and Now from which that glance is operating." The conception of the Here and Now is borrowed from Husserl. Interestingly, after his immigration to the United States, Schutz acquainted himself with American philosophy and sociology, and in later writings (Schutz, 1962:9) substituted W. I. Thomas's "definition of the situation" for the Here and Now. Briefly, Schutz is primarily interested in the subjective aspect of defining a situation, suggesting that the actor's biography and his choosing among various interests jointly determine which elements of the situation are relevant.

The conception of the definition of the situation has been at the heart of much recent sociology. The sense of its use, however, has varied considerably from one sociologist to another. For example, except for *Asylums*, Erving Goffman's abiding concern has been with the character and changes of the "external" aspects of the definition of the interaction situation. He seems to get much closer to Schutz with his discussion of biography and personal identity as situational components in his excellent *Stigma* (1963b:51–66). Harold Garfinkel in a very early paper, "Conditions of Successful Degradation Ceremonies," (in Manis and Meltzer, 1967) treats a certain type of *rite de passage* as a radical transformation in the definition of the situation. Peter Berger's discussion in several of his works of the phenomenon of alternation (in Berger and Luckmann, 1966) refers to the way in which changes is viewpoint (or definition of the situation) impel one to reconstruct his biography. A recent book by Peter McHugh (1968), *Defining the Situation,* deals with the emergence and relativity of situational definitions in terms going well beyond Schutz but, also, certainly indebted to him. McHugh's discussion of these temporal (emergence) and spatial (relativity) parameters of definitions analyzes them into component properties. In his treatment of the properties of relativity, he makes use of such Schutzian concepts (elaborated, however, by Garfinkel) as typicality, likelihood, and congruence.

Let us return to the particulars of Schutz's argument. What the term situation refers to is a particular physical and sociocultural environment in which the actor has a physical, social, and moral position as determined in part by his biography. To say that the definition of the situation is partly biographically determined means that the actor has a history—that his unique stock of knowledge at hand is the accumulation of his previous experiences. Schutz (1962:9) states that any situation "includes certain possibilities of future practical or theoretical activities which shall be briefly called the 'purpose at hand'." This immediate interest at hand is never isolated from others. Rather, it is always an "element within a hierarchical system, or even a plurality of systems, of interests which in everyday life we call our plans—plans for work and thought, for the hour and for our life" (Schutz, 1964:125). This system of interests changes from situation to situation and its loose organization does not preclude internal conflicts.

Beyond its biographical determination, the situation, then, is further defined by the actor's choosing among the disparate interests that exist. "This choice will state the problem or set the goal in respect to which the world we are living in and our knowledge of it are distributed in zones of various relevance" (Schutz, 1964:125).[1] In the everyday world, then, relevance is to be understood as problem relevance—that is, relevance to the actor's project or interest at hand. A single zone (or domain) of relevance always refers to a set of related problems, for every problem has outer fringes that may become subject to questioning and inner horizons that are also only *temporarily* unproblematic. To return to an earlier point (and close a circle), the very formulation of a problem determines what is to be taken for granted and what is to be questioned. Both of these spheres are known to us through typifications. Schutz uses the concept of typifications to refer to the mode of our knowledge of the everyday world. It is these typifications that are the constitutive units of the domains of relevance. More on typifications later.

Schutz distinguishes among four zones of decreasing relevance. First, we have a part of the world that is "within our reach." It can be observed by us and to some extent can be altered by our actions. In order to operate successfully in this sphere of primary relevance, we have to understand its structure. Second, there are other areas that provide the conditions under and the means by which we must work at gaining our goals in the sphere of primary relevance. We cannot dominate these fields; we have merely to be familiar with the possibilities they hold. Next, there are the regions of the relatively irrelevant that *for the present* have no connection with our immediate interests. These are just taken for granted insofar as they do not change or upset the more relevant sectors. Finally, certain fields are absolutely irrelevant because *we believe* that no change in them could possibly effect our purpose at hand. With respect to this zone we employ a "blind belief in the That and the How of things" (Schutz, 1964:124–125). Schutz emphasizes that these relevance zones are not to be seen as divided by boundaries. Rather, the various regions interpenetrate and create a multitude of transitional areas. These relations would be better depicted in a three-dimensional topographical map, with its contours showing peaks

1. The background to Schutz's zones of relevance is Heidegger's notion of regions of care.

and slopes, than in the standard two-dimensional political map, with its well-defined governmental borders.

Schutz distinguishes between two ideal typical systems of relevances, the intrinsic and the imposed. Intrinsic relevance derive from our chosen interests. If we decide to undertake a certain project, we become bound to a system of relevances intrinsic to that project. However, it remains true that we may at any time choose to shift our interest to a new project with a different set of intrinsic relevances. Imposed relevances are those we have no possibility of choosing. Their imposition derives from such events as are involved in the human condition (such as Heidegger's thrownness), in one's physical condition (disease, race), and so on. These relevances remain somewhat unclear to us, partly as a result of their being imposed (Schutz, 1964:124–125).

In the above treatment, I dealt with the hierarchical order in which domains of relevance are arranged *from the point of view of the actor.* According to Schutz, various social groups also value certain activities (or principles) and organize on a vertical dimension the zones of relevance that correspond to these valued activities. This set of relevance structures ordered in terms of superiority and inferiority differs from group to group. To refer to this social ordering of domains of relevance, Schutz makes use of Scheler's notion of the "relatively natural conception of the world" of an in-group. Burkhart Holzner (1968) has discussed a similar conception, namely, that of an epistemic community. In any event, it is this socially approved and unquestioned way of life of a particular group that is formed by the hierarchy of domains of relevance. Apart from the ordering of the domains of relevance into a relatively *natural conception of the world,* certain other things can be said about the formal structure of these domains. First, separate domains are essentially heterogeneous. The standards of excellence in one domain do not apply to other domains. Furthermore, the structure within and between the domains is continually in flux. It might happen that the system of typification constituting a relevance domain could lose their taken-for-granted character and be permeated by a heterogenous domain. Or, the order among domains may at any moment cease to be taken for granted and another may be substituted (Schutz, 1964).

What kinds of groups are considered complex enough to have elaborated relevance structures? In a distinction somewhat analogous to that between imposed and intrinsic relevances dealt with above, Schutz differentiates *existential* from *voluntary groups.*[2] In the first case, the individual member is born into a social heritage that involves a preformulated system of relevances and typifications. However, with volun-

2. Both of these sets of ideal types are in turn clearly related to Linton's well-known distinction between ascription and achievement, to which Schutz (1964:242) acknowledges his debt.

tary groups that one chooses to join, the relevance structures are not yet fully formed. There is a dynamic element involved here in that members must work together toward arriving at a common definition of the situation. Nearly every group has some form of relevance structure—from a marriage to a business enterprise, from a club to a nation to Western culture (Schutz, 1964:252–254). It should be added that Schutz (1962:14; 1964:233) does give us some hints as to the relative importance he ascribes to various social units. He reasons that as language is a most important typifying medium, the relevance structures prevailing in what he terms a linguistic in-group are of special significance to members of various social groups.

In that the individual is always, to use Simmel's phrase, at the intersection of social circles, it is still up to him to define his private situation with respect to his various group affiliations. To repeat an earlier point, the relation in the individual's mind of the various domains of relevance stemming from different group associations cannot be adequately represented by a two-dimensional system of coordinates. The proper means of expressing the overlap of the various domains of relevance in the actor's consciousness is by a three-dimensional topographical map with infinitely diversified contours and configurations.

It was said above that our knowledge of the social world is always in the form of typifications. This statement requires one important qualification. While most of our knowledge of the world is indeed typical, in one kind of relationship, the We-relation, an actor can experience the Other in his uniqueness. Within the realm of contemporaries with whom we share a community of time, Schutz delineates "consociates," those with whom we also share a community of space, from "mere contemporaries." This face-to-face relationship between consociates need not be especially intimate for the Other to be experienced in his uniqueness. It is only necessary that some signs of mutual recognition be exchanged between the partners in the interaction. Yet, typicality intrudes into even the We-relation; for knowledge of the Other's individuality can be only partial. In Schutz's (1962:17) words:

> In such a [face-to-face] relationship, fugitive and superficial as it may be, the Other is grasped as a unique individuality (although merely one aspect of his personality becomes apparent) in its unique biographical situation (although revealed merely fragmentarity). In all the other forms of social relationship (and even in the relationship among consociates as far as the unrevealed aspects of the Other's self are concerned) the fellow-man's self can merely be grasped ... by forming a construct of a typical way of behavior, a typical pattern of underlying motives, of typical attitudes of a personality type, of which the Other and his conduct under scrutiny, both outside of my observational reach, are just instances or exemplars.·

The process of typification consists of ignoring what makes a particular object unique and placing that object in the same class with others that share some trait or quality.[3] As noted above, types are always formed in relation to some purpose at hand, and it is this immediate interest that determines which traits will be equalized and what "individuality" will be ignored. However, it may be that we have no other purpose than to be with the Other in interaction. In this case, lacking special interests, we are more likely to know the Other in his uniqueness (Schutz, 1962:8). Note that whether certain objects or aspects of objects are seen as individual or as typical depends on the purpose in the *subject's* mind. For even if an actor *transcends* the type through which his partner in interaction is understanding him, the partner can always bring another type into play for perceiving his fellow (Schutz, 1967:191–192). This new type that the partner uses may relate to an unchanging purpose at hand or the purpose itself may change.

According to Schutz, our knowledge of other persons, in the form of typifications, derives its ultimate validity from direct experience in the face-to-face relation. He approvingly quotes Scheler (Schutz, 1967:165) to the effect that "the experience of the We ... in the world of immediate social reality is the basis of the Ego's experience ... of the world in general."[4] That is, the ideal types that we use as interpretive schemes for knowing others gain the greatest meaning from the immediate experiences between consociates. It is only in the direct We-relation that one can gain the immediate experience of others necessary for constituting types. (For a type is simply a set of characteristics formed by anonymization, that is, by omitting the subjective meaning of directly experienced individuals who have gone to make up the type. The anonymity or generality of the type is increased by the number of unique individuals it subsumes.) Moreover, in that mere contemporaries are always apprehended by means of types and not directly, the types themselves cannot be changed or refined in relations with contemporaries. In contrast to the direct We-relation, there is the They-relation between contemporaries; here one's partner is always an "ideal type." If information inconsistent with one's "type" of a contemporary is received, a more adequate, preconstituted type may be substituted for the

3. Among active sociologists, John McKinney has probably dealt most thoroughly with the process of typification. Although he has concentrated (following Howard Becker) more on constructed, second-order types used by social scientists, he has recently turned to the analysis of existential types in the tradition of Schutz. See McKinney's "Sociological Theory and the Process of Typification" in McKinney and Tiryakian (forthcoming).

4. One can notice here a strong convergence of Schutz's analysis of the origin of our knowledge of others in the We-relation and Cooley's ideas about the personality-molding effect of the primary group.

unsatisfactory type. But the unsatisfactory type cannot on the basis of the They-relation be refined to include the "deviant" contemporary within its bounds. For Schutz (1967:185), ideal types are "carried along with and modified by the We-relationship as it develops. In the process they cease to be mere types and 'return to reality' again.

Now, having made these neat distinctions between the We- and They-relation, Schutz proceeds to befoul the picture by telling us that these two types of relations are merely poles on a continuum. The dimension underlying this continuum of relations runs from concrete individuality on the We end of the scale to anonymous types on the They end. Between the poles there are several distinguishable regions.[5] For example, in what is called the indirect We-relation is included the relation I have with a friend with whom I once shared a face-to-face relation but who has since moved out of the range of direct interaction. I assume that this contemporary's subjective state has not changed since I last saw him, even though "I know very well that he must have changed through absorbing new experiences or merely by virtue of having grown older" (Schutz, 1967:182). I can also apprehend a contemporary by means of some cultural object that he has manufactured. But, in fact, the subjective experience of this other self, this producer, can be known only because I had previously stood beside a man who was making the same product, and I knew what was going on in his mind as he worked. These two examples, intermediate between the We- and They-relationship poles, are referred to by Schutz as indirect We-relations. Though both are relations with mere contemporaries, the first seems quite concrete and the second clearly involves subjective meaning. Furthermore, indirect relations such as these can alter our ideal-typical knowledge of others. As Schutz (1967:193) says later in his treatment; "The ideal types that are continually being constructed in everyday life are subject to constant adjustment and revision on the basis of the observer's experience, *whether the latter is direct or indirect.*"[6]

We have already distinguished relations with consociates, where the Other is apprehended in his uniqueness, from those with mere contemporaries, who are known by means of more or less anonymous types. We have also noted that there are many shadings between these two polar types of relation. Now let us look closer at some of these intermediate relations and examine the kind of ideal types formed to deal with them. We have already offered above a case exemplifying the region near the We-relation pole of the continuum—my contemporary

5. These are discussed briefly in Schutz (1967:180–181).
6. Italics mine.

who has been my consociate in the past. Very near the other end of the continuum we saw that certain cultural artifacts could carry the subjective meaning of their producer. Now, another region to be found near that of "my absent friend" is that of my contemporary whom I have never met, but who is being described to me by my consociate. This relation is obviously less concrete and more anonymous than that with my absent friend. Next, there are those anonymous individuals who fulfill a certain function in social space, such as the postal clerk who processes my letter. Finally, there are collective entities that are anonymous to me but whose function and organization I know; for instance, a corporation or state.

Even more anonymous than my relations with contemporaries are my relations with those who lived in the past, my predecessors, and those who will live after my death, my successors. Even though they can never be bodily present for me, predecessors can be apprehended in much the same way as contemporaries. There is, however, one radical difference between relations with predecessors and those with contemporaries. With the latter, I always shared that very general ideality, "contemporary civilization." This sharing is obviously lacking with predecessors. At best, my knowledge of predecessors will be very vaguely formulated in terms of general kinds of "human experience" (Schutz, 1967:209–211). As for the realm of successors, we can have no certain knowledge of them by means of ideal types. The single thing we can be sure of is that we will have some successors (Schutz, 1967:214).

Schutz discusses several kinds of ideal types that are used to represent the various relations we have with our contemporaries.[7] We will discuss only the most important, the personal ideal type and the course of action type which Schutz makes use of in his later works. Potentially the least anonymous of all types, the personal ideal type is formed of "another person who is expressing himself or has expressed himself in a certain way" (Schutz, 1967:187). This type can be as concrete as "my absent friend" or as anonymous as "some postal clerk." The course of action type refers to the expressive process itself, or to the product of that process on the basis of which we can make inferences about the process. The "stamping and forwarding of letters" will serve as an instance of this kind of type. As the examples imply, the course of action and the personal types are intimately related. The course of action type serves as the objective meaning of an action, that is, the type is "what is being done" or "what has been done." The personal ideal type, on the other hand, tells us the subjective meanings in the mind of the person who executes a certain action. Because the action itself is objective, the

7. Some of these are discussed in Schutz (1967:196–201).

subjective experience of the person acting must be adequate to the objective meaning already defined. To put it differently, one cannot define "the ideal type of a postal clerk without first having in mind a definition of his job" (Schutz, 1967:187). Since the course of action type is prior, the personal ideal type is to be seen as derivative.

Knowledge of things in general, as distinct from the knowledge other persons we have been discussing, can be constituted out of our own experience, but for the most part it comes from the experiences that others have and pass on to us. This is known as socially derived knowledge. This kind of knowledge has several typical sources. First, there is the eyewitness who communicates his immediate experience to me. I believe his report on the basis of two idealizations that are typically used in common-sense thinking to overcome differences in individual perspectives. To begin with, there is the "interchangeability of standpoints." That is, I assume that if I exchange places with my fellow man, "his 'here' becomes mine, I shall be at the same distance from things and see them with the same typicality as he actually does; moreover, the same things would be in my reach which are actually in his" (Schutz, 1962:12). Also, there is the idealization of the "congruency of systems of relevance." Here, I accept without question

> that the differences in perspectives originating in our unique biographical situations are irrelevant for the purpose at hand of either and that he and I, that "We" assume that both of us have selected and interpreted the actually or potentially common objects and their features in an identical manner or at least an "empirically identical" manner, i.e., one sufficient for all practical purposes (Schutz, 1962:12).

It seems that these two idealizations are at the core of much of Garfinkel's work. Many of his experiment-demonstrations have been concerned with the role of these principles and the violation of them or rules or understandings based on and/or reducible to these principles. For example, in his study (in Harvey, 1963:220–226) of "trust," he devised two demonstrations in which the aim was precisely the breaching of these idealizations. Further, his analysis of the "routine grounds of everyday activities" shows that the assumptions of "the interchangeability of standpoints" and "the congruency of systems of relevance" are integral parts of the common-sense world (1967:55).

For Schutz, these idealizations must be altered in some respects for the other typical sources of socially derived knowledge. The insider reports his immediate experience, though not necessarily directly to me, of an event that has some place in a system of relevances that is different from my own. I believe his report because I assume that his unique relevances allowed him to "know the even better" than I could have, had I observed it. In this case, though I do not assume our relevances to be entirely congruent, they are also not contradictory. It is just that his unique perspective permits him to have special insight that I do not have. Next, there is the analyst who offers me some *opinion* about some piece of knowledge. The facts themselves can be either immediate to him or socially derived; as long as they are organized by a system of relevances similar to my own, I am likely to accept his opinion. Finally, there is the commentator's opinion that is based on information from the same sources available to the analyst. However, the commentator groups facts according to relevance structures quite different from my own. I will tend to trust his opinion insofar as it allows me to form a clear picture of his deviant system of relevances (Schutz, 1964:132).

There is one final aspect of common-sense knowledge that we shall treat briefly. This is the whole area of signification and sign relations. In general, significative devices serve to tell us of representational meanings. This mode of knowledge obviously interlocks with our central mode of knowing, typifications. Thus, the signs or symbols we use and their meanings are shared with some social group and characterized by their typicality. The basic process underlying representational pairing is that of appresentation. This process is the means by which, when we apperceive an object, though we really only see its frontside, we know by analogies – built up from our total experience – what its backside looks like (Schutz, 1962:294–296). Two types of representational vehicles, marks and indications, do not necessarily presuppose intersubjectivity. First, there are marks that I left behind in a world that was once within my reach. If I return to that world, these marks will serve as "subjective reminders" of the original motives or reasons for which they were designated. For instance, I use a bookmark to remind me of where I stopped reading. Indications occur in the following form: if I perceive a certain fact A as occurring, I expect it to be accompanied in the past, present, or future by the existence of fact B, even though my motive for pairing A and B remains opaque. Indeed, when there is "clear and sufficient insight into the nature of the connection between the two elements, we have to deal not with the referential relation of indication but with the inferential one of *proof*" (Schutz, 1962:311). Hence, because we know the logical relationship between a tiger's footprint and his presence in the area, the former is not an "indication" of the latter. Most "natural signs," however, such as smoke representing fire, are considered to be indications.

There are two types of referential terms, signs and symbols, that do presuppose the existence of fellow men. Signs are those facts in the outer world "whose apprehension appresents to an interpreter cogitations [including feelings, thoughts, volitions] of a fellow man" (Schutz, 1962:319). For instance, not only body movements and speech are signs, but also any products of our bodily actions. Symbols are used to apprehend the experience of the transcendence of the common-sense world of everyday life. That is, the appresenting part of the symbolic pair is a fact that exists within our everyday world, while the appresented refers to an ideal that transcends our common-sense experience. Schutz (1962:332) distinguishes two broad levels of symbols.

> There are first sets of appresentational references which are universal and can be used for symbolization because they are rooted in the human condition. . . . Secondly, [there are] the particular forms of symbol systems as developed by the various cultures in different periods.

An example of a universal form of symbol is the opposition of the male and female principle. In one particular manifestation, this opposition can be seem in the traditional Chinese balance wheel, with Yang above Yin.

This concludes our treatment of Schutz's analysis of the foundations of knowledge in everyday life. We have seen how our choosing of an "interest at hand" is basic to the organization of socialized typifications into subjective domains of relevance that channel our action. Further, we have seen that our apprehension of others in the various realms comes through our knowledge of typical objective actions and typical signs of their subjective meaning.

While Schutz did not see himself as working in the sociology of knowledge, in the last decade his unique contributions have redirected inquiry in this field. Not only did he help to broaden this previously narrowly defined field, his influence is also being felt in such other quite divergent fields of sociology as methodology and deviance.

Normative and Interpretive Paradigms in Sociology*

This chapter forms a transition between the conventional approaches to the study of social phenomena predominant in contemporary sociology and the quite different approaches explored in the remaining chapters in this volume. Its purpose is to lay the groundwork for these chapters by showing how the approaches taken in them stem from fundamental theoretical and methodological difficulties pervading conventional sociology. Our concern, however, is not with particular conceptual or logical difficulties and unclarities in specific theories or with methodological defects in various empirical studies. Such shortcomings are common in all disciplines, and clearing them up is part of the normal work in any field. Rather, we are concerned with more fundamental troubles inherent in the assumptions underlying conventional sociological inquiry irrespective of that inquiry's specific theoretical or methodological orientation.

*Portions of this paper are adapted from Wilson (1970) by permission of the American Sociological Association.

I wish to acknowledge the valuable comments and suggestions of Howard N. Boughey, Lloyd H. Fitts, Melvin Pollner, J. Michael Ross, Thomas J. Scheff, Tamotsu Shibutani, Charles B. Spaulding, Bruce C. Straits, Paul Wuebben, and, particularly, Aaron V. Cicourel in developing the argument.

I owe Harold Garfinkel and his students D. Lawrence Wieder and Don H. Zimmerman a special debt. The importance of Garfinkel's influence will be apparent to readers familiar with his writings and lectures (e.g., 1952, 1959b, 1967). However, I remain responsible for any defects in this formulation of the ideas or in the scholarly foundations.

Kuhn (1962) has referred to such a set of pretheoretical notions underlying research as a "paradigm," and the particular assumptions underlying conventional sociology may be called the "normative paradigm."[1] In the first sections of this chapter we will outline the basic notions of the normative paradigm and indicate how they underlie such widely divergent perspectives as operant-conditioning theories of behavior and conventional sociological theories employing the notions of culture, social structure, and socialization. In the second section, we will outline an alternative perspective based on the notion of social interaction as an interpretive process. Then, in the third section, we will examine the methodological problems inherent in the normative paradigm if, indeed, social interaction is an interpretive rather than a rule-governed process. Finally, we will sketch rather briefly some implications of the interpretive paradigm for the study of social phenomena that are explored more extensively in the chapters that follow.

At the outset it is important to note that the central concern of sociology under both the normative and interpretive paradigms is with action as opposed to nonmeaningful behavior.[2] That is, at the most elementary level, the phenomena of interest to sociology are regularities and changes in selected features of behavior that are meaningful to the individuals involved. In order to emphasize this focus, the term action is often used to refer to behavior that is meaningful to the actor.[3] Further, actions do not occur as isolated events but rather are linked to each other as one actor responds to and anticipates the actions of others, and this is so even when an action is performed in solitude. Any particular action, then, is embedded in a process of interaction involving several actors responding to each other's actions.

In this view, large-scale social phenomena, such as organizations,

1. The term normative is used here not in the sense of a prescriptive theory that specifies an ideal norm of conduct to which persons should aspire, but rather to indicate the strategic role of norms in conventional sociological explanation. Moreover, the term paradigm is somewhat of a metaphor, given the diffuse nature of sociological inquiry.

2. Some work in fields such as demography and social psychology may fall outside this definition, but by most criteria work of that sort is marginal to the core of sociology. Attempts to relate such work to sociology typically involve introducing the idea of meaningful behavior, even if in disguised form, as, for example, in Duncan's discussion (in Faris, 1964:37–82) of the importance of technology in the ecosystem.

3. The most explicit formulation of the concept of action is, of course, found in Weber (1947), Parsons (1937, 1951, and in Parsons et al, 1961:32), and Parsons and Shils (1951). While most sociologists are not as explicit as Parsons, inspection of both empirical and theoretical work shows clearly the pervasive concern with meaningful behavior, that is, with actions and patterns of action. Thus, even would be behaviorists such as Homans (1961), when they deal with social phenomena, use common-language categories of meaningful action to identify the "behavior" they seek to explain, and they suggest no other definition of their phenomena, much less provide explicit criteria and demonstrate that these are satisfied in their work.

institutions, and conflict, can be seen as patterned interrelationships between the actions of individual actors in interaction with one another. It should be observed that this view does not commit the sociologist to a version of psychological reductionism.[4] Nor do complex patterns of sociological interest need in themselves be meaningful to the actors. For example, the rate of theft in a group may not even be known to the members of the group; nevertheless, an individual act of theft is behavior meaningful to the members, and the rate expresses a regularity in these actions that can be taken as a phenomenon for sociological investigation. Thus, complex social phenomena are seen as patterned arrangements of interactions among individual actors. The process of interaction, then, is at the logical core of sociological interest, even though for some purposes, particularly of a macrosociological sort, this is often left implicit.

The Normative Paradigm

The normative paradigm consists of two major orienting ideas: interaction is essentially rule governed, and sociological explanation should properly take the deductive form characteristic of natural science. In the first part of this section we will elaborate these ideas more fully. In the second we will show how they are incorporated in two quite different theoretical approaches to social interaction.

INTERACTION AS RULE GOVERNED

In the major current theoretical approaches in sociology, the relevant features of a pattern of action are accounted for ultimately in terms of dispositions that have been acquired by the individual, such as attitudes, sentiments, conditioned responses, and need dispositions, on the one hand, and sanctioned expectations to which the individual is subject, on the other.[5] In common sociological terms, such sanctioned expectations are called role expectations, and an organized set of role expectations applying to a particular actor is termed a status. The role expectations of

4. That is, sociology is committed to what Nagel (1961) has called the "ontological thesis" of methodological individualism, in that social phenomena are taken to be patterns of interrelated actions of individuals. However, as Nagel points out, this does not entail a commitment to reductionism.

5. See Inkeles (in Merton et al, 1959:249–276) and Homans (1964) on the necessity for "psychological" concepts, such as dispositions, in sociological analysis. On the importance of rules, see Homans (1961:13), Coleman (1968), and of course the traditions drawing on Linton (1936), Parsons (1937, 1951, and in Parsons et al, 1961:30–79), Parsons and Shils (1951), and Merton (1968). A similar formulation of the normative paradigm is provided by Cicourel in Chapter 6 in this volume and in Sudnow (1969), and by Blumer (1966).

any one status are thought of as differentiated with respect to the statuses occupied by other individuals with whom the occupant of the first is interacting. Consequently, interaction between individuals is subject to the role expectations of their respective statuses (Merton, 1968:422–424; Gross et al., 1958; Oeser and Harary, 1962, 1964). Looked at in this way, interaction is studied in terms of the relations between the individuals' dispositions and role expectations, role conflict, conformity and deviance, and sanctioning or reinforcement processes.

As Inkeles (in Merton et al., 1959:249–276) and Homans (1964) have noted, in order to account for patterns of action in terms of dispositions and expectations it is necessary to adopt, implicitly or explicitly, a model of the actor that indicates how dispositions are acquired and modified and how the actor's dispositions are related to observed action (for example, that actors seek to optimize gratification, or that they repeat reinforced actions and avoid those that have been punished). The interaction observed in any particular situation, then, is accounted for by identifying structures of expectations and complexes of dispositions such that actors having the properties specified in the theorist's model would act in the observed manner when subject to these dispositions and expectations.

The Concept of a Rule. Common to the notions of both expectation and disposition is the idea of a stable linkage between the situation of an actor and his action in that situation. In the case of a disposition, the linkage is a tendency for the actor to behave in some definite fashion in a particular situation. In the case of an expectation, the linkage is an imperative supported by sanctions: the actor should behave in some specified way in a given situation and will be rewarded for complying or punished for not complying. Such a linkage, whether it is a disposition or an expectation, may be called a rule, and can be represented by an ordered pair (S, A), where S is a specified situation and A is a particular action linked to S by a disposition or an expectation. In sociological terms, a disposition is a rule that has been learned or internalized, while an expectation is a rule that has been institutionalized in a social system. Within the normative paradigm, interaction is viewed as rule governed in the sense that an observed pattern of action is rendered intelligible and is explained by referring to rules in the form of dispositions and expectations to which actors are subject.

The Assumption of Cognitive Consensus. It is important to note that situations and actions are not single events with unique locations in time and space; instead, the same situation can recur, and actions can be repeated. This means that specific occasions and behaviors with unique locations in time and space must be treated as instances of situations and actions. Consequently, to say that a dispositional rule links a situation S and an action A is to say that on any occasion that is an instance of S, the actor has a tendency to engage in behavior that can be treated as an instance of A, and, similarly, *mutatis mutandis*, for expectational rules.

It is clear, then, that the way in which an actor discriminates situations and actions is critical. For if a particular rule (S, A), whether a disposition or an expectation, is in fact operative on a given occasion, then that occasion must be discriminated by the actor as an instance of the situation S, since if the occasion is responded to as an instance of some other situation, say S', then a different rule, say (S', A') would be operative. Similarly, on any given occasion the concrete behavior of one actor must be recognized by another as either an instance of the action A or an instance of some other action, for otherwise such processes as reinforcement and sanctioning could not operate as mechanisms for the acquisition and stabilization of dispositions and expectations. It follows that if social interaction is to be stable, the different participants must discriminate situations and actions in virtually the same way. Otherwise rules could not account for stable, coherent interaction over time and across situations, and the explanatory function of rules would disappear. Thus, theories within the normative paradigm require an empirical assumption of substantial cognitive agreement among interacting actors. Typically this takes the form of an assumption that the actors have been socialized into a common culture that includes a system of symbols and meanings, particularly a language. Disparate definitions of situations and actions do occur, of course, but the assumption of cognitive consensus is retained by treating such divergences as differing subcultural definitions or idiosyncratic deviations resulting from accidents of individual biography.

Consequently, the study patterns of action under the assumption that interaction is rule governed leads to some form of an assumption that, at least within identifiable subgroups, the actors discriminate situations and actions in very nearly the same way (see, for example, Warriner, 1969). Whether it is made explicit or remains implicit, this assumption of cognitive consensus is an essential element within the normative paradigm.

EXPLANATION AS DEDUCTIVE

The second fundamental assumption of the normative paradigm is that explanations of patterns of action should follow the deductive model characteristic of the natural sciences. In this form of explanation, empirically described facts are explained by showing that they can be deduced logically from assured theoretical premises in conjunction with already given empirical conditions. For sociological explanations, the assumed theoretical premises would consist of the assumptions embodied in the model of the actor together with whatever strictly sociological postulates are adopted. The given conditions would then be features of the social phenomenon that are taken as established and not problematic for the investigation at hand. While this model is only infrequently employed in a serious way in substantive sociological inquiry, it stands as the major ideal underlying current methodological and theoretical discourse.[6]

TWO EXAMPLES

We turn now to two quite different theoretical approaches to be study of social interaction. The first, operant-conditioning theory, is relevant because its leading ideas are incorporated in several criticisms and proposed alternatives to conventional sociological approaches (Homans, 1961; Blau, 1964; Coleman, 1964, 1968b; Baldwin, 1967), and the theory itself has been applied to social interaction by Skinner (1957). Consequently, it is of considerable interest to find that operant-conditioning theory displays clearly the basic assumptions of the normative paradigm.

The Skinnerian Actor. The basic unit of analysis in operant-conditioning theory consists of an organism in a stimulus situation, or, in our terminology, an actor in a situation. The analysis itself is concerned with the probability that the actor will display a particular behavior pattern in that situation, and it seeks to account for the magnitude of this probability in terms of the way the actor was previously reinforced in that situation. For example, if a pigeon is conditioned in a Skinner box to peck at a target when a light is on, the situation consists of being in a Skinner box with the light on, the behavior pattern consists of pecking at the target, and the tendency of the pigeon to peck when the light is on is specified by some probability to be determined empirically by the observer as a function of the pigeon's reinforcement history (Skinner, 1953).

6. On the deductive pattern of explanation, see Kaufman (1944:68-69), Hempel and Oppenheim (1948), and Nagel (1961). Suppes (1957) provides an introduction to logic, emphasizing applications to mathematics and science, For a briefer introduction, see Quine (1965). Strong statements of the position that sociological explanation should follow this pattern may be found in Homans (1964, 1967), Zetterberg (1965), Rudner (1966), and Blalock (1969:1-3). More typically, however, sociologists express this position obliquely, as in Dubin (1969: passim, and especially 166, 170-171), Greer (1969:123), Parsons (1937:6, 24, 1960:468), Merton (1968:41, 150, et passim), Smelser (1968:14-15), Gibbs (1968), and Wallace (1969:3). For the prevalence of the "natural science model," see virtually any introductory text or methods book. However, it is perhaps surprising to note that Lazarsfeld (in Merton et al, 1959:39-78) appears to dissent: his discussion of the notions of a universe of indicators, interchangeability of indicators, and the drift of indicators is incompatible with the logic of deductive explanation.

The concept of action, in the sense employed in this chapter, is perhaps not properly used within the context of operant-conditioning theory. Consequently, we will use the term behavior pattern instead of action to refer to the pattern of behavior in which the observer is interested. Clearly, however, the notion of behavior pattern occupies the same place in relation to the concept of a rule as does the notion of action, and when in fact the theorist is interested in explaining human social interaction, the question of the relation between behavior patterns and actions becomes critical.

What is really of interest, however, is the manner in which the Skinnerian actor incorporates the notion of a rule and the central place that rules have in explanation. In the example given above, the observer can be thought of as concerned with the ordered pair (pigeon in the Skinner box with the light on, pigeon pecks at the target) and with the probability that the behavior pattern designated by the second term occurs whenever the situation designated by the first term occurs. Thus, at the very heart of operant-conditioning theory is the notion of a rule, in the form of a disposition associated with the actor through the mechanism of the actor's reinforcement history.

In order to carry out this kind of analysis, the observer must specify objectively what features of a particular concrete occasion are linked with what characteristics of the actor's behavior on that occasion. In these terms, any occasion having these same features is an instance of the "same situation," and any behavior of the actor having these same characteristics is an instance of the "same" behavior pattern. Thus, the situation and the behavior pattern are specified by the observer in terms of properties of specific concrete occasions and behaviors that are linked as a result of reinforcement. In addition, of course, the observer must supply nontautological criteria for identifying those features of the occasion immediately following the actor's behavior that constitute "reinforcement." Within this model, a disposition is such a linkage between a situation and a behavior pattern together with the probability that the actor will display the behavior pattern in that situation. Knowledge of the actor's reinforcement history, then, specifies the actor's dispositions at any given time, and from these his behavior patterns can be explained or predicted.

Although the main focus of operant-conditioning theory is on the acquisition and modification of dispositions, expectations also play a critical part in the form of reinforcement contingencies. For example, in training the pigeon the observer establishes a stable connection between the situation of the pigeon's being in the Skinner box with the light on, on the one hand, and the behavior pattern of the pigeon's pecking at the target, on the other such that whenever the pigeon displays this behavior pattern in this situation, some specified reinforcement schedule is applied. The formal structure of contingent reinforcement, then, is that of an expectation: a rule, conformity to which is supported by sanctions. The critical theoretical importance of such expectations lies in the assumption that the stable features of actors' behavior patterns result from stable characteristics of their reinforcement histories, which in turn must depend on exposure to stable reinforcement contingencies, that is, to stable expectations.

Thus, the behavior patterns of the Skinnerian actor are rule governed. Knowing the actor's dispositions and the reinforcement contingencies, or expectations, to which he is exposed allows one to deduce an explanation of his current behavior pattern and predictions concerning changes in his behavior patterns. Moreover, when this model is applied to human social interaction, it is assumed (Skinner, 1957) that the actors belong to a "verbal community" within which they are trained to respond to verbal behavior in similar ways. Thus, an explicit assumption of cognitive consensus is found in the most elementary theory that might be constructed within the normative paradigm.

Conventional Sociological Theories. As Homans (1964) has noted, the models of the actor employed in most contemporary sociological theories are implicit if not ad hoc. Consequently, it is impossible to give one or even a few examples that would accurately characterize them all in detail. However, the overwhelming tendency is to use some version of the notion of a socialized actor. The most explicit formulation of this has been developed by Parsons and Shils (1951), but essentially the same ideas are employed by other sociologists, often with different terminology and without commitment to Parsons' total conceptual scheme.

Parsons and Shils (1951:115) define a need disposition of an individual actor as a learned "group of orientations" all following a pattern involving the discrimination of an object or group of objects, the cathecting of an object or group of objects, and a tendency to behave in a fashion designed to get the cathected relationship with the object [or group of objects]." Thus, in this model, a situation is composed of a group of discriminated objects such that the actor has a tendency to behave in a definite fashion toward these objects. In the case of socialized human actors, the discriminations of objects are assumed to be mediated by a system of symbols shared with other actors. Consequently, the underlying notion of a linkage between a situation, composed of discriminated objects, and action is fundamental to this model, but need dispositions are seen as embedded in a symbolic process that allows the introduction of fairly elaborate psychological mechanisms, including defenses and internalization of values and expectations. With this model, the action of an actor on any given occasion is explained through the assumption that the actor behaves so as to try to optimize gratification relative to his need dispositions (Parsons and Shils, 1951: 123-124).

With the introduction of symbolic processes, communication between actors becomes possible, and the notions of expectation and sanction become important in a way not possible when these concepts are treated simply as reinforcement contingencies. In particular, actors are viewed as internalizing values and expectations, which means that these become part of their need dispositions, in the process generally called socialization. With this, then, arises the possibility of a shared culture of legitimate expectations that are not merely sanctioned but are also constitutive of the actors' systems of need dispositions. However, as Parsons (1951) has noted, such internalization is never perfect, and the actor need not be regarded merely as an automation "programmed" by his culture. Rather, the shared cognitive and normative culture provides for one aspect of the dispositions and expectations confronting an actor, along with others emerging from the actor's personal and necessarily idiosyncratic biography.

Sociological analysis, of course, is not confined to explaining the actions of one actor in a single situation but is also concerned with the properties of large-scale patterns of action involving numerous actors in many situations. However, dispositions and expectations retain their central place in the analysis. Since the action of each actor in any particular situation is explained by referring to the dispositions and expectations to which he is subject, properties of large-scale social patterns must result from the characteristics of the systems of expectations and dispositions to which the actors are subject. This means not that every regularity is taken to be normatively prescribed or the result of shared dispositions, but only that the regularity results from actors' attempts to optimize gratification within particular structures of dispositions and expectations that effectively define their interests.

For example, Parsons has been especially concerned with the characteristics a normative system must have if a social system is to exhibit stability, and he has argued that dispositions and sanctioned expectations must be complementary and that the system of expectations must exhibit a certain structure (Parsons, 1960). Insofar as the normative system is not characterized by these properties, the social system will be incompletely integrated and thus display tendencies toward unregulated conflict, tension, and patterned deviance. Similarly, Merton (1968) has addressed the question of why some societies exhibit particular differential rates of deviance between various categories of actors, for example, the reported higher crime rates among the lower- as compared with middle-class individuals. As elaborated by A. E. Cohen (1955, 1966), Cloward (1959), Cloward and Ohlin (1960), and Short and Strodtbeck (1965), this results in a model of normatively constrained differential opportunity structures that affect crime rates through both differential socialization and differential access to legitimate and illegitimate roles. Further, to the extent that labeling theories of deviance (Lemert, 1951; Becker, 1963; Scheff, 1968) do not adhere rigorously to a symbolic-interactionist position, they are readily assimilated as useful though minor additions to such structural theories (A. E. Cohen, 1966; for more detailed discussion, see Zimmerman, 1969). Finally, the recurring debates over the place of conflict in sociological analysis (Adams, 1966; Horton, 1966; Williams, 1966; Coser, 1967; Demerath and Peterson, 1967) all take for granted the assumptions that actors acquire characteristic purposes and motives, that is, dispositions, by virtue of their differential locations in society, and that they act in response to organized structures of expectations supported by sanctions. The disagreements center on the extent to which expectations are internalized (normative consensus or its absence) and the empirical degree of integration of societies (such as whether subgroups in fact have conflicting or coinciding interests).

The Interpretive Paradigm

The conception of interaction as an interpretive process proposed by Blumer (1966) and in earlier statements by Blumer (1954, 1956, and in Rose, 1962:179–192), Turner (in Rose, 1962:20–40), and others (e.g., G. H. Mead, 1934; Mills, 1940; Garfinkel, in Scher, 1962:689–712; 1964), differs sharply from the normative paradigm. Turner (in Rose, 1962:23), for instance, directly contrasts the normative role model with the concept of role-taking:

> *The idea of role-taking shifts emphasis away from the simple process of enacting a prescribed role to devising a performance on the basis of an imputed other role.* The actor is not the occupant of a stratus for which there is a neat set of rules—a culture or set of norms—but a person who must act in the perspective supplied in part by his relationship to others whose actions reflect roles he must identify.

A role, in Turner's formulation, is a coherent pattern of behaviors. The actor is assumed to have a tendency to perceive the behaviors of others in such patterns, and "it is this tendency to shape the phenomenal world into roles which is the key to role-taking as a core process in interaction" (Turner, in Rose, 1962:22). Further, "the unifying element [by which behaviors are seen as a pattern] is to be found *in some assignment of purpose or sentiment to the actor"* (1962:28). In short, one actor perceives the behavior of another as a meaningful action expressing some purpose or sentiment embodied in a role.[7] On the basis of this perception of what the other is up to, the actor then devises his own course of action. Moreover, Turner (in Rose, 1962:22) notes,

> Since the role of alter can only be inferred rather than directly known by ego, testing inferences about the role of alter is a continuing element in interaction. Hence the tentative character of the individual's own role definition is never wholly suspended.[8]

As a consequence, the perceived purpose and meaning in the other's action are always provisional and subject to revision in the light of subsequent events in the course of interaction. Thus, what was initially seen as one role may later be seen in retrospect as having actually been a very different role, resulting in a thoroughgoing reinterpretation of the actions the other was performing all along.[9]

Blumer (1966:540) develops this same conception of interaction using somewhat different terminology. He suggests that in interaction

> the participants fit their acts together, first by identifying the social act in which they are about to engage and, second, by interpreting and defining each other's acts in forming the joint act. By identifying the social act or joint action, the participant is able to orient himself; he has a key to interpreting the acts of the others and a guide for directing his action with regard to them. . . . [The participants] have to ascertain what the others are doing and plan to do and make indications to one another of what to do.

Further, Blumer (1966:538) notes the tentative character of a participant's formulation of what he and the others are about: "In the flow of group life there are innumerable points at which the participants are *re*defining each other's acts." Thus, Turner's view of social interaction coincides with Blumer's. Both conceive of interaction as an essentially interpretive process in which meanings evolve and change over the course of interaction.

Documentary Interpretation and Indexicality. In order to see clearly

---

7. No assumption is made here that the actor first sees the behavior of the other as an array of raw sense data and then assigns meaning and purpose to it. Rather, what is seen is the action of the other with its perceived purposes and sentiments. For a discussion of the difficulties with the notion of raw sense data and the correlative assumption that such "data" are uniquely and completely determined by physical stimuli, see Gurwitsch (1964:Parts I, II, III) and Dreyfus (in Edie, 1967:31–47).

8. Turner's use of such terms as inferred and testing inferences should not be misconstrued as positing a rationalistic model of the process, since "inference" in this context does not necessarily mean strict logical deduction but can include other criteria, such as aesthetic or moral appropriateness as well.

9. As Parsons (1937) has emphasized, the very notion of an action requires the idea of the actor's end or purpose. That is, for an action to be perceived, purpose and meaning must be perceived. Thus, a change in the perceived meaning or purpose entails a change in the action that is perceived.

the methodological implications of the interpretive paradigm, it will be useful to employ the sharper and more powerful formulation based on Garfinkel's (in Scher, 1962: 689–712; 1964) use of the notions of documentary interpretation and indexicality.[10] Documentary interpretation consists of identifying an underlying pattern behind a series of appearances such that each appearance is seen as referring to, an expression of, or a "document of," the underlying pattern. However, the underlying pattern itself is identified through its individual concrete appearances, so that the appearances reflecting the pattern and the pattern itself mutually determine one another in the same way that the "part" and the "whole" mutually determine each other in gestalt phenomena (Gurwitsch, 1964). This mutual determination of appearances and underlying pattern is referred to by Garfinkel as indexicality, and a particular appearance is called an indexical particular.[11] A central characteristic of documentary interpretation is that later appearances may force a revision in the perceived underlying pattern that in turn compels a reinterpretation of what previous appearances "really were." Moreover, on any given occasion present appearances are interpreted partially on the basis of what the underlying pattern projects as the future course of events, and one may have to await further developments to understand the meaning of present appearances. In this sense, documentary interpretations are retrospective and prospective.

In these terms, role-taking in interaction is a process in which the participants engage in documentary interpretation of each other's actions such that the underlying pattern consists of the context of their interaction, including their motives, purposes, and sentiments (that is, their respective roles), of which the particular actions are seen as expressions. Each action in the course of interaction, then, is an indexical particular that is understood by the participants in terms of the place of the action in the context of what has gone before and what they see as the future

10. The concept of documentary interpretation was borrowed and somewhat transformed by Garfinkel from Mannheim (in Kecskemeti, 1952:52–63). Further discussion of the parallel between Garfinkel's formulation and that of Blumer and Turner may be found in Wieder (1964). The term indexical is taken from Bar-Hillel (1954), who defines an indexical expression as one that depends for its meaning on the context in which it is produced. The term indexical particular then, is a generalization of indexical expression to include nonlinguistic as well as linguistic events. See Garfinkel and Sacks (in McKinney and Tiryakian, forthcoming) for an extended discussion.

11. Strictly speaking, the concept here should be called essential indexicality to indicate that it is in principle impossible to eliminate the dependence on context in such situations. When the gestalt "part-whole" interdependence is absent, the indexicality can be removed by appending a suitable description of the context that is independent of the particular appearance. This idea is expressed by Garfinkel in various places by the assertion that indexicality is irremediable.

course of the interaction. Moreover, this context itself is seen for what it is through the same actions, it is used to interpret. That is, on any particular occasion in the course of the interaction, the actions that the participants see each other performing are seen as such in terms of the meaning of the context, and the context in turn is understood to be what it is through these same actions. Further, what the situation on any particular occasion is understood to have been may be revised subsequently in the light of later events. Consequently, what the situation "really was" and what the actors "really did" on a particular occasion are continually open to redefinition.

It is apparent that in the interpretive view of social interaction, in contrast with the normative paradigm, definitions of situations and actions are not explicitly or implicitly assumed to be settled once and for all by literal application of a preexisting, culturally established system of symbols.[12] Rather, the meanings of situations and actions are interpretations formulated on particular occasions by the participants in the interaction and are subject to reformulation on subsequent occasions.[13]

Methodological Implications. It is now possible to draw the methodological implications of a crucial observation made by Blumer (1966:542). If the fundamental process in interaction is documentary interpretation in the form of role-taking, through which actions are seen as they are in terms of the actor's perception of the context,

the study of interaction would have to be made from the position of the actor. Since action is forged by the actor out of what he perceives, interprets, and judges, one would have to see the operating situation as the actor sees it, perceive objects as the actor perceives them, ascertain their meaning in terms of the meaning they have for the actor, and follow the actor's line of conduct as the actor organizes it—in short, *one would have to take the role of the actor* and see the world from his standpoint. [Emphasis added.]

That is to say, in order to understand and follow the course of interaction, the researcher must engage in documentary interpretation, and

---

12. For a critique of this aspect of the normative paradigm, see Bittner (1964) and Wieder (in Chapter 5 in this volume).

13. It is important to note that while the interpretive paradigm has been formulated partially in symbolic-interactionist terms, not all versions of symbolic interactionism are based on this paradigm. For example, the term significant symbol is frequently used to refer to a gesture that calls out the "same response" in the user and the recipient. To the extent that such a notion is actually employed in a manner similar to the concept of culture, the normative rather than the interpretive paradigm is involved, even though the terminology is somewhat different from the usual formulations. It is perhaps convenient to refer to symbolic-interactionist formulations consistent with an interpretive conception of interaction as radical symbolic interactionism. In particular, Blumer and Turner are not entirely consistent on this matter.

D

in particular he must do so in order to identify what action is performed at any given moment.[14]

The central premise of this argument is that there is no way of seeing an event as an action and of describing its features other than through the documentary method of interpretation. Because actions are constituted and have their existence only through the participants' use of the documentary method of interpretation, the researcher has access to these same actions as intended objects of description only through documentary interpretation.

Moreover, this conclusion holds whether the researcher relies on only his own observations or uses reports by informants, organizational or historical records, or survey respondents' replies to questions. To the extent that accounts from such sources are treated as descriptions of patterns of action or of expectations or dispositions in which the researcher is interested, these accounts are documentary interpretations on the part of the individuals providing the information, and in order to construct his own description as a basis for analysis, the researcher must see through these reports to identify the underlying pattern they reflect.[15] That is, the researcher's description is itself a documentary interpretation.[16]

Descriptions based in this way on documentary interpretation may be called *interpretive* descriptions. Thus, a major consequence of viewing social interaction as an interpretive process is that depictions of interaction in terms of the meanings of the actions, whether these depictions be the participants' own or the researcher's, must be construed as interpretive descriptions. The importance of this conclusion, as will be seen below, is that the characteristics of interpretive description are incompatible with the logic of deductive explanation.[17]

14. This is so even using fixed observational categories such as Bales's (1951). Invariably, to classify an action as an instance of a particular analytical category, such as "gives support, . . . ," the observer must impute motives or sentiments to the actor, identify the other actors to whom the act was directed, and perhaps impute some sentiments or motives to the recipients of the act in response. That is, the observer must decide the meaning of the behavior in its context. It is also worth pointing out the close connection of Blumer's statement with the concept of *Verstehen* developed by Weber (1947).

15. For a more extended discussion, see Cicourel (1964, 1968).

16. The only way for the researcher to avoid this is to relinquish interest in the pattern of action by employing descriptive categories based on features that are invariant over all possible reinterpretations of the actions. That is, the features on which the description is based would have to be independent of the entire range of meanings that could be imputed to the concrete behaviors. But then the concept of action would become irrelevant, and, in fact, it would not be definable within such a system of categories.

17. This point was noted by Blumer (1954, 1956). However, the use of the concept of essential indexicality allows a much sharper statement of the argument, since it places the discussion in a clear logical context (Bar-Hillel, 1954; Quine, 1960, 1961). It should be

Deductive Explanation and Modes of Description

In the deductive form of explanation, facts are explained by showing that they can be deduced logically from assumed theoretical premises and already given empirical conditions.[18] Descriptions of the phenomenon enter into such an explanation at two points: as the given empirical conditions and as statements of the facts to be explained. Consequently, commitment to the deductive form of explanation entails commitment to a mode of description that satisfies the logical requirements of deductive argument. The notion of a valid deductive argument, however, rests on the assumption that the meaning of each assertion entering into the argument is independent of occasions of its use, that is, that the assertion is a "statement" and not an essentially indexical expression (Carnap, 1937:167-168; Bar-Hillel, 1954:365-366, 378; Quine, 1960:42, 44, 227; 1965:5-8).[19] In particular, each description entering into deductive explanation must be treated as having a stable meaning that is independent of the circumstances in which it is produced. A description satisfying this condition as well as the usual criterion of intersubjective verifiability will be called literal, in the sense that the description itself is to be taken in a strictly literal fashion.[20] Thus, deductive explanation in any strict sense is appropriate and meaningful only when the descriptions of phenomena can be treated as literal. A central question, then, concerns the conditions under which descriptions can be taken as literal.

THE CHARACTERISTICS OF LITERAL DESCRIPTION

Literal description is taken for granted in the natural sciences, and problems of description tend to be treated mainly as practical matters of competent technique rather than as posing fundamental methodological questions of concern to practicing scientists. However, as Schutz (1962:53) has observed, "intersubjectivity, inter-communication, and language are simply presupposed" as resources taken for granted for the conduct of research in the natural sciences. That is to say, science is a

---

mentioned that Buckley (1967) has also sharply criticized theories within the normative paradigm. However, it would seem that little is gained by employing a general systems metaphor unless the fundamental descriptive problems are solved.

18. In practice, deductive explanations are never presented in fully rigorous form. Rather, the point is that such explanations can always be made more rigorous should one so desire: that is, implicit premises can be made explicit, informal definitions can be made more precise, and omitted logical steps can be supplied.

19. The term statement in formal logic is used to refer to a declarative sentence that is unequivocal and has the same truth value on all occasions of its use. Quine (1960:1933ff) uses the term eternal sentence in just this sense. Thus, all sentences that are not eternal in Quine's sense are indexical in Bar-Hillel's usage.

20. In Quine's (1960) terms, a literal description is an eternal sentence that adequately paraphrases an observation sentence.

fundamentally social enterprise, so that scientific descriptions are the products of research activities conducted by members of a particular scientific community and consist of accounts of those activities that are provided and understood by competent members of that community. The conduct of research and communication of results, moreover, depend on common-sense knowledge that is taken for granted by the members of the relevant scientific community, and one's competence as a member of that community, consists partially in being seen as having command of this body of presumptively shared common-sense knowledge.[21] It is impossible, then, for a researcher to give a complete account of his research activities; instead he must rely on common-sense understandings that he and his colleagues assume are taken for granted by all competent members of the fraternity.

Consequently the question is how descriptions can be treated as literal by members of a particular scientific community, that is, as independent of context and intersubjectively verifiable. As an initial approach to the problem, the following is proposed. Any description of a phenomenon is based on perceived features that the phenomenon displays to the observer. A literal description, then, amounts to asserting that on the basis of those features the phenomenon has some clearly designated property, or what is logically the same thing, belongs to some particular well-defined class of phenomena. For members of a scientific community to treat a description as literal, they must take it for granted that the following are enforceable criteria for the products of research activity.

1. A description of a phenomenon as an instance of a class specifies explicitly the particular features of the phenomenon that are sufficient conditions for counting it as belonging to that class.
2. The features on which the classification is based are demonstrably recognizable by any competent member of the relevant scientific community independently of the other members.

"Feature in this context means either a part of the phenomenon specified by further descriptions meeting the above two criteria or an aspect of the perceived phenomenon taken for granted as a matter of common sense, that is, perceivable by all competent members of the relevant scientific community. Thus, an attempt to clarify what a particular feature is must either take the form of further literal description or resort to "what any competent person can see," such that to question

---

21. On the crucial importance of implicit, unexplicated procedures in natural scientific research, see Bridgeman (1927, 1936, 1950, 1951), Campbell (1920, 1921, 1928, 1935), Kaufman (1944), and Kuhn (1961, 1962). For a review of Bridgeman's and Campbell's writings on this matter, see Handel (1968).

the appearance of the feature is to render questionable one's status as a competent member of that particular scientific community. Literal description, then, depends on a body of common-sense knowledge, taken for granted by scientific colleagues, as an essential resource.[22]

Further, "sufficient conditions" is meant in its full logical sense. Consequently, all phenomena exhibiting the same features must be identified as members of the same class, and membership of a phenomenon in that class can be denied only by showing that certain of the alleged features on which the classification was originally based were actually not present at the time the classification was made. Except for such a demonstration, a literal description can be revised only in the direction of making it more refined and never in a way that denies the original classification. In particular, a literal description stands as true irrespective of what else might be said about the phenomenon, and thus what the description means depends in no way on the context of other features the phenomenon might also display. For example, under the assumption that the measurements were done competently, the assertion that a certain body has a mass of 3.52 ± 0.03 grams at a particular time must stand as a stubborn fact that cannot be altered by other statements that might be made about the body. Of course the theoretical significance of this fact will depend heavily on other facts, as well as on the theoretical

22. This formulation may suggest a possible alternative to Quine's (1960) reliance on stimulus meaning that is more in accord with his continual insistence that the adequacy of a paraphrase of a given sentence is always relative to the purposes for which the original sentence was uttered. The basic trouble with the notion of stimulus meaning is that Quine (1960:34) is forced to treat the concept of stimulus as a logical universal, which invites the question of how two concrete occurrences are recognized as the "same" or "different" stimuli. It should be noted, however, that this does not vitiate Quine's critique of synonymy and the related notion of analyticity, since his argument goes through even if there are no stimulus synonymous sentences.

In this connection, it should be noted that Katz (1966) and Lewis (1969) have attempted to answer Quine's critique of synonymy and analyticity. Katz's effort fails because he assumes the existence of a dictionary in which each word has a finite entry that exhaustively establishes its meanings. The meanings of sentences, then, are built up from words by grammatical rules. This is untenable since it provides no way of handling indexical sentences, and there is the further problem of what language the dictionary is to be written in so as to avoid circularity or infinite regress.

Lewis's analysis, on the other hand, runs into difficulty because it relies on the notion of a possible world: a sentence is analytic if and only if it is true in every possible world. However, as Lewis himself notes (1969:207), any clear explication of the concept of possible world rests on a prior notion of analyticity, so that "possible world" must be left a primitive term. While Lewis may not view this as a problem for some philosophical purposes, it nevertheless reinforces Quine's argument that there is no absolute universal distinction between analytic and nonanalytic sentences in an actual natural language and, likewise, no absolute notion of synonymy. Rather, whether a sentence is to be treated as analytic, or two sentences as synonymous, is a matter to be determined on the particular occasions of use in terms of the purposes and intentions of the users.

framework employed by the investigator.[23] The fact itself, however, cannot be denied without challenging the competence with which the original observations were made.

Finally, the enforceable character of the criteria of literal description means that, while demonstration of conformity to them frequently may be omitted, the members of the relevant scientific community take it for granted that they may legitimately be called upon to show explicitly that any description offered as literal in fact satisfies the criteria.

Thus, scientific research is a practical activity, which is embedded, as is any practical activity, in a context of implicit common-sense knowledge and is carried on by members of a particular scientific community for the purpose of developing descriptions that can serve as the bases for eventual theoretical understanding. In particular, when explanation is taken to be deductive in form, the practical purpose at hand in research is the production of descriptions that can be treated as literal. The criteria of literal description, required for the conceptual and logical clarity of deductive explanation, then, are imposed as enforceable canons of criticism for the products of scientific research.[24]

THE DESCRIPTION OF INTERACTION

The phenomena of interest in sociological investigation are patterns of action, which consist ultimately of interactions between particular actors. Even when the explicit concern is with macroscopic phenomena, these are comprised of patterns or regularities in interactions within some population. In a fundamental way, then, sociological investigation depends upon descriptions of interactions, and, if sociological explanations are to be deductive, these descriptions must be taken to be

23. With respect to social phenomena, Kaplan (1964) uses the somewhat unfortunate terms act meaning and action meaning to refer to the distinction between the empirical meaning of a descriptive statement (Smith did thus-and-such) and the theoretical significance of this (why it is important or interesting that Smith did thus-and-such rather than something else).

24. The emphasis on conceptual and logical clarity as enforceable canons of criticism for deductive explanation contrasts markedly with the conduct of everyday practical affairs. In practical situations, insistence on conceptual and logical clarity beyond the point needed to facilitate the business at hand is typically rejected, bringing forth such epithets as hair splitting and logic chopping. That is, in practical activities, one must be only as precise and rigorous as is necessary to accomplish the present purposes; to insist on more is to be seen as an obstructionist or some other objectionable social type. For a fuller discussion, see Garfinkel (1960).

It should also be noted that there is considerable tolerance in scientific work for ambiguity. The history of science shows many instances in which concepts have turned out to be obscure and theoretical arguments have been found to be logically inadequate. Uniformly, however, recognition of such difficulties has generated strenuous efforts at clarification, resulting in major advances in mathematics, important empirical and theoretical discoveries, and sometimes fundamental scientific revolutions.

literal. Under the normative paradigm, the question of literal description can be dealt with by invoking implicitly or explicitly the assumption of a shared system of symbols and meanings, for such a complex of shared symbols could be used to provide context-free and unambiguous descriptions of situations and actions (Warriner, 1969). If, however, social interaction is essentially an interpretive process, then, as we have seen, descriptions of interaction are necessarily interpretive descriptions. But if at this most fundamental level the only way an observer can identify what actions have occurred is through documentary interpretation, then descriptions of interaction are not intersubjectively verifiable in any strong sense, since the interpretations of different individuals will necessarily agree only when they are able to negotiate a common social reality,[25] nor are such descriptions independent of context.

In describing interaction interpretively, the observer necessarily imputes an underlying pattern that serves as the essential context for seeing what the situations and actions are, while these same situations and actions are a necessary resource for seeing what the context is. Thus, the observer's classification of the behavior of an actor on a given occasion in the course of interaction as an instance of a particular type of action is not based on a limited set of specifiable features of the behavior and the occasion but, rather, depends on the indefinite context seen as relevant by the observer, a context that gets its meaning partly through the very action it is being used to interpret. Moreover, though the behavior of an actor on a given occasion may be classified as an instance of some particular type of action, this classification is indefinitely revisable on the basis of later events or further information.[26]

It is, for example, a familiar experience in social interaction for individuals to explain what they really meant by some previous gesture, and such reinterpretations frequently are accepted at face value, thus sharply altering the course of interaction. In observational studies of interaction, it is not uncommon for the observer to understand what the events recorded in his notes really consist of only in the light of subsequent events and often only after he has left the field altogether.

25. See the suggestive empirical studies by Scheff (1968) and Emerson (1969).

26. This does not mean that behavior has no literally describable or "objective" consequences. Rather, the point is that the behavior and its consequences take on sociological relevance only when subject to interpretations by actors in the society. For example, there is frequently no doubt that, in literally describable terms, a certain object has disappeared from a particular place. The socially relevant questions, however, are whether the object was borrowed, stolen, or removed by someone with a socially acknowledged right to do so, and the effect the actors see the vanishing of the object as having on their plans, purposes, and projects. But specification and analysis of these requires interpretive rather than literal description. Thus, Nagel's discussion of this matter (1961:475–476) misses the essential point.

Similarly, in survey research the meaning of a set of items or an index often becomes clear only after the analysis has begun to take definite shape and a clear story line has started to emerge, in which case the index receives its meaning from the way it fits into the emerging pattern of findings, but the pattern of findings partly depends on seeing the index as measuring a particular thing.

Clearly, then, the description of interaction cannot be treated as literal. Rather, to understand what is meant by a particular description, it is necessary to see it in the light of what else has been said about the interaction. Thus, in order to establish the meaning of a description of an action, the observer must rely not only on a body of common-sense knowledge shared with his colleagues but also on his grasp of the common-sense understandings shared by the participants in the interaction itself.[27] Consequently, in order to communicate to his colleagues, the observer must evoke in them the context for any given descriptive statement so that they will see it in the same light he does.

Moreover, it should be evident that since larger group, organizational, institutional, or cultural patterns are themselves comprised of regularities perceived by the observer in interactions among actors, the description and analysis of such patterns are thoroughgoing interpretive processes. Consequently, such macrosocial patterns are no more susceptible to literal description than are the particular interactions entering into them.[28] Of course, an observer, whether participant observer, historian, or survey analyst, generally has a wider range of events and a

27. This is crucial in view of Quine's (1960) insistence that the adequacy of a paraphrase of a given sentence (that is, a description of that sentence in terms of its meaning) always depends on the purposes intended by the person using the sentence. Thus, descriptions in the natural sciences are often indexical expressions but can be paraphrased, if needed, by appropriate statements through reliance on the taken for granted shared competence of scientific colleagues, though as Quine (1960:227) notes, this is seldom actually done in practice. However, this strategy is not available when the objects being described are themselves actions, often in the form of utterances, for in this case the adequacy of the description or paraphrase depends on the participant's intentions and purposes, that is, on its meaning to the actor, which is what one is trying to describe in the first place.

28. If such patterns could be described literally, these descriptions would in turn provide literal descriptions of aspects of the component actions, which, as has been noted, implies that these latter descriptions would have to be invariant over all possible imputations of meaning to the original concrete behaviors, thus rendering them irrelevant for the study of action. It should be noted that, as a consequence, to invoke features of the social context as conditions that help "structure" specific situations (Blumer, in Rose, 1962:187; Blumer, 1966:541) is to provide a further interpretation. That is, when the observer seeks to study the way differing perspectives or definitions of situations are related to features of the social context (for example, group membership, status, and social background characteristics), both the dependent and the independent variables are identified by interpretive rather than literal description. While this is perfectly legitimate and necessary for understanding patterns of action, it does not provide a basis for literal description.

broader context to interpret them than do any of the individual participants, and thus his descriptions may sometimes be seen as more com-
prehensive, penetrating, and "objective," than the participants' own
accounts. This, however, does not warrant a claim to literal description,
since the mutual determination of event and context remains, and the
observer's account of what in fact happened at particular times and
places is subject to continual revision in the light of unfolding events,
further information, and reflection.

The Study of Interpretive Processes

It is evident that if social interaction is an interpretive process, descriptions of interaction cannot be literal and sociological explanations of
patterns of action are not deductive in any strict sense.[29] Thus, a commitment to deductive explanation, as assumed within the normative
paradigm, is incompatible with the study of patterns of action. This does
not mean that explanations of social phenomena employing the notion of
rule-governed action are meaningless or trivial. Rather, as Weber (in
Shils and Finch, 1949:50-112) and, more recently, Kaplan (1964:363-
367) have shown, interpretation of patterns of action in terms of the
purposes and situations of the actors is a defensible and significant form
of explanation.[30] Indeed, explanation in such terms is what is called for
in countless situations in everyday life and has been the substantial goal
of much of scholarship since the time of the first historian. Clearly,
though, a major theoretical and methodological reorientation is needed if

29. A similar conclusion has been reached following Wittgenstein (1953) by Winch
(1958) and Louch (1966). Moreover, the same result is implied by Quine's critique (1960,
1961) of the notion of synonymy and Dreyfus's critique (in Edie, 1967:31-47) of artificial
intelligence.

In terms of Kaplan's (1964) distinction between logic in use and reconstructed logic,
sociological explanations of actions cannot properly be reconstructed in deductive form if
social interaction is taken to be an interpretive process. In this light, attempts to formulate
deductive explanations in sociology would seem to have an ad hoc and metaphorical
quality to them, with their persuasiveness often resting more on the imagery invoked than
on logically compelling grounds. From this point of view, polemics such as Homans's
(1964, 1967) are fundamentally misguided. Indeed, Homans's own efforts at deductive
explanation (e.g., 1961) can be seen as resting heavily on metaphor and ad hoc reinterpretations of supposedly firm concepts and underlying principles. This, of course, does not
mean that his explanations are necessarily bad ones, but only that they cannot be treated
as deductive in any serious sense.

30. A great deal of confusion concerning Weber's views has been created by the
practice of translating the German *Wissenschaft* as "Science." In its original sense,
science meant rational intellectual discipline, or scholarship, which would be adequate
renderings of the German. The word science as it tends to be understood today, however,
has a much narrower sense and is a translation of the German *Naturwissenschaft*, primarily physics, chemistry, biology, etc. If, in the translations of Weber, one systematically
substitutes scholarship and scholar for the words science and scientist, his work takes on a

D*

the interpretive character of conventional sociological inquiry is to be recognized explicitly rather than suppressed in an essentially unrealizable attempt to follow the intellectual model of the natural sciences.[31]

Of central interest here is that conceiving of social interaction as an interpretive process opens up the possibility of treating the interpretive process itself as a phenomenon for investigation. In such inquiries, the documentary method of interpretation is not taken for granted as a resource in the study of patterns of action but is viewed as a topic for investigation in its own right.[32] It is this opportunity that has been followed up in various ways in the remaining chapters in this volume.

A central theme running throughout this book is that meanings and definitions of situations are constituted and have their objectivity established through the interpretive processes of interaction rather than by reference to a body of culturally given common definitions. This raises a variety of problems. One concern is with the structure of interaction on a particular occasion, not in terms of conventional notions such as roles, norms, sanctioning processes, common definitions, and culturally given social categories, but rather in terms of the operation of interpretive processes. The chapters by Zimmerman and Pollner, Wieder, Zimmerman, Cicourel, Spier, and Turner touch upon this question from several different points of view, exploiting, and sometimes challenging, ideas drawn from phenomenology, modern linguistics, and ordinary-language philosophy. The chapters by Cicourel and Manning raise in addition the question of what it is to become a competent participant in an interaction event, that is, a competent member thus posing in new ways the question of socialization. All of the chapters raise in some form the question of how it is that members produce and sustain the *sense* that they act in a shared, orderly world, in which actions are concerted in stable, repetitive ways that are recognizable and reportable.[33] Thus,

---

very different and, it may be argued, more consistent cast from the usual contemporary readings. In particular, Parson's (1937) discussion of Weber and ideal types appears to be seriously misled by the attempt to construe Weber as moving toward a view of sociology as a science in the narrow sense of the term. Similarly, Merton (1968:28–29) fails to observe that Weber's remarks on the continual replacement of present ideas and interpretations by new ones apply with equal force to all forms of scholarship, and thus Weber need not be construed as referring to science in the narrow sense.

31. See also the discussion of these issues in Habermes (1966) and the references therein.

32. Failure to recognize this shift in topic is the source of the fundamental misunderstanding evidenced by writers such as Coleman (1968a) and Denzin (1969). See the lucid dissection of Coleman's remarks by Israel (1969). While Denzin's discussion is generally sympathetic, he also has apparently failed to grasp this central point. For example, he states (1969:922) that in ethnomethodology "the method of documentary analysis is set forth as a preferred strategy." Rather, the point is that there is no other way to do conventional sociology, and the thrust of ethnomethodological interest is to study the properties of the interpretive process itself.

social organization is not treated as an objectively existing structure. Rather, the question is raised of how it is that the members establish repetitiveness, stability, regularity, and continuity over space and time as features of their social world that are taken by themselves and anyone else as objective matters of fact rather than creatures of fantasy or whim. This in turn poses the fundamental problem of reflexivity (Garfinkel, 1967:7-9). On the one hand, the objectivity and reality of what is happening on any given occasion depends on the members seeing the present occasion as located within a stable, objective social order. On the other hand, the members' sense that the features of the social order are objective and real is an accomplishment of the members on that same occasion. Thus, the organized, factual character of any occasion depends reflexively on itself. As Garfinkel and Sacks (in McKinney and Tiryakian, forthcoming) have noted in another context, this is not to say that the world is not real; rather it indicates the manner in which it is real. The member's sense that he lives in a real world shared in common with others is the foundation of his being in the world. Consequently, to tamper with the reflexivity by which this sense is accomplished is to disorganize the member's world in the profoundest sense possible. This also means, however, that the problem of understanding the reflexive nature of interpretive processes is centrally important, and it lies behind more explicit concerns of the chapters that follow.

In conclusion, adoption of the interpretive paradigm radically transforms the nature of the social world. On the one hand, it leaves intact the primordial questions addressed by layman and scholar alike of what people do and why they do it, though the answers to these can no longer be seen as having some kind of scientific warrant. On the other hand, it makes available for study a vast realm of problems that cannot even be formulated within the normative paradigm, the study of interpretive processes themselves.

33. Or, in Garfinkel's terms, accountable.

The Everyday World as a Phenomenon*

Introduction

In contrast to the perennial argument that sociology belabors the obvious, we propose that sociology has yet to treat the obvious as a phenomenon. We argue that the world of everyday life, while furnishing sociology with its favored topics of inquiry, is seldom a topic in its own right.[1] Instead, the familiar, common-sense world, shared by the sociolo-

*Adapted with minor revisions from Don H. Zimmerman and Melvin Pollner, "The Everyday World as a Phenomenon," in Harold Pepinsky, ed., *People and Information.* Copyright © 1970 by Pergamon Press and used with their permission.

We are indebted to Aaron Circourel, Harold Garfinkel, Harold Pepinsky, and D. Lawrence Wieder for their critical reading of the first draft of this chapter. In addition, we thank our fellow conferees, and the members of a graduate seminar in ethnomethodology at the University of California at Santa Barbara for their many helpful comments. Thomas P. Wilson patiently read many portions of the final draft and provided a number of timely suggestions that helped us through several difficult sections. Dorothy Smith, Matthew Speier, and Roy Turner made a number of helpful suggestions. We gratefully acknowledge the insightful comments of these friends and colleagues. We are alone responsible for wheatever defects this chapter may possess.

Our debt to Harold Garfinkel is a special one. He made available to us funds from Air Force Grant AF-AFOSR-757-66, of which he and Harvey Sacks are coprincipal investigators. More importantly, as will be evident throughout the chapter, his work and counsel furnished us the critical resources from which we have drawn so heavily.

1. The phenomenological studies of Schutz (1962, 1964, 1966, 1967) and the seminal investigations of Garfinkel (1959a, 1967, and in Shneidman, 1967:171-187) and Sacks (1963, 1966, unpublished) have been directed precisely to the task of making the world of everyday life available to inquiry as a phenomenon in its own right. Studies by Bittner

gist and his subjects alike, is employed as an unexplicated resource for contemporary sociological investigations.

Sociological inquiry is addressed to phenomena recognized and described in common-sense ways (by reliance on the unanalyzed properties of natural language),[2] while at the same time such common-sense recognitions and descriptions are pressed into service as fundamentally unquestioned resources for analyzing the phenomena thus made available for study. Thus, contemporary sociology is characterized by a confounding of topic and resource.

Below, we suggest how an analysis may procede, respecting the distinction between the social world as topic of, and resource for, inquiry. The distinction between topic and resource requires further discussion as an introduction to the concerns of this chapter.

TOPIC AND RESOURCE

In terms of both the substantive themes brought under examination and the formal properties of the structures examined, professional and lay sociologist are in tacit agreement. For example, while the sociologist and the policeman may entertain very different theories of how a person comes to be a juvenile delinquent, and while each may appeal to disparate criteria and evidence for support of their respective versions, they have no trouble in agreeing that there are persons recognizable as juvenile delinquents and that there are structured ways in which these persons come to be juvenile delinquents. It is in this agreement— agreement as to the fundamental and ordered existence of the phenomenon independent of its having been addressed by *some* method of inquiry—that professional and lay sociologists are mutually oriented to a common factual domain.

The agreement indicates sociology's profound embeddedness in and dependence upon the world of everyday life. Not only does the attitude of everyday life[3] furnish the context of sociological investigation, it also seems to furnish social-scientific inquiry with a leading conception of its order of fact and program of research. The factual domain to which sociological investigation is directed is coterminous, with but mild variation, to the factual domain attended by lay inquiries. For instance,

---

(1961, 1963, 1965, 1967a, 1967b), Churchill (1966), Cicourel (1964, 1968, and in this volume, Moerman (unpublished), Pollner (forthcoming), Shegeloff (1967), Speier (1969), Sudnow (1965, 1967), Turner (1968), Weider (1969, and in Douglas), and Zimmerman (1966; in Hansen, 1969; in Douglas; in Wheeler, 1970) have taken the above cited corpus of theory and research as a point of departure.

2. See Garfinkel (1967: especially Chapter 1), Garfinkel and Sacks (in McKinney and Tiryakian, forthcoming), and Sacks (1963).

3. See below, "The Attitude of Everyday Life."

status hierarchies, race relations, organizational structure, and juvenile delinquency are of interest to both professional and lay inquirer. Each mode of inquiry accords the phenomena formulated under these and a long list, of other titles the status of independent structures of accomplished activities whose properties are objectively assessable.

It is readily acknowledged by professional and lay inquirers alike that some methods of investigating and accounting for the presumptive domain of investigation are more suitable than others. Indeed, the very notion of the suitability of procedures testifies to the incorrigibility of the domain to which those procedures are to be applied. Concern with suitability is the product of an implicit and fundamental faith that the referents of investigation are possessed of a determinate structure, which may be exposed by the judicious selection and use of *a* method. Through one technique or another, the received social world is available as a topic of investigation. The social world is attended to as a domain whose stable properties are discoverable by *some* method. Key methodological questions turn on the choice of an appropriate method.

SOME OBJECTIONS

One may ask at this point, "So, what?" So what if lay and professional sociologists are oriented to a common fact domain? After all, the operations of social scientists are less subject to bias, distortion, unreliability, and a whole host of methodological devils characteristic of everyday methods of fact assembly and testing. After all, the assumption of an independent and objective domain whose properties are presumptively amenable to description by law or lawlike formulations — in short, the assumption of the existence of a natural world — is not peculiar to sociology. It is an indispensable assumption for any type of scientific investigation. Given such an assumption (even if shared by laymen), the operations of academic sociology are deemed far more likely to produce an objective, empirically adequate description of common phenomenon than are the operations of lay members. In response to a "So what?" of this type, we introduce the following considerations.

Sociology's acceptance of the lay member's formulation of the formal and substantive features of sociology's topical concerns makes sociology an integral feature of the very order of affairs it seeks to describe. It makes sociology into an eminently *folk discipline* deprived of any prospect or hope of making fundamental structures of folk activity a phenomenon. Insofar as the social structures are treated as a given rather than as an accomplishment, one is subscribing to a lay inquirer's version of those structures. The "givens" of professional inquiry, the fundamental availability of the social structures to study as such, are then coterminous with the "givens" of lay inquiry.

Indeed, the common orientation of lay and professional sociology generates the sort of argument mustered in support of a "So what" attitude, and that argument reveals the profundity with which sociology's phenomenon is essentially a member's phenomenon. The "so what" argument assumes sociology to be a disciplined investigation that is fully *competitive* with members' relaxed investigation. This assumption has been stated in one way or another by sociology's favored philosophers (e.g., Nagel[4]), practitioners (e.g., Lazarsfeld[5]), and theorists (e.g., Merton[6]). Such an assumption leaves unexplicated members' methods for analyzing, accounting, fact-finding, and so on, which *produce* for sociology its field of data.[7] Indeed, as the competitive argument has it, those notoriously loose procedures, whatever they are, are destined to be replaced by the operations of sociology as means for securing scientifically warranted depictions of society's orderly ways.

Sociological investigations have been depicted above as honoring the same preconceptions about the social world that lay investigations honor, and as directed to the presumptive order of fact to which lay members direct their investigations. It is the intent of this chapter to elaborate a few of the implications of this characterization and to suggest the outline of a paradigm that will permit a principled recognition of the distinction between topic and resource.

We propose to suspend conventional interest in the topics of members' practical investigations and urge the placing of exclusive emphasis on inquiry into practical investigations themselves, lay or professional. The topic then would consist not in the social order as ordinarily conceived, but rather in the ways in which members assemble particular scenes so as to provide for one another evidences of a social order as-ordinarily-conceived. Thus one would examine not the factual properties of status hierarchies, for example, but the *fact* of the factual properties of status hierarchies: one would ask how members provide for the *fact* that status hierarchies are factual features of the members' world. Similarly, instead of treating statistical rates as representations of trends, processes, and factual states of the society, one would ask how members manage to assemble those statistics, and how they use, read, and rely on those statistics as indications of the states of affairs they are taken to depict.[8] But such conjecture anticipates our exposition. Let us therefore

4. Nagel (1961: especially Chapter 1).
5. Lazarsfeld (1949); see also Toby (in Barron, 1964:25–26).
6. Merton (1957: 68–69 et passim).
7. See the discussion below of the occasioned corpus.
8. See Zimmerman (in Wheeler, 1970) for an analysis of the socially organized arrangements whereby bureaucrats in a public assistance agency provide for the factual character of a variety of records of, and reports on, the circumstances of applicants for assistance.

outline what is to be offered in support of our proposals in the balance of this chapter.

OUTLINE OF THE CHAPTER

We shall begin with a consideration of the formal properties of the social world as it is encountered by lay members under the attitude of everyday life. We shall then turn to a consideration of the properties of the social world as it is encountered by the sociologist (and the ways in which common-sense attitudes and assumptions permeate actual investigatory procedure). These characterizations will reveal the deep similarity to which we have alluded above. Finally, we shall provide an outline of what may be involved in examining socially organized activities, while attempting to maintain a principled respect for the distinction between the world of common sense as a resource and the world of common sense as a topic.

The Attitude of Everyday Life

According to Schutz,[9] the world, as it presents itself to the member operating under the jurisdiction of the attitude of everyday life, is a historical, already organized world. It did not appear with the member's birth; it will not perish with his death. From the beginning, the world is experienced *pretheoretically* as the prevailing and persistent condition of all the members' projects. It furnishes the resistant "objective structures," which must be reckoned with in a practically adequate fashion if projects of action are to be effected successfully.

The attitude of everyday life sustains particular doubts, but never global doubts. Indeed, that the existence of the world is never brought into question is an essential requirement for any particular doubt. That is, from the perspective of the attitude of everyday life, the world and its objective constitution are taken for granted[10] from the outset. Not only is the global existence of the world taken for granted, the thesis that the world presents itself to alter essentially as it does to ego—with due allowance for different temporal, spatial, and biographical perspectives—is also merely assumed.[11] The world is *experienced* as an intersubjective world, known or knowable in common with others.

9. Most of Schutz's work was devoted to articulating the formal properties of the "attutide of everyday life." An overview of that work may be found in Maurice Natonson's and Aron Gurwitsch's introductions to Schutz (1962; 1966).

10. Schutz's (1962: 207–259) paper "On Multiple Realities" is particularly relevant here.

11. Schutz (1962:10–13 et passim) termed these presuppositions the "thesis of reciprocal perspectives." The two basic presuppositions subsumed under this heading consisted in the idealization of the "interchangeability of the standpoints" and the idealization of the

The member takes for granted that the social world and, more specifically, the aspect of it relevant to his interest at hand, is actually or potentially assembled or assembleable by rule or by recipe. That is, he may know, or take it that he could determine by inquiry, the rules or recipes whereby he and others might gear into or understand some activity. Put another way, the member assumes that such structures are actually or potentially locatable and determinable in their features by recourse to such practices as asking for or giving instruction concerning a given matter. Everyday activities and their perceived connected features present themselves with the promise that they may be understood and acted upon in practically sufficient ways by competent employment of appropriate proverbs, paradigms, motives, organizational charts, and the like.[12]

Under the attitude of everyday life, the features of this known- in common world are addressed with pragmatic motive.[13] What is known or knowable about its organization awaits recognition or discovery precipitated by the occurrence of particular projects who execution depends on coming to terms with more or less circumscribed features relevant to the anticipated action. Accordingly, under the auspices of members' practical interests in the workings of the everyday world, the member's knowledge of the world is more or less ad hoc, more or less general, more or less fuzzy around the periphery. The member finds out what he needs to know; what he needs to know is relative to the practical requirements of his problem. His criteria of adequacy, rules of procedure, and strategies for achieving desired ends are for him only as good as they need to be.

The social structures that present themselves under the attitude of everyday life are for the member only minutely of his doing. They are encountered as resistive to his wish and whim, and they transcend their particular appearances. As omniprevalent and pervasive conditions and objects of members' projects, the world is available for practically adequate investigation and description. From the standpoint of the member, the world and its exhibited properties are not constituted by virtue of their having been addressed. For the member operating under the atti-

"congruency of relevances." The operation of these presuppositions is a requisite condition of the possibility of an intersubjectively available world. Garfinkel (1967:Chapter 2) has enumerated in concise terms the presuppositions constitutive of the attitude of everyday life in addition to furnishing field demonstrations of their role in the maintenance of perceivedly stable environments.

12. Schutz's (1964:91–105) description of the "stranger" is a particularly dramatic example of the problems encountered by one for whom the validity of that "promise" is not assured as a matter of objective necessity. Garfinkel (1967:Chapter 1) proposes, as we shall, that practices whereby the rational properties of descriptions of one sort or another are made observable are to be rendered problematic.

13. Schutz (1962:208–209 et passim).

tude of everyday life, the world offers itself as an a priori resistive, recalcitrant, and massively organized structure into which he must gear himself.[14]

The formal properties of the social world encountered under the attitude of everyday life are the formal properties that Durkheim attributed to the social structures that were to be sociology's topic.[15] For both lay and professional investigation, the social world presents itself as an exterior field of events amenable to lawful investigation. For both lay and professional investigation, however, the fundamental "facticity" of those structures—their very presence as orders of affairs that, to borrow Merleau-Ponty's phrase, are "always already there"[16]—is an unexplicated and invisible premise, condition, and resource of those investigations.

It is in this sense that sociology retains the presuppositions native to the field of data it seeks to describe, as presuppositions of *its* investigations of that field. As a consequence, the phenomenon to which explanatory effort is directed is the nature and operation of objective social structures of activity. Yet the availability of social structures to inquiry in the first place is masked over the course of inquiry by and through which the features of such structures are made available. The work by which the objectivity of described structures is displayed, detected, and accounted for in concrete, practical situations is disengaged, tacitly but with enormous effort, from its recognized products.[17]

We now offer several brief examples of the way in which the presuppositions of the attitude of everyday life are tacitly employed as resources of professional investigation.

Sociology and the Attitude of Everyday Life

When the features of the world encountered under the attitude of everyday life are incorporated as first principles of professional investigation, a vast order of activity is immediately excluded from consideration as a phenomenon. In addition, investigations predicated on those principles are rendered profoundly akin to investigations carried out by lay inquirers.

14. Schutz's papers "On Multiple Realities" (1962: especially 218–229), "Choosing Among Projects of Action" (1962), and "The Dimensions of the Social World" (1964) are particularly relevant.

15. Specifically, Durkheim (1938:13) defined a social fact as "every way of acting, fixed or not, capable of exercising on the individual an external constraint."

16. Merleau-Ponty (1962:vii).

17. Garfinkel and Sacks (in McKinney and Tiryakian, forthcoming).

This affinity is revealed dramatically by the status accorded lay formulations.[18] Because the referent of lay and professional accounts and
descriptions is identical—the world of everyday life—lay formulations
are often compared to professional formulations. Depending upon the
nature of the criteria and the rigor with which they are applied, lay
formulations are typically regarded as erroneous and hence of no particular value to professional investigation. The notorious looseness of
lay investigative procedures, for example, often stands as the grounds
for dismissing formulations produced by the man in the street.[19] Thus,
what might otherwise be attended to solely as a phenomenon is treated
as a mistaken or otherwise faulted theory or account.

Since lay formulations are often treated as propositions about the
world[20] that are of interest to the sociologist, the possibility remains that
lay formulations may be correct for some referents. In those areas where
members' formulations are judged, explicitly or implicitly, to correspond
with the state of affairs whose features the formulation describes, the
researcher may treat the lay member as a vital auxiliary to the research
enterprise. Not only may the researcher address his inquiry to the
presumptive world to which members address their inquiries, he may
treat the members' descriptions about its various aspects as he would
the report of a colleague. Answers to a researcher's question may be
treated as a truncated research report.

Whether lay formulations are recognized as true or false, conflicting
or complementary vis-à-vis professional formulations, the fact remains
that in order for lay formulations to be the subject of such judgments
entails that they be treated on a conceptual par with professional formulations. Once lay members' accounts are the object of evaluation, the
professional investigator has implicitly raised the lay member to the
status of a professional colleague (however incompetent). That such
status will be accorded the lay member is assured once the features of
the world as it appears under the attitude of everyday life are adopted as
an unquestioned point of departure for professional investigation. It is

18. We have in mind here such devices as rules, categories, typifications, idealizations,
attitudes, and imputed and avowed motives by the use of which members depict or
account for the orderly features of everyday activities.

19. As in Toby's (in Barron, 1964:25–26) "classroom demonstration" of the unreliability of personal experience as adequate evidence for accepting or rejecting propositions
about the social world. In citing this example we are not advocating personal experiences
or other common-sense investigative procedures as the grounds upon which to assess the
adequacy of propositions. As will become clear later in this chapter, what we are proposing is that common-sense methods for making features of the social world observable must
be subject to investigation as phenomena in their own right rather than alternatively relied
upon and criticized in the course of sociological inquiry.

20. Or standing on behalf of implicit propositions about the world.

only then that lay accounts are seen to be directed to the same structures that are of concern to professional sociologists. If the attitude of
everyday life is permitted to furnish the structures that are the topics of
sociological investigation, then the very availability of these structures
to inquiry cannot be treated as a topic in its own right.

The preceding remarks may be illustrated by reference to several
domains of sociological and social-scientific interest with different methodological and conceptual orientations. Our purpose is to sketch[21] how,
under the attitude of everyday life, investigators in each of these fields
employ categorizations, descriptions, and formulations as unquestioned
(save on the narrowest technical grounds) resources for inquiry.

DEMOGRAPHY

For demographers the fundamental recordability of items of demographic interest such as sex, age, birth, and death is not problematic. While
issues of accuracy and reliability of data are prominent methodological
concerns,[22] the methods through and by which features such as normal
sexedness are routinely displayed, detected, and recorded in concrete
situations of categorization remain an unexplicated and invisible resource of demographic inquiry.[23]

Though the investigator relies upon the work whereby members,
including the investigator, *do* sex and age, and *do* recording of such
properties, and *do* the demonstration that such recording was done in
accord with the ideals governing the procedures of counting and categorizing, the *doings* are specifically severed from the subsequently produced distributions and interpretations of them. For the demographer, as
for the members he counts, sexedness is not a matter of theoretical

21. To support our argument fully, a much more detailed and documented account of
social-scientific practice is required than is presented below. The discussion that follows
thus stands as a statement of our conception of these practices rather than as evidence for
the adequacy of our conception. The reader may dispute our version of social science
practice, but he will at least have available the kinds of issues to which we are addressed.

22. For example, assessment is made or advocated of "errors of classification" or
"errors of coverage" (failure of complete enumeration) in census data. With respect to
errors of classification, issues of the veracity of respondents (exaggeration, falsehoods,
etc.) and the conscientiousness of interviewers are relevant. See Bogue and Murphy
(1964).

23. Garfinkel's (1967:Chapter 5) study of an intersexed person documents the management of sexual status through the examination of the practical troubles encountered by one
for whom such status could not be taken for granted, and the practical remedies devised by
this person to deal with such troubles. In contrast to studies directed to the consequences
for social conduct of presumptively stable sexual status, Garfinkel's study investigates the
managed course of situated presentation and identification of the features of normal
sexuality, that is, how sexuality is made to happen "in commonplace settings as an
obvious, familiar, recognizable, natural, and serious matter of fact" (1967:180). In so
doing, Garfinkel brought under examination the very availability of sexual status to both
lay and professional inquiry.

interest or speculation. The fact that persons are of one or the other sex; that persons are (or should be) recognizable at a glance as the one which they happen to be; that errors of identification may be symptomatic of a faulted social competence, an impaired sensory apparatus, or an encounter with a "freak of nature"; that displays of sex are presented as a natural matter of fact without plan or effort; all these are assumptions fundamental to the work of furnishing objective descriptions of an objective world.[24]

In effect, the demographer presupposes the operation of a normative order local to the society in question. The normative order is presupposed by the demographer as an enforceable schema of interpretation and guide to action used by members to present themselves in a particular fashion and to recognize the presentations of others in stable ways. Members are presupposed to comply with a normative order and, in so doing, to produce demographically relevant properties, independent of the varied demographic work (lay and professional) of making those properties observable in concrete, practical situations.

That the work of lay or professional demography is founded on the supposition that, in principle, the categories in use and the counts of events and persons falling within them may correspond in assessable ways to "real" distributions of events and persons ought not to be treated as a warrant for evaluating the success of either enterprise but merely as a further aspect of the phenomenon. The question is not how adequately the varied methods of lay and professional demography permit approximation to "real distributions," but how any achieved dis-

24. For a detailed consideration of other properties see Garfinkel (1967:110–133). These features as accomplished correlates of displayed sexedness provide for the perceived invariance of sexual status to any and all situational exigencies, and hence to the procedures through which males and females are counted and categorized. These and other features are definitive of the objectivity or fundamental "facticity" of a person's sexual status. As such, they furnish the sense and warrant of the assumption that the sex of a person or the sex composition of a collectivity are facts that await discovery, not creation. As such, these features provide for the perceived interdependence between the depiction of the sex composition of a population and the categorizing and counting procedures through which the distribution was assembled, on the one hand, and the "actual" or "real" population parameters, on the other. Indeed, it is these correlates of displayed sexedness that induce the notion of "real" parameters of a population's sex composition in the first place. And, in turn, the fundamental facticity of sex and sex composition as properties of persons and populations, respectively, prompt the demographer to take precautions to gauge the efficacy of categorizing and sampling procedures in terms of their ability to approximate the features of the real distribution. The presumptive facticity of sex is thus a point of departure for demographic inquiry. Yet, as Garfinkel's study (1967:Chapter 5) of an intersexed person reveals, on every actual occasion of categorization the facticity of one's sexual status will require an enormous, albeit unnoticed, effort to ensure its appearance as a constituent feature of the display of sexedness. For demographers and sociologists in general to ignore the features of that effort as a topic in its own right is to treat sex precisely as a member does—as an obvious, objective furnishing of the world.

tribution, including its reference to, and accompanying claims to adequate estimation of, a "real" distribution, is accomplished as a socially enforceable "finding" in the first place.

Surveys and Ethnographies

Use of lay formulations is notoriously prevalent in survey analysis. The respondents' answers to questions regarding past, present, and projected biography, background features such as age and sex, interactional patterns, and mental life are accorded the status of protocol observations about those items. Answers to questions may thus be used as reports made by a colleague or assistant.[25] In this light, methodological discussions of reliability and validity may be seen as responses to the need to devise assurances to the researcher and to his colleagues that members' formulations are not done haphazardly. In this sense, reliability and validity procedures are ways of arguing for the trustworthiness and internal consistency of such reports, ways of arguing that upon the occasion of a report (that is, an answer to a researcher's question) the respondent was in effect answering as a scientist whose subject matter happened to be his own life.[26]

Community, organizational, and tribal ethnographies are also well known for their reliance on informants' reports, particularly insofar as these reports formulate otherwise unobservable or difficult to observe aspects of the "inside life" of various social settings. When ethnographers assemble *their* descriptions of settings, by reference to informants' formulations, the members' description and the ethnographer's description have an identical status in relation to the events reported on. The member's formulation, like that of the ethnographer, is a possible re-

25. The respondent is implicitly conceived as furnishing a researcher with a descriptive report on the workings of his life as if he, the respondent, were a coinvestigator. In a good deal of contemporary research the respondent is an invaluable partner in that the events he reports are often those to which he alone has access, as in the case of his own mental life.

26. Goode and Hatt, for example, consider the problem of the truth of responses to questionnaires. They suggest that the problem of truth involves "that dim sphere in which the respondent is not giving the facts but is not really certain that these are not the facts. All of us reconstruct our personal history to some extent, especially in areas involving our self-conception. Only very careful probing can ever separate fact from fiction, and for some respondents even this will not be adequate" (1952:162). Among the devices available to the researcher for separating "fact from fiction" is the sieve question which "sifts out those who should not be answering the question because they do not possess the necessary knowledge or experience" (164). The problem for the sociologist is thus one of getting the respondent to perform competently, to perform according to rules governing correct scientific procedure. Similar conceptions of the sociologist's task are embedded in most discussions of questionnaire construction and administration. See, for example, Hyman (1955:149–172). For a general critique of conventional conceptions regarding the use of questionnaires see Circourel (1964).

construction of the setting, that is, a version of the setting's reigning norms and resident attitudes, and it is often the case that the ethnographer must rely on the member's formulation as the definitive characterization of the setting.[27] As in survey research, the fact that members are able to do formulations — to describe in recognizably orderly ways — is an uninvestigated resource.

Even if we ignore the strange catechistical[28] relation that obtains between researcher and those he seeks to study, a plethora of unexamined, but nonetheless relied upon, procedures remain. The methods through which the production of recognizably reasonable talk is achieved, the methods through which responses are provided and appreciated as answers to the intended sense of questions, the methods through which understanding is displayed and detected as the occasion it is intended to be, the methods through which the occasion will later be demonstrated to have met the ideals of interrogation and description, are but a few tacit resources of social scientific investigation.

We may also mention the various methods of documentary interpretation[29] through which members' talk and activities are located as concrete instances of behavior indexed by the sociologist's terminology. The procedures through which informants' reports about what ought to be done, the good reasons for doing it, and what the doing of it will accomplish are transformed into illustrative instances of norms, roles, attitudes, and beliefs. These are essentially ways of seeing the society that stands behind situated actions.

For example, a group member's declaration "I have a report prepared by Miss Smith on the expenditures to date"[30] may be coded as an

27. A fairly common strategy of ethnographers consists in the use of an informant's report as corroboration of the analyst's report. Thus Becker (1963) notes that job security as a muscian comes from the number and quality of established connections. He states, "To have a career one must work; to enjoy the security of steady work one must have many 'connections' " (105). This is immediately followed by the statement of a musician, "You have to make connections like that all over town, until it gets so that when anybody wants a man they call you. Then you're never out of work" (105). The use of informants' reports as corroborative evidence is similar in many ways to the use of a professional colleague's research findings as corroborative evidence. So, too, the grounds upon which lay formulations are criticized (for their ambiguity, vagueness, reliance on poor sampling procedure, and so on) are similar to the criteria used to assess the adequacy of professional reports.

28. Sacks (1963) considers, by way of an illuminating parable, (a) the nature of the question-answer relation that obtains between sociologist and lay members and (b) the implications of employing a version of a member's answers to a researcher's questions as the researcher's description of the domain to which the questions refer. One of Sacks's major recommendations is that describing or, more appropriately, "doing describing" ought to be treated as a problematic phenomenon in its own right, just as any other activity of a member would be treated as problematic.

29. Garfinkel (1967:Chapter 3).

30. Bales (in Layarsfeld and Rosenberg, 1955:349).

instance of Bales's category "*gives orientation*, information, repeats, clarifies, confirms" and finally as an instance of the attempt to resolve the "problem of orientation" which is a problem, according to Bales, of most groups. Similarly, a delinquent boy's comment on his relations with adult fellators "It's OK, but I like the money best of all"[31] may be treated as an instance of "affective neutrality." According to Reiss, however, the comment becomes, upon another transformation, an instance of the norm presumptively governing the boy's participation in homosexual relations, which specifies that the partners "should remain affectively neutral during the transaction."[32]

The work through which researchers make correspondence between norm and concrete instance and, more generally, between textual assertions, on the one hand, and tables and talk, on the other, is unexplicated.[33] Often the reader is implicitly asked to employ his competence as a lay member and to use "what anybody knows" as a background scheme of interpretation in order to locate the correspondence between conceptual formulation and empirical illustration, thus to see the society-in-the-talk.

Whether members' formulations are treated as descriptions of socially organized activities or as events that reflect the operation of those organized activities, the assumption prevails that the structures of activity are invariant to the operations through which their properties are made observable. Demographers, survey researchers, ethnographers, and others whom we have not had occasion to mention, address their inquiries to the very structures to which members' inquiries are addressed. The mutuality of orientation is dramatically revealed when lay formulations are included as an integral part of a researcher's description. The methods through which concrete situations of interrogation, categorization, and description are assembled are members' methods. As with members, the method through which the fundamental availability of socially organized activities to investigation is accomplished is systematically excluded from consideration as a topic in its own right. The possibility of an everyday world with all of its familiar furnishings is, with but a few notable exceptions, a problem for neither lay nor professional investigators. It is because of this neglect, which we proposed earlier, that sociology has yet to give serious attention to the "obvious." In the section that follows, we suggest how the obvious may be investigated.

31. Reiss (in Becker, 1964:201).
32. Reiss (in Becker, 1964:200).
33. Garfinkel (1967:94–103).

An Alternative Phenomenon

Our efforts to this point have been directed largely to an adumbrated critique of sociology's conception of its problematic phenomena. We have argued that current practice in the field confounds topic and resource. As a consequence, sociology apparently is in the position of providing a professional folklore about the society that, however sophisticated, remains folklore. Such a critique would be merely querulous were it not directed toward the delineation of a positive alternative. The alternative we shall propose is not conceived as a remedy to the kinds of troubles we have pointed out. Instead, it turns those troubles into a phenomenon. To do so requires more than a rewriting of manuals of research procedure and redefinition of criteria for adequate theory. It requires no less than a paradigmatic shift — to borrow presumptiously from Kuhn.[34] This shift has already been specified in detail in the seminal work of Harold Garfinkel.[35] Following his lead, we offer here suggestions for a perspective on the study of a domain of phenomena systematically overlooked prior to Garfinkel's investigations.[36] With respect to these phenomena, Garfinkel proposes that

> in contrast to certain versions of Durkheim that teach that the objective reality of social facts is sociology's fundamental principle, the lesson is taken instead, and used as a study policy, that the objective reality of social facts *as* an ongoing accomplishment of the concerted activities of daily life, with the ordinary, artful ways of that accomplishment being by members known, used, and taken for granted, is, for members doing sociology, a fundamental phenomenon.[37]

If the "objective reality of social facts" is to be transformed from a principle to an object of inquiry, then it will first be necessary to suspend the relevance of contemporary conceptions of what sociological problems are and how they may be solved. The suspension is not predicated on the notion that such conceptual schemes are in error. It is simply that

---

34. Kuhn (1962).

35. See Garfinkel (1967). In this work, Garfinkel reports a number of cumulative discoveries which have led to this shift. See his discussion of "the unsatisfied programmatic distinction between and substitutability of objective for indexical expressions" (4–7); the "essential reflexivity of accounts" (7–9); the "etcetera" property of rule-use (18–24); the bases of "common understandings" (24–31 and 38–42); the "documentary method of interpretation" (76–103); and the on-going situated accomplishment of the objective properties of objects and actions in society as accounting practices (11–18 and 116–185).

36. See Garfinkel and Sacks (forthcoming) for an account of the reasons inherent in the social science approach (characterized as "constructive analysis") for overlooking these phenomena. See also Garfinkel (1967:31–34) for a statement of research policies which have served as a critical resource in the formulation of the central ideas of this paper.

37. Garfinkel (1967:vii).

these schemes take as an unexplicated point of departure and resource the very order of affairs to be treated as problematic. To treat the objective reality of social facts as problematic is to treat

> every feature of sense, of fact, of method, for every particular case of inquiry without exception, as the managed accomplishment of organized settings of practical actions, and . . . particular determinations in members' practices of consistency, planfulness, relevance, or reproducibility of their practices and results . . . as acquired and assured only through particular, located organizations of artful practices.[38]

Indeed, conventional schemes, or more specifically the ways in which such schemes are employed as methods for analyzing the orderly properties of social activities, are themselves of interest as phenomena.[39] Under the jurisdiction of the alternative conception to be recommended below, each social setting and every one of its recognized features is construed as the accomplishment of the situated work of displaying and detecting those features at the time they are made visible. We may now consider this alternative conception, specified in terms of what we call the occasioned corpus of setting features.

THE OCCASIONED CORPUS OF SETTING FEATURES

The features of a setting attended to by its participants include, among other things, its historical continuity, its structure of rules and the relationship of activities within it to those rules, and the ascribed (or achieved) statuses of its participants. Under the attitude of everyday life, these features are "normal, natural facts of life." Under the attitude of everyday life, these features are objective conditions of action that, although participants have had a hand in bringing about and sustaining them, are essentially independent of any one's or anyone's doing.

When viewed as the temporally situated *achievement* of parties to a setting, these features will be termed the occasioned corpus of setting features. By use of the term *occasioned* corpus, we wish to emphasize that the features of socially organized activities are particular, contingent accomplishments of the production and recognition work of parties to the activity. We underscore the occasioned character of the corpus in contrast to a corpus of member's knowledge, skill, and belief standing prior to and independent of any actual occasion in which such knowledge, skill, and belief is displayed or recognized. The latter conception is usually refered to by the term culture.

By use of the conception of an occasioned corpus, we mean to transform any social setting and its features for the purposes of analysis by bringing them under the constituent recommendations comprising

38. Garfinkel (1967:32).
39. See, for example, Bittner (1965).

this notion, that is, to examine a setting and its features as temporally situated accomplishments of parties to the setting. The nature of this transformation may be seen in the contrast between a setting and its features as it is encountered by the analyst under the attitude of everyday life, and as it is by the analyst's operating in terms of the recommendations of the occasioned corpus.

From the member's point of view, a setting presents itself as the objective, recalcitrant theater of his actions. From the analyst's point of view, the presented texture of the scene, *including* its appearance as an objective, recalcitrant order of affairs, is conceived as the accomplishment of members' methods for displaying and detecting the setting's features. For the member the corpus of setting features presents itself as a product, as objective and independent scenic features. For the analyst the corpus *is* the family of practices employed by members to assemble, recognize, and realize the corpus-as-a-product.

Accordingly, from the point of view of the analyst, the features of the setting as they are known and attended to by members are unique to the particular setting in which they are made observable. Any feature of a setting — its perceived regularity, purposiveness, typicality — is conceived as the accomplishment of the work done in and on the occasion of that feature's recognition. The practices through which a feature is displayed and detected, however, are assumed to display invariant properties across settings whose substantive features they make observable. It is to the discovery of these practices and their invariant properties that inquiry is to be addressed.[40] Thus, instead of an ethnography that inventories a setting's distinctive, substantive features, the research vehicle envisioned here is a *methodography* (to borrow Bucher's term)[41] that searches for the practices through which those substantive features are made observable.

IMPLICATIONS AND RECOMMENDATIONS

Let us state more succinctly what is entailed by the notion of the occasioned corpus and the kind of research recommendations it delivers.

1. The occasioned corpus is a corpus with no regular elements, that is, it does not consist of a *stable* collection of elements.
2. The work of assembling an occasioned corpus consists in the ongoing "corpusing" and "decorpusing" of elements rather than the situated retrieval or removal of a subset of elements from a larger set transcending any particular setting in which that work is done.

40. See, in particular, Garfinkel and Sacks (in McKinney and Tiryakian, forthcoming) and footnote 43, below.
41. Bucher (1961:129).

3. Accordingly, from the standpoint of analysis done under the auspices of this notion, the elements organized by the occasioned corpus are unique to the particular setting in which it is assembled, hence ungeneralizable to other settings. That is, for the analyst, particular setting features are "for the moment" and "here and now."

Elements. By the term elements we mean those features of a setting that members rely upon, attend to, and use as the basis for action, inference, and analysis on any given occasion.[42] The designation "member" should be read as referring either to those persons for whom the setting is an arena of practical activities or to an outside observer whose task it is to bring that setting under rational analysis, when either attends a given setting under the attitude of everyday life. Such features may encompass the biographies of the setting's personnel, its reigning norms, the setting's history, the latent functions of activities within it, and so on. Thus, elements are as diverse as ways of talking in and about settings, and include the ways of talking characteristic of lay and professional members alike.

Assembling the Corpus. The proposal that the occasioned corpus is not a stable collection of elements may be explicated by consideration of paragraph two above. The availability of a particular element is conceived to be the consequence of a course of work through which it is displayed and detected, regardless of the recalcitrance and obviousness the element may appear to possess when viewed under the jurisdiction of the attitude of everyday life. In fact, the very obviousness of the features of a setting, such as a family's appearance in the evening as the same family to which one said goodbye that morning, is itself an element that remains to be concertedly accomplished as a constituent feature of a setting's appearances. Thus, for the purpose of analysis, a setting's features (or, in the terms of the occasioned corpus, its elements) are not independent of, and cannot be detached from, the situated work through and by which they are made notable and observable.

By this proposal a given setting's features are not referable for their production and recognition to "cultural resources" transcending a particular occasion. The analyst cannot have recourse to such explanatory devices as a shared complex of values, norms, roles, motives, and the like, standing independent of and prior to a given occasion. On these

---

42. Thus, an element when viewed from the member's point of view consists in the recognized features of a particular setting. From the point of view of the analyst, an element consists in the practices whereby the recognized features of a setting are displayed and detected. For the member the setting may present itself as an objective, determinate state of affairs. For the analyst, the setting consists in methods that make that objectivity observable.

considerations we are led to specify the occasioned corpus as a corpus with no regular elements. In consequence of this specification (in conjunction with the other specifications of the occasioned corpus) we are able to retain as a *phenomenon*, but exclude as a *resource*, members' invocation of such notions as the common culture as a means of detecting and arguing the orderly features of a given setting.

Uniqueness of Elements. Because a setting's features are viewed as the accomplishment of members' practices for making them observable, the elements of the occasioned corpus are treated as unique to the particular setting in which it is assembled. These elements may not be generalized *by the analyst* to other settings. Within this framework, for example, one would not be interested in constructing typologies of one or another class of social settings, although the members' work of constructing such typologies would be eligible for treatment as a phenomenon.

Under the auspices of the attitude of everyday life, settings, such as that of the previously mentioned family, maintain their perceivedly stable features over time and may be conceived as instances of, say, families-in-general, or families-of-this-or-that-type. From the standpoint of the occasioned corpus, a family's temporal and typal features are its own situated accomplishments. The ungeneralizability of a setting's features follows from the paradigm principle that a feature's typicality is an accomplished typicality. A feature's temporal identicality is an accomplished identicality. Perhaps the most concise way of stating this position is to note that when viewed as the assembling of an occasioned corpus, no setting is conceived as a product. Each setting and every one of its features consists of the way in which the setting and its features are displayed and detected.

On the basis of the three numbered paragraphs set forth above and the preceding discussion, we can now further specify the notion of the occasioned corpus.

4. The work of assembling an occasioned corpus mentioned in paragraph two above makes reference to the family of *practices* and their properties, by which a particular occasioned corpus is assembled, revised, invoked, and used to recognize and account for a setting's rational, that is, orderly, properties.[43]

5. The fact that members take for granted, insist upon, and talk about features of a world and knowledge of those features of a world and knowledge of those features transcending any particular

---

[43]. Garfinkel and Sacks (in McKinney and Tiryakian, forthcoming) have specified several invariant properties of the practices. When treated as a set of constraints that any practice must satisfy, these properties furnish an apparatus with which to locate additional practices.

here-and-now situated appearance, (that is, a corpus *with* regular elements) is preserved intact and made a feature of the work of assembling an occasioned corpus. Members' orientation to the properties of transsituational events and relationships (for example, their typicality, regularity, and connectedness) and their reference to general knowledge of those events and relationships is treated from this perspective as a feature and accomplishment of members' work. As the analyst views it, such work by members consists of assembling and using an occasioned corpus as a background schema and condition of competent interpretation and action.

Members' Practices. Paragraph four sets forth the order of phenomena to be investigated. The chief purpose of the notion of the occasioned corpus is to "reduce" the features of everyday social settings to a family of practices and their properties.[44] This reduction builds into the framework of analysis a principled recognition of the distinction between topic and resource, and thereby severely restricts the analyst's reliance upon his common-sense knowledge of his subject matter as an unanalyzed resource. In this respect, the notion of the occasioned corpus serves much the same purpose as the incongruity procedures employed by Garfinkel in his earlier work, namely, to "produce reflections through which the strangeness of an obstinately familiar world can be detected."[45]

The Strangeness of a Familiar World. The everyday world as known under the attitude of everyday life is indeed transformed upon impact with the reduction imposed by the occasioned corpus. The familiar world does become strange. But nothing in that world is lost in the transformation, and much is gained.

As was indicated in paragraph five, every feature of the world of everyday life is maintained intact. The typicality of that world, its historical continuity, its order, its furnishings, and the rest, are preserved. The members of that world, lay and professional alike, may continue to address it in the same way and to deliver their ordinary accounts of its features. What *is* changed by recourse to the notion of the occasioned corpus is the status accorded the features of that world, and the accounts, explanations, and stories that accompany encounters with it. They are made available as

44. The term reduction is borrowed from Husserl (1962). While the notion of an occasioned corpus partakes of Husserl's program, the order of phenomena revealed by its use is by no means offered as equivalent to that which appears by virtue of the use the phenomenological reduction.

45. Garfinkel (1967:38).

phenomena in their own right. Let us complete the "recovery" of the common-sense world within the reduction of the occasioned corpus.

6. The occasioned corpus is thus conceived to consist in members' methods of exhibiting the connectedness, objectivity, orderliness, and relevance of the features of *any* particular setting as features in, of, and linked with a more encompassing, ongoing setting, typically referred to as "the society." The work of the occasioned corpus is the work of displaying the society "in back of" the various situated appearances constituent of everyday, located scenes.

The General Phenomenon. Although paragraph three informs us that the generalizability of particular setting *features* accomplished through ›the work of assembling an occasioned corpus must be radically restricted, paragraphs three through six have specifically provided for the immense generality of members' *procedures* for assembling and employing particular setting features, so as to recognize and account for particular scenes and the articulation of those scenes within an "objective societal context." It is to the discovery of those procedures that the notion of the occasioned corpus directs us.

DISCUSSION

The social world, when considered under the reduction imposed by the occasioned corpus, is a radical modification of the one known to contemporary sociological investigation. Topics constituted by virtue of the reduction are not simple transformations of current sociological interests. The reduction does not generate research that may be regarded as an extension, refinement, or correction of extant sociological inquiry. The concerns of studies carried out under the auspices of the occasioned corpus are not and cannot be the concerns of members whose disciplines do not view any and every feature of ordinary activities as the temporally situated accomplishment of the work through and by which those features are made observable. The reduction constitutes as its phenomenon an order of affairs that has no identifiable counterpart in contemporary social science. That is because the phenomenon includes as constituent features the topicalizing of the world, modes of theorizing its, order, inquiries into its properties and presentations of analyses about its formulable features by whomsoever, wherever, and whenever that work is done. Social-scientific investigation is itself an integral feature of the order of affairs transformed into a phenomenon by the reduction recommended in the notion of the occasioned corpus.

In short, we intend the notion of occasioned corpus to organize for study the various practices members employ to sustain the sense of an objective structure of social activities, a society, *exhibited from* the vantage point of particular situations. The features of that society, from this perspective, are to be found nowhere else, and in no other way, than in and upon those occasions of members' work, lay and professional, through which those features are made available.

This chapter has been frankly programmatic. However, the basic ideas constituting "the program" continue to generate research, which gives indication of accumulating at an increasing rate in the future. Accordingly, we conclude with brief reference to a series of researches that have either contributed to the development of the basic framework[46] to which we have given *a* particular formulation or have taken this framework as a point of departure.

Ongoing Research

In distinctive ways each of the studies reported below is an attempt to distinguish between the social world as a resource and the social world as a topic. As such, they represent research carried out under the perspective whose distinctive features we have attempted to specify here in some detail. For expository purposes and for those purposes alone, we shall present these studies as if their method consisted in turning some conventional topic of sociological inquiry on its head by "application" of the reduction. In fact, this was rarely the case. That studies were undertaken in formal organizations, in halfway houses, in traffic courts, etc., should not be taken to indicate that they were studies of a particular formal organization.

In our view each study is ultimately concerned with discovering the properties of the practices whereby parties to a setting, regardless of its substantive character, make that setting available to one another as the kind of setting they take it to be. In presenting these studies, our exposition will attempt to specify — albeit in general terms — the ways in which they are relevant to our discussion of the reduction imposed by the notion of the occasioned corpus.

ORGANIZATIONAL BEHAVIOR

Given the recommendation of the occasioned corpus that any feature of a setting is to be treated as an accomplishment, actions in a bureaucratic setting, for example, are not of interest for the ways in which they are governed by rule, formal or informal, but rather for the ways in which they are detected and displayed as actions-in-accord-with-a-rule. Thus,

46. The framework is that developed in the previously cited works of Harold Garfinkel.

one would suspend, as Zimmerman has,[47] the relevance of accounts attempting to explain bureaucratic action by reference to rule, in favor of examining how organizational action in any one of its particular appearances is made to appear as actions which are referable to a program providing for their production.[48]

Bittner[49] has similarly suspended the relevance of theorists' accounts of organizational order that appeal in one way or another to formal models of organizational structure, for example, flow charts developed by parties to that organization. Instead, Bittner has searched for the ways in which members employ organizational models as devices for analyzing, and making observable on particular occasions, an organization as an ensemble of coherent and unified actions.

Guided by the same perspective, Wieder[50] is examining how rules – in this case, the collection of rules known to sociologists as the "convict code" – are employed by paroled ex-addicts in concert with staff members in a halfway house, as explanatory and persuasive devices for analyzing various kinds of activities in the setting, and how the very existence of those rules and the warrant for their use is made observable by members for members.[51]

COMMON UNDERSTANDINGS

In addition to the studies by Garfinkel which we have had occasion to mention, we note his radical revision of the problem of common understandings.[52] Briefly, a sociologically popular explanation of common understandings argues that they consist in measured amounts of shared agreement on substantive issues. Mead's[53] famous definition of the significant symbol – a gesture that calls out the same response in an auditor that it calls out in its producer – is perhaps the archetypical solution for sociologists to the problem of how members manage to understand one another.

Under the jurisdiction of Garfinkel's policy recommendation from which the notion of the occasioned corpus is derived,[54] conventional versions of sign-referent relations, such as Mead's, are suspended as

47. Zimmerman (in Douglas).
48. To speak of the *appearance* of action as in accord with a rule does not imply that the action was "really" otherwise, that it merely appeared to be so but was in fact otherwise. Further, if an appearance of "conformity" is found by members to be deceptive, the ways in which *that* finding is accomplished is equally a phenomenon.
49. Bittner (1965).
50. Wieder (1969).
51. See also Garfinkel (1967:Chapters 6, 7; in Shneidman, 1967:171–187).
52. Garfinkel (1967:Chapters 1, 2).
53. G. H. Mead (1934).
54. Garfinkel (1967:31–34).

E

potential explanations of a common understanding. By virtue of the suspension, the problematic character of common understandings is shifted to a concern with members' methods for analyzing "how" (for example, metaphorically, or narratively) another spoke, and to the methods whereby members display and detect the fact that they understand.[55] Sacks, for example, has provided a detailed analysis of how members manage their talk so as to *display* that they understand another's utterances, as well as recognize that display when it is produced by the other. The conceptual apparatus of Sacks's analysis, incidentally, is a product of his continuing studies of members' methods for producing recognizedly rational talk in naturally occurring conversations.[56] By treating the commonplace particulars of talk as problematic (as formal linguistic analysis, psycholinguistics, and sociolinguistics do not), Sacks has been able to uncover elegant formal operations employed by members to assemble and analyze those particulars. Cicourel,[57] employing the version of the problem of understanding as it is developed in the work of Garfinkel and Sacks, is studying how children acquire and use interpretive operations to organize the intelligible features of their own actions and to analyze the actions of others.

MEMBERS' FORMULATIONS

As a final example, we return to the topic of members' formulations. In accord with the preceding recommendations, members' formulations are not given a privileged exemption, nor are they conceived here as descriptions *of* or propositions *about* some domain (That *members* conceive of formulations as being formulations *of* or *about* some field of events is quite another matter.) From our point of view, formulations are constituent features of the settings in which they are done. A formulation's good or bad sense, success in illuminating the order of affairs it depicts, truth or falsity, recognizability as being *about* the order of affairs whose features it describes, and so on, are contingent accomplishments of the settings in which they are done. As phenomena, members' formulations cannot be assigned a truth value by the analyst. As phenomena, they cannot possibly be treated as poor competition or convenient resources for scientific inquiry. As phenomena, the rational properties of formulations are entirely and exclusively the concerted achievement of members acting in particular practical situations.

In line with this approach, Pollner[58] is currently examining the ways

55. Garfinkel (1967:24–31).
56. Sacks (1966). See also Moerman (unpublished), Schegeloff (1967), Speier (1969), and Turner (1968).
57. Cicourel (Douglas and Sacks, forthcoming).
58. Pollner (forthcoming).

in which the defendant in traffic court provides (or fails to provide) a recognizably (to the parties concerned) rational, coherent, and complete account concerning the circumstances of his charged violation and why he should receive lenient treatment. The criteria by which these properties of such accounts are assessed are being investigated as integral features of the setting within which they are offered.

Concluding Remarks

We have argued that there is a fundamental convergence between lay and professional sociological inquiry. Both modes of inquiry subscribe to formally and substantively identical conceptions of social fact. Each mode presupposes the existence of objective structures of activity, which remain impervious to the procedures through which their features are made observable. Further, each mode of inquiry addresses the same substantive domain. The list of sociological topics overlaps substantially with members' everyday concerns. In short, the properties of the attitude of everyday life are firmly entrenched in, if not constitutive of, professional sociology's resources, circumstances, and topics.

The world that stands as the condition and object of lay investigations is thus much the same world known to professional investigation. The ways in which it is problematic for the lay member are also the ways in which it is problematic for the professional. Similarly, the ways in which its features are glossed over by lay members are the ways in which they are glossed over by professionals.

We noted several consequences of this shared orientation to the social world as an object of investigation. For example, by virtue of mutual subscription to the fundamental facticity of the social world, common-sense descriptions (or more generally, formulations of the orderly properties of socially organized activities) are rendered either competitive with or a resource for professional investigations. We have recommended a perspective that demands treating as problematic what in lay and professional sociological investigations alike is treated as a stable and unquestioned point of departure.

The distinctive features of the alternative perspective, which we offer here, reside in the proposal that the objective structures of social activities are to be regarded as the situated, practical accomplishments of the work through and by which the appearance-of-objective-structures is displayed and detected. The apparent strangeness of this perspective is due to the fact that it introduces a strange and hitherto largely unexplored domain of inquiry – the commonplace world.

PART TWO

Constructing Situational Meanings: Language, Meaning and Action

On Meaning By Rule

Those who examine existential, phenomenological, or ethnomethodological social science "from the outside," frequently note that they differ from other orientations in their insistence on examining social reality from the "actor's point of view." Yet such an insistence seems quite similar to the now long-standing sociological interest in the definition of the situation, the life space of the actor, the actor's orientation to his situation, and the more general notion of culture as a cognitive map of the societal member's world. Traditional interest in the actor's point of view is perhaps most explicitly conceptualized in the field of language and cognition, where the analyst is interested in language as a method for "discerning how people construe their world of experience from the way they talk about it" (Frake, in Gladwin and Sturtevant, 1962:74).

The explicitly subjective interests of the field of language and cognition can be seen in Brown's (1958:230) formulation of the Whorfian hypothesis.

> Each language embodies and perpetuates a particular world view. The speakers of a language are partners to an agreement to perceive and think of the world in a certain way—not the only way. The same reality—both physical and social—can be variously structured and different languages operate with different structures.

This passage, however, also points to the ways in which existential, phenomenological, or ethnomethodological interests depart from those of symbolic interactionism, as in Strauss's (1959:15–25) treatment, and anthropological or structural semantics.[1] Members of both of these latter

1. Structural semantics is a major effort in the growing concern among social scientists, and anthropologists in particular, to take the findings, theories, and phenomena of linguistics into account in their own studies. This concern is known, in part and in whole, as

schools have proposed that the semantic aspects of language, like the grammatical aspects, have a rulelike character in the game-theoretic sense of rules. The promise of such a proposal is great if it is correct, for it would follow that the meaning of any object or event in a society for its members could be determined by an analysis of the semantic rules of the language that is spoken in that society.

The theoretical treatment of language as containing a cognitive map is appropriate, however, only if the semantic aspects of language have in fact rulelike properties. It is over this issue that existential, phenomenological, or ethnomethodological analyses and that of at least some symbolic interactionists and structural semanticists part company. Over this issue what each means by the actor's point of view appears quite different. It has been the recurrent finding of ethomethodology that, because everyday language use is characterized by the use of indexical or occasional expressions,[2] everyday language is used in such a way that it is inappropriate to conceptualize its use in terms of a rulelike semantics. That is, in everyday talk persons constantly use expressions the sense of which is relative to the place in which it is spoken, what the hearer knows about the speaker, the time at which it is spoken, and an indefinitely extendable collection of other contextual matters.

Every theorist who deals with the semantic aspects of language is faced with the choice of assuming the stability of everyday language use or directing his attention to the indexical properties of everyday language use. The theorist's choice between these alternatives has critical consequences for his solution to fundamental theoretical problems such as the problem of intersubjectivity and the problem of the identicality of perceptual objects in time and space. In more general terms the theorist's choice between these alternatives constrains the character of his theorizing about what members of a society can and cannot experience. Further, the theorist's choice has extensive consequences for what his theory makes observable in contrast to what it rules out of order as investigatible phenomena.

The consequences of proposing a rulelike semantics rather than focusing on the indexical properties of everyday language use may be seen by examining the nature of a society that members would experience if they did speak with a rulelike semantics. By constructing theoretical puppets that do nothing other than what a specific theorist proposes, we will see

anthropological linguistics, language and culture, language *as* culture, componential analysis, cross-cultural studies of cognition, cognitive anthropology, ethnoscience, ethnolinguistics, ethnographic semantics, structural semantics, etc.

2. For the definitive formulation of indexical expressions and their import for social science see Garfinkel (1965) (1967:pp 4–7) and Garfinkel and Sacks (in McKinney and Tiryakian, forthcoming). They are further developed in Garfinkel's lectures delivered from 1966 to 1970.

that rulelike theories of signs do indeed solve many important theoretical and methodological problems which have puzzled philosophers and social scientists for centuries. However, it will also be seen that such formulations also have the consequence of proposing absurd societies that do not correspond to the experiences of any theorist. Moreover, electing the choice of a rulelike semantics is done at the expense of making the *activity* of using rules for applying names theoretically nonobservable. That is, questions pertaining to invariant or variable sense of rules for applying names are not posed as investigatable phenomena from the standpoint of rulelike theories of semantics. Instead, those rules have the status of what Garfinkel has called ideals[3] wherein what the activity of using rules amounts to is settled by theoretical fiat.

The actual activity of using rules is an important domain to exclude from one's empirical interests for it is here that empirical adequacy of a rulelike semantics must ultimately be assessed. Ethnomethodological studies that have empirically investigated the ways in which rules are actually employed find that persons continually discover the scope and applicability of rules in the developing occasions in which they use them (Garfinkel; 1967:18–24; Zimmerman, forthcoming). This suggests that the claim that the use of a name accords with rules of proper usage applicable in all situations does not mean that the name has a stable sense in all occasions in which it is employed, since those rules of correct usage can vary in their sense depending on the particular way the rules are used "this time." Thus, the adequacy of explicating the meaning of everyday language use by detecting and elaborating a set of rules of correct usage is directly questionable as an empirical matter. Ongoing ethnomethodological studies by Garfinkel and his students of phenomena of the activity of rule use, especially in regards to language, will doubtless further clarify this matter.

Moreover, further difficulty can be detected in a rulelike semantics by an examination of the circumstances that name users face in deciding between alternative names for an object. When we examine the situation of choosing we will see that no finite set of rules or criteria for applying names can be stated for a wide range of objects-in-situations with which societal members must routinely deal. Lack of finitude in sets of rules or criteria undermines the logical structure of a rulelike semantics because of the inherent *gestalt* properties of any list of rules.[4] Finally, some of the ways that societal members actually employ names which are ruled

---

3. In his lectures at U.C.L.A.(1965–70); Berkeley (1966); Harvard(1967–68); and at the Purdue Symposium on Ethnomethodology(1967).

4. The discussion here of the character of lists of rules is cognate to Garfinkel's detailed discussions of "swarms of indexical particulars" which he has presented in lectures delivered in 1967–1970.

E*

"out of order" by a rulelike semantics but which are of interest for existential, phenomenological, or ethnomethodological studies will be indicated.

We will begin by considering in detail two major types of structural semantics represented by four figures — Goodenough, Lounsbury, Frake, and Conklin. Then we will extend their theories by applying the method of puppetry and critically examining three major points: their treatment of criteria for using names, the extent to which a definite set of criteria could be employed by name users, and the extent to which meaning is determined by criteria of proper use. In this connection the findings of ethnomethodology will be contrasted with the theoretical apparatus of structural semantics.

Goodenough and Lounsbury's Structural Semantics

These two theorists are considered together because both draw heavily on a phonemic analogy as the basis for their theories and both use the work of Charles Morris as a theoretical resource.

Although the member of a society is seen by Lounsbury (1956:190–191) as confronting, in every situation of action, an infinitely large number of features or stimuli that could be potentially relevant to his action, that member does not treat every "objectively" different situation in a different manner. Instead, he is responsive to a limited number of features that he has learned to perceive, be alert for, and act upon. By responding to a limited number of features, he "classifies" his environment by his action toward it.

A principal way in which the member of a society classifies his environment is by naming objects. Those features that are relevant to his naming of objects become those features that are relevant to his treatment of those objects. One has, then, an environment with an infinite number of features or stimuli, a subset of those features that are relevant to the member, and a name for indicating those relevant features.

In Goodenough's more formal terms, the relevant features are paired with, though not equivalent to, significatum, which is defined by Goodenough (1956:195) in the following passage:

> The significatum of a linguistic form is composed of those abstracted contextual elements with which it is in perfect association, without which it cannot properly occur. Its conotata are the contextual elements with which it is less frequently associated. Significata are prerequisites while conotata are possibilities and probabilities. Only the former have definitive value.

He then gives us an example:

> What do I have to know about A and B to say that A is B's cousin? Clearly

people have certain criteria in mind by which they make the judgment that A is or is not B's cousin. What the expression *his cousin* signifies is the particular set of criteria by which this judgment is made.

A name, then, is coupled to a set of criteria or conditions that must be met if the name is to be properly used. Presumably, though not described by either Goodenough or Lounsbury, the member would check out the features of his environment against the criteria of the name. If he found a match between the two, the name could be properly used. As will be seen, Bruner explicitly provides for this procedure as used by an actor. It is important to note that what the name is coupled to is invariant to the occasion of its use; that is, the meaning of the name is exactly the same every time the name is uttered.

Both Goodenough (1956:196–197, 205) and Lounsbury (1956:191–192) provide for the characteristics of the criteria by making use of a phonemic analogy. Just as phones are unique events, denotata are the unique events that are referred to by a specific occasion of the use of a term. In both cases, differences between phones and differences between denotata may or may not be perceptible differences to persons using the phones or the names. In the same manner, kinsmen in a combinatorial analysis of kinship are the unique individuals designated by a kin term on some occasion of its use.

Just as a phone type is a class of phones heard and transcribed as the same by the phonetician, a kin type is a class of kinsmen given the same designation by the ethologist. In terms of denotata, the analog would be a set of objects described as the same by an observer in the most refined description he could give. The refinement of his description is assumed to be more precise than members of the society under study would care to give and use, and probably more refined than they are capable of giving and using. It is also assumed that the description includes everything the members of the society would say.

A phoneme, as a class of noncontrastive phone types that share a distinctive bundle of phonetic features that members of a society are presumed to use in discriminating between sounds, is analogous to a kin class. That is, a kin class is a class of kin types that are not contrasted terminologically and that share some distinctive features that the members of the society are presumed to use in deciding what relationship they have to some other member. For example, uncles is a kin class in our society—all parents' brothers are designated uncles (that is, they are not contrasted terminologically). Similarly, a significatum is also a bundle of distinctive features—a set of necessary and sufficient conditions that an object must meet to be properly signified by the sign, name, or lexeme in question.

The analyst, confronted with a native term and specific occasion for its use, employs some *etic* descriptive technique for recording the occasions of the term's use — some recording technique that makes very fine discriminations and does not require a member's understanding of the society. Thus, he *begins* his analysis with the analog of a phoneme and its allophones (or, better, a series of phones known to be instances of the phoneme) rather than having its discovery as the *goal* of his inquiry. His task is to find those features that consistently discriminate between the arrays of objects given different names.

In this manner, the analyst finds a rule for assigning specific objects to one of two complementary terms. Two terms are said to be complementary if a single significata (criterion) is used to assign objects to one name or the other. A complementary set of terms belongs to the same paradigm. Two terms may also be initially seen as members of the same paradigm if they refer to some portion of a field of objects that may be referred to by some more general term. For example, if the denotata of cars and tractors are included within the denotata of machine, then cars and tractors belong to the same universe of discourse and can be analyzed as members of the same paradigm.

The paradigm will usually have more than one dimension. Thus, the objects under its jurisdiction will have more than one feature that is relevant to their proper naming. To this, Lounsbury adds the qualification that the analysis be applied to the same "semantic field," which requires that all items being considered have at least one feature in common. This avoids the problem of metaphoric extension of the terms into areas having different kinds of denotata, thereby making unitary definitions impossible. In other words, one could not state a single set of rules that would locate the possible items but would have to state several sets of rules.

Since both Lounsbury and Goodenough draw on C. W. Morris's work on signs, we can turn to Morris (1946:7) for a further explication of features of signs and "their objects" and the manner in which these two are connected. His basic definition of a sign follows:

> If something, A, controls behavior towards a goal in a way similar to (but not necessarily identical with) the way something else, B, would control behavior with respect to that goal in a situation in which it were observed, then A is a sign (7).

Since a behavioral organism may not respond to the sign itself but to "the object it presents" after some chain of behaviors, Morris (1946:10) modifies the above definition:

> If anything, A, is a preparatory-stimulus which in the absence of stimulus-objects initiating response-sequences of a certain behavior-family causes a disposition in some organism to respond under certain conditions by response-sequences of this behavior-family, then A is a sign.

That is, if *A* can stand proxy for *B* as a stimulus for setting off a course of action with *B* as a goal, then *A* is a sign for *B*. The organism is called an interpreter and the disposition to respond the interpretant. He describes (1946:17) the object toward which the course of action is directed as

> Anything which would permit the completion of the response-sequences to which the interpreter is disposed because of a sign will be called a *denotatum* of the sign. A sign will be said to *denote* a denotatum. Those conditions which are such that whatever fulfills them is a denotatum will be called a *significatum* of the sign.

Thus we are dealing with two features of the interpreter's environment that are coupled by his action—the sign that initiates the action and the significatum, that set of terminal conditions under which the response-sequences to which the organism is disposed can be completed. The import of Morris's definition of a sign and its signification for structural semantics is that the signification is the relevant *goal features* of the object in his portrayal. They define the actor's interest in the object.

Morris proposes that a language has five major features: (1) the language is composed of a plurality of (2) interpersonal signs (signs having the same significatum for a number of interpreters), (3) which are systematically interconnected, and (4) which are producible as well as interpretable by members of the interpreter family. It is the fifth feature that is of particular interest here.

> The signs which constitute a language are plurisituational signs, that is, signs with a relative constancy of signification in every situation in which a sign of the sign-family in question appears. If the term 'odor' e.g., signified differently each time the sign occurred it would not be a sign in a language even though at a given occurrence it was interpersonal. A sign in a language is thus a sign-family and not merely a unisituation sign-vehicle (Morris, 1946:35).

In other words, the referent, the thing the sign is coupled with, is invariant to the occasion in which the sign is used.[5]

In summary, this type of structural semantics provides that what ego presents to alter is a set of lexemes (items of vocabulary) within some domain of discourse.[6] Although both ego and alter must "agree" to what the relevant domain of discourse is for their conversation to have intelligibility, how this agreement takes place is not provided for in the

5. Morris is not consistent on this matter. Although in some passages he speaks of the relative constancy of signification, in no place does he provide for how actors could deal with relative constancy. He provides only for how they would deal with absolute constancy of signification.

6. The notion of a domain of discourse is not explicit in the work of Lounsbury or Goodenough, but it is directly implied by Goodenough's advice that the analyst insist that the informant speak "literally" and by Lounsbury's rule that the analyst deal with a single semantic field. A domain of discourse includes the semantic field, the terms used to refer to it, and the way in which the terms are related to their meanings.

theory. That is, there must be some way alter knows that ego is speaking of kinship in order for alter to recognize a term such as father correctly.

In this scheme the status of the presented term as a member of a pair (term-object) is like that of a sign (name) in a language. That is, it stands proxy for its object in setting off courses of action toward that object. Ego can present the object to alter *through* its name. Ego, in choosing a name within a domain of discourse, is confronted with a fixed set of alternatives from which to make a choice. Once the domain is fixed, the chosen name can mean only a limited (finite) number of things.

Further, what ego presents to alter by use of a name is not the denotata but the significata. Given the attentiveness of the members to a limited set of stimuli, those features that discriminate between various denotata may be available only to the analyst. In any case, what ego presents to alter through the use of a name is the necessary and sufficient conditions for properly using the name.

Each time the name is used within the same domain of discourse, the same "object" is presented to alter. Although each occasion of use of the name may present different denotata, differences between denotata are not relevant to alter's consummation of a course of action directed toward the object in question as long as relevance· is defined by the domain of discourse of the initiating name. Thus, properly described, the object consists of nothing other than those features that satisfy the necessary and sufficient conditions.

Inasmuch as it is asserted that the tie between name and object is cultural, that tie is normative. Although it is not explicit in their discussion, Goodenough and Lounsbury must therefore have some conception of semanticalness that parallels grammaticalness in structural linguistics.[7] Therefore, the members would have some conception of "properly named" and would be sensitive to and negatively sanction occasions of "improper naming." Presumably, frequent improper usage of names would render a conversation unintelligible. Before exploring the consequences of this theory, the work of Frake and Conklin will be reviewed.

Frake and Conklin's Structural Semantics

In their studies, Frake and Conklin focus on such things as the diagnosis of disease and the features of color categories rather than on the analysis

7. Lounsbury acknowledges that the actor's concern for proper usage of names would be observable when, for example, ego's relation to some other person was under dispute, as it might be in the settlement of claims to ego's inheritance of that person's property. Such an occasion also makes the criteria for the proper use of a term explicit as well as observable. Personal communication, spring, 1964.

of kinship of Goodenough and Lounsbury. For these types of phenomena, Frake (in Gladwin and Sturtevant, 1962:74) insists that the only possible method of investigation is to discern "how people construe their world of experience from the way they talk about it." He differentiates this method from the method used by Goodenough and Lounsbury—the discovery of distinctive features. A series of studies using the methods of Frake and Conklin is intended to provide a map of the world from the members' point of view.

Frake (1961:114) begins by taking some area of experience that is a frequent topic of conversation among the members of some society and looks to the way they talk about it. In the area of diseases, for example, he states:

> Every culture provides a set of significant questions, potential answers, and procedures for arriving at answers. The cultural answers to these questions are *concepts* of disease. The information necessary to arrive at a specific answer and eliminate others is the *meaning* of a disease concept.

It is the analyst's task to find these questions and answers. He notes the kind of questions the members ask about the phenomenon in question and the alternative kinds of answers these questions can elicit. Then the analyst seeks to find how the members decided between alternative answers.[8]

Among the set of questions the member can ask, one subset demands the name of the object in question. For the topic of disease, answering a question with a disease name is diagnosis.

> Subanun diagnosis is the procedure of judging similarities and differences among instances of 'being sick,' placing new instances into culturally defined and linguistically labelled categories (Frake, 1961:115).

The minimal utterance that can answer the question "What kind of an X is that?" is taken by Frake to qualify as a single name for an X.

Before considering the criteria for naming X the analyst must ascertain that the name was selected from a set of contrasting alternatives. Two names contrast if only one can correctly be applied to a particular set of features. In Conklin's (in Gladwin and Sturtevant, 1962:124) terms, the two names can be contrastive only if they also belong to the same lexical set. A lexical set

> consists of all semantically contrastive lexemes which in a given, culturally relevant context share exclusively at least one defining feature.... The semantic range of all such lexemes defines the *domain* of the lexical set (1961:120).

For Frake the domain is defined by the situation in which the utterance is given.

Essentially it is a matter of determining with what a term contrasts in a

---

8. For one explication of this method see Black (1963).

particular situation. When someone says, "This is an *X*," what is he saying it is *not*?

If *X* is to have a determinate meaning under these conditions, alter must know what else ego might have said. That is, the possible events must be delimitable and specifiable. The disease world or the plant world as cultural (rather than as medical or botanical) phenomena must exhaustively divide into a set of mutually exclusive categories (Frake, 1961:131, and in Gladwin and Sturtevant, 1962:79). As we shall see in the last section of this chapter, this point is of great importance.

To obtain the criteria of interest the terms must be arranged in a taxonomy. The more complex taxonomies divide phenomena in two dimensions. The vertical dimension is arranged so that each level is more general than the one below it and includes the lower levels. The horizontal dimension discriminates between objects at the same level of generality. Further, Conklin specifies that definitions of the categories included within the taxonomy are achieved through the conjunction of these dimensions or, more specifically, through the conjunction of the values along the several dimensions.

The values of the dimensions are equivalent to the rules or criteria the members use for assigning one name rather than another to a particular object. From the point of view of the member, an "instance" of the object is matched against the defining attributes of the conceptual category and treated as equivalent to other "instances" that also occupy that category.

While one could use the distinctive-features method or, possibly, even methods of studying stimulus discriminations used in experimental psychology of perception,[9] Frake (1961:123) prefers to ask informants about the criteria they use because of the lack of relevant *etic* recording procedures[10] in most areas of ethnography and the lack of procedures of perceptual testing in the field. For example,

---

9. However, it is not at all clear that the study of stimulus discriminations would be relevant for this purpose. The very project that Frake undertakes would have to be achieved, and with great precision, before the study of stimulus discrimination could be undertaken. That is, the experimental psychologist would have to be provided with a set of *culturally relevant* dimensions along which the stimulus arrays could be varied. Only then could he vary the phenomenon in such a way as to transform it (for the subjects) from one object to another. Experimental psychologists have traditionally worked with phenomena much less complex than the diagnosis of disease, and the techniques for manipulating such objects are probably not available.

10. Conklin (in Gladwin and Sturtevant, 1962:90) emphasizes that if one merely records any discriminable differences between objects that are given different names, the analyst will be able to find many such differences. Only some subset of these differences, however, may be used by the member of society as criteria that differentiate between objects for him and as criteria that are used by him in identifying objects and assigning names. This is in direct contrast to the methods of Goodenough and Lounsbury.

One can simply ask his informants about meanings: "What is an uncle?" "How do you know he is an uncle and not a father?" Such procedures yield the culture's explicit definitions or *criteria* of categories.

In theory, the members must be able to specify these criteria, since they are part of their cultural equipment; they learned the criteria from their fellow members, and they identify and give a name for an object in the presence of others (Frake, in Gladwin and Sturtevant, 1962:75, 78). This last point is of special importance, since, if the member incorrectly identified the object, presumably his fellows would point out to him the features the object lacked to be called that object. In this way the member would be told again what the criteria were. For a clarification of this conception of criteria we must turn to Bruner, who is cited by Frake and Conklin as the source of their concepts.

Bruner characterizes the actor's world as an infinite multiplicity of potentially, uniquely discriminable objects and events. But, if the actor were to be responsive to this potential multiplicity, the world as containing objects for his treatment and contemplation would be impossibly complex. To treat his world in an efficacious, intelligible manner, the actor must be able to view "the same object" as that same object, even though, in terms of stimulus display, the presented object varies from perspective to perspective and from moment to moment. The actor must also be capable of seeing "two different objects" as equivalent—as *the same kind of thing* or *amounting to the same thing*—if he is to treat them in the same way and if he is to indicate them to someone else via a common language that has *any* limitation in vocabulary. The actor's "problem" is solved through his capacity to categorize. In fact, for Bruner (1956:12), the actor's capacity to think in the first place is based on his capacity to categorize.

> Categorizing is the *means by which the objects of the world about us are identified*. The act of identifying some thing or some event is an act of "placing" it in a class.

That is, the *seeing* of the object as an object depends on categorizing it. In this sense, the categorizing of stimuli is the objectivizing of one's experimental environment.

The act of categorization or identification involves the scanning of the stimulus input in the attempt to find in that display those features that match the specifications of a category. The identification, or recognition of the objects as such, is made when there is a "fit" between the properties of a stimulus input and the specifications of a category. For example, the actor might have the category "apple" with the specifications "round, red, and shiny." Any object he scanned that matched these specifications would be seen, identified, and recognized by him as "an apple."

The specifications of the category are referred to as criterial attributes. Any features of objects that vary from event to event may be used as criterial attributes (that is, any object features that may be used by the actor to discriminate between events may also be used by him in the identification of those events). Object features are construed as varying along dimensions; for example, an object might have the dimensions of roundness, redness, and shininess. Attributes are equivalent to these dimensions.

> Any attribute which when changed in value alters the likelihood of an object being categorized in a certain way is . . . a criterial attribute for the person doing the categorizing (Bruner, 1956:31).

Use of attributes in this way is seen by Bruner as the inference from a feature of the environment to the identity of an object with that feature. Once the identity of the object is established, further inferences are possible.

> We . . . regard a concept as a network of sign-significate inferences by which one goes beyond a set of *observed* criterial properties exhibited by an object or event to the class identity of the object or event in question, and thence to additional inferences about other *unobserved* properties of the object or event (Bruner, 1956:244).

For example, one infers from a set of symptoms the disease of a patient. Then one is able to further infer the patient's responsiveness to certain courses of medication, the likelihood of his death, what his insides look like, etc. However, these further inferences as actual features of the named object are not referred to by Frake and Conklin.

What Frake and Conklin do for Bruner's theory of cognition is to convert criterial attributes into features of a culture by incorporating them into the corpus of cultural or common-sense knowledge. Thereby, every member of the society in question identifies objects by use of the same cognitive methods. Use of the same methods of identification guarantees a world known in common as the result of the application of these methods. The normatively required character of these methods provides Frake and Conklin with a solution to the problem of intersubjectivity by reference to the features of the normative order.

In the view of Frake, Conklin, and Bruner, then, what ego presents to alter is any utterance that can answer alter's question "What kind of an X is this?" This is not to say that the only kind of interaction that goes on between ego and alter is of the question-answer form, but that the term used by ego could be used as an answer to that question and the term would have an identical meaning as when used in an answer. The utterance or name is selected from a fixed set of alternatives provided by "a kind of X."

The status of the name as a member of the pair name-object is as a word from a subset of a common language, that is, a word selected from language used to talk about "that kind of situation" (a specific situation of diagnosis, an occasion of ordering a meal, etc.). Frake's conception of the situation of use of a term is perhaps his most important notion, but it is also the least explicated. It is important because it defines for the user and the hearer both the sense of the question "What kind of an X is this?" and the range of alternatives from which an answer can be selected (its taxonomy).

What ego presents to alter through the use of a name is the *claim* that an object was encountered that met the criterial attributes of that named category of objects. That is, ego presents to alter a member (any member) of that class of objects or, put in other terms, any object having the features of that named category.

While in Lounsbury, Goodenough, and Morris's account there is a three-member set — name, necessary and sufficient conditions, and features of the denotata — in Frake and Conklin we find a two- and four-member set. That is, it is a four-member set from the name user's point of view — name, category, criterial attributes, and features of the input — while for the hearer the set has two members. For the hearer, name and category are simultaneous, and criterial attributes are equivalent to relevant object features. The import of having a two-, three-, or four-member set will be discussed below. From the hearer's point of view, the coupling between name and object (as criterial attributes or relevant features) is a normative, that is, a cultural, one. The hearer is taught how to use the term by being taught its criterial attributes; he assumes that ego uses the term in the same way he does and would negatively sanction ego if this were not so. He also assumes that when he uses the term the other expects the same of him.[11]

In many important respects, the theories of Frake, Conklin, Goodenough, and Lounsbury are the same. All have the following conceptions.

The use of a name is the method members of a society have of presenting objects to one another and is their method for indicating the features of that object. That is, ego could present alter with some object by using that object's name, for example, by telling him "there is a rock in the path you are taking" ego presents to alter's plans about his walk the existence of a rock that he might take into account. The name can also be used by ego to objectivize "a something" in alter's environment, i.e., to provide the identity of "a something" by using its name to point out its features. For example, by saying to alter "that's a rock in your

11. These assumptions that members make are referred to by Garfinkel as the "constitutive accent" of the "attitude of daily life" (in Harvey, 1963).

path," ego tells him the features it has (in this case the feature of hardness and that it will injure his foot if he kicks it.)

The "thing" presented or indicated by the use of the name is a set of relevant features. These are alternatively called significata (necessary and sufficient conditions for using the name) or criterial attributes (features used by members to infer the identity of objects). These features have two properties of special importance.

First, they are features known to the name-using members as features of their own culture. What the members know about a named world they know together and they know because they were taught. What they have learned as relevant are those features that an object must have if the use of the name is to be correct. They have learned a "grammar" of meanings. This grammar is enforced and legitimately enforceable in interactions in which the names are used. Thereby, relevant object features are always sanctionably relevant object features. It is these sanctionably relevant object features that the structural semanticist uses in assembling his paradigm.

Second, the features obtain their relevance from the domain of discourse within which the name is used on *specific occasions of its use*. The notion of a domain of discourse is required by a theory of structural semantics to provide the relevance of features used for discriminating between objects. That is, for every different array of objects there is, potentially, a different set of features discriminating one member from another. Therefore, relevant features always apply to one assembled set of objects rather than to another. For the members, the domain of discourse selects the specific meaning on this occasion of use from the numerous possible meanings that the term can have by locating the object referred to within some specific and repetitive array of objects with which the named object relevantly varies. By providing the actors, as parties to an interaction, with a fixed set of alternative names and meanings to use on that occasion, the domain of discourse (or a paradigm and its semantic field) provides them with a map or schema of interpretation that can be used to both recognize any event that does happen and to exhaustively anticipate all the events that might happen. If the structural semanticist were to provide a paradigm for all the domains of discourse available to the members of a society, he would have provided a set of all the possible events that could happen in that society as, and in terms of, what the members could recognize and act upon. How the members recognize which one of a set of possible domains of discourse is relevant to a given occasion of interaction is not provided for by the theorists, though Frake does say that "the situation" marks the relevance of a domain.

A major difference between the theorists is their method. On the one hand, the theorist can ask the members directly how they differentiate between named objects. On the other hand, with the distinctive features approach, the theorist[12] can interrogate an informant about features of objects (about features of persons who are called by a given kin name, for example) while using some theory of that kind of object to guide the interrogation. The theory guides the interrogation by providing the theorist with those features of that kind of object that can be eligible as relevant features.

The theorist does not ask the informant to give him these features directly; instead he asks him to characterize the objects in terms of expressions whose meanings are known to both the informant and the theorist (the terms used to enable the theorist to characterize persons by way of kintype notation, for example). Then the theorist can use these terms and their directly implied meanings to find those features that discriminate between objects given different names. For example, if a person with one name is characterized as "Father's Brother" and a person with another name is characterized as "Mother's Daughter," there is the direct implication that between these two persons there is a difference of sex and generation, among other things. Howsoever the theorist came by this characterization, the directly implied features of characterized objects must be available to members of the society the theorist is dealing with in order for his theory to be correct. That is, in the example above the members must recognize the difference of sex and generation between persons given the names in question. If they did not recognize these things, the terms in which the members described the society to the theorist were not terms that, in fact, were known to both analyst and informant. The theory the analyst used as a guide must also be a theory that correctly provides for relevant features in the society he is dealing with, if he is to be dealing with the "real cognitive features." Otherwise, he may miss those features that the members really use. As long as there are no procedural errors of these two types, the method of distinctive features is a possible way of permitting the members of a society "to tell about" relevant object features. In this respect it does not essentially differ from the procedure of asking directly "How do you know X is your uncle?"

Alternative Societies Encompassed by the Theories

Further features of the theories of signs provided by structural semantics may be obtained by applying a method described by Schutz (1962:40–43) in which the theorist constructs puppets who do nothing

12. Of course the theorist need not actually interrogate the informant himself. Lounsbury uses the results of ethnographer's interrogations.

other than enact the society or circumstances described by the theorist. Within this method the only thoughts, feelings, and perceptions that the puppet has are those depicted by the theorist. Although Schutz intended his description of this method as an account of how some classical sociological theorists, notably Weber, did their work, the method can be applied to theories that have already been stated as a method of obtaining further but unstated consequences of any theory.

A Theorist's Society That Consists of Talk: A Theory of Corresponding Marks

Application of the method of puppetry to the theoretical statements of Goodenough and Lounsbury results in actors and the objects of their action consisting in courses of talk. Within the procedures employed by these two theorists, the society is made available for analysis only through the members' talk about that society and only through their talk. That is, such distinctive features of kinship, as seniority of generation, age, consanguineal or affinal relationship to ego, and even sex, are matters available to most members of the society through the person's reputation and presentation. One knows these things about specific persons through what is said about them. For example, you could hardly "see" that someone was older than you if older meant only born prior to you, as it does in Goodenough and Lounsbury's theory. That is, as long as the theorist retains the notion that denotation refers to those features that are invariably associated with the correct use of the name and these features are observable circumstances, then one could "see" age only by having been present at a birth. Most members, especially members younger than the person in question, would have to be told about someone's age, since they could not see it for themselves.[13]

Inasmuch as for Goodenough and Lounsbury the significatum of a sign is that set of features that permit the completion of a course of action that was originated by a sign (and in their treatment these features are verbal attributions), their statements are quite consistent with a reconstruction of their theory as a description of a society consisting of talk. There are a series of consequences about the society in which the member lives that follow from this way of understanding such theories.

1. Members are courses of talk — nothing more. A sleeping member would be either a "long pause" or no member at all. This is intended in

13. In Goodenough and Lounsbury's terms, members' assertions that "he is wrinkled," "he is bald," "he is toothless," etc., would be connotations, not denotations of someone's age and thereby not the real referents of the term.

the same sense that an actor as a course of action is intended in some sociologists' theories (Talcott Parson's, for example). The society would then be the talking that goes on.

2. Object features consist only in the features that members talk about (verbally attribute, note, point out, and argue about) as features that give evidence that the name of the object has been correctly applied. These same features also exhaustively define the actor's interest in the object, inasmuch as they constitute the object for the actor. They define the objects of his affect and action and they define the uses the object can be put to in whatsoever way the actor might use them to accomplish whatsoever project he might entertain.

3. When the name is used, its referent is the set of rules for its correct application and nothing more. There is no reference to a visually perceived object. Within this theory the object consists in the rules. Thereby, the name and its referent stand in exact and exhaustive equivalence, just as one side of an equation stands to the other. Hence, the theory is called a theory of corresponding marks.

4. Socialization in such a world would consist in learning the names of objects and their corresponding features by being taught those names with those features. These same features would be available to the members' memory if they were asked to characterize the object. There would be no ostensive defining available to these members.

5. Speakers would be differentiated by
(a) their pronouncement ("I'm Jack"),
(b) attribution ("That's Jack"),
(c) the character of their utterances,
(d) the character of utterances directed toward them.
6. Occasions would be differentiated by
(a) naming them,
(b) the character of the utterances pronounced there.
These last two would mark the domain of discourse.

7. Correct usage would be defined by the theorist, on behalf of the members, by consistency and consistency alone. Once a name (thereby object) was introduced, everything that was said about it would have to be compatible with the criteria or features of that name. But no lies in the sense of false naming would be possible since, with no perceptual world as the reference for his naming, whatever the member says is "just so." The member could say, "I said it, therefore it is."

8. The member has "no problem" in knowing his fellows' minds in that with no perceptual world there are no perspectives. Whatever one member says is available to the others in terms of its criteria in the same

way that it is available to the announcing member. Thereby, the problem of intersubjectivity is solved for the theorist by providing for the simultaneity of the stream of consciousness for all actors who are in each others' presence. In effect, they *are one*. This can be so, of course, only if the only events in the society are talk and, thereby, everything the members do is observable.

These features present the analyst with some enviable consequences. (1) The analyst must take his own imagery as specifically irrelevant. Since in social science most of this imagery is available for presentation to others only through the use of metaphor or analogy, the analyst's stance here is a solution to troubles, not a problem. When an object is red, tall, and thin, it is to be treated as *equivalent* to its having the features X,Y,Z. Equivalent here does not mean that they are replaceable by X, Y, and Z, but that what the theorist might know ostensively about red, thin, and tall is to be "put out of action." This is the same as treating the world you are attempting to represent from the stance of a blind man who has been kept in a straightjacket and who has no way of addressing his world except by means of his hearing and speaking. This also means that the analyst may approach his subject matter under the ideal scientific assumption that he knows nothing about what he is studying and what he ends up knowing will be only and exactly what he discovers while studying.[14] There would be no fringes of accompanying meaning to his assertions, which is presently neither specified nor specifiable. This ideal is not realizable elsewhere in social science. (2) Not only is the analyst's own knowledge of his affairs irrelevant to the character of his findings, what his fellow analysts know about the world they live in is also irrelevant. The findings depend for their adequacy only on their methods of production. They need not make good sense nor correspond to a society as known in the manner of common sense. (3) The findings are fully compatible with the built-in presuppositions of the computer, which treats all inputs as marks, that is, the computer "assumes" the exhaustiveness of expressions given to it as inputs.

But in order for the assumption of society as talk to provide a viable method, actors would have to provide the justification for every identification they made, to satisfy the analyst. When the theorist addresses an empirical society, he might encounter utterances that require a perceptual base of interpretation for their intelligibility. If, for example, the

14. That is, he knows nothing when he begins and knows nothing more than what he discovers when he finishes, except other propositions that have been already admitted into the corpus of scientific knowledge. For a discussion of this aspect of scientific rationality see Garfinkel (1960:76).

actors said of each other, "he doesn't recognize what he is seeing," or "he said it was a rock when we could all see that it was a house," the analyst operating within the confines of a theory of corresponding marks could not *see* what they were saying.

There would be, however, some kinds of naming for which this method would be relevant. The naming, identifying, and teaching about ghosts, gods, devils, and hallucinations, either occurring naturally or drug induced, at least as these phenomena appear in some societies, would be compatible with conceiving the object as a set of attributed criterial features.

An alternative way of understanding names and objects they name becomes relevant once the theorist assumes the relevance of the perceptual world but still maintains the basic tenets of structural semantics. For reasons I hope will be apparent below, I will call this elaboration a theory of tokens.

A Theory of Tokens

Tokens involve a three-member set: the token (name), the rules for its application, and the objects to which it is applied. The proposal that criterial attributes are matched against the features of a perceptual world in Frake, Conklin, and Bruner's theories warrants the consideration that a theory of tokens is an extension of their theories. A name is treated as a token when a person to whom the name is delivered assumes that the token was selected by a correct application of selection rules (criterial attributes, for example) when the actual course of selection is not, or cannot be, directly observed by him. The theory of tokens differs from the theory of corresponding marks in that one member of the system is not a restricted set of alternatives, that is, the "objects" are not so limited. What gives this system the appearnace of limitation are the courses of action that can be directed toward the objects. In other words, the user has a limited set of tokens that can be applied to objects. The limitation of the number of tokens can be seen as providing a limited set of alternatives for the actor, if and only if the means or methods whereby he "fits" the tokens to the objects are seen by those who "interpret" the token as specifically irrelevant to the meaning of the token. An example that fits these specifications is the phoneme from the point of view of the member of a society.

If one treats the produced sound in an utterance as an instance of a phoneme, the unique sound may be viewed as utilized by the members of a society as tokening a phoneme. Distinctive features would then be rules for correctly producing and recognizing sounds as instances of phonemes. The actual physical manipulations of a member's vocal apparatus would be his methods, and the acoustically described sounds that these same members could potentially utter would be the objects that are "fitted" to the phonemes.

From the point of view of the member, what the descriptive linguist describes is *one* of the possible methods of producing a recognizable language sound. That is, by describing the sound phonetically, the linguist provides his readers with a notation that can be read as instructions for reproducing that sound. But among the members of the society whose speech the linguist intends to describe, will be persons who do not use the method indicated in phonetic notation but who still produce, to the members' satisfaction, "the same sound." For example, members would recognize that some sound produced by a man who had no upper lip, or had a slit trachea and a speaking device, or was a ventriloquist and didn't close his lips, as a [p] sound, even though it was not bilabial. From the members' point of view, the methods used in producing that sound were not relevant to the sanctionable character of the sound. Thereby, the actual sound tokens the intended phoneme.

The features of a theory of names as tokens are as follows:

1. There is a limited set of tokens but not a limited set of objects to which they are applied.

2. Their methods of application are not relevant to the identity of the token. That is, the token remains invariant to the way in which its rules are applied.

3. Interest in the tokened object is nevertheless defined by the token's criterial attributes. That is, the criterial attributes or rules of application define the relevant features toward which a course of action can be directed.

4. To recognize a name as a token is to assume that the criteria or rules for applying the name were in fact correctly applied, although one does not specifically know how those rules were applied. One does not know how the rules were applied because whatever method is employed by the token user is covert. That is, his fellow members cannot see its use and must thereby treat his actions in terms of their products rather than treating them in process. This would restrict the area of relevance of a theory of tokens to those actions that can be analyzed down to the point where process can no longer be seen. Below the level of observability, any variation in the actor's method is inconsequential, that is, *structurally* inconsequential. At this level of activity any method is

legitimate. Many grammars, in the most general sense of that term, have this character.[15] But for this possibility to have viability the following condition must hold.

5. The methods or schemas of interpretation used by the actors must require the same "inputs" and make the same "outputs" for such a condition to persist (that is, for a variety of methods to be in use. Each method must require exactly the same information to make a correct identification or prediction of the object, and each must, at least usually, come up with the same answer. Otherwise, I would be dumbfounded when you are able to identify a man as, say, uncle, but I do not, when I know you know no more about him than I. If this condition is met, a variety of componential solutions to the same problem is a possibly accurate portrayal of what is "really going on" in a society.[16]

6. Unlike the case of corresponding marks, a lie is possible here. For example, one could say, while pointing to a wastebasket, "That is a rock before me," and be sanctioned for that usage. Under a theory of corresponding marks, the wastebasket that was pointed to cannot be "seen," so sanctioning on this account could not be treated under the theory.

7. Finally, since the methods, criteria, or schemas of interpretation cannot be shown or demonstrated in process to neophyte members of a society, these methods must be discovered by "experimentation" by each member. Frake (1964:119) provides for this process in the following passage:

> A person learning to speak and behave in a culturally appropriate manner is "just fiddling with a set of rules which allow him to use terms (and otherwise behave) the way others do."

It is easy enough to see that some kinds of methods are learned in that fashion (for example, learning how to make correct pronunciations of words). The procedure of learning the meaning of a rule by having that rule illustrated for the neophyte by means of examples seems much more common, however. But any use of rules that makes their employment observable and open to question extends beyond a theory of tokens.

---

15. Ostensive definitions of the single-sketch variety (like the picture in a dictionary) also match the theory of tokens. The sketch stands as a "something like this" rule for recognizing the object. Yet, it is accompanied with no procedures for putting the rule into practice.
16. One of the critical arguments between structural semanticists about their own works focuses on their finding that there may be a number of apparently valid but different analyses of the same semantic data. For some of the consequences of this result, see Wallace and Atkins (1960:75–79) and Burling (1963, 1964).

Criteria As Ideals And Criteria In Use

The theoretical apparatus of structural semantics construes criteria for using names properly as a set of ideals that are matched against the experienced world. The experienced world is encountered as verbal attributions in the case of a theory of marks and as perceptually available objects in the theory of tokens. The theoretical apparatus would terminate analysis at the point at which consistent verbal attributions are obtained for a theory of marks or where members' stated criteria are obtained for a theory of tokens. Termination of the analysis at these points idealizes members' use of names and rules in such a way that the use of names appears to mean the same thing in all occasions in which they are used. However, it is important to note that workers in this area have not attended to the full range of methodological implications of their conceptual apparatus in collecting empirical materials. Frake, in fact, has collected some materials that, as I will indicate, would require a different kind of conceptualization.

If one examines the activity of employing criteria for using names or titles, he finds that the particular sense of the criteria are specific to the cases in which the criteria are employed. Rather than having a stable meaning across a set of cases that are classified by their use, criteria are matched against cases by elaborating the sense of the criteria or the case to encompass the particular occurrences that the name or title user faces. (Garfinkel, 1967:18–24; Leiter, 1969; Wieder, 1969; Zimmerman, in Garfinkel and Sacks, forthcoming). Frake (1961:125) hints at this circumstance.

> This is not to say that the evaluation of cues of a particular illness as exemplars of diagnostic criteria is always easy or consistent. Informants operating with identical diagnostic concepts may disagree in a particular case, but they rarely disagree in the verbal definitions of the concepts themselves.

One might wonder about what identicality means when "identical" concepts applied to the same events produce inconsistent results. In light of paradoxes like this, ethnomethodologists would turn the problem the structural semanticists pose on its head. They would propose instead that the successful elaborative showing that some criteria for applying a name do indeed apply in this particular case is achieved by means of providing ad hoc grounds. Thus, the appearance of this particular case as identical with others is acheived for members party to the demonstration. The sense of "identical" is thus not a logical identity but is instead what Garfinkel would call a "for all practical purposes" identicality.

Frake (1961:126) incidentally notes some uses of diagnostic criteria that are more suitable to conceptualization within a "practical logic" than within the kind of logical apparatus he employs.

For any derivative disease, a given prodome is a necessary but not a sufficient criterion. If the evidence of other criteria overwhelmingly points to a contrary diagnosis, one must conclude — since the criteriality of the prodrome cannot be discounted — that the previous diagnosis, or current information about it, is erroneous. Thus an informant insisted that an inflammation on my leg was an inflamed insect bite . . . rather than an inflamed wound . . . even though I had told him I thought it originated as a 'minor cut.' I simply, according to him, had not noticed the prodromal bite. In such cases the existence of the prodrome is deduced from its criteriality to a diagnosis eventually arrived at on other grounds. Our data would have been much improved had we earlier recognized the importance of these *ex post facto* classificatory decisions as evidence of criteriality.

Rather than merely taking ex post facto decisions as valuable sources of information on what a member's criteria are, one can emphasize the fact that "criteria" employed in this way fundamentally alter the meaning of criteria and of necessary and sufficient conditions. In uses like the case of Frake's insect bite, it would appear that criteria are used not to determine what category of disease one has but instead as prescriptions for reconstructing what must have occurred. The availability of reasonable reconstructions like "Frake had not noticed the insect biting him" makes it possible for the informant to proceed with the diagnosis while claiming that this case had the features of other cases diagnosed as belonging to the same category. Ethnomethodological studies of the employment of criteria have found that the use of such ad hoc procedures as elaborating the sense of a rule so that how the rule fits in this case can be seen, reconstructing some feature of an event so that it can be seen that it fits the prescriptions of the rule, ignoring some aspect of an event that does not fit the rule, and proceeding to classify an event while some "critical" aspects are left undetermined are essential, unavoidable practices. Whenever persons are confronted with having to make a choice and cannot rely on leaving this case in the status of undecided they will employ these practices.

If "criteria" have these properties, then the analyst's ability to state a set of "criteria" would not explicate how societal members go about the task of assigning names to objects. But, even if we overlook the difficulties posed by "criteria" which have an indefinite sense, there is considerable doubt that a finite set of even indefinite criteria is employable in most occasions of applying names to objects.

The Domain of Discourse As Providing A Limited Set Of Alternatives

The meanings of names that result from a structural semantic analysis appear to be invariant in all the occasions in which the terms are employed, at least in the sense that the same "criteria" would be said to be relevant to the meaning of the name in every case in which it is employed. However, this apparent stability of the meaning of names is dependent on the repetitive and standardized character of the situations that members encounter. Frake (in Gladwin and Sturtevant, 1962:79) has argued that a limited set of characteristics intended by the use of a name is possible because not any object could contrast with another in any particular setting.

> In writing rules for classifying hamburgers I must say something about hot dogs, whereas I can ignore rainbows. Two categories contrast only when the difference between them is significant for defining their use. The segregates 'hamburgers' and 'rainbows,' even though they have no members in common, do not function as distinctive alternatives in any uncontrived classifying context familiar to me.

To say this, Frake must rely on his sense of "what any member knows" about likely purchasable objects at a hamburger stand. The domain of discourse for this setting would be defined by all the purchasable items. While it seems clear that no member would "reasonably expect" to purchase a rainbow at a hamburger stand, it seems just as clear that there would be a large number of objects that he might "reasonably expect" to purchase yet could not specify. From the purchaser's point of view, his "reasonable expectation" extends to any object he sees as possibly sold at that place. He sees that his request will be judged by the seller in terms of its "reasonableness." He sees as well that some requests would be seen as strange, some as not strange but still not available at this particular hamburger stand, and some as reasonable and available. Each of these boundaries is not distinct for him, yet each is important.

If he requests a "most strange" object, he will be thought mad, perhaps dangerous, and persons will not wish to wait on him; this is known to him and provides a fearful possibility. For example, he might think that to request a used Ford at a hamburger stand would put him in this position. He might fear that the counterman would ask, "Do you know where you are?" or "Would you like me to call the police?"

A bad move on the purchaser's part can rupture the competence others assume of him and are willing to continue to assume of him to the point that he gives evidence of lack of competence (Garfinkel, in Harvey, 1963). Requesting "reasonable objects" is, from his point of view, a serious matter. Yet as serious as his concern is about the difference between reasonable requests and unreasonable ones, the member does not know specifically where that boundary is. He may be totally committed to complying with a domain of discourse without being able to find its fringe.

When he approaches a hamburger stand he could perhaps count on the availability of and reasonableness of hamburgers. He might think as well that candy bars are reasonable but perhaps not available. But what about sno cones, stick licorice, cotton candy, felt caps, pennants, balloons, beef jerky, and a host of other things? We have seen these things available at some hamburger stands but not all. Although we would rarely request them at an expensive restaurant that specializes in hamburgers, we might at a hamburger stand in an amusement park. When we approach an establishment that sells hamburgers we see some of what is available and from that *try* to imagine what else goes with those things. But what goes with those things as we imagine them, which in turn defines the domain of discourse, is not something that merely presents itself to us; it is something we *do* and know we can err in doing. And in doing it, we find a vast area of possibilities and probabilities.

If, from the members' point of view, the domain of discourse has no precise boundaries, objects defined within the domain of discourse do not have a fixed set of attributes in the sense used by structural semantics. This is so because the criterial features or significata described within structural semantics are intended as those features that are actually used to differentiate one object from another. Yet if members confront situations whose contents cannot be enumerated in advance, then just how one object contrasts with another is something that is, for members, to be discovered over the course of some particular situation. What members might mean when they apply a name would then have a definite sense for a particular temporally located situation but would have no necessary stable connection to other situations in which the name was used.

For every new object added to the set of possible objects there is potentially a new attribute needed to differentiate it from other members of the set. For every object that has been in the set, but is there no longer, there is a potential loss of an attribute. For a member who could not specify the boundaries of a domain, no limited set of object features would be possible. The "best" the member could do would be to use whatsoever features of objects that seemed to differentiate members of the domain as seen and imagined from his present perspective, while "holding in reserve" usable features that might become necessary should the apparent boundaries of that domain be altered as he views it from more perspectives. For the name user, no particular set of criteria that would apply in all cases could be stated.

Criterial Attributes As Defining The Significance Of A Name And Defining The Actor's Interest In The Object

Structural semantics treats meanings of names as known to every member of a society in a like manner. That is, the name has an identical meaning not only every time it is used but for every member speaking to any other member. Yet we never suppose this when we converse with someone. In every case we have some notion of what the other knows about what we are talking about, and in every case we formulate that as part of the meaning of the utterance. Even when we deal with strangers there are things we know about what they know that we would not attribute to some other person. Specifically, we attribute to the stranger a knowledge of the situation we presently share with him.

When we refer to some object in a shared environment, for example, we may refer, by use of a name, to any feature we suppose the other knows that object has. When I say to you, a friend and a frequenter of my house, "We are getting the green chair upholstered," I expect you to understand much more than what it takes for an object to be green and to be a chair. Instead, I expect you to remember *that* green chair with the hole in it that sits in my front room. I have used the name green chair as a tag or mnemonic device for an object we both know.

When we use names in this way, we depend on the experience the other has had with the object in question and the features of that experience that he will see as relevant to our naming. What he will understand by our naming is never fully predictable, for we never fully know what experience he has had, nor do we fully know what plans and projects he has that will determine what he sees as relevant. Even for the case of an object in front of both of us, his experience of that object differs from mine since he sees it from There and I see it from Here. Thus, the meaning of a name used as a mnemonic device depends on what the speaker attributes to the listener and upon "something more." The something more is the speaker's knowledge that what he has attributed to the listener is necessarily incomplete. The something more is therefore not known to the speaker as content.

Every shared experience I have had with someone else provides for this kind of usage of names. And this sharing need not have been simultaneous, that is, I need know only that what I have done, or where I have been, or whom I have known is also part of the experience of the other, though at other times than for me. Consider that there are a group of people who know my uncle Jack. I say to them, "Uncle is coming." What I intend to convey to them is not his status as uncle but merely that it is he who is coming. How he stands to me with respect to kinship and how that might be defined in terms of significata or criterial attributes is not relevant to me or to those who hear my remark.

It might seem that such usage depends on reference to specific objects. In some cases it does, but this is still important because the world is, for any actor, not simply populated by typical persons with typical motives doing typical things in typical places but is populated by his wife, his child, his job, his old car, and his house as well. For each of these things there is for him a set of persons with whom he shares this experience.

But this kind of usage can be involved when a specific *that one* is not referred to. Consider the following utterances:

"I wish I had an uncle."
"I wish I had a rich uncle."
"As his uncle, I hardly feel responsible for what he did."
"He is my uncle, so I can expect to get the job."

If I were to say these sentences, would I be assuming that you know no more than the fact that I am referring to someone who is male, one generation above me, and ablineal to me? In fact, are these features even particularly relevant to what I am saying? Surely I mean more than that and expect that you will understand more than that. What I am talking about and what interest I have in the object named uncle above has little to do with the criterial attributes of the name uncle, except as they are part of all the things I assume you know about uncles in this society.

By using the name uncle I may make reference to the variety of typifications of uncles and their relationships to nephews that I understand are typically, though not inevitably, current in the society in which I and the hearer of my remark live. I depend, in my usage, on the likelihood that he has heard and knows the rough equivalent of the stories and characterizations of uncles and their nephews that I have heard, and that in his recognition of *what we are talking about.* he will see which of these "stories" is being referred to.

The sense of the title uncle is thus not restricted by the criteria for properly using that term but can instead be used as a vehicle for "recovering" whatever can be said about uncles by the parties who say and hear the term. How members go about the task of seeing what the other is saying by relying on and actively developing a sense of what the other could be talking about has been a principal phenomenon of ethnomethodological interest. We find that members engage in a course of understanding what the other is saying by seeing what he is saying as making pointed references to such things as "what has been talked about thus far," "what will have been talked about in the end," "what someone like that could mean," and "what I can see in the present setting that he could be talking about" (Garfinkel, in Scher, 1962; McHugh, 1968; Garfinkel and Sacks, in McKinney and Tiryakian, forthcoming; Leiter, 1969; Wieder, 1969). By employing a body of practices like these, which

F

have been collected under the title of the documentary method of interpretation by ethnomethodologists, members are able to discover a
particular sense of an expression, the sense of which varies with the
occasions in which it is employed.

Conclusions

We have examined and elaborated the theoretical apparatus of structural
semantics and then compared that apparatus with the interests and
findings of ethnomethodology. We have seen that the construction of
"cognitive maps" that members of a society employ in recognizing the
events around them and employ in hearing what their fellow members
mean when they employ names involves the reconstruction of members'
talk to provide necessary and sufficient criteria for using names properly.
These reconstructions result in substantive descriptions of what members "have in mind" when they look and describe.

From the standpoint of ethnomethodology these apparently definitive
descriptions appear as idealizations of what members are doing when
they employ categories and use criteria. Ethnomethodologists have
found that, when one directly examines the activity of employing criteria
for using names or titles, one finds that the particular sense of the
criteria are specific to the cases in which the criteria are employed.
Rather than having a stable meaning across a set of cases that are
classified by their use, criteria are matched against cases by elaborating
the sense of the criteria or the case to encompass the particular occurrences the name user faces. Explicating what members mean by their
terms by stating criteria for using those terms would then be an inappropriate method, since criteria vary in their meaning over the occasions in which they are used. When we examine the indeterminate and
developing character of the situations that members face when they
employ names, it appears that no definite set of criteria for using names
could be stated in any case. Further, when we examine some of the
common ways in which members employ names or titles for something
they assume they know in common, what they could be talking about is
not constrained by whatever criteria they might state for properly using
names.

Thus, under an ethnomethodological analysis, structural semantic
analyses appear to be idealizations of what members are actually doing
when they look and describe. It is also the case, however, that by
focusing on how members actually use titles, names, categories, and
criteria in ongoing situations, the possibility of producing substantive
transsituational descriptions of such things as "definition of the situ-

ation," "life space," "the actor's orientation to his situation," and "cognitive maps" is abandoned as the analyst's task and becomes instead a further instance of the work that members do in making the *orderly* properties of the settings in which they act visible to each other.*

* Ed. Note. The exact nature of the ethnomethodological approach to transsituational phenomena is presented by Don Zimmerman and Lawrence Wieder in Chapter 12 of this volume.

The Acquisition of Social Structure: Toward a Developmental Sociology of Language and Meaning*

How members of a society or culture make sense of, or assign sense to, their environment over time is central to the persistent problem of how social order is possible. Conventional introductory tests in sociology such as Broom and Selznick's (1963) view the socialization of the child in standardized ways as basic for social control and the emergence of human society or social order. But these tests do not ask or reveal how the internalization of others' attitudes and the inculcation of norms in the child serve as "blueprints for behavior" in some developmental sense. The idea of "adequate" socialization simply makes casual reference to the importance of social interaction and language. References to the emergence of a social self, to norms, or to rules for deciding appropriate and inappropriate behavior according to vague but unspecified schedules of reward and punishment do not ask what is "normal" rule development. The conventional or "normal" view in sociology, to use Thomas Kuhn's (1962) notion of normal science loosely, does not ask how language and meaning appear in children according to developmental stages such that a progressive sense of social structure or social organization emerges as essential to conventional abstract theo-

*This paper was prepared under the support of a small grant awarded by the Faculty Research Committee, University of California, Sanata Barbara, and the Social Sciences Research Council.

ries about learning to follow the "rules of the game" (Williams, 1960; Bierstedt, 1957; Gibbs, 1966). Nor do sociologists view the development of language and meaning as essential for deriving measures of everyday social organization.

Recent work in linguistics and language socialization and research on the properties making up everyday practical reasoning suggest radical changes in conventional sociological conceptions of norms, socialization, and the acquisition of rules by children. In this chapter I will draw upon these advances to outline a sociological conception of the developmental acquisition of rules by children. Such a perspective is a necessary prerequisite to more precise measurement of social organization as opposed to measurement by fiat (Cicourel, 1964).

Theory of Language and Linguistic Descriptions

Although the literature on language and linguistic analysis cannot be summarized in this paper, an understanding of some of its elementary notions is needed to reveal the sociologist's use of these materials in pursuing his concern with language and meaning in the measurement of social organization. A recent book by Katz (1966: 110–112) provides a convenient statement of modern linguistic theory with which to commence the discussion.

The theory of language consists of three subtheories, each of which corresponds to one of the three components of a linguistic description and provides a statement of the organization of that component in a linguistic description. We use the terms *phonological theory, syntactic theory* (which together comprise *grammatical theory*) and *semantic theory* to refer to these subtheories. We use the terms *phonological component, syntactic component,* and *semantic component* to refer, respectively, to the three corresponding parts of a linguistic description. The phonological component is a statement of the rules by which a speaker deals with the speech sounds of his language; the syntactic component is a statement of the rules by which he organizes such sounds into sentential structures; and the semantic component is a statement of the rules by which he interprets sentences as meaningful messages.

The syntactic component of a linguistic description is a set of rules that generates an infinite class of abstract formal structures, each of which describes the syntactic organization of a sentence. It is the source of the inputs to both the phonological and semantic components. The phonological component operates on such formal objects to determine their phonetic shape, while the semantic component operates on them to determine their meaning. Both the phonological and semantic components are, therefore, purely interpretive: they relate the abstract formal structures underlying sentences to a scheme for pronunciation, on the one hand, and to a representation of conceptualization, on the other. The absence of a connection between the pho-

nological and the semantic components accounts for the generally acknowledged fact about natural languages that sounds and meanings are arbitrarily
related.

Particular linguistic descriptions must show how semantic interpretations are connected to phonetic representations of a given natural language. The elegance of modern linguistics for sociologists cannot
rest, however, with ideal formulations about the tacit knowledge actual
speakers possess about their language (Chomsky, 1965; Chomsky and
Halle, 1965), nor with the idealization assumed when ignoring dis-
tractions in speech, false starts, paralinguistic intonational features,
jokes, memory limitations, antinomies, ironies, and the like. Chomsky's
work on generative grammar refers to a system of rules that enables the
linguist to assign structural descriptions to sentences under the assumption that a speaker who has mastered the language has internalized the
grammar regardless of his awareness of its rules. The concern, therefore,
is not with the speaker's reports and viewpoints.

> Thus a generative grammar attempts to specify what the speaker actually
> knows, not what he may report about his knowledge. Similarly, a theory of
> visual perception would attempt to account for what a person actually sees
> and the mechanisms that determine this rather than his statements about what
> he sees and why, though these statements may provide useful, in fact, com-
> pelling evidence for such a theory.
> To avoid what has been a continuing misunderstanding, it is perhaps worth
> while to reiterate that a generative grammar is not a model for a speaker or a
> hearer. It attempts to characterize in the most neutral possible terms the
> knowledge of the language that provides the basis for actual use of language
> by a speaker-hearer. When we speak of a grammar as generating a sentence
> with a certain structural description, we mean simply that the grammar
> assigns this structural description to the sentence. When we say that a
> sentence has a certain derivation with respect to the particular generative
> grammar, we say nothing about how the speaker or hearer might proceed, in
> some practical or efficient way, to construct such a derivation. These ques-
> tions belong to the theory of language use—the theory of performance
> (Chomsky, 1965:8–9).

In stressing what Katz calls the epistemology of linguistic descriptions
and a theory of language rather than performance (viewed as falling
within psychology), Chomsky (1965: 10) relies heavily upon "acceptable
utterances," or what I will call a "normal form" of everyday usage or
"utterances that are perfectly natural and immediately comprehensible
without paper-and-pencil analysis, and in no way bizarre or outlandish."
The sociologist, however, must be interested in competence *and* performance or situated usage, for it is the interaction of competence and
performance that is essential for understanding everyday activities. Imputations of competence by members to each other and the recognition

of this competence are integral elements of projected and "successful" social action. Normal-form social behavior is comparable to the notion of acceptable utterances. Chomsky's statement that generative grammar seeks to specify "what the speaker actually knows" suggests a strong theory about everyday common knowledge. Yet such a notion remains vague and ambiguous in work on generative grammar and is almost totally divorced from the socially organized settings of communication. The critical issue for the sociologist would be what everyday speaker-hearers assume everyone knows. Thus members' tacit knowledge about "what everyone knows" is integral to normal-form behavior.

A central concept of this chapter is that interpretive procedures, as opposed to surface rules (norms), are similar to but in many ways different from Chomsky's distinction between deep structure (for rendering a semantic interpretation to sentences) and surface structure (for designating phonetic interpretation to sentences), for interpretive procedures are constitutive of the member's sense of social structure or social organization. The acquisition of interpretive procedures provides the actor with a basis for making sense of or assigning meaning to his environment (it provides a sense of social structure, thus orienting him to the relevance of surface rules). This fundamental distinction between interpretive procedures and surface rules seldom recognized in conventional sociological theories. The conventional way of suggesting the existence of interpretive procedures is to refer to the "definition of the situation." But in using this phrase, the sociologist does not attempt to specify the structure of norms and attitudes, nor does he indicate how internalized norms and attitudes enable the actor to assign meaning to his environment or how such norms and attitudes are developmentally acquired and assume regulated usage. The traditional strategy of the sociologist is to endow his model of the actor with the ability to assign meanings, but only after assuming that internalized attitudes and norms provide automatic guides to role-taking. The internalization of norms is assumed to lead to an automatic application of rules on appropriate occasions. Appropriateness, however, is not explained, nor is it viewed as developmentally and situationally constrained. When deviance is said to arise, it is deviance vis-à-vis the idealized surface rules as conceived by members and/or sociologists. But surface rules or norms presuppose interpretive procedures and can be consulted only after the fact (as written rules or social customs) for revealing the detection and labeling of deviance.

The problem of meaning of semantic interpretations of sentences (as bounded by formal grammatical rules or across open tests) is similar to the idea of inherently meaningful internalized norms and attitudes; there is an implication that a lexicon exists with obvious meanings for all competent users. But linguistic or philosophical constructions such as that presented by Fodor and Katz (1963), Katz and Postal (1964), or Katz (1966), are not very useful because lexical entries in dictionaries and search procedures for obtaining semantic categories of language are of little use to an anthropologist or a sociologist who is dealing with members' natural speech, in which the attribution of meaning in every-day settings is by reliance upon "what everyone knows." Cryptic utterances are generated under the assumption that their situated meanings are obvious. In field and laboratory settings respondents or subjects and researchers continually use "what everyone knows" to ask questions, give instructions, write down "satisfactory" answers, and interpret the content of responses or conversations. Members in natural conversations obviously engage in similar uses of "what everyone knows." The reliance on assumed common knowledge facilitates practical exchanges. We are dealing with oral lexicons whose connection with written dictionaries is unknown and often remote or irrelevant. The acquisition of this oral lexicon by children, and a grammar that permits manipulations and efficient usage of the lexicon, are embedded in a semantic field that can be understood only by reference to the acquisition of interpretive procedures or a sense of social structure. The developmental acquisition of interpretive procedures presumes that a semantic input to sound and syntax means that initial or simplified interpretive procedures precede or accompany the acquisition of grammar.

Two problems require clarification here. (1) The establishment of a lexicon and rules for transforming lexical items into detached cognitive meanings (as opposed to situated or actual social scenes) must be separated from the interpretive procedures that make lexical items relevant in actual social contexts. The idea of performance requires an extension of dictionary meanings into their socially organized use in unfolding action scenes (see Gumperz, 1966). (2) Interpretive procedures are always operative within or in reference to social settings, and their necessary use in making norms recognizable and relevant in particular and general cases means that semantic issues are not independent of syntactic, phonological, and ecological features or of situated body movements and gestures. Further, the properties making up interpretive procedures are not hypothetical but can be derived from behavioral manipulations of socially organized settings. Thus, interpretive procedures are not to be equated to or confused with deep-structure syntactic rules, despite a suggested similarity in function. Finally, the necessary reliance upon a presumed corpus of common knowledge ("what everyone knows") is not to be confused with intended or truncated substantive issues that emerge in actual exchanges between members. The members' use of and reliance upon this presumed corpus are invariant properties of interpretive procedures.

The Acquisition of Language and Meaning

The problem of meaning for the anthropologist-sociologist can be stated as that of how members of a society or culture acquire a sense of social structure that enables them to negotiate everyday activities. But the developmental acquisition of interpretive procedures and surface rules by children cannot ignore a theory of language acquisition consistent with linguistic theory. Recent work (McNeill, in Smith and Miller, 1966: 15–84; Lyons and Wales, 1966) stressing the necessity of coordinating the formulation of linguistic theory with studies of language acquisition requires supplementation by the anthropologist-sociologist; the semantic input to phonology and syntax becomes more than a function of an existing lexical domain formalized by a dictionary with appropriate search procedures for deciding or assigning meaning to utterances. A reference to the competence and performance activities of native speakers requires some commitment to how the former is detectable through the latter in empirical studies, and how both depend upon a developmental acquisition of interpretive procedures for acquiring and retrieving (or invoking) an appropriate vocabulary or terminology in actual encounters. Thus a child's vocabulary is filtered by his interpretive procedures, and its retrieval depends upon the same structure vis-à-vis recognition decisions as to appropriateness in unfolding interaction. A reference to the child's exposure to and imitation of adult speech cannot ignore either the role of interpretive procedures in assigning relevance to that speech or the retrieval or stored information triggered by auto stimulation and/or the perception and interpretation of an environment of objects over time.

The proposal that children acquire a rich and intricate grammatical competence in about thirty-six months (from around eighteen months to fifty-four months of age) suggests a parallel assertion about the development of interpretive procedures prior to and during this period of language development. For the anthropologist-sociologist, the semantic input to the phonological and syntactic components during the acquisition of grammar must go beyond a reference to (1) branching rules dealing with grammatical functions and grammatical relations and (2) subcategorization rules dealing with syntactic features for subcategorizing lexical categories. The syntactic component of a grammar is said to be made up of a base that generates deep structures. These deep structures take on semantic interpretations from lexical items in sentences

F*

and from the grammatical functions and relations that these lexical items
possess in the underlying structures. A transformational part of grammatical theory that is solely interpretive maps deep structures into surface
structures. Chomsky (1965:141–142) provides a succinct statement of
the form of grammar:

> A grammar contains a syntactic component, a semantic component, and a
> phonological component. The latter two are purely interpretive; they play no
> part in the recursive generation of sentence structures. The syntactic com-
> ponent consists of a base and a transformational component. The base, in
> turn, consists of a categorical subcomponent and a lexicon. The base gener-
> ates deep structures. A deep structure enters the semantic component and
> receives a semantic interpretation; it is mapped by the transformational rules
> into a surface structure, which is then given a phonetic interpretation by the
> rules of the phonological component. Thus the grammar assigns semantic
> interpretations to signals, this association being mediated by the recursive
> rules of the syntactic components.
>
>   The categorical subcomponent of the base consists of a sequence of con-
> text-free rewriting rules. The function of these rules is, in essence, to define a
> certain system of grammatical relations that determine semantic in-
> terpretation, and to specify an abstract underlying order of elements that
> makes possible the functioning of the transformational rules. . . .
>
>   The lexicon consists of an unordered set of lexical entries and certain
> redundancy rules. Each lexical entry is a set of features (but see note 15 of
> Chapter 2 ['If we regard a lexical entry as a set of features, then items that
> are similar in sound, meaning, or syntactic function will not be related to one
> another in the lexicon']. Some of these are phonological features, drawn from
> a particular universal set of phonological features (the distinctive-features
> system). The set of phonological features in a lexical entry can be extracted
> and represented as a phonological matrix that bears the relation 'is a' to each
> of the specified syntactic features belonging to the lexical entry. Some of the
> features are semantic features. These, too, are presumably drawn from a
> universal 'alphabet,' but little is known about this today, and nothing has been
> said about it here.

Chomsky's formulation stresses the role of the syntactic component
of grammar in assigning meaning to the lexicon of its base and the
signals produced by the transformation of deep-structure into sur-
face-structure phonetic interpretations. If syntactic rules governed the
lexicon and the context-free rewriting rules for defining the grammatical
relations determining semantic interpretations, then the structure of social interaction (or the scenic features of social settings) would not
possess independent status but would always be "known" to members
of a society vis-à-vis grammatical rules. Hence social reality would be
generated by universal features of language possessed by all competent
("normal") humans. Cultural differences would presumably stem from
some as-yet-unknown higher-order grammatical rules that would permit

variations in expression but would remain consistent with universal features of a grammar's three components. The semantic component and its subserviance to syntax in Chomsky's formulation is obscure and suffers from improverished development. I shall assume that it can be ignored and shall offer a different construction—one that claims an interaction between the particular grammatical forms actually used in daily social exchanges (not the ideal context-free forms used by some linguists) and the interpretations of language performance that can be made independently of syntactic structures or where syntactic knowl-dependently of syntactic structures or where syntactic knowledge is either misleading or of limited use. Hence formal syntactic rules can be generated in cultural settings or can remain oral traditions; once they are available and used in socially prescribed and sanctioned ways, however, they constrain (although not completely) interpretations assigned by members. The existence or lack of constraints remains an empirical problem only barely touched by researchers. Without getting involved in a Humboldt-Sapir-Whorf hypothesis discussion, I think the issue can be clarified if we ask how new recruits to a society are socialized and how they acquire a sense of social structure. The fact that recent work on developmental psycholinguistics has used a generative grammar model for studying the acquisition of syntax provides additional material for examining the syntax-semantic correspondence and for suggesting what properties an independent semantic component might contain.

The significance of taking a developmental approach to problems of interpretive procedures and surface-rule acquisition is that adults are continually supplying children with lexical items or categories whose meaning can be decided only partially by reference to adult oral and written dictionaries, and where instructions by adults to children about meaning are not equivalent to an adult's use of written dictionaries. Oral dictionaries of the young child had been called holophrastic (McNeill, in Smith and Miller, 1966:63) because their words are presumed to stand for sentences. Such words reveal the need for a notion such as in-terpretive procedures for understanding the child's ability to decide simple appropriateness. Instructions to a child require making proble-matic adult notions of "what everyone knows." Hence Chomsky's pro-posals can be examined in natural languages by treating the socialization process as an experimental setting within which performance generates exchanges useful for clarifying how competence might be attributed to children. Adult instructions, therefore, presume competence and syntac-tic, phonological, and semantic relevances. Brown and Bellugi, in Lenne-berg, 1964) also suggest that a world view (or culture-bound world view) is communicated by these instructions, but they do not state how the child's conception of social structure is developed.

I am assuming that "world view" is an observer's loose way of talking about culture-bound substantive attitudinal types of orientations to one's environment, and not a specification of universal properties of interpretive procedures for acquiring a general sense of social structure. It seems reasonable to propose that the particular substantive outcomes generated by interpretive procedures are culture bound that permit the recognition of normal forms of objects and events, or the presence of danger, a sense of fairness or injustice, etc., in cultural settings. Interpretive procedures prepare the environment for substantive or practical considerations in which a world view is presumed to be an abstract, central, orientational schema. But the world view (or related world views) of a particular culture is not an invariant orienting schema, and like the class of attainable grammars (Chomsky, 1965: 35), it is not to be equated with universal features of interpretive procedures necessary for an adequate stipulation of how social order is possible and sustained over time. The generation or production of social structures, their maintenance, and their change over time, therefore, can be observed in the child's developmental and innovative acquisition of interpretive procedures and surface rules.

The view that the young child speaks an esoteric language fluently and not merely produces an inadequate or incomplete adult language that can be analyzed with categories of adult grammar (McNeill, in Smith and Miller, 1966: 16; and in Lyons and Waler, 1966: 99–115) is relevant for describing the acquisition of interpretive procedures. The child's conception of the social world should not be studied by imposing as-yet-unclarified adult conceptions of normal social structures. Although initial interpretive procedures do not permit the child to comprehend adult humor, double entendres, antinomies, and the like, they do generate esoteric childhood social structures in which it is possible to fear stuffed animals on display in a museum, be whisked away by witches at night, and believe in the existence of Batman and Robin.

The sociologist cannot rest with a description of the child's performance in social settings; he must explain behavioral activities with a model of how the child's interpretive procedures and surface-rule competence generate behavioral displays. The notion that the child possesses a simple grammar that generates telegraphic speech (Brown and Fraser, in Cofer and Musgrave, 1963:158–197; Brown and Bellugi, in Lenneberg, 1964; McNeill in Smith and Miller, 1966) implies that the child's sense of social structure (his interpretive procedures and surface-rule competence) generates childhood conceptions of social organization. It is difficult to convince the four-year-old child that the "monsters" and "bad guys" are not going to "somehow" inflict their nasty deeds upon him, in the same way that it is difficult to convince him of the dangers of crossing the street. Although the child initially acquires simple properties of interpretive procedures and surface rules which permit him to detect restricted classes of normal forms in voice intonation, physical appearance, facial expressions, cause and effect, story beginnings and endings, simple games, and the like, he finds it difficult if not impossible to understand exceptions, and explanations of them often terminate with "that's just the way it is." Adult descriptions of the "why" of everyday life to children provide a rich source of information on adult notions of simplified social stuctures. As has been suggested by McNeill in Smith and Miller, 1966:51 with regard to the child's early speech (its severely limited grammatical competence, which does not reflect the operation of transformational rules) the child's ability to comprehend subtleties in social organization (particularly surface rules involving possession of property, privacy, or combined interpretive procedures and surface-rule subtleties contained in antinomies and jokes) requires adult transformations of meaning. The child is forced to suspend the relevance of appearances, for example, when he is told that something is poisonous when it "looks like candy."

But I am only speculating about developmental problems in the acquisition of interpretive procedures and surface rules. We have little or no empirical information or even consistent and imaginative theoretical formulations about the child's acquisition of the properties of interpretive procedures. Therefore, a discussion of interpretive procedures from the vantage point of adult competence is necessary.

SOME PROPERTIES OF INTERPRETIVE PROCEDURES

The use of the term rules (or legal and extralegal norms) in everyday life usually means various prescriptive and proscriptive norms (R.T. Morris, 1956; Bierstedt, 1957; Williams, 1960; Gibbs, 1966). I have labeled such norms surface rules. In this chapter I shall treat norms in everyday life and scientific rules of procedure as legal and extralegal surface rules governing everyday conduct and scientific inquiry, in keeping with recent work in ethnomethodology (Garfinkel, 1967). By ethnomethodology I mean the study of interpretive procedures and surface rules in everyday social practices and scientific activities. Hence a concern with everyday practical reasoning becomes a study in how members employ interpretive procedures to recognize the relevance of surface rules and convert them into practiced and enforced behavior. Scientific research, as do legal and extralegal norms, has its ideal or normative conceptions of how inquiry is conducted, as well as its implicit or intuitive strategies followed by individual researchers and promoted by different "schools."

Paradigms of "normal science" (Kuhn, 1962) emerge in different fields to define temporally enforceable strategies of research and bodies of acceptable propositions. As Michael Polanyi (1958) has argued, the scientist's success in his research relies heavily upon "tacit knowledge" that cannot be articulated into surface rules. Interpretive procedures in everyday life and in scientific research, however, are not "rules" in the sense of such general policies or practices as operational definitions or legal and extralegal norms, where a sense of a "right" and "wrong" pre- or proscriptive norm or practice is at issue. Instead, they are constitutive of all inquiry yet exhibit empirically defensible properties that "advise" the member about an infinite collection of behavioral displays and provide him with a sense of social structure (or, in the case of scientific activity, provide an intuitive orientation to an area of inquiry). I assume that interpretive and surface rules govern normal science in the same sense in which everyday social behavior requires that members generate and use "acceptable" descriptive accounts about their environments; scientists seek accounts that can be viewed and accepted as recognizable and intelligible displays of social reality. Scientific procedures orient the researcher's conception of normal-science surface rules in normative or actual practice.

The child cannot be taught to understand and use surface rules unless he acquires a sense of social structure, a basis for the assigning meaning to his environment. The acquisition of language rules is like the acquisition of norms; they both presuppose interpretive procedures. The child must learn to articulate a general rule or policy (a norm) with a particular event or case said to fall under the general rule (Rawls, 1955). There are no surface rules for instructing the child (or adult) on how the articulation is to be made. Members of a society must acquire the competence to assign meaning to their environment so that surface rules and their articulation with particular cases can be made. Hence interpretive procedures are invariant properties of everyday practical reasoning necessary for assigning sense to the substantive rules sociologists usually call norms. Surface rules, therefore, always require some recognition and cognition about the particulars that would render given rules as appropriate and useful for understanding and dealing with actual behavioral displays. Hence all surface rules carry an open structure or horizon vis-à-vis some boundable collection of meanings until they are linked to particular cases by interpretation procedures.

Linking interpretive procedures and surface rules presumes a generative model in a loose sense of Chomsky's work on generative or transformational grammar. The interpretive procedures prepare and sustain an environment of objects for inference and action vis-à-vis a culture-bound world view and the written and "known in common" surface rules. Just as a generative grammar is not a model for a speaker or a hearer (Chomsky, 1965:9) but a basis for revealing how actual use is possible, the idea of generative or praxiological (Kotarbinski, in Nagel et al, 1962:211–223; Hix, 1954; Garfinkel, 1956) social structure is not a model for well-socialized members of a society but an attempt to show (1) how the acquisition of interpretive procedures and surface rules is necessary for understanding members' everyday activities and (2) how members and researchers assign structural descriptions to all forms of social organization. An analogous generative or praxiological perspective is suggested in the remark by Goodenough (1957, as reprinted in Hymes, 1964:36): "As I see it, a society's culture consists of whatever it is one has to know or believe in order to operate in a manner acceptable to its members, and do so in any role that they accept for any one of themselves." Stated another way, what must be known about the properties of interpretive procedures and surface rules in order to program subjects' actions (in field and experimental settings) for such behavior to be recognized as "normal" or routine (or unusual or bizarre) social activity by members?

Our present knowledge of the nature of interpretive procedures is sparse. I do not want to suggest or claim the existence of a "complete" list (or of any "list") but will simply describe a few properties to facilitate further discussion.

1. *The Reciprocity of Perspectives.* Schutz (in Natanson, 1953:302–346; and in Bryson et al, 1955:135–203) describes this property as consisting of (1) the member's idealization of the interchangeability of standpoints whereby the speaker and hearer both take for granted that each (*A* assumes it of *B* and assumes *B* assumes it of *A*, and vice versa) would probably have the same experiences of the immediate scene if they were to change places, and (2) that until further notice (the emergence of counterevidence) the speaker and hearer both assume that each can disregard for the purpose at hand any differences originating in their personal ways of assigning meaning to and deciding the relevance of everyday life activities, such that each can interpret the environment of objects they are both attending in an essentially identical manner for the practical action in question. A corollary of this property is that members assume, and assume others assume it of them, that their descriptive accounts or utterances will be intelligble and recognizable features of a world known in common and taken for granted. The speaker assumes that the hearer will expect him to emit utterances that are recognizable and intelligible, and the speaker also assumes that his descriptive accounts are acceptable products and will be so received by

the hearer. Finally, the hearer assumes that the speaker has assumed this property for the hearer, and expects to comply with the tacit but sanctioned behavior of appearing to "understand" what is being discussed.

2. *The Et Cetera Assumption.* To suggest that speakers and hearers sanction the simulated "understanding" of each other implies something more than a reciprocity of perspectives. Garfinkel (1964:247–248) suggests that the understanding goes so far as to require that a speaker and hearer "fill in" or assume the existence of common understandings or relevances of what is being said on occasions when the descriptive accounts are seen as "obvious" and even when they are not immediately obvious. The tolerance for utterances viewed as not obvious or not meaningful depends upon further properties and their reflexive features. The et cetera assumption serves the important function of allowing things to pass despite their ambiguity or vagueness, or allowing the treatment of particular instances as sufficiently relevant or understandable to permit viewing descriptive elements as "appropriate." What is critical about the et cetera assumption is its reliance upon particular elements of language itself (lexical items or phrases or idiomatic expressions or double entendres, for example) and paralinguistic features of exchanges for "indexing" (Garfinkel, 1967) the course and meaning of the conversation. I return to this problem below. But notice that neither the reciprocity of perspectives nor the et cetera assumption imply that consensus exists or is necessary; rather, they indicate that a presumed "agreement" to begin, sustain, and terminate interaction will occur despite the lack of conventional notions about the existence of substantive consensus to explain concerted action.

3. *Normal Forms.* Reference to a reciprocity of perspectives and to the et cetera assumption presumes the existence of certain normal forms of acceptable talk and appearances upon which members rely for assigning sense to their environments. Thus, on occasions when the reciprocity of perspectives is in doubt (when the appearance of the speaker or hearer, or the talk itself, is not viewed as recognizable and intelligible such that the et cetera assumption cannot overcome discrepancies or ambiguities), efforts will be made by both speaker and hearer to normalize the presumed discrepancies (this is similar in sense to the reduction of dissonance or incongruity; see Festinger, 1962; Brown, 1965; and in Brown et al. 1962:1–85). But, unlike the social-psychologist's interest in dissonance, the anthropologist-sociologist's attention must be directed to the recognition and description of normal forms, and to how members' linguistic and paralinguistic behavior reveals the ways in which interpretive procedures and surface rules are called into question and the ways in which the social scene is sustained as dissonant or is restored to

some sense of normality. Competent members (those who can expect to manage their affairs without interference and be treated as "acceptable types") recognize and employ normal forms in daily interaction under the assumptions that all communication is embedded within a body of common knowledge or "what everyone knows" (Garfinkel, 1964:237–238).

4. *Retrospective-Prospective Sense of Occurrence.* Routine conversation depends upon speakers and hearers' waiting for later utterances in order to decide what was intended before. Speakers and hearers both assume that what each says to the other has, or will have at some subsequent moment, the effect of clarifying a presently ambiguous utterance or a descriptive account with promisory overtones. This property of interpretive procedures enables the speaker and hearer to maintain a sense of social structure despite deliberate or presumed vagueness on the part of the participants in an exchange. Waiting for later utterances (which may never come) to clarify present descriptive accounts, or "discovering" that earlier remarks or incidents now clarify a present utterance, provides continuity to everyday communication.

The properties of interpretive procedures have been ignored because sociologists have taken them for granted when pursuing their own research, particularly research in their own society. Hence the sociologist invokes the properties of interpretive rules as a necessary part of making sense of the activities and environment of members he studies, and his use of these properties is derived from his own membership in the society, not from his professional training or from knowledge gained from research. Members use the properties of interpretive procedures to clarify and make routive sense of their own environments, and sociologists must view such activities and their own work) as practical methods for constructing and sustaining social order.

Garfinkel (1966) has suggested that the properties of practical reasoning (what I am calling interpretive procedures) be viewed as a collection of instructions to members by members, and as a sort of continual (reflexive) feedback whereby members assign meaning to their environment. The interpretive procedures, therefore, have reflexive features linking their properties to actual scenes such that appropriate surface rules are seen as relevant for immediate or future inference and action. The reflexive features of talk can be viewed as saying that the properties of interpretive procedures, as a collection, are reflexive because they are necessary for members to orient themselves (1) in the presence of but not in contact with (driving a car alone) other members (2) during face-to-face or telephone exchanges, and (3) in the absence of actual contact with others. The properties of interpretive procedures provide members with a sense of social order during periods of solitary living and they are integral to actual contact with others (though the contact may vary from walking alone in a crowded street, to sitting on a bus but not conversing, to actual exchanges with others). Within talk and in the absence of talk, reflexive features of interpretive procedures operate to provide a continuous feedback to members about the routine sense of what is happening. Hence physical features of the ecological scene, the members presence or absence, the existence of conversation or its absence, and features of talk within conversation all provide the participants with continuous "instructions" for orienting themselves to their environment and deciding appropriate inferences and action.

5. *Talk Itself as Reflexive*. Talk is reflexive to participants because it is seen as fundamental to "normal" scenes. I am not referring to the content of talk but simply to its presence during speech and the expectation that particular forms of speech will give a setting the appearance of something recognizable and intelligible. The timing of speech (as opposed to deliberate or random hesitation and alterations of normal-form intonational contours) and the timing of periods of silence or such occasional reminders of normal speech as "uh huh," "I see," "ah," and "oh," reflexively guide both speaker and hearer throughout exchanges. The observer must also make use of reflexive features to assign normal-form significance to a scene or sequence of scenes as a condition for deciding the content of talk. Talk provides members with information about the appropriateness of occasions. Garfinkel notes that talk is a constituent feature of all settings because members count on its presence as an indication that "all is well" and because members also use talk as a built-in feature of some arrangement of activities in order to produce a descriptive account of those same arrangements. Thus the member's accounting of some arrangement relies upon the talk itself as a necessary way of communicating the recognizable and intelligible elements of the scene. Talk is continuously folded back upon itself so that the presence of "proper" talk and further talk provide both a sense of "all is well" and a basis for members to describe the arrangement successfully to each other.

6. *Descriptive Vocabularies as Indexical Expressions*. In recommending further reflexive features of the properties of interpretive procedures I draw upon Garfinkel's discussion of how members take for granted their reliance upon the existence and use of descriptive vocabularies for handling bodies of information and activities, where the vocabularies themselves are constituent features of the experiences being described. The vocabularies are an index of the experience. But the experiences, in the course of being generated or transformed, acquire elements of the vocabularies as part of the generative process and permit the retrieval of

information indexed by selected elements of the original vocabularies. Garfinkel uses catalogues in libraries as an example of this reflexive feature of practical reasoning. The titles used to index reports to facilitate a search for something are invariably part of the vocabulary that went into the terminologies or vocabularies of the very experiences they describe. The catalogues are terminologies or vocabularies of the experiences they describe. Several years ago Bar-Hillel (1954) noted the necessity of indexical expressions in ordinary language, stating that context is essential but that different sentences might require knowing different common knowledge or presumed common knowledge to give it some kind of interpretation. Thus it might be necessary to know where the utterance was made, who made it, and its temporal character. The significance of conversational or written indexical expressions, however, cannot be stated as merely a problem in pragmatic context; rather, it requires some reference to the role of "what everyone knows" in deciding the indexicality of the utterance or some part of the utterance. The significance of descriptive vocabularies as indexical expressions lies in their providing both members and researchers with "instruction" for recovering or retrieving the "full" relevance of an utterance; suggesting what anyone must presume or "fill in" to capture the fidelity of a truncated or indexical expression whose sense requires a specification of common assumptions about context (time or occasion of the expression, who the speaker was, where the utterance was made, and the like). Brown and Bellugi (in Lenneberg, 1964:146–147) suggest elements of this problem in discussing parental expansions of children's speech.

> How does a mother decide on the correct expansion of one of her child's utterances? Consider the utterance "Eve lunch." So far as grammar is concerned this utterance could be appropriately expanded in any one of a number of ways: "Eve is having lunch"; "Eve had lunch"; "Eve will have lunch"; "Eve's lunch," and so forth. On the occasion when Eve produced the utterance, however, one expansion seemed more appropriate that any other. It was then the noon hour, Eve was sitting at the table with a plate of food before her and her spoon and fingers were busy. In these circumstances "Eve lunch" has to mean "Eve is having lunch." A little later when the plate had been stacked in the sink and Eve was getting down from her chair the utterance "Eve lunch" would have suggested the expansion "Eve has had her lunch." Most expansions are responsive not only to the child's words but also to the circumstances attending their utterance.

Brown and Bellugi are concerned with how the mother decides the appropriateness of expansions under situational constraints. But there are several problems here: the child's telegraphic utterance viewed as a reflection of a simple grammar of less complexity than adult grammar, thus endowing the child with limited competence; the adult expansion that encodes elements of social organization not coded by the child's telegraphic utterance; the child's utterance as indexical to children's grammar; and the adult's various expansions decided according to the indexicality deemed appropriate to the situational constraints or context. We should not confuse children's normal forms and the child's ability to recognize and use indexical expressions with the adult's stock of normal forms and typical usage of indexical expressions for encoding broader conceptions of social organization than those possessed by the child. When Brown and Bellugi (in Lenneberg, 1964:147–148) suggest that a mother's expansion of a child's speech is more than teaching grammar, that it is providing the child with elements of a world view, there is the presumption of a developmental acquisition of social structure. Hence the child's creation of social meanings not provided by an adult model would parallel the creation of children's grammar not based exclusively upon a model provided by an adult but generated by innovative elements of the child's deep-structure grammar. The child's creative attempts at constructing social reality or social structure and grammar can be viewed as generated by a simple conception of indexicality stemming from developmental stages in the acquisition of the properties of interpretive procedures and deep-structure grammatical rules. The acquisition of interpretive procedures would parallel the acquisition of language, with the child's interpretive procedures gradually replaced or displaced by adult interpretive procedures.

A necessary condition of animal and human socialization, therefore, is the acquisition of interpretive procedures. Sufficient conditions for appropriate use of language and interpretive rules in actual settings include (1) the acquisition of childhood rules (gradually transformed into adult surface rules), and (2) interpretive procedures and their reflexive features as instructions for negotiating social scenes over time. Hence members are continually giving each other instructions (verbal and nonverbal cues and content) as to their intentions, their social character, their biographies, and the like. *The interpretive procedures and their reflexive features provide continuous instructions to participants such that members can be said to be programming each others' actions as the scene unfolds.* Whatever is built into the members as part of their normal socialization is activated by social scenes, but there is no automatic programming; the participants' interpretive procedures and reflexive features become instructions by processing the behavioral scene of appearances, physical movements, objects, gestures, sounds, etc., into inferences that permit action. The progressive acquisition of interpretive procedures and surface rules is reflected in how children and adults interact, or how children interact with other children. Children continually rehearse their acquisition of social structure (and language) in ways reminiscent of adults rehearsing for a play or translating a written play into a live production. But in the latter cases the interpretive procedures and surface rules are already built-in elements of the actors, while in children it is possible to observe different stages of complexity over time. For example, the child's ability to learn surface rules governing a game follows a developmental sequence, and his ability to decide the relevance and applicability of surface rules is always a function of the development of interpretive procedures.

The child's conception of "fairness" in games or play or family settings cannot be specified by reference to surface rules. Nor will any conception of norms now available in the sociological literature provide a basis for explaining how the child learns eventually to distinguish between games and their normal forms, and everyday life activities and their normal forms. What seems plausible despite little or no empirical evidence is that children acquire interpretive procedures prior to their use of language, and they develop normal forms of voice intonation and expect their usage by others. Children are able to recognize and insist upon normal-form spacing in speech and to develop their own indexical expressions.

The child's acquisition of social structure, therefore, begins with a simple conception of interpretive procedures and surface rules, and his stock of common knowledge is expressed initially in the form of single lexemes whose meaning by parents is usually judged by reference to imputations of childhood competence and adult meanings. Inasmuch as our knowledge of adult recognition and usage of meanings is unclear, a word about this problem is in order before going on to strategies for the semantic analysis of adult speech that could be useful for following the development of meaning in children.

Kernel and Fringe Meanings and Their Situational Embeddedness

Earlier I remarked that members obviously are capable of carrying on conversations endlessly without recourse to a written dictionary by invoking an oral dictionary derived from common knowledge. The field researcher must obviously utilize the same oral dictionary in deciding the import of his observations despite the possibility of asking natives for definitions or referents. The child's acquisition of language, interpretive procedures, and surface rules is complicated by exposure to limited oral dictionaries in different households, but we are still rather ignorant about the sequence of development here. I assume that the acquisition of meaning structures and the use of lexical items is governed by the development of interpretive procedures. Interpretive procedures, therefore, filter the acquisition and use of lexical items intended as idexical semantic inputs and outputs. Hence the use of an *etic* framework presupposes an *emic* perspective (following the usage of Pike, 1954); the researcher's use of formal grammatical or semantic (dictionary) categories provides an etic framework imposed upon unclarified emic elements used by both subjects and researcher. If we assume that children's language, interpretive procedures, surface rules, and common knowledge as opposed to adult conceptions are contrastive sets that overlap because of developmental stages of acquisition, then our theories must include their developmental organization and reorganization as well as rules for their contrast. Modern approaches to the problem of meaning in philosophy, linguistics, psychology, and anthropology, however, do not deal with the problem of knowledge as socially distributed (Schutz, in Bryson et al, 1955:195– 196).

> Some things can be supposed as well known and self-explanatory and others as needing an explanation, depending upon whether I talk to a person of my sex, age, and occupation, or to somebody not sharing with me this common situation with society, or whether I talk to a member of my family, a neighbor, or to a stranger, to a partner or a nonparticipant in a particular venture, etc.
>
> William James has already observed that a language does not merely consist in the content of an ideally complete dictionary and an ideally complete and arranged grammar. The dictionary gives us only the kernel of the meaning of the words which are surrounded by "fringes." We may add that these fringes are of various kinds: those originating in a particular personal use by the speaker, others originating in the context of speech in which the term is used, still others depending upon the addressee of my speech, or the situation in which the speech occurs, or the purpose of the communication, and, finally, upon the problem at hand to be solved.

Members' common knowledge permits typical imputations of behaving, dress, talking, motives, social standing, and the like to others in everyday exchanges, and each developmental stage in the socialization process alters and utilizes interpretive procedures and surface rules, language, and nonverbal behavior.

A characteristic feature of speech is its embeddedness or entification (Cambell and Walker, 1966) as the dialogue or written document unfolds. Initial use of speech presupposes kernels and fringes embedded in past experiences, or it may rely upon a written dictionary for structuring the assignment of meaning to early parts of exchanges and in later dialogue. I will mention only three general contexts within which the problem of embeddedness or entification is basic to semantic analysis.

1) The construction of written reports intended for general audiences

or the preparation of a radio script or news broadcast does not permit immediate face-to-face exchanges between members; the use of embedded terms or phrases is usually restricted. Radio announcers with their own "show" may presume an audience with whom embedded talk may be used, particularly if the program consists of music designed for adolescent consumption. Radio stations with programs directed to Negro audiences invariably presume their listeners are socialized to highly embedded speech. A news broadcast, therefore, would rely upon normal-form speech.

2) Strangers meeting for the first time must rely upon appearances and a minimum of embedded speech, but interpretive procedures continually provide information as to the interpretation of appearances, initial speech, and nonverbal behavior. The reflexive features become operational indicators of the sense of what is "happening." As strangers continue talking they may begin to develop embedded usage that can sustain particular relationships between them and evoke particular meanings with truncated expressions on later occasions. Embedded terms and phrases become indexical expressions carrying fringe information that encodes meaning structures considerably beyong kernel or denotative meanings. When strangers meet, therefore, conversations can remain superficial, relying upon appearances to make the setting recognizable and intelligible, or the exchanges can lead to progressive embeddings and elaborations that interlace the biographies of the speakers. The recursive folding back of speech by members that creates embedded talk is reflexive because such talk and accompanying nonverbal behavior provide instructions indicating that the relationship is or is not evolving into something more intimate. Embeddedness leads to the use of and reliance upon double entendres, antinomies, and parodies, thus enabling members to sanction indexical expressions as evidences of intimacy, or "friendlier" relations.

3) Acquaintances not only presuppose and use normal-form expressions when conversing with each other, they demand embedded expressions to insure and reaffirm the existence of past relationships. Treating embedded terms and phrases as indexical expressions enables members to talk about things not present (Hockett, in Spuhler, 1959; Hockett and Asher, 1964) and fill in "what everyone knows" to create or sustain a normal form. Intimates' use of embedded speech relies upon connotative meanings built up over time. A componential analysis of such speech leading to denotative meanings presumes preliminary knowledge (or conjectures) by the researcher of interpretive procedures and surface rules. Members' use of terms from everyday social organization for the researcher's benefit become somewhat arbitrary abstractions or artificially constructed indexical expressions that are not clearly

articulated with actual use by particular members on specifiable occasions of talk. If we wish to ask natives for denotative meanings about the use of kin terms it might be more appropriate to have them begin with childhood practices rather than with adult usage. The problem is similar to one posed by Brown and Bellugi on how we decide the appropriateness of a child's utterance; without contextual cues for deciding the sense of social structure required for inference and action, the expression's relevance cannot be clarified. The elicitation procedures of componential analysts or ethnosemanticists are not always clear on this point. Frake (1961, and in Gumperz and Hymes, 1964:127–132), however, does link abstract procedures to actual arrangements.

In each of the above general conversational settings, members must assume the existence of an oral dictionary of "what everyone knows." The use of embedded terms and phrases in converstaions generates meanings for indexing particular social relationships between members and becomes reflexive for members by instructing them on the unfolding relevance of lexical items in the course of attributing structure and "sameness" to social objects and events. The measurement of social organization must include how embedded speech and its reflexive features enable members to mark off and identify settings into relevant categories for generating and deciding upon the appropriateness and meaning of communication. How members accomplish the task of assigning relevance to their environments enables the researcher to find measurement categories in everyday behavior. In addition to how members employ categories signifying quantity (Churchill, 1966), the problem is also how members utilize particular social categories in situationally bounded sequences, under the assumption that normal forms of language and meaning prevail. The particular use of categories and the assumption of normal forms permits members to "close" the stream of conversation such that sets are created permitting exclusion and inclusion of linguistic and paralinguistic behavior into meaningful inferences about "what happened." The "closing" operations presume that members have "frozen" temporally constituted imputations of meaning; interpretive procedures and their reflexive features generate a basis for "freezing" surface structures into socially meaningful sets. Hence interpretive procedures and their reflexive features generate "sameness" or equivalence in social objects and events in temporally and socially organized contexts according to the social relationships of participating members.

To summarize, members' linguistic and paralinguistic behavior is transformed by interpretive procedures and their reflexive features into instructions to participants; the unfolding interaction leads to a continuous programming of members by members. Hence interpretive procedures and their reflexive features lead to behavioral outcomes within unfolding situational constraints. Members, therefore, impose "measurement" on their environments by the articulation of interpretive procedures and their reflexive features with emergent social scenes.

The child's acquisition of social structure, therefore, begins with simple interpretive procedures and their reflexive features, facilitating the leaning of lexical items and the development of an oral dictionary consisting of simple denotative meanings. The situated indexicality of early vocabulary is both grammatical and semantic, because it is assumed that the child with pivotal grammar is not using lexical items as indexical of adult sentences but is expressing telegraphic sentences of his ability to assume and refer to past experiences and/or objects not present. The researcher must restrain himself from imposing measurement categories intended for adults as relevant "closings" for children's speech. This is difficult to avoid when we are not entirely clear about the nature of children's grammar and lexical domain. Attempts to develop measurement categories by examining the child's speech must follow the dictates of a developmental model and not simply what a researcher assumes is "obvious" vis-à-vis adult meanings. Thus when adults seek to convince children that çrossing the street can lead to dreadful consequences, the child's response or behavior is not exactly unequivocal; the child may laugh at the suggestion. Attempts to explain death also pose difficult problems for adults because we are not clear when interpretive procedures development is adequate for the comprehension of death, especially when it involves the child or his parents. Recent developments, however, suggest some directions we might pursue in the analysis of conversational materials, and I now turn to a brief examination of work that is sometimes called contrastive analysis.

CONTRASTIVE ANALYSIS AND THE MEASUREMENT OF SOCIAL ORGANIZATION

When the speaker commits himself to linguistic and social categories, he provides the hearer, himself, and an observer or researcher with information about what he intends. The commitment, however, may be a compromise between what the speaker felt had to be said, what he did not want to say, what he was incapable of saying because of limited vocabulary, intelligence, or the constraints of speaking with a stranger, etc. Utterances ordinarily have a normal form, but the information they carry for all concerned are not unequivocal facts leading to direct and obvious analysis. The analysis will vary with the kind of theory utilized. I have argued for a developmental theory of social knowledge because a cross-section of adults in a particular culture or society does not reveal the invariant conditions making up members' utilization of social structure, for we are dealing with well built-in members who, like Chomsky's acceptable grammatical sentences, are usually committed to masking the ambiguity and problematic character of situational constraints that make up the construction of social reality.

In examining utterances or descriptive accounts of members of a culture or society it is critical to recognize that our reliance upon "what everyone knows," much less a written dictionary, presumes that a world view is built into the message. When logicians or philosophers of language analyze sentences disengaged from their context of occurrence and the biography of the speaker-hearer, the unstated presumption and reliance upon normal forms obscure the implicit ways in which the standardized character of the culture or society is presumed as obvious to members. The assumption here of kernel or denotative relevance (but not fringe or connotative relevance) by logicians or philosophers of language (or science) seeks clarity by constructing social reality to fit the narrow form of analysis already judged to be logically adequate. The fringes that become attached because of the occasion of the utterance, the biography of the speaker-hearer, the social relationships assumed, and the like presume a world view. The substantive content of the communication exchanged is built into the linguistic and social categories employed, as is the normal form of paralinguistic intonational contours emitted, the appearance of the participants, and so forth. The observer is provided a similar basis for assigning structural significance to the descriptive accounts. Our analysis presumes a theory that tightens the organizational space in which the exchange occurs; we can rule out certain contrast sets, include alternatives that are likely until further evidence is identified, and decide that the choice of categories by participants carries particular kernel and fringe meanings despite the restrictions of the code itself, the skills or lack of skills of the participants, and so on. The problem is similar to the problem of the parent's expanding the child's utterance; the expansion must be responsive to the child's words as well as to the circumstances attending their utterance. Deciding appropriateness presumes knowing something about the parent's conjectures about the child's development. But in dealing with adults qua adults we presume, as do participants, that each is a well built-in member of the society capable of producing "acceptable" grammatical sentences in Chomsky's sense. Situational constraints can be simulated in experimental settings, but natural settings defy explicit pre-programming; members must use interpretive procedures and reflexive features as instructions for negotiating all scenes and programming each other successfully through encounters. Contrastive analyses must somehow deal with this problem of appropriateness.

Contrastive analysis has emerged in anthropology via ethnographic studies that depart from traditional ethnographies (Conklin, 1955, 1959; Goodenough, 1956, and in Hymes, 1957:36–39; Lousbury, 1956; Frake, 1961, and in Gladwin and Sturtevant, 1962:72–85). Consider the following statement Lounsbury, 1956:161–1962):

(1) Semantic features may be recognized in more than one way in a language. Some may be recognized overtly, with separate phonemic identities, while others may be recognized covertly, merged with other semantic features in various jointly and simultaneously shared phonemic identities.

(2) For a single semantic feature there is sometimes a mixing of the two manners of linguistic recognition: some features emerge, so to speak, at some points to find separate identity in the segmental structure of a language, but are submerged at other points, being identifiable only as possible contrasts between various already irreducible segments. . . .

(4) The description of the componential structure of contrasting forms is an important part of linguistic analysis, whether or not the contrasts have any correlates in the segmental structure of forms.

Both Lounsbury and Goodenough stress the importance of kernel or denotative meanings, while lacking a theory that would explain how researchers or members are capable of communicating denotative meanings in some pure form without necessary references to or use of fringe or connotative meanings, and the interpretive procedures generating both. Hymes (1962) suggests a more general framework when he describes the ingredients for developing an ethnography of speaking as knowledge of the kinds of things to be said, in specifiable message forms, to certain types of people, in appropriate situations. In describing the contrastive analysis developed by componential analysts or students of ethnographic semantics, I shall confine myself to Frake's (1961, as reprinted in Hymes, 1964:127) more general and useful viewpoint: "Of course an ethnography of speaking cannot provide rules specifying exactly what message to select in a given situation. . . . But when a person selects a message, he does so from a set of appropriate alternatives. The task of an ethnographer of speaking is to specify what the apppropriate alternatives are in a given situation and what the consequences are of selecting one alternative over another." The specification of appropriate alternatives presupposes that natives used as informants are all competent members of the society and hence have acquired "normal" interpretive procedures for deciding appropriateness and assigning relevance or a sense of social structure to situations. Specifying appropriate alternatives is a post hoc activity imposed by the researcher upon the actor's retrospective decisions about "correct" choices.

Contrastiveness depends upon the temporal structuring attributed to unfolding scenes by members and upon members' use of social categories for linking the particulars of actual events to explanations provided by general rules. A further element needed for an ethnography of speaking is evident in the earlier quoted statement by Goodenough (1957, as reprinted in Hymes, 1964:36): "As I see it, a society's culture consists of whatever it is one has to know or believe in order to operate in a manner acceptable to its members, and do so in any role that they accept for any one of themselves"; there remains the problem of "what anyone has to know or believe."

The specification of alternatives and the presumed classes from which they are chosen require generating rules to structure and transform an environment of objects into meanings that "close" the stream of behavior into possible alternatives such that choice reflects both the member's and the researcher's perspectives. To assume that the only valuable framework is one that imposes a denotative structure determined by the researcher and divorced from members' actual intention and usage reduces the actor to a rather simple "dummy." An example would be the child of three years, who is capable of simple grammatical construction and comprehension, telegraphic utterances, and interpretive procedures permitting only simple denotative comprehension of temporally impoverished social interaction, or a sense of social structure with little or no temporal continuity. Elicited denotative meanings would then generate indexical expressions disengaged from fringe meanings used by members in their generation, but the source of the researcher's structural descriptions of members' behavior would be misleading but self-contained packages of meaning or "blueprints for behavior." Situational constraints and unfolding contingencies are eliminated or minimized, and normative structure becomes the ethnographic focus.

The general procedures leading to contrastive analysis have been stated by Fake (1961, as reprinted in Hymes, 1964:199–200):

Analytic derivation of meanings ideally yields *distinctive features:* necessary and sufficient conditions by which an investigator can determine whether a newly encountered instance is or is not a member of a particular category. The procedure requires an independent, *etic* (Pike, 1954, p. 8) way of coding recorded instances of a category. Examples are the "phone types" linguistics and the "kin types" kinship analysis (Lounsbury, 1956, pp. 191–192). The investigator classifies his data into types of his own formulation, then compares "types" *as though* they were instances of a concept. From information already coded in the definitions of his "types", he derives the necessary and sufficient conditions of class membership. Thus by comparing the kin types of English "uncle" (FaBr, MoBr, FaSiHu, etc.) with the kin types in every other English kin category, the analyst finds that by scoring "uncle" for features along four dimensions of contrast (affinity, collaterality, generation, and sex) he can state succinctly how "uncles" differ from every other category of kinsman. . . . (When analytically derived features are probabilistically, rather than necessarily and sufficiently, associated with category membership, then we may speak of *correlates* rather than of distinctive features. A correlate of the uncle-nephew relation is that uncles are usually, but not necessarily older than their nephews.)

To arrive at rules of use one can also direct attention to the actual stimulus discriminations made by informants when categorizing. . . . Perceptual attributes relevant to categorization, whether distinctive or probabilistic, are *cues*. Discovering cues in ethnographic settings requires as yet largely unformulated procedures of perceptual testing that do not replace the culturally relevant stimuli with artificial laboratory stimuli (cf. Conklin, 1955, p. 342).

When Frake notes that (1) informants may be asked about meanings directly in each case he outlines above and (2) a specific coding device constructed by the researcher is a necessary part of distinctive-features analysis, he presupposes that Goodenough's definition of culture has been satisfied, that the researcher knows how members operate in a manner acceptable to other members. To uncover "cues," the researcher must have a firm grasp of "what everyone knows" and takes for granted when conversing with members of the culture, or what members assume each "knows" when conversing with each other. The elicitation procedure is designed to construct a written dictionary, but it ignores the necessary existence of a tacit oral dictionary for normal-form social interaction. The researcher must acquire and use the culture's particular interpretive procedures (analogous to a particular language) and world view to decide the relevance or oral and written dictionaries; an oral dictionary is activated vis-à-vis situational constraints and the fringes that members attribute to actual scenes. The use of elicitation procedures to identify lexical items and their denotative meanings and the initial learning of rules governing usage of lexical items are similar to how a child learns to be a bonafide member of his culture. The researcher, however, presumably learns at a faster rate of speed and acquires fringe meanings rapidly through day-to-day living; he has the ability to employ adult interpretive procedures in a different culture in a way the child cannot. Hence the initial elicitation procedures utilized when the researcher has only limited access to the native language and everyday practices give way more and more to an approximation of native interpretive procedures and surface-rule usage.

The acquisition of the knowledge and skill enabling the researcher to perform "like a native" makes it more and more difficult to employ simplified elicitation procedures and, simultaneously, complicates the researcher's procedural rules for deciding "what happened." The more successfully the researcher can perform verbally and nonverbally like a native, the more he will take for granted and be exposed to practiced and enforced, rather than normatively oriented, everyday activities. The problem is like that of articulating general rules or policies with particular cases said to fall under general rules (Rawls, 1955). General rules are presented to children as general kernel or denotative meanings, diffuse as to application and requiring continual explanation in each specific case. The child's initial acquisition of interpretive procedures does not permit him to learn or make the necessary interpretations for linking general rules with particular cases except on a rote basis; he lacks the ability to justify the articulation according to adult procedures. Adults can make the articulation only by invoking implicit interpretive procedures, despite the common assumption that general surface rules are the basis for designating the conditions under which particular cases can be said to fall under the general case. The general rule cannot specify the many fringes, the contingencies surrounding the actual articulation. For example, laws pertaining to juveniles for deciding delinquency are linked to actual persons and events by the utilization of interpretive procedures by agents of social control (Cicourel, 1968). The initial etic coding procedures used by componential analysts for specifying denotative meanings generate an abstract skeleton; the perception and interpretation of particular cases as falling under initial general rules requires moving away from denotative meanings and incorporating more and fringes based upon the use of interpretive procedures, and their reflexive features. The researcher relies upon "what everyone knows" or upon his ability to perform as a competent member of the culture of society.

Frake was unable to use distinctive-feature analysis for his work on the diagnosis of disease among the Subanun. He (Frake, 1961, as reprinted in Hymes, 1964:201) proposes instead procedures parallel to those employed for determining a system of nomenclature: "We collect contrasting answers to the questions the Subanun ask when diagnosing disease. By asking informants to describe differences between diseases, by asking why particular illnesses are diagnosed as such and such and not something else, by following discussions among the Subanun themselves when diagnosing cases, and by noticing corrections made of our own diagnostic efforts, we can isolate a limited number of diagnostic questions and critical answers." Frake moved from a presumed etic formulation to an emic or member's perspective by following actual practices and normative descriptions, and therefore relies more and more upon "what everyone knows."

> The Subanun ask "Does it hurt?" (*mesait ma*). The contrasting replies to this question are, first, an affirmative, "yes, it hurts"; second a denial of pain followed by a specification of a contrasting, non-painful, but still abnormal sensation, "No, it doesn't hurt; it itches"; and, third, a blanket negation implying no abnormal sensation. Thus the Subanun labels a number of con-

trasting types of sensation and uses them to characterize and differentiate diseases (Frake, 1961, as reprinted in Hymes, 1964:203).

The outputs of contrastive analysis described by Frake are levels of terminological contrast, and the resulting tables are cross-tabulated outcomes obtained by running diagnostic questions (in the particular example discussed here) against a range of contrasting answers. Neither the elicitation strategies nor the terminology contrasts, however, specify procedures used by members for generating utterances that have their own built-in contrasts for competent members of the culture or society. The developmental question relevant here is how children construct and employ contrastive sets and recognize their appropriateness in actual settings. The elicitation procedures described by Frake suggest how the researcher cuts into a presumed adult normal flow to make contrastive sets explicit. Although Frake does not seek to pinpoint members' procedures for transforming social settings into "instructions" for inference and further action, a recent work does begin by making members rules central to the analysis.

Sacks (1966) is interested in finding relationships that go beyond a recursive analysis of single sentences, attempting to link members' language categories by transcending sentences to include some indeterminate text ranging from one word to N pages. A central interest is how members "do describing" and "recognize a description." The ways in which members produce and recognize descriptions are seen as necessary steps in arriving at criteria for "correct sociological description." Sacks's work, therefore, follows the tradition of insisting upon emic constructions as basic to etic descriptions.

A central notion in Sacks's work is called a membership categorization device. Devices consist of various categories, or a collection of categories (actually used and recognized by members as "acceptable"), plus rules of application. The general idea is to pair a device (containing at least one category) with a population (containing at least one member). An example of a device would be "sex," consisting of the categories male and female. A collection of categories is said to "go together" because members "recognize" them as such. The researcher, performing like a member, presumably follows members' relevances about "what everyone knows" in deciding that a collection of categories "go together." Sacks uses the phrase "members' knowledge" for Schutz's notion of "what any knows" or socially distributed common knowledge. Thus Sacks implicitly employs the same concept of a "well built'in" or a normally socialized member employing normal-form kernel or denotative and fringe meanings. Although Sacks does not discuss it, his analysis tacitly assumes that his subjects possess and successfully employ interpretive procedures, surface rules, and reflexive features.

His research procedures appear inductive when seeking to show how members are likely to hear utterances in particular ways. The potential elegance of the formulation lies in the possibility of developing rules of application or what Sacks calls, for example, an "economy rule," a "consistency rule," "hearers maxims," and "viewers maxims." Members' ability to connect different categories and thus arrive at meanings "everyone knows" and sanctions suggests ways for revealing the application of interpretive procedures and surface rules within specific cultural or societal settings.

In a series of dittoed lecture notes, Sacks illustrated in 1966 the above notions with a two-sentence story taken from a book on children's stories. The sentences, produced by a child of two years, nine months, are: "The baby cried. The mommy picked it up." Briefly, Sacks argues that native speakers of the English language will hear the two sentences as saying that the mommy is the mommy of the baby, despite the absence of a genitive in the second sentence. The idea, however, is to discover ways of revealing how members' common knowledge about how things "go together" in order to enable the researcher to develop rules for explaining how members make sense of their environment and decide the referential adequacy of their utterances. Thus, the two sentences can be seen as an "adequate description" because members will connect "baby" with the device "family" rather than, say, "stage of life" (baby, child, preteen, teenager, young adult, etc.). "Mommy" will also be connected with the device "family" (mommy, daddy, brother, sister, baby, etc.), thus "locking in" two categories from two different sentences on the assumption that the hearer constructs a coherent picture by the indicated pairings. A contrastive principle is presumed when Sacks notes that a hearer would not expect to hear "short-stop" instead of "mommy." The notion of an economy rule is coined to describe how a single category (from a device) is recognized by a member as being an adequate reference for a person. Thus "baby" is presumed to be an adequate reference to some speaker-hearer. The "consistency rule" states that if a population is being categorized, and one category from some device has been used to categorize a first member, and the same or other categories from the same collection can be used to categorize further members of the population, then the rule holds. In the above two sentences, then, the fact that "baby" can be said to refer to the device "family" leads to the use of the consistency rule, suggesting that the category "mommy" is a relevant mapping by reference to the same device. A hearer's maxim would, therefore, direct a member to hear "baby" and "mommy" as belonging to the same device. Following my earlier remarks, norms or surface rules, therefore, are used by members to order (explain the particular) activities they observe, and are integral features of how rules of application are linked to the use of categories by members.

Sacks's procedures tacitly presuppose unstated normal-form usage of interpretive procedures and their reflexive features; the various maxims and rules can be viewed as applied instructions for concrete social scenes. Sacks's formulation is similar to the notion of the indexicality of different categories; categorization devices reflect how members generate and recognize indexical expressions. A particular category serves as an index of unstated devices. Actual choices would then become realized in the course of interaction, and their measurement by the researcher would become a function of assumed linkage with other categories presumed to be distinctive features and contrastive sets. The speaker uses interpretive procedures and their reflexive features to generate appropriate categories and assign them situational relevance. The hearer receives instructions for programming his own attributions of meaning and generating responses. The identification of categories, and the connection between devices deemed appropriate by maxims and rules, can be viewed as a research strategy for operationalizing members' use of indexical expressions. When linked to the theoretical concepts of interpretive procedures, their reflexive features, and the indexicality of expressions, Sacks's inductive procedure becomes a possible basis for measuring conversational material.

Sacks's work includes many additional features about conversations which I cannot cover in this chapter (how characteristic beginnings and endings help members recognize their observations as intelligible, how different sequences of talk are tied together by characterisitic locations in speech, and so forth). Contrast sets are developed in the course of analyzing the conversational material, and thus remain implicit until substance is designated by reference to a particular piece of conversation. Sacks draws upon his own common knowledge of how members are likely to "hear" or "see" things, and carefully examines hundreds of different texts for their opening lines, closing lines, ironies, antinomies, and the like, thus using the implicit notion of members' common knowledge as an inexhaustible reservoir of categorization devices for "locking in" categories and how members make sense of their environment. The problem of what is "heard" and the nonverbal elements of conversations are not explicit features of Sacks's analysis, but he relies upon these features when attempting to describe transcripts he has heard over and over again.

Although the strategies described above do not make explicit reference to the temporally constituted character of all exchanges, the use of

G

normal forms, and the role of nonverbal cues, contrastive analysis provides the researcher with an empirical procedure for identifying (contrast sets and categorization devices during) different developmental stages in the acquisition of interpretive procedures and their reflexive features. A developmental model of how the child acquires and modifies the corpus of knowledge we have called an oral dictionary or "what everyone knows" and of how he uses this knowledge in routine indexical expressions should help unravel existing gaps in our knowledge of how competent adults construct and sustain social order through their everyday actions.

Concluding Remarks

Throughout this chapter I have argued that interpretive procedures and their reflexive features provide us with basic elements for understanding how the child's acquisition of social structure makes social order possible. I assume that the properties making up interpretive procedures are analogous to claims about linguistic universals, acquired early in life and fused with the acquisition of language. I have tried to separate the acquisition of interpretive procedures from their development in a particular culture in order to stress their analytic status as paralleling the existence of linguistic universals independently of the learning of a particular language. The notion of world view and the acquisition of interpretive procedures in a particular culture suggests how the child becomes oriented to both generic and substantive cultural recognition and use of normal forms in his environment. Interpretive procedures and their reflexive features provide the child with a sense of social-structure competence necessary for tackling the performance that includes the everyday usage of a particular language and world view. Actual performance means the transformation of verbal and nonverbal materials into instructions whereby members program each other's unfolding action. Hence much of performance depends upon the unfolding social stiuation that cannot be automatically preprogrammed by built-in competence. The invariant status of interpretive procedures, for example, enables a normal child to acquire language in a family of deaf parents, and the interpretive procedures and their reflexive features enable deaf persons to acquire a sense of social structure that is nonverbal.

A developmental model suggests that the problem can also be stated comparatively across species; preprogrammed competence and the acquisition of language and interpretive procedures become less and less determinate of performance as we encounter more complex organisms with more and more emphasis placed upon expanding developmental stages of "imprinting" and the contingencies of action scenes for structuring actual behavior. Intra- and intercultural substantive differences in child rearing must be separated from the invariant development stages of language and interpretive procedures.

Pursuing the developmental notion further, I suggest that commonly held conceptions in anthropology and sociology about the fundamental role of a common value system require modification for explaining how social order is possible. The idea that concerted action is possible because norms and common value orientations generate consensus has been a long-standing thesis in the literature. The argument presented earlier states that members are quite capable of concerted action despite the absence of consensus, during explicit conflict, or as children where it is not clear that even norms are known or understood, much less elements of a common value system. I am sàying not that values do not enter into the picture of that they are unnecessary but that their role in generating, sustaining, or changing action scenes is always dependent upon the properties of interpretive procedures. The usual argument that a common value system exists and consists of a oral tradition in an esoteric society is also extended to pluralistic societies on the grounds that a common core of values also exists despite different ideological positions.

The idea of what is or should be desirable about objects, ideas, or practices is not invariant to concerted social interaction or social order. The relevance of general norms and values becomes central on ceremonial occasions or after conflict situations, where some attempt at structuring or restructuring "what happened" or "what should have happened" becomes a key group activity. I am suggesting that values, like surface rules or norms or laws, are always general policies or practices whose articulation with particular cases remains an empirically problematic issue dependent upon how interpretive procedures structure unfolding action scenes so as to generate bounded conceptions of "what happened." Thus actual choices between alternative courses of action, objects of interest, the morality of members' actions, desired ideals of life, and the like, occur within the context of interpretive procedures and their reflexive features. The interpretive procedures provide for a common scheme of interpretation that enables members to assign contextual relevance; norms and values are invoked to justify a course of action, "find" the relevance of a course of action, enable the member to choose among particulars for constructing an interpretation others can agree to or an interpretation designed to satisfy the imputed interests or demands of others. The property of normal forms is invariant to a given culture or soiety, but its empirical relevance is always culture bound and necessarily includes commitments to normative or value-oriented conceptions of appropriateness. Day-to-day living requires tacit commitment to some normative order; that order is built into what members assume to be known in common and taken for granted in their everyday activities. References to norms and values in mundane activities is necessary for deciding which particulars of action scenes will be identified and used for articulating concrete cases with general policies or rules. The central developmental question becomes that of how adults routinely expose children to the normative order, as opposed to a practiced and enforced order that reflects norms and values as idealized general policies or rules invoked after the fact to explain or justify activities governed by the contingencies of an unfolding action scene. The moment-to-moment programming each member accomplishes for himself and others reestablishes the normative order because of post hoc linking with general policies or rules. In attempting to socialize children this as yet ambiguous process of linking particular cases with general policies or rules becomes a perpetual laboratory for discovering how social order is made possible through the child's acquisition of social structure.

Words, Utterance, and Activities*

It is increasingly recognized as an issue for sociology that the equipment that enables the "ordinary" member of society to make his daily way through the world is the equipment available for those who would wish to do a "science" of that world.[1] This might be formulated as the sociologist's "dilemma," but only so long as a notion of science is employed that fails to recognize the socially organized character of *any* enterprise, including the enterprise of doing science. A science of society that fails to treat speech as both topic and resource is doomed to failure. And yet, although speech informs the daily world and is the sociologists's basic resource, its properties continue to go almost unexamined. Linguistic models have had some recent influence on the development of sociolinguistics, but it is still not at all clear that any specifically linguistic properties of talk can be related to central sociological concerns.[2] If we take sociology to be, in effect, "a natural history of the social world," then sociologists are committed to a study of the

* Work on this paper during the summer of 1969 was supported by a research grant from the Canada Council. I would like to acknowledge many helpful suggestions made by members of the Sociolinguistics Research Laboratory at the University of British Columbia, in particular, Bruce Katz and Stan Persky.
    1. Some particularly relevant discussions of this issue are to be located in Cicourel (1964), Garfinkel (1967), Garfinkel and Sacks, "On Formal Structures of Practical Actions," in McKinney and Tiryakian (forthcoming), Blum, "The Sociology of Mental Illness," and Moerman, "Analyzing Lue Conversation: Providing Accounts, Finding Breaches, and Taking Sides," in Sudnow (1969), and in Chapter 4 in this volume.
    2. A discussion of the import of contemporary linguistic theory for sociology is to be found in Chapter 6 in this volume.

activities such a world provides for and of the methodical achievement of those activities by socialized members.

In 1955, the British linguistic philosopher J. L. Austin set foot on sociological territory when he claimed a concern with the "business" of any utterance considered as a piece of talk. In the course of beginning to map out the configurations, Austin identified an important class of utterances which he termed *performatives*.[3] A crucial test an utterance must meet to gain membership in that class is described as follows: "If a person makes an utterance of this sort we should say that he is *doing* something rather than merely *saying* something." Austin (1961:222) gives the following examples of what would count as performative utterances.

Suppose for example, that in the course of a marriage ceremony I say, as people will, "I do" – (sc. take this woman to be my lawful wedded wife). Or again, suppose that I tread on your toe and say "I apologize." Or again, suppose that I have the bottle of champagne in my hand and say "I name this ship the *Queen Elizabeth*." Or suppose I said "I bet you sixpence it will rain tomorrow."

This sounds like a promising beginning, in that it sets out to provide some rigorous connection between talk (utterances) on the one hand, and activities (doing) on the other. More than that, it suggests that at least some talk can be analyzed *as* the doing of activities, thus taking us at once beyond the naive view that perhaps at best talk merely "reports" activities. If Austin substantiates his claims, then, the links thus established between the utterances and activities are very much the business of sociology. In this chapter I shall consider Austin's treatment of performative utterances in some detail, although I shall not do so in the spirit of providing an exposition or critique of Austin's work as an end in itself. My concern, rather, is with the elaboration of arguments that may underpin some actual procedures – primitive though they may be – for "taking apart" stretches of talk in the examination of its constituent activities. Later in the chapter I shall provide some transcribed talk as data and attempt a brief demonstration of how such materials may be analyzed in a sociologically relevant way so as to elucidate commonplace and recurrent activities. Indeed, very briefly I shall try to indicate how "substantive findings" may be derived from such an analysis, but let me emphasize that the point of the chapter is not so

3. Austin's work on performatives is treated at great length in Austin (1965) and more briefly in "Performative Utterances" in Austin (1961). This is the place to acknowledge my great indebtedness to Austin's writings. In developing a critique of his concept of performative utterances here, I am biting the hand that has fed me for several years. I would like to make it quite clear that my perfunctory treatment of Austin's concept, in the service of elaborating some tools useful for conventional analysis, does no justice to the power and richness of *How To Do Things with Words*. The book is a sociological gold mine, waiting for prospectors.

much to present a set of findings as to demonstrate and discuss possible procedures for "analyzing utterances into activities."[4]

I.

Before looking further into Austin's treatment of performatives, let me suggest what might be their potential importance for sociological analysis in purely formal terms. Suppose for a moment that an exhaustive list of performative "verbs" could be constructed, and that a formula could be provided to identify a performative utterance constructed out of an appropriate verb form; for example, if "to bequeath" were an item in the list of performative verbs, then a corresponding utterance might be constructed along the following lines:

I bequeath + [object name] to [person, kin or organization term]
yielding, for example,
I bequeath [my watch] to [Jehovah's Witnesses].

If such a list and such a set of formulas could be provided, we should have achieved the following: *we should be in a position to scan transcripts of talk and formally identify items as instances of activities, where the name of the activity would be derivable from the performative verb* (for example, the activity of bequeathing). I assume this would be a significant sociological achievement in that it would provide the analyst with a tool with which he could systematically analyze transcribed conversations into at least one class of their constituent activities and identify mechanically some of the things persons *accomplish* through "talk." Indeed, presumably such a resource would provide the ultimate in contemporary sociological validation of methods, in that it could be fairly readily computerized.

Unfortunately, Austin's own elaboration of performatives provides at least two grounds on which such a procedure must fail. An examination of those grounds will, I believe, enable us to grasp both the fundamental usefulness of the notion of performatives and the ultimate failure of Austin's treatment to come to terms with social-organizational parameters of activities. I shall discuss briefly each of these gounds in turn.

1. THE EXISTENCE OF "IMPLICIT" AND "PRIMITIVE" PERFORMATIVES

The development of a mechanical procedure for the extraction of performative utterances from a transcript, and hence the mechanical identi-

4. I borrow the phrase from the unpublished lectures of Harvey Sacks. Although I have tried to keep the record of specific borrowings straight, I have taken too much from Sacks to hope that a few footnotes will be an adequate measure of his writings as a resource.

fication of a set of activities, depends upon both the "listable" character of performative verbs (which would therefore need to be finite in number) and the ability to generate an unambiguously identifiable formula from any item in the list. Leaving aside the problem of constructing such a list, this requirement fails on the grounds that the formulaic appearance of a suitable verb form is not a necessary condition for the identification of a performative utterance. Thus Austin (1965: 32–33) notes:

> It is both obvious and important that we can on occasion use the utterance 'go' to achieve practically the same as we achieve by the utterance 'I order you to go': and we should say cheerfully in either case, *describing subsequently what someone did,* [emphasis added] that he ordered me to go. It may, however, be uncertain in fact, and so far as the mere utterance is concerned, is always left uncertain when we use so inexplicit a formula as the mere imperative 'go,' whether the utterer is ordering (or is purporting to order) me to go or merely advising, entreating or what not me to go. Similarly, 'There is a bull in the field.' may or may not be a warning, for I *might* just be describing the scenery and 'I shall be there,' may or may not be a promise. Here we have primitive as distinct from explict performatives; and there may be nothing in the circumstances by which we can decide whether or not the utterance is performative at all. Anyway, in a given situation, it can be open to me to take it as *either* one or the other. It was a performative formula — *perhaps* — but the procedure in question was not sufficiently explicitly invoked. Perhaps I did not *take it as* an order or was not anyway *bound* to take it as an order. The person did not *take it as* a promise: i.e. in the particular circumstance he did not accept the procedure, on the ground that the ritual was incompletely carried out by the original speaker.

So much, then, for the mechanical recognition of performative utterances. But there is more to be learned from this discussion than the mere fact that no mechanical recognition procedure can be derived from Austin's analysis. Consider, for instance, the precise form of the initial condition for admission of an utterance to the class of performatives, as quoted earlier in the chapter: "If a person makes an utterance of this sort *we should say* [emphasis added] that he is *doing* something rather than merely *saying* something." The situation invoked here is not that of the doer of the activity but of the potential reporter of the activity and what he "should" say in giving such a report. Similarly, in elaborating the problems of implicit and primitive performatives, Austin again, as a test of the character of the original utterance, appeals to the situation of "describing subsequently what someone did." In terms more familiar to sociologists, it appears that Austin is preoccupied with the giving of *warranted accounts* of events. Thus, I take it that the following hypothetical example is in the spirit of Austin's analysis.

A, returning from church, where he has just heard *B* utter the words "I do" at the appropriate moment in a wedding ceremony, meets *C,* an old friend of both *A* and *B*. *A* tells *C* has just seen *B*, and *C* asks, "Oh, what was he doing?" Now, according to Austin, it would be "odd" for *A* to reply, "He was just saying a few words," *under the condition that it could be said*, "He just got married." I assume that it is indeed a basic fact of daily life that "reports" or "descriptions" are so constrained, and that behavioral or technical descriptions of events would frequently be treated as bizarre, humorous, in bad taste, or in some way incompetent. Nevertheless, there is a deeper issue here that I must briefly explore. In order to do this I want to make some changes in my hypothetical example.

A reads in the newspaper that *B* has recently married. He meets *C* (who has been out of town) on the street and says, "Say, *B* just got married." Now given that *A* was not present at the wedding — and indeed may never have been present at any wedding, being quite vague as to the structure of such an occasion — he certainly cannot be *reporting* on an utterance he did not hear. In this case we might be inclined (to use Austin's own criterion) to say that *A* was "bringing *C* up-to-date," "announcing" that *B* had got married, or whatever. Announcing, after all, is surely plausible business for an utterance to do.

Austin himself, in a classic paper, has provided for the possibility of an utterance's constituting an act of "excusing" or "justifying," where one condition of the utterance's doing that work is that *it occurs in the context of the following upon an "accusation."* Thus:

You dropped the tea-tray: Certainly but an emotional storm was about to break out: or, Yes, but there was wasp (1961:124).

Suppose, then, that in the face of an accusation a person answers, "He ordered me to do it." Austinian logic would require us to treat such an utterance as *doing* the activity, "excusing" or "justifying." What then of his treatment of utterances like "He ordered me to do it" as derived from, dependent upon, and reporting on an earlier employment of a performative? In looking at some piece of talk as the "later" report which serves as evidence for the "earlier" existence of a performative utterance, Austin appears to claim that utterances can be treated as reports or descriptions *without reference to the interactional location of the utterance in question.*

Consider, then, the following difficulty which seems to be entailed by Austin's treatment of performatives.

We should find it "odd" to say that Jones had "uttered a few words" in the circumstances that what Jones did could be seen as "getting married." Should we not also find it odd to say that *A* was "describing" some earlier talk of *B*'s as a performative, in the circumstance that what *A* was doing was "providing an excuse"?

In short, Austin's treatment of "explicit" performatives as model
G*

forms to which other (related) utterances are to be assimilated as "implicit" or "primitive" varieties leads him to overlook the "business" (the character *as an activity*) of utterances that he is inclined to treat as reports or descriptions of other utterances. "Context" and "convention," which are invoked to characterize the work of explicit performatives and as criterial for seeing other utterances as "weaker" forms of performatives, cannot be permitted to go off duty when we seek to analyze other classess of utterances. Indeed, Austin himself is finally led to take explicit notice of describing as an activity, itself to be seen as a *located phenomenon*, when he argues that

The total speech act in the total speech situation is the *only actual* phenomenon which, in the last resort, we are engated in elucidating (1965: 147).

It may be, of course (as I shall discuss in some detail in the data sections of the chapter), that *this* kind of recognition severs—or at least greatly weakens—the link between formulas for *doing* activities and the procedure whereby we decide *what* activity has been done: remember that at some point Austin's solution to the problem is simply to participalize the performative verb to locate a "name" for the activity achieved by the performative utterance (for example, "I apologize" is doing "apologizing."

At this point I shall turn to the second ground (provided by Austin's own analysis) for undercutting the possibility of a "mechanical" procedure for identifying instances of performative utterances.

2. THE CONVENTIONAL SUPPORTS OF PERFORMATIVES

Recall that the issue is the possibility of locating members of a class of performative utterances (and hence activities) on the basis of developing some formula providing for their recognition. Even if the first objection to such a possibility (the existence of "implicit" and "primitive" performatives) did not exist, such an approach would still fail. For, as Austin notes, the successful employment (indeed, the existence) of utterances having a performative force depends upon two conditions, which we might refer to as social-organizational supports. The two conditions, as Austin states them are

a. *There must exist an accepted conventional procedure having a certain conventional effect, the procedure to include the uttering of certain words by certain persons in certain circumstances.* (1965:26).

b. *The particular persons and circumstances in a given case must be appropriate for the invocation of the particular procedure invoked.* (1965:34).

This seems reasonable enough, in that it argues that it is not the mere stringing together of words into utterances that automatically produces activities but that utterances are to be examined as being situated. Thus, I may say as many times as I wish, "I bequeath the Crown Jewels to my son," but I have bequeathed nothing, and therefore have not performed an act of bequeathing, since the Crown Jewels are not mine to dispose of. Austin is fond of pointing out that utterances embedded in jokes or state plays do not carry their normal performative force: an actor and actress do not "in fact" become man and wife by nightly going through a representation of a wedding ceremony.

It is a sufficient objection to locating instances of performative utterances by formula, then, to note that two appearances of the "same" utterance may not count as two instances of the "same" activity (if one is spoken within the framework of a stage play, for example). But again, there is surely more to say about utterances and their settings than can be generated by considering how performatives may "fail" for want of some proper "fit" between situational elements. Thus, to mention a possibility without pursuing it in any detail, "doing a joke" may be achieved precisely by virtue of the fit between utterance and setting; the utterance "I promise" may come off as a successful joke, where it would be perverse to see it as merely an instance of a spoiled "promise."

For the sociologist, further, Austin's two conditions can be faulted on the grounds that they simply take for granted matters that persons in the society may have to decide, negotiate, or assert as premises for bringing off activities. Thus, granted that the events of a stage play do not have the force of the activities they mere depict, *that it is a stage play* must itself be made demonstrable as a framework for viewing. The "brute fact" of being a stage play is not in itself a guarantee that at least some represented activities may not be fully consequential. Thus, to take a gross instance, if you and I decide to rehearse a scene from a script on the sidewalk downtown, wherein I press a gun in your ribs and say "This is a stick-up," the "brute fact" that it is, after all, a play, will not necessarily prevent my being cut down by a passing armed policeman. Even "happenings" and other advanced forms of "spontaneous" theater take place at announced times in announced places. Pirandellian tricks depend for their effect upon their being viewed as theatrical devices; a literal "confusion" between depicted and "for real" events is no part of the theater that trades upon realism and spontaneity.

I shall now provide some transcribed pieces of talk and employ them for a discussion of some elementary procedures for analyzing activities. Although I still plan to travel a little further with Austin, I think the journey will be more eventful if it leads us to confront the concrete problems of dealing with actual bits of interaction.

II.

Here, then, is a piece of talk pulled out of a transcript made from a tape-recorded occasion. I shall deliberately withhold any description of the occasion or the setting for the moment, since issues concerning their relevance are part of what we have to discuss.

BERT: Yeah, yeah, that's correct. I uh uh really did know im and uh he was with me in the Alexander Psychiatric Institute in in Alexander, Western Province. I I don't remember his name but we uh we always buddied around together when uh we were at the hospital and we always (( )) French. And uh I saw him out at Western City about three weeks ago, and I said to 'm, "Hello, howarya doing?" He said "I don't know you – who are you?" "Well, lookit," I said, "You *must* know me." He says, "No, I don't know you." Now he was with another fellow there too – waal he didn't want to admit that he was in a mental hospital uh in a hospital – he didn't want to admit it to the other fellow that was with him. So he just walked off and that was it. He wouldn't say hello to me. He wouldn't say nothin!

ROB: What was you view there? Do you have your own views on that? A touchy point.

BERT: Uh.

?: (( ))

JAKE: Perhaps he didn't like the idea of being in that place. Maybe he didn't want/

BERT: Well no he had to say it – there was another fellow with him you see/

JAKE: Well he didn't want to admit/

BERT: Who hadn't been in a mental hospital probably, and he *was* in the hospital. He didn't want *him* to know.

ART: You mean he

?: This other guy

COUNS: But he

BERT: Oh, oh never been in a hosptial

BERT: He didn't want to know his friends.[5]

Now, given such materials as these, the practical issue is: How might they be taken apart in a sociologically relevant way – that is to say, as a demonstration of their orderliness? An initial paradox seems to be that as societal members we find that such materials are often terribly obvious, if not trite (and I imagine that the reader was able to find sense in the talk on the basis of a very rapid reading, despite the fact that he has no personal knowledge of Bert and the other speakers); while as sociologists, confronted with the task of obtaining some leverage in providing an analytical description, the very same set of utterances become forbiddingly opaque. It becomes opaque, I believe, under the condition that as sociologists we suppose that we must locate instances (or indicators) of concepts posited by an explicit theory; and yet we obviously have no such theory to guide us in analyzing talk in any detail. Thus an

5. This transcript was supplied to me by Anthony Crowle.

elementary problem might be formulated as: What are we to attend to as units — words, sentences, utterances?

Let us assume that we are agreed for the moment that we want to locate and look at instances of activities. The problem still remains. I take it that Austin did not doubt that we can *recognize* activities; indeed, his method of operation seems to require, first, the collection of a number of performative utterances, treated as non-problematic in itself, after it has been explained what shall count as a performative utterance, and, then, the search for formal criteria that distinguish the class of performatives from other classes of utterances. Of course, if we isolated the formal criteria, we should then have no problem in scanning further candidates of performatives to decide their membership status; but that scarcely solves the problem of how we assemble out first collection of utterances on the basis of which the formal criteria are to be derived.

As a solution to the vexed problem of the relation between the shared cultural knowledge (members' knowledge) that the sociologist possesses and the analytical apparatus that it is his responsibility to produce, I propose the following:

A. *The sociologist inevitably trades on his members' knowledge* in recognizing the activities that participants to interaction are engaged in; for example, it is by virtue of my status as a competent member that I can recurrently locate in my transcripts instances of "the same" activity. This is not to claim that members are infallible or that there is perfect agreement in recognizing any and every instances; it is only to claim that no resolution of problematic cases can be effected by resorting to procedures that are supposedly uncontaminated by members' knowledge. (Arbitrary resolutions, made for the sake of easing the problems of "coding," are of course no resolution at all for the present enterprise.)

B. The sociologist, having made his first-level decision on the basis of members' knowledge, must then *pose as problematic* how utterances come off as recognizable unit activities. This requires the sociologist to *explicate the resources* he shares with the participants in making sense of utterances in a stretch of talk. At every step of the way, inevitably, the sociologist will continue to employ his socialized competence, while continuing to make explicit *what* these resources are and *how* he employs them. I see no alternative to these procedures, except to pay no explicit attention to one's socialized knowledge while continuing to use it as an indispensable aid. In short, sociological discoveries are ineluctably discoveries *from within the society.*

Now leaving the programmatics aside, let me cite once again Austin's admonition that "the total speech act in the total speech situation is the *only actual* phenomenon which, in the last resort, we are engaged in elucidating." Supposing we decide to take this seriously, how do we bring it to bear on the data presented above? What, for example, is "the total speech situation" of the talk recorded and transcribed?

Consider the possibility that more than one technically correct description of the occasion of the talk might be provided. Thus I could propose that a tape recording was made of Bert and a few acquaintances sitting around having an evening's chat. Another possible description of the occasion is as follows: A number of former mental patients voluntarily attended an evening group discussion sponsored by a mental health association; the discussion was in the charge of a counselor whose instructions were to help members of the group discuss their problems. As between these two possible descriptions I offer the latter as the more useful, employing the following criterion: the latter description characterizes the occasion as that occasion was organized, announced, and made available to the participants; an act of self-identification as a "former mental patient" was any member's entitlement to attend, and his entitlement to see that his fellow participants (apart from the "counselor") were likewise "former mental patients."

Why does this matter? It matters, I argue, in that it provides participants with an orientation and a set of criteria for contributing and recognizing activities. Whatever one says during the course of the evening may be treated as "something said by a former mental patient," not on the "technical" grounds that after all one *is* such a person but on the grounds that that identification is occasioned and thereby warranted as relevant.

Presumably this does not end a characterization of the "total speech situation" of any unit of speech smaller than the whole conversation. Thus consider Bert's remark "So he just walked off and that was it." I assume that in order to see the sense of this remark it is necessary to notice its ties to at least the earlier parts of the utterance from which it is extracted. Notice, for instance, that given its position in the utterance, the "he" in the remark "So he just walked off and that was it" can be given a determinate reading by hearers (and now readers). Put crudely, then, one task of an analysis such as this is to make explicit just what features of the occasion and the talk are appealed to as providing for the force of an utterance or the character of an activity.

I hear Bert's remarks in this portion of the talk as constituting a "complaint," or "doing complaining." In so identifying it, I am unable to locate any obvious syntactic properties that might be seen as structural correlates of complaints, nor do I have any operational means for identifying its boundaries. I take it that Bert may have begun his complaint in an utterance previous to the first utterance given here; and I further assume that Bert's last utterance given here (but not the end of the talk), "He didn't want to know his friends," is in some sense "part of" the complaint. I know of no a priori reason an activity should be expected to require so many words or so many utterances; in any piece of data being considered it will be an issue to note the boundedness of an activity.

I now want to look at the production of a recognizable complaint in some detail, to look at the resources and components of Bert's complaint. I use the term resources carefully, since I take it that there is an issue of bringing off an activity in such a way that one's hearers can bring to the talk the necessary equipment and materials to make out its intended character.

Commonsensically there is no difficulty in saying that the basis of Bert's complaint is a "snub." More specifically, I take it that Bert's account is of "a former mental patient being snubbed," and thus is produced as an instance of "the kind of thing that can happen to a former mental patient."

Let us assume for the moment that a snub or slight, in the form of a refusal of recognition, can happen to "anyone." For the person to whom it has happened, such an event can presumably constitute a puzzle—that is to say, it is an event requiring an explanation. If I walk down the corridor and meet a colleague I encounter in such circumstances daily, and if we exchange greetings, then an interactional routine will have been achieved that—*for members*—is nonproblematic. Thus, if you are accompanying me at the time and you ask "Why did that guy smile at you?" I assume that an answer such as "He's a colleague of mine," will be sufficient, that is, that it would be "odd" for you to persist, "I know that, but why did he smile at you?" A snub becomes a puzzle, presumably, just because such a nonproblematic routine is breached.

Now if after being snubbed one makes that event the basis of an anecdote for others, one thing they may do, it seems, is to offer possible "explanations" or queries directed to uncovering "what happened." One readily available explanation has the consequence of inviting you to reconsider the event, to see that it wasn't a snub after all, perhaps that "there was some mistake"—that it wasn't who you thought it was. He looked remarkably like an old friend, but you caught only a glimpse, and it was probably a stranger. I mention this routine treatment because if we look carefully at Bert's first utterance we can see that Bert orients to the possibility of this being forthcoming from his hearers, and forestalls it: "I uh uh really did know im." The reader should notice here the interplay between common-sense knowledge offered as how I make out what is going on, and sociological concern, in that I take it as an analytical responsibility to account for the remark "I uh uh really did know im," while having recourse to members' knowledge in providing the substance of my account.

Now if we look at Bert's first utterance as a unit, it seems that it (a) recounts the occurrence of the snub, and (b) provides an explanation for it. Nevertheless, at the same time it is via the character of the explanation that I see that Bert is constructing a complaint. In effect, this leads us to consider the "mechanics" of doing an activity. If Bert is to bring off a successful instance of a complaint, he must build it out of components that will provide for its recognition by hearers who are presumed to be—like Bert, and like readers—"experts" in constructing and recognizing a repertoire of activities. In looking at the talk in detail, then, we are discovering how the materials at hand are made to serve the requirements of certain invariant properties of activities. The following considerations lead me to argue that the explanation provides for Bert to be seen as "complaining."

a. Recall Austin's requirement for the successful achievement of a performative utterance, that "the particular persons and circumstances in a given case must be appropriate for the invocation of the particular procedure involved." How is that relevant to the present issue? In the first place, since we are not analyzing as data the talk that took place between Bert and his acquaintance upon the occasion of the snub, we are hardly in a position to characterize that "total speech situation" in a way that a transcript of the occasion might permit. What we have, rather, is Bert's characterization of the occasion, developed as a resource for constructing a complaint. In effect, then, we are dealing with the societal member's concern with providing for the "appropriateness" of the "particular persons and circumstances" as features that will properly orient hearers to the sense of the occasion—that is, orient them to a sense of the occasion that will enable them to recognize what Bert is *now* doing. This permits us to ask: *How* does Bert provide such an orientation?

Notice first, then, that Bert does not simply tell his listeners that he was snubbed by "an acquaintance," "an old friend" or "a guy I knew," although presumably any of these would have been a sufficient and proper indentification of the party to allow for what happended to be seen as a snub. Bert identified the snubber as a man who "was with me in the Alexander Psychiatric Institute." Now I take it that this identification is not warranted simply by its literal correctness, since a range of possible "correct" identifications is always available (in this case, for example, "a fellow I used to know in Western Province") and it is not a matter of indifference which item of a set of possible items is selected. One thing we can note about the identification selected, then, is a relevance provided by the occasion, by the presence of this collection of hearers, in that the party mentioned is mentioned now as "one of us." Beyond that, the identification of the snubber as "he was with me in the Alexander Psychiatric Institute" provides that Bert himself could be seen by the other party as a "released mental patient."

   b. Bert tells his listeners that on recognizing the other party he said to him, "Hello, howarya doing?" Now given that he has already indicated *that* (and *how*) they were acquainted, a greeting is seen to be in order and to require a greeting in return, since an exchange of greetings is a procedure permitted among acquainted persons; and upon one party's offering a greeting the other is taken to be under obligation to return it. In short, I take it that Bert is invoking what I have just stated in the form of a "norm," and that it is by reference to such a procedure that it becomes "obvious" to his listeners that "something was wrong" when instead of the greeting the greeted party returned with "I don't know you — who are you?" That this is the case is further provided for by Bert's remark "He wouldn't say hello to me. He wouldn't say nothin!" As I understand Bert's remark, assumption of shared knowledge that a greeted acquaintance has an *obligation* to respond with a greeting is both a requirement and a resource for seeing how Bert is entitled to say "He *wouldn't* say hello to me," in that he is thus enabling his listeners to find the "absence of a greeting" as a motivated act.[6]

   So far, then, all we have seen is an account of a breached norm, the norm that requires acquainted persons to acknowledge one another upon meeting face-to-face. This component of the account constitutes the occurrence of a "trouble," in this case, a snub.

   c. If we look further at the utterance we find that Bert claims to see *why* he was offered a slight by an acquaintance who owed him at least the return of a greeting. Thus, Bert remarks: "Now he was with another fellow there too — waal he didn't want to admit that he was in a mental hospital uh in a hospital — he didn't want to admit it to the other fellow that was with him. So he just walked off and that was it."

   Now the interesting question to ask is: *How does this come off as an explanation?* To set it up with heuristic naïvité, what could Bert be talking about in saying of the other party "He didn't want to admit . . . that he was in a mental hospital?" How does the question of making an admission arise? To put the question in somewhat different form, we may ask: Are there any resources that Bert's listeners (as well as ourselves) might bring to bear on this remark to see in it the sense it is presumably intended to have (as grounds for the refusal to return a

6. On the notion of "relevant absences," see Sacks, unpublished lectures and research notebooks. Compare Schegloff's discussion of "conditional relevance" in Schegloff (1968).

greeting)? How might it be seen that a returned greeting would be, or would lead to, an "admission to the other fellow" that he had been in a mental hospital? To put it differently, and in common-sense terms, it might be argued that it would have been entirely inconsequential for Bert's former fellow-patient to have responded, for example, "Pretty good, thanks. How's yourself?"

I take it that Bert is able to trade upon an "obvious" feature of "chance encounters," namely, their informational value. The paradigm case is suggested by the following hypothetical conversation.

A: Who was that guy who waved from across the street?
B: Oh, just a fellow I knew in the Marines.
A: Really? I didn't know you were in the Marines! When was that?

Bert's friend, then, could be depicted as motivated to refuse an acknowledgment of the acquaintance on the grounds that it might have opened him up to "explaining" to his companion "who" Bert was—where the relevant sense of "who" would require a reference to the basis of their being acquainted. But beyond that, there are other norms relating to the situation of renewing acquaintance that are possibly being invoked here.

An issue in the orderly conduct of conversation may be termed "the distribution of speaker's rights."[7] Thus Sacks has pointed out with respect to questions and answers as paired units that a potentially infinite chain of utterances may be produced under the auspices of the following rule: *The questioner has a right to talk again when an answer is returned,* that is, when the answerer finishes his turn at talking the right to speak passes back to the questioner, *and the questioner has a right to ask another question* (thus providing for another answer and a further question; and so the cycle may be repeated, as court transcripts nicely indicate). Similarly, Schegloff (1968) has indicated that within the structure of a telephone call the caller may select the first topic for talk. With respect to face-to-face social contacts among the acquainted it appears to be the case that a simple exchange of greetings—"hello," "hello"—may constitute an adequate "conversation," and the parties may separate without breach of the relationship. However, it further appears to be the case that the initial greeter has the right to talk again when a greeting is returned, and that he thus becomes a "first speaker" with respect to rights of topic selection. If this is the case, then (as I take it Bert and his listeners could see), to acknowledge a greeting by returning a greeting is to open oneself up to the initial greeter's developing a

7. See Sacks, "On Formal Structures of Practical Actions," in McKinney and Tiryakian (forthcoming); see also Speier (1968).

conversation and to his initiating a topic. In the cited incident, Bert would have had the right to so talk, providing that his acquaintance did not attach the opening of topical talk to the utterance returning a greeting.

If we shift our attention for the moment from the initiation of talk to the issue of the *management of relationships,* conversations can be seen as having sequential properties; that is, when related parties meet, the conversational possibilities may be constrained by "what happened last time" or by events that have intervened. Thus, persons employ opening slots in conversations to "bring one another up-to-date," or — when the passage of time has been considerable, or "circumstances" have changed — to talk over "when we last saw each other," or, as in reunions, to "talk over old times." Notice again that I am suggesting this not as an analysis independent of members' knowledge and members' concerns but as integral to them, and I take it that it is a commonplace experience to "look forward to" or "avoid" persons with whom such conversations are to be expected.

In this connection it is relevant to note that Bert's development of the situation permits his hearers to see that indeed "bringing up-to-date" might have been in order, in that this was apparently a first meeting since the hospital days, and in a city more than a thousand miles from the hospital. In short, the locational and temporal features of the occasion are not simply descriptive but are *explanatory*: a "reunion" would have "normally" been in order, and a reunion could be seen as precisely what a former mental patient who is "passing" could anticipate as a threat.[8] Returning a greeting, then, is not without cost.[9] For Bert's acquaintance, the return of a greeting, carrying with it an acknowledgment of their relationship, would have entitled Bert to develop talk about what each had done "since the hospital," etc. Thus potential conversational partners may avoid eye contacts, give signs of "being in a hurry,"

8. Stan Persky pointed out to me the importance, for the account, of the encounter being seen as "the first since the hospital." An instance of the fulfillment of such a threat is contained in the following account given me by a former mental patient, in response to my asking if he would greet "fellow former patients" he might meet on the street:

Al: Yes I do. I stop and say hello to them and one case I came across was . . . we used to buy our groceries from the New Market Store and he was the manager — of the New Market Store. Well, he went out to State Hospital. I met him out there and I said hello to him out there and talked to him for a while. A year later I met him downtown in Western City. He was with his wife and I said, "Oh, hello, Mr. Robbins. Remember me out at State Hospital? And his wife looked at me and said, "He's never been out in State Hospital." But there was no mistaking it. It was him. (laughs) I thought that was quite funny.

Data taken from Turner (1968).

9. Compare the anecdote cited by Schegloff to make the point "that conversational oaks may out of conversational acorns grow," in Schegloff (1968:1094).

or balk at the first interchange, where the "danger" is seen to be located at some later (and unspecifiable) spot in the conversation that mutual acknowledgment may generate.

d. To recapitulate, I have suggested that the visible breach of a norm requiring acquainted persons to acknowledge one another, or at least return a proffered greeting, has constituted a trouble for Bert—he has been snubbed. Bert saw and made available to his hearers an explanation of the snub; it was by no means a case of mistaken identity but rather a matter of "deliberate" (motivated) refusal to "know a friend" on the part of one who might find that the cost of an acknowledgment would be disclosure to a companion that he had been a "mental patient."

But—and this I suppose to be crucial—it isn't the mere fact that the snubber had been a "mental patient" that constitutes *Bert's* embarrassment or chagrin: for Bert the complaint-worthy item is presumably *that he sees that he himself had been identified as a "former mental patient;"* the snubber's own problems stemmed from *Bert's* former-patient status.

This I take to be the feature of the account that constitutes it as a complaint, where the complaint could be formulated, for example, as "He wouldn't talk to me because I've been a mental patient." The complaint, then, is directed to the recurrent kinds of "troubles" that persons can find themselves inheriting along with an unwanted categorial indentification—in this case the identification that constitutes the tie between participants to the group talk and that is taken by them to generate the occasion in the first place. The complaint thus becomes a *category-generated activity,* providing for any members of the category (such as Bert's hearers) to see that "what happened to him" could happen to "us."

Earlier in the chapter I mentioned briefly that the analysis of talk into activities here presented could be seen to provide for at least a suggestion of "substantive findings." What I have in mind is that the preceding discussion permits some comments on the traditional sociological literature on former mental patients and their "problems," a literature which, with few exceptions beyond the writings of Erving Goffman, establishes as its framework of inquiry a set of psychiatric assumptions concerning the character of such "problems."[10] On the basis of the analysis presented here I believe I am warranted in suggesting that the categorical identification "former mental patient" (as used by former mental patients

10. I am thinking particularly of *Stigma*, (Goffman, 1963b), but the structure of interactionally generated problems is a theme in all of Goffman's writings. It is interesting to note by contrast that when Freeman and Simmons (1963:233), in a book-length study of the "problems" of former metnal patients, turn their attention to the issue of "stigma" it is to note the embarrassment created for "the family" by having a former mental patient in their midst.

themselves and by others) does the work of organizing and structuring accounts of persons' behavior and difficulties. That is to say, under the conditions that a person can be categorized *as* a former mental patient, such an identification can and will be used by members as explanatory and predictive of what such persons "do."

For persons in the rehabilitative professions, such an identification provides the auspices for searching out (and finding), for example, residual illness, bizarre behavior, having a relapse, etc. "Former mental patients" themselves, on the other hand, make use of their membership in the category to both locate and explain a set of interactional "difficulties" that they provide accounts of as recurrent events in transactions with friends, family, neighbors, etc. Notice that although I have constantly appealed to membership in the category "former mental patient" to elucidate what I took it participants to the talk were orienting themselves to, I have not *as part of my own analytical apparatus* attributed any special properties to such category incumbents, on the grounds (hopefully clear by now) that the invocation of the category as part of the "total speech situation" is the only relevant feature for my purposes.

What I want to note, then, is that a plausible view of at least one class of "problems" of "former mental patients" is that such problems are generated out of the same raw materials that provide for "normal" interactional routines, in particular, the invocation of norms governing such matters as meeting an old friend. It is in finding that such norms may be breached systematically, and the breach accounted for by the identification "former mental patient," that Bert is able to propose that "what happened" constituted a complaint-worthy event. Further, not only is it the case that such persons may find their "problems" cut from the same cloth that allows "normals" to manage relationships in a satisfactory way, it also seems to be the case that "former mental patients" employ the same standard methodical procedures for "giving accounts," "constructing complaints," etc., as are available to "anyone." Even persons who claim that their lives have been "ruined" as a consequence of time spent in the mental hospital may still retain intact their grasp on "how to do things with words" — *their* claims, in effect, validating *my* claim.

III.

A few concluding remarks about words, utterances, and activities. A traditional sociological approach treats speech either as a source of "hidden" realities — such as values, attitudes and beliefs — waiting for the sociologist to ʼuncover them, or as the reporting of members' "perceptions" of social facts, to be verified or falsified by "scientific" procedures. The initial value of Austin's work is that it at least brings our attention back to the fact that, as persons go about their business, some of that business is done (and not merely reported upon) *in* and *through* talk. It also helps us to see that an inventory of "norms" or "role expectations" fails to come to terms with the fact that members may (and do) assert, argue, hint at, deny, undercut, etc., the "relevant" situational features of accountable actions, *upon the occasion of giving accounts*. Some recent sociological writings do stress the "negotiated" or "emergent" character of interaction but usually fail to demonstrate how the structure of any given piece of talk can be displayed as an interlocking set of activities. Without linked demonstrations, of course, such programmatic statements must resemble "advice" given at a level of generality, which leaves the researcher still facing the crucial problem of how to analyze the tapes or transcripts that constitute his data. Too often such theories of interaction become the rugs under which the data are conveniently swept. The reader who wishes to utilize such "theoretical" writings is typically left to ask "Now what do I do?" It is in the hope of avoiding another such exhortation that I have attempted to spell out in some detail what an analysis of talk into its constituent activities might look like.[11]

In building upon and departing from Austin's work I have argued:

a) That all and anỹ exchanges of utterances — defining an utterance for the moment as one speaker's turn at talking — can in principle be regarded as "doing things with words";

11. A few sociologists have recently tried to develop models based on premises derived from transformational grammer. Despite the intrinsic interest of such work, and the cogency of the arguments, such writings differ from the work of linguists proper in one crucial respect; they fail to tie their theoretical arguments to the analysis of particular instances of data. Thus, whatever insensitivity to social structure the sociologist may find in some lingquistic treatments of the deep structure of sentences, at least the linguist typically spells out in detail the steps whereby he arrives at his analysis, thus permitting his colleagues to pinpoint their criticisms and requiring them to demonstrate the basis of alternative treatments of the same data. It is for this reason that I have taken the space to spell out rather literally how I "hear" talk in the transcript presented above. Readers are free to perform their own analyses of the data in alternative to mine. In this connection I cannot resist quoting Gilbert Ryle's comment (in Chappel, 1964:26) on his ʼproblems in arguing the "stock use" of an "ordinary" expression with his colleagues: "One's fellow-philosophers are at such pains to pretend that they cannot think what its stock use is — a difficulty which, of course, they forget about when they are teaching children or foreigners how to use it, and when they are consulting dictionaries." The point, I take it, is that our concern in treating interaction is not to see how ingenious we can be in torturing alternative senses out of utterances, but that our task is to characterize their employment as it is located in the talk — such as we may (and do) find ourselves engaged in. Wittgenstein (1958:18) might almost have had traditional sociology in mind when he spoke of "the contemptuous attitude towards the particular case."

b) That there is no a priori reason to suppose that syntactical or lexical correspondences exist between units of speech and activities:

c) That in constructing their talk, members provide for the recognition of "what they are doing" by invoking culturally provided resources;

d) That "total speech situations" are to be elucidated as the features oriented to by members in doing and recognizing activities, and assessing their appropriateness;

e) That in undertaking such elucidations, sociologists *must* (and do) employ their own expertise in employing and recognizing methodical procedures for accomplishing activities;

f) That the task of the sociologist in analyzing naturally occurring scenes is not to deny his competence in making sense of activities but to *explicate* it;

g) That such explication provides for a cumulative enterprise, in that the uncovering of members' *procedures* for doing activities permits us both to replicate our original data and to generate new instances that fellow members will find recognizable.

I would particularly like to emphasize this last claim that the sociological apparatus that emerges from the detailed study of interaction is a set of descriptions of *methods* and *procedures* (for accomplishing and locating activities). Work that is currently proceeding along these lines suggests that the logic of the "programming" whereby socialized members "produce" social structure will result in a more viable central core for a "scientific" sociology than the existing common-sense division of the discipline into "substantive fields."[12] The building of this core as an empirical enterprise depends upon the sociologist's recognition that he has no choice but to reflect upon and analyze the social order to which he himself subscribes.

12. I am thinking of work such as Sacks, "The Search for Help," in Sudnow (1969), Garfinkel (1967), Blum, "The Sociology of Mental Illness," in Sudnow (1969), Zimmerman and Pollner, in Chapter 4 in this volume, Speier (1968a, 1968b), Cicourel (1968), Turner, "Some Formal Properties of Therapy Talk," in Sudnow (1969), Bittner (1967a, 1967b), Schegloff (1968), Smith (1969), Moerman, "Being Lue: Uses and Abuses of Ethnic Identifications," in American Ethnological Society (1967:153–169), and Moerman, "Analyzing Lue Conversation," in Sudnow (1969). In this last work Moerman makes a similar argument with respect to the "resource" character of what the sociologist may state as formal "norms."

The Everyday World of the Child

I. A New Look at the Empirical Content of Childhood Socialization

Sociology considers the social life of the child as a basic area of study in so-called institutional analyses of family and school, for example. What is classically problematic about studying children is the fact of cultural induction, as I might refer to it. That is, sociologists (and this probably goes for anthropologists and psychologists) commonly treat childhood as a stage of life that builds preparatory mechanisms into the child's behavior so that he is gradually equipped with the competence to participate in the everyday activities of his cultural partners, and eventually as a bona fide adult member himself. This classical sociological problem has been subsumed under the major heading of socialization.[1] In studying the organization of culture and society it seems quite natural to inquire into the process by which a new entrant acquires the status of a member in the eyes of others in his surrounding cultural milieu (unlike those entrants who arrive as adults, as "strangers"[2] or immigrants, tourists and the like, the child enters upon the scene with a clean slate, because the process takes place without the underlay of previous cultural experience).

The classical formulation of the problem of socialization has centered on treatments of the child's entry and incorporation into culture as a *developmental process*. Its working paradigm[3] has been to ask questions

---

1. The standard works that present the classical formulation of socialization include: Elkin (1960), Child, "Socialization," in Lindzey (1954), Aberle, "Culture and Socialization," in Hsu (1961), Aberle and Naegele, "Middle Class Fathers' Occupational Role and Attitudes Toward Children" in Bell and Vogel (1969), Brim (1959), Bossard and Boll (1948), Sears, Maccoby, and Levin (1957), Maccoby, (1961), and most recently Clausen (1968). For a complete list of references to this field see Clausen (1968:3–17, 18–72).

2. On the notion of a cultural "stranger" see Schutz (1962:9).

3. By the notion of a working paradigm I have in mind what is meant by Kuhn (1962).

about child development, such as the general one: How does the child internalize the norms, values, attitudes, etc., of others in his society?[4] Traditional anthropological ethnography has asked in addition: How does the child develop particular skills in social and economic ways of life?[5] Psychologists have focused on maturational growth and on personality development.[6] Lately, researchers from all these disciplines have become interested in the development of language skills.[7]

I would like to propose an approach that differs sharply from the developmental one found in the classical formulations of socialization research. This approach sets aside questions of development yet retains the substantive interests of adult-child interaction central to the study of socialization.

I propose a simple definition of socialization that if acceptable to developmentally oriented research would imply the investigation of a hidden frame of analysis altogether: *socialization is the acquisition of interactional competences.* We can readily admit to the fact that children acquire "a sense of social structure," to use Cicourel's phrase.[8] That is, for the child to develop from a newborn entrant to a participating member in social arrangements around him, he must undergo a learning process over the course of growing up through successive stages of life. However, to study this implicitly recognized acquisition process, presupposes a good knowledge of the features of interactional competences that are acquired. That is, what in fact are children developmentally acquiring? An investigation of the concrete features of competent interaction is nothing more or less than a study of what children normally and routinely do in their everyday activities, and as such it is not a study at all in the development of competence but a study in descriptive interactional analysis. It is my firm belief that no investigation of acquisition processes can effectively get underway until the concrete features of interactional competences are analyzed as topics in their own right. Without this preliminary step, which deliberately refrains from treating the topic of development, discussions of social competence must necessarily remain too vague and abstract to be of any direct use in empirical socialization research.

4. See, for example, Parsons and Bales (1955) and Miller and Swanson (1958).
5. See, for example, Whiting (1963) and Margaret Mead (1930).
6. See, for example, Kluckhohn and Murray (1948), Murchison (1931), Erikson (1950), Hsu (1961), and Hoffman and Hoffman (1966).
7. See Piaget (1965, 1960). Along these lines see Brown (1958). These studies in "cognitive socialization" are antecedents to the newer fields of psycholinguistics and sociolinguistics, in which language socialization has become a central research focus. See Brown and Bellugi in Lenneberg (1964:131–161), and Brown and Fraser, in Bellugi and Brown (1964:43–79). See also Ervin-Tripp and Slobin (1966), McNeill, in Smith and Miller (1966:15–84), Lyons and Wales (1966), and Saporta (1966).
8. See Chapter 6 in this volume.

The target phenomena I propose to examine, interactions and concerted activities, are not customarily the subject of childhood socialization research. I refer to those sorts of interactions and activities that are *naturally situated* in the stream of everyday life. Naturalistic interactions and activities regularly take place by means of one very dominant mode of human communication, namely, talk. The centrality of talk in the everyday organization of human activity has been stressed in various analytic arguments throughout this volume (see especially the chapters by Turner, Zimmerman and Pollner, and Cicourel)—it is perhaps the major contribution by so-called ethnomethodologists to the history of modern sociology, a discipline that has remained oddly sluggish in recognizing the central role of speech in the organization of group life.[9]

Talk and its conversational properties (including, where necessary, accompanying nonspoken aspects of interaction such as gestures, facial organization, and ecological spacing) therefore comprise an altogether new set of empirical dimensions in the study of childhood social organization. It can easily be shown how investigators of childhood socialization have regularly relied on the speech communications of cultural participants in making inferences about "childrearing practices," though the speech practices themselves are never treated explicitly as analytic topics in their own right, directly relevant to the abstractions that are constructed about organized native knowledge presumably underlying childrens' and parents' situated courses of action.[10]

This new direction in childhood socialization encourages the generation of topical analyses dealing with problems in how children talk to other children and how they talk with parents and other adults. These constitute, in part, problems in conversational analysis, a field most notably developed in recent years by Sacks,[11] and also by Schegloff,[12] Turner,[13] Moerman,[14] and others. Unlike past researchers who have

9. The ethnomethodological researchers aside—Garfinkel (1967) having been the first to note this peculiar failing in sociology—the work of Erving Goffman is perhaps a notable exception. See his statement on the nature of spoken interaction in Goffman (1967:33–38).

10. See the first page of Chapter 7 in this volume for the same criticism. I have documented this more fully in Speier (1969:6–12).

11. See Sacks (1966a). See also the various series of his lectures delivered at the University of California at Los Angeles, Department of Sociology, 1966 and 1967. Later series of lectures are now found at the University of California at Irvine, Social Science Division. Sacks has summarized his dissertation, "The Search for Help," in Sudnow (1970).

12. See Schegloff (1967, 1968).

13. See Turner (1968) and Turner, "Some Formal Properties of Therapy Talk," in Sudnow (1970).

14. See Moerman, "Analysis of Lue Conversation: Providing Accounts, Finding Breaches, and Taking Sides," in Sudnow (1970). In the same volume see also Speier, "Some Conversation Problems in Interactional Analysis."

only noted in passing the most general significance of language (as in symbolic interactionism), this new direction in studying speech as the living performance of language has emphasized the *methods* participants use when building talk and practical activity around each other. By methods is meant what others in this volume have often alluded to as the *procedural basis* for everyday interactions, or, as Turner puts it in Chapter 7 in this volume, our enterprise consists of "the uncovering of members' procedures for doing activities," talking or "doing things with words" being a major component of those procedures.

Our task in research, then is to gather "samples" (and at this point no sampling rules can be evinced) of concrete instances of natural interactions involving children. What can we explicate about the formal properties of those conversational procedures, for example, that we find participants using in the concrete instance coming before our analytic scrutiny?

The reader accustomed to the conventional paradigm in childhood socialization will not find hypothetical inquiries about "socialization influences and aims," nor problems in the social-structural basis for the child's "internalization of norms," etc. He will find, instead, that the interactional orientation to childhood organization will supply a frame of reference that precludes the posing of such abstract problems, and that in fact such problems as are found in the classical formulations will be dissolved and replaced by a whole new set of analytic considerations. In searching out the procedural properties of children's conversational interactions, a vast variety of studies in childhood social organization could be attempted, encompassing parent-child interactions in everyday household activity, adult-child interactions in other families' homes, in public places, in schools, or interactions exclusively among children themselves. Children's exclusive contacts constitute problems of study in what might be called the organization of "children's culture," and as such open up a wholly new sociological domain.[15]

In this reformulated context for studying children's everyday activity the notion of development takes on a new shape. The temporal scale is vastly reduced to interactional units of *occasioned and situated activity*. The focus now is upon developing sequences of interaction from one moment to the next, rather than upon stages of development in the child's life; on the way interactants build a social scene and build a conversation together, episodically, beginning with procedures for opening and entering into copresent interactions, next for sustaining them around practical purposes using conversational resources for so doing, and finally for terminating the interaction or shifting into new activities

15. This domain of study, the social organization of children's culture, is the subject of Speier and Turner (forthcoming).

or situations along natural junctures. The notion of development, then, enters into the analysis of interactional sequences moving naturally through time as participants do and say things methodically together. Children presumably have sufficient competence to cooperate in interactional development over a great variety of social circumstances. As interactants they must be able to employ conversational procedures with those they routinely encounter in everyday life. What conversational resources are available to children and to their interlocutors when routine interactions arise and take shape? That is, how are such procedures for interacting employed resourcefully by participants as they go about their talking and acting and their everyday practical achievements?

In the discussion that follows I will attempt to demonstrate how a concrete instance of data in the child's everyday life can be analyzed so as to yield some key issues in the organization of childhood activity. These issues will form the basis for the general analysis in the remainder of the chapter.

II. Treating an Instance as an Opening Gambit

Outside his house he found Piglet, jumping up and down trying to reach the knocker.
"Hallo, Piglet," he said.
"Hallo, Pooh," said Piglet.
"What are *you* trying to do?"
"I was trying to reach the knocker," said Piglet. "I just came round—"
"Let me do it for you," said Pooh kindly. So he reached up and knocked at the door.
"I have just seen Eeyore," he began, (Pooh continues to explain his story about Eeyore when he interrupts himself)—
"What a long time whoever lives here is answering this door."
And he knocked again.
"But Pooh," said Piglet, "it's your own house!"
"Oh!" said Pooh. "So it is," he said. "Well let's go in."[16]

I will open with an analysis of a piece of data from the study of children's everyday activities. From it I hope to generate a few important issues that I will take up in more detail in the sections following this one. These issues will center on the analysis of interactional development as a sequence of conversation, and on the nature of some of the conversational resources used by participants in that sequence. I take it that the instance is typical of a mundane routine that children confront in daily life, namely, calling on their friends. Children's contacts often involve and sometimes require the intervention of adults. This is a point

16. A. A. Milne, *Winnie the Pooh* (New York:E. P. Cutton & Co., 1954), p. 75.

about the organization of childhood to keep in mind when examining the instance I am about to present.

The following complete event took place in an encounter between a neighborhood child and a household mother. I was a guest in this home and at the time of the interaction was alone in a bedroom whose window was situated in a favorable position to overhear and record the entire sequence. It lasted for about one minute. The ecological arrangement is very important for an interpretation of the data. This house, on a street of private attached homes in San Francisco, has a front gate off the street that is always locked and that leads onto a tunnel or passage that has a staircase at the far end going up to the front door of the house. The staircase turns and a caller at the front gate at street level cannot see the front door one flight above. To gain entry a caller must always ring the bell at the gate first. This is a standard architectural arrangement for many homes in this city. It structures an interaction between caller and door-answer in such a way that neither party can see the other unless the answerer descends the staircase and turns the corner to look down the passageway at the caller. The entire passage and staircase are actually outdoors. The following transpired:

1. Caller: (Boy rings bell and waits for an answer to his ring.)
2. Mother: Who's there?
3. Caller: Can your son come out?
4. Mother: What?
5. Caller: Can your son come out?
6. Mother: What do you want?
7. Caller: Can your son come out?
8. Mother: (pause) Who is it?
9. Caller: Jerry. Can your son come out?
10. Mother: Oh— No he can't come right now. (Closes the front door.)
11. Caller: When do you think he could come out?
12. Mother: (Silence, since mother has not heard, having closed the door before the boy spoke utterance 11.)
13. Caller: (leaves)

I want to make the following points about this piece:

1. One of the features of family arrangements consists of an ecological containment of members inside the confines of a physical setting, commonly thought of as a residence. Family members therefore carry on their household activities in a home territory. In this instance we find that home territories have entrance points, such as doors and front gates. Those who are bona fide residents of the territory have the right of free

passage into their own homes (as Piglet points out to the forgetful Pooh) and in fact need not knock or ring to ask permission to be granted entry. In the case at hand, adults have keys, and others wishing entry, such as household children, ring, wait for vioce identification, and without further question get passage by means of an electric button pressed by the door answerer. This does *not* constitute asking for and receiving permission where household members are concerned but merely requests clearance, a form of mechanical security to control the entry of *outsiders*. In other words it is an inconvenience to children of the house who may not own a key to the gate, the price paid for such security measures in big cities. But where nonhousehold members are concerned, entry does indeed involve the granting of permission to come in through the front door (guests are treated as temporary household members and therefore the simple clearance pattern of ring-voice identification-entry applies).

2. A child wishing to call on another child must attend to this problem of entering another home territory (whether gates, locks, closed front doors, or some other physical arrangements exist). Now as far as conversational interaction or a state of talk goes, *the child must be prepared to identify himself as a caller and likewise the person on whom he is calling*. He must therefore have at his disposal the conversational resources to make such relevant identifications as necessary conditions, perhaps, for paying a visit to another child or getting him to come out to play.

3. As the data shows, the opening of the interaction is founded upon the principle of getting an adequate identification from the caller *as a second step in the sequence*, the first being the summoning of a household member by the bell-ring. The structural parallel is to that of the opening sequences of telephone calls, as analyzed by Schegloff.[17] Where in telephoning activity the answerer speaks first after hearing the ring summon him, so too in the household entry situation in our data. But unlike the telephoning interaction, here the answerer provides a question that calls for explicit identification from the caller: "Who's there?" Unlike the telephone answerer, who cannot know where the caller is located, the door-bell answerer knows precisely his location and thereby presumably his most general intention: to speak to some member of the house and possibly to gain entry.

4. Now the boy caller in the data hears the mother's call for an identification, but rather than supplying it with an *identification term* he relies on voice recognition to do this identificational work. But it does

17. I borrow the notion of a summons from the detailed investigation of opening sequences of telephone conversations made by Schegloff (1968).

not. His question, moreover, is his reason for being there. Instead of identifying himself in the terms of reference carried within his utterance, he offers an identification of the one he is calling on, the thirteen-year-old boy of the house: "Can your son come out?"

5. What can be gathered from this question? The caller could have made an identification by using the boy's first name (*FN*), but instead he has selected a term from an altogether different set of possible calling terms. He uses what I might call a *relational term* that is one of a number of such terms applying to members of a unit of social membership called "family." The selection of "your son" is interactionally viable because the caller has performed an analysis of his interlocutor, the mother of the house. Hearing (not seeing) her as the mother, because either he is familiar with her voice or he assumes any woman's voice will typically be that of the mother of the house, he transforms his own identification term for his friend, a *FN*, used to address him, into relational terms for the benefit of the answerer. In other words, when a child talks to another child's mother he can refer to his friend in terms of his relationship to her as her son. Now another consideration about this selection procedure suggests itself, namely, that when a neighborhood child doesn't in fact know the name of a boy on the block he has played with in the past, he can formulate an identification using familial relationships in households. This is a conversational resource to accomplish the purpose of his call. Perhaps he just wants *someone* to play with.

6. The mother's failure to make voice identification leads her to ask the boy to repeat his first utterance. After he does, she still cannot identify him, so she then goes on to inquire about the purpose of his call: "What do you want?" The caller repeats himself for the third time, still waiting at the front gate and out of sight, and the mother calls once more for an identification of the caller. This is preceded by a brief pause in which she appears to be scrutinizing the voice for familiarity. It brings the boy's identification: "Jerry. Can your son come out?" He selects *fn*, but he doesn't employ a parallel term for the rest of his utterance, and continues to identify the boy of the house in family-relationship terms. I cannot prove it, but I would speculate that he does not know the *FN* of the boy of the house.

7. The mother then grasps fully the purpose of the call and what its interactional consequences might be, that her son is being asked to go outside and play. However, at that moment she knows that her son is playing with another child in the house, and also that he has not discerned the occasion of the caller's visit. This raises the next interesting point for our discussion. Instead of relaying the matter to her son, she instead tells the caller herself that he can't come out. Two aspects of this

suggest themselves for consideration of the nature of adult interventions in children's contacts and on the nature of children's rights. On the one hand, this mother has the entitlement, as does presumably any mother, to make decisions about contacts between her child and other children. On the other hand, she does not feel obligated to inform her son of the event *before closing it off* on her own. Finally, she does not show obligation to the caller to provide for future contacts by saying "Come back later," for example. So, in no sense has she assigned herself the responsibility of being a go-between in a fully developed way. Her intervention then might be characterized in terms of the parental rights she typically exercises to *answer for or talk for* her child. In this way we see that a child has restricted rights as a speaker, given that we do indeed find in many different situations that parents enforce their entitlements to speak for their own children. Needless to say, the restriction of rights to speak is intimately connected to the restrictions on responsibilities, such as the child's presumed responsibility to take appropriate courses of action or to make suitable interactional decisions where other children are concerned. By talking for her son, a mother can practice interactional control over household activity.

8. Finally, the sequence terminates when the caller places a question designed to provide for future contact, and, recognizing that the answerer has retreated inside the house, leaving only silence, he takes leave of the front gate, never having gained entry.

III. Some Basic Conversational Resources for Children's Interaction

In this section, the major part of my analysis, I want to convert the findings of the previous data analysis into some key issues on the nature of children's conversational resources in everyday interactional circumstances.

There appear to be two classes of conversational resources of the most general significance for interaction. One has to do with the problem of referring to things, persons, and events in the world, or what we might simply call the problem of reference. The other class pertains to the problem of assigning serial and temporal order to interactional occurrences. This problem deals with the sequencing of events that participants perform over the passage of time. Accordingly, I will refer to these two resources in terms of *two procedural classes: (1) referential procedures and (2) sequential procedures*. In the pages that follow I will offer a very general description of some of these procedures. They provide interactants with adequate instruments for communicational competence. For lack of space, in this chapter, I will concentrate on referential procedures and only barely mention those pertaining to sequential phenomena. It should be kept in mind, however, that both sets of procedures are empirically coextensive, because conversationalists make referential talk only within unfolding sequential structures of conversation. While sequencing can be broken down into component steps taken in serial order on the smallest scale (a single two-person exchange, for example), it can also be comprehended in larger proportions approximating what might be thought of as bounded units of activity to the participants (a dinner, a visit, a play of a game, etc.). For this reason sequential problems for interactants may involve different and broader kinds of interactive attentions than referential ones; in face, a conversation does appear to require referential continuity for its interactional development.

IV. Referential Procedures

The problem of reference as it pertains to human speech abilities has been discussed and known about for a long time in linguistics, linguistic philosophy, and psychology. In one of the more recent treatments, one that explores the biological foundations of language production, by the way, Lenneberg defines the problem as man's cognitive organization of the relation between words and things. Lenneberg (1967:329) inquires into "the role that our capacity for naming may play in man's organization of cognition." In the naming function in cognitive reference, Lenneberg (1967:332) argues, words are treated as labels for what he calls a categorization process. He says in this regard:

> The words that constitute the dictionary of a natural language are a sample of labels of categories natural to our species; they are not tags of specific objects . . . most words may be said to label realms of concepts rather than physical things. This must be true for otherwise we should have great difficulty in explaining why words refer to *open* classes.

With respect to this notion of open classes, Lenneberg (1967:332) points out that the child's early use of terms of reference for family members constitutes a cognitive categorization process.

> The infant who is given a word and has the task of finding the category labeled by this word does not seem to start with a working hypothesis that a specific, concrete object (his father) uniquely bears the name *daddy*; instead, initially the word appears to be used as the label of a general and open category, roughly corresponding to the adult category *people* or *men*.

I would like to propose that the framework of cognitive organization that Lenneberg offers is inadequate for our understanding of the problem of reference because it neglects the basic fact that referential activity is

H

organized interactionally. The child is not merely a "cognitive organizer," so to speak. He interacts with others in his household environment. He is required to attend to and identify their social presence in some contextually relevant and correct way. What a child learns to "think" about the naming process is from the start dominated by the actions of his words that are produced for the hearing and subsequent words and actions of others. That is, his words do things; they have powers that take effect in the arena of actions. Children learn very early in life that what they say has interactional consequences. It does not take very long for a child to systematically use terms such as daddy or mommy that apply as names of unique persons who stand in particular social relationships to him. Nor does it take very long for the child to know that other terms may be used as appropriate alternatives for those same familial persons, and still further, that other terms may not be appropriate alternatives for them. The point I am making is simply that naming or identifying are conversational phenomena if they are at all to be regarded as social phenomena, and that the relationship between words and social figures, for example, requires our understanding of interactional events where such relationships become used, known, and tested by everyday interlocutors.

It appears to be the case that children are confronted with interactional problems of reference even before they acquire minimal linguistic skills to speak competent sentences in their native language. Holt (1969:62) offers some illustrations in his experience that nicely point out the very early interactional basis for referential talk:

> One day, when Danny . . . was very small, I was watching him play. He had not really begun to talk; there were only half-a-dozen or so "words" that he could say. At this time he was much interested in a big alarm clock. . . . Seeing the clock on the mantlepiece, he began to make an insistent, one-syllable noise, which he kept on making until someone gave him the clock. It seemed clear that he was not just saying "clock", or some baby equivalent of "clock". What he was saying was, "I want that clock, I need that clock, give me that clock!"

Despite the child's linguistic incompetence—his word was not correct as a label for the object—he was able to interactionally accomplish a request by his speech. Holt (1969:63) gives another illustration, this one showing how a child can refer not just to physical objects like clocks or persons but to courses of social action as well.

> Some of Tommy's first words were not names of things, but other kinds of words. When he was still little enough to be carried around a good deal of the time, he used to show where he wanted to go to whomever was carrying him by pointing his hand in the desired direction and saying, imperiously, "Way!" When he said this tone, I used to answer, "Way," and then add, using my language, "Shall we go over this way?" Another of his early words was

"Down". If he was being carried, "Down" meant "Put me down." If he wasn't being carried, "Down" meant "Pick me up."

V. Selecting an Identification by Means of Social Categories

Early uses of referential procedures involve the application of social category terms for addressing, for referring *in absentia*, and for distinguishing what persons appropriately can be called. The child at a very early stage in life is confronted with one very basic problem of reference, practically speaking – how to go about selecting an identification for another. The following material illustrates the very young child's first attempts at using referential procedures. It is from the notes of a mother reported by Church (1966:217,235,243– 44,259).[18]

> a. at 11 months: Whenever Ruth sees an infant or a child in a carriage, or even a toddler, she says "Hi, babee."
>
> b. at 11 months: If I scold Ruth and slap her hand for doing something she shouldn't, she either hits her own hand or mine and says in a scolding tone, "Da-da-da", which means "bad", I think, in addition to "Daddy" and some other things. But while "da-da" means several things, "Ma-ma" now means only "mother".
>
> c. at 15– 16½ months: When Ruth sees any of our friends who have babies, she says, "Baby, baby", whether or not the baby is present.
>
> d. at 17– 18 months: It isn't confusing yet to Ruth that I am "Mother", "Ellen", and "Mommy" or that my husband is "Karl,", "Daddy", or "Father". . . . Lately she calls me "Mommy Ellen".
>
> e. at 19 months: Ruthie connects couples. Whenever she hears someone's name, she adds the name of the spouse and the baby. Example: "Herb-Elaine and baby Janet".

Geertz (1961:34) reports about a Japanese family household in which a mother, separated from her husband, returned with her small son to her parent's home:

> Tuti's son Ta, aged one and a half, was the pet of his grandmother, who still had children of her own aged about 10 and older. Ta called his grandmother "mother" and his grandfather, "father", partly following the usage of his own mother toward them and partly because he was taught so by the affectionate grandmother. His own mother he called by her name, a familiar practice usually only permissible toward kin younger than oneself.

This child appeared, then, to have solved the task of selecting an identification for other household members by using referential terms for them interactionally mobilized by those around him; that is, he called his grandparents what his mother called them and his grandmother what his grandmother instructed him to call her. From this illustration we find

18. See also Weir (1962).

that referential procedures and terms are not found by the analyst by looking for kin terms in the family, for example, that are used only in accordance with consanguinal rules of address, as anthropologists refer to them. The Javanese child called his biological mother by her proper name and used the biological kin terms normally reserved for the parent-child relationship for nonparents. A similar case would be in our own culture when a husband addresses his wife with "mother" in the presence of his children. He is calling *their* mother what he knows is a term of reference used by *them*.

The child's problem in using referential procedures in the family household appears quite complicated from the start because of the wide range of alternative selections of social categories that he can make in given interactional circumstances; that is, who can be called what in the presence of relevant others, when speaking either to or about them. It is important to distinguish between situations where referential procedures are used for those present or absent to the speaker. One way of conceptualizing this distinction is to say that the child learns to use different procedures when he talks *to* others as compared to when he talks *about* others. A four-year-old boy expressed the relevance of this distinction when his father overheard him speaking to his mother, using his father's first name, which was not common practice for him to do. The father asked the child when he called him by his name and when he called him "daddy." The child replied: "I call you daddy when I'm telling you something." His father then inquired further into when he called him by his first name and the child replied: "When I'm talking about you."[19] The point I want to stress here is that probably the child very rarely used this *in absentia* procedure as an optional way of referring to his father, but that it was part of a real repertoire of possibilities apparently governed by the child's perceived social constraint upon proper forms of address for his father.

Schneider (1968:83–84) has spelled out the range of normal alternatives for referential terms in American kinship. It should dispel any idea that socialization to referential procedures is based upon the acquisition of only a few basic terms for identifying and calling others in the household. He says:

> The first point which must be made is that there is a wide variety of *alternate* terms and usages applicable to any particular kind of person as a relative. To put it another way, there are far more kinship terms and terms for kinsmen than there are kinds of kinsmen, or categories of kinsmen.
>
> Mother may be called "mother", "mom", "ma", "mummy", "mama", "old woman", or by her first name, nickname, a diminutive, or a variety of other designations, including unique or idiosyncratic appellations, sometimes re-

19. Author's field notes.

lated to baby-talk. Father may be called "father", "pop", "pa", "dad", "daddy", "old man", "boss", or by his first name, nickname, a diminutive, or a variety of less commonly used designations, including unique or idiosyncratic appellations, sometimes related to baby-talk. Uncles may be addressed or referred to as uncle-plus-first-name, first name alone, or uncle alone. And so, too, aunts. Grandparents may be called "grandma", "grandpa", "gramma", "grapa", "nana"; last names may be added to distinguish "Gramma Jones" from "Gramma Smith". Cousins are addressed by their first name, nickname, a diminutive, or other personal forms of designation, or as cousin-plus-first-name ("Cousin Jill"). Son may be called "son", "sonny", "kid", "kiddy", "boy", or by his first name, nickname, or diminutive, or other forms of personal designation. And daughter may be called "girl", "sister", "daughter", by her first name, nickname, a diminutive, or sister-plus-first-name ("Sister Jane"), as well as idiosyncratic and personal forms. "Kid" as a form for child does not distinguish son from daughter. Brother may be "brother", brother-plus-first name, first name alone, nickname, diminutives, or personal forms. Sister may be "sister", sister-plus-first-name, first name alone, nickname, diminutives, or personal forms.

What I want to stress about this list of possible referential alternatives is not that the researcher can simply make a list of them, as Schneider has done, but that he can also search out their *systematic procedural basis* in family interaction. That is, by examining their conversational use he can attempt to describe the child's practices of selecting identifications for others in the family household.

A further procedure that a child can use involves his knowing an identification term for all the family members as *a unit of membership*. That is, he can refer to his family as "my family" or "our family," or his family's residence as "my house" or "our house," which adds the locational or territorial aspect to the referential procedure. Schneider points out that "members of the family" can be differentiated from "the family as a cultural unit."[20] That is, in some sense the child learns that all of his relatives (another identification term for a whole collection of familially related persons), are referentially distinguishable with respect to the unit he calls "family." The latter constitutes for the child a stable set of categories used in everyday interaction with household members. In cases where extended relatives, such as grandparents or uncles, are permanent household residents, the child presumably acquires suitable methods of reference that take on additional categorials. In other words, the composition of the unit he calls his family consists of various stable identifiable members whose daily presence establishes interactional re-

20. Schneider (1968:30–31). The following bit of data is instructive on this issue. It is shortly after Christmas and a mother is visiting another mother's home, during which visit she asks the young boy of the house what he got for Christmas. He brings up a particular gift:

quirements for the child's use of referential procedures. In other words, referential demands are placed upon his speech interaction relative to each and every member.

To summarize the discussion so far, one major problem in the child's socialization to family life is how he competently used referential terms for relevant others in the family membership unit. The correct use of referential procedures for naming others comprises one part of the child's cultural apparatus pertaining to typical family arrangements and to the structure of social relationships these arrangements encompass.

I would like to consider more closely the reciprocal and relational aspects of categories. In a recent paper Goodenough (in Banton,1965:1-24) states that individuals have a number of different social identities, and that rights and duties are operative according to whatever identity they assume in interactional circumstances. The interactional environment for the enactment of a particular identity is criterial for member's interpretations of it, because rights and duties are interactionally achieved on the spot, and Goodenough correctly attacks the sociological convention of treating rights and duties as properties of *an* actor in a particular status rather than as properties of interaction of actors in concrete situations. Goodenough offers a clue to referential procedures when he refers to "identity selection", or how a member comes to possess a particular social identity as a recognizable social fact in everyday interaction. Given a multiplicity of identities, and given that he has more available to him than he can occupy at any one time, the task of an interactant is to "select from among his various identities those in which to present himself" (Goodenough, in Banton, 1965:37). We quote Goodenough's elaboration of the selection problem at length

36. Child 4½ years:	No I didn't get the boots from Santa. I got it from my friend.
37. Mother:	From grannie, she's your friend.
38. Child:	They are our friends.
39. Mother:	Yes, but they are also our relatives. There's a difference you know.
40. Child:	They are not in our family are they?
41. Mother:	Yes they are. Grannie is so in our family, just like nana is in our family.
42. Child:	Is she in our family?
43. Mother:	Not in our family of you, daddy, and Alan, but she's in our family.
44. Child:	How could she be in our family?
45. Mother:	She's daddy's mommy.
46. Child:	Because she, because daddy was born with grannie. Is that why?
47. Mother:	Yes.

(SFT 4, M. Nowakowsky, transcriber.)

An analysis of utterance 43 would exhibit some features of the family membershipping process, that is, of counting the members, listing them, as in one unit collection at home versus another unit collection for those not in the household.

because it provides a preliminary basis for the next part of our discussion, namely, a specific consideration of Sacks' analysis of the problem of categorization. Goodenough (in Banton, 1965:38) says the following:

Several considerations govern the selection of identities. An obvious consideration is an individual's (or group's) qualifications for selecting the identity. Does he in fact possess it? He may masquerade as a policeman, for example, donning the symbols that inform others of such an identity, and yet not be one. People often pretend to social identities for which they are not personally qualified, but such pretence is usually regarded as a serious breach of one's duties to fellow-members of one's peace group, duties that attach to one's identity as a member of a human community.

Another consideration is the occasion of an interaction. For any society there is a limited number of culturally recognized types of activity. The legitimate purposes of any activity provide the culturally recognized reasons for interactions, and they in turn define occasions. The same individuals select different identities in which to deal with one another depending on the occasion. For example, I may call upon someone who is in fact both my physician and my personal friend because I wish to be treated for an illness or because I wish to invite him to dinner. The purpose that specifies the occasion for the interaction determines whether I assume the identity of 'patient' or 'personal friend' in approaching him.

The setting, as distinct from the occasion, might also seem to be an obvious consideration in identity selection. For example, the same individual may or may not assume the identity of chairman of a meeting depending on what other persons are present, but here we are really dealing with the factor of qualifications for assuming an identity, already mentioned. Or again, when I invite my physician friend to dinner, how I approach him depends on whether or not one of his patients is a witness to the transaction, but this is not so much a matter of identity selection as it is a matter of choosing among alternative ways of honoring one's duties and exercising one's privileges. I suspect that settings are more likely to affect how one conducts oneself in the same identity relationship than to govern the selection of identities, but this is a matter requiring empirical investigation.

An important consideration is that, for any identity assumed by one party, there are only a limited number of matching identities available to the other party. If two people enter an interaction each assuming an identity that does not match the one assumed by the other, they fail to establish a relationship. The result is ungrammatical, and there is social confusion analogous to the semantic confusion that results from story-completion games in which no one is allowed to know anything but the last word that his predecessor in the game has written down. We take care to employ various signs by which to communicate the identities we wish to assume, so that others may assume matching ones and we can interact with mutual understanding. Any pair of matching identies constitutes an identity relationship.

It is noteworthy that different identities vary as to the number of identity relationships that are grammatically possible for them within a culture. But in all cases the number appears to be quite limited. Thus in my culture the identity relationships 'physician-physician', 'physician-nurse', 'physician-patient' are grammatical, but there is no such thing as a 'physician-wife' relationship or a 'physician-employee' relationship. The physician must operate in the identity 'husband' with his wife and in the identity 'employer' with his employees.

Finally we must consider that the parties to a social relationship do not ordinarily deal with one another in terms of only one identity-relationship at a time. The elderly male physician does not deal with a young female nurse in the same way that a young male physician does, and neither deals with her as a female physician does. In other words, identities such as old adult, young adult, man, and woman are as relevant as are the identities physician and nurse. Some identities are relevant to all social interactions. In my culture, for example, I must always present myself to others as an adult and as a male. This means that I am ineligible for any identity that is incompatible with being adult and male. Among the various identities that I do possess and that are compatible with these two, not all are compatible with one another, nor are they always mutually exclusive as to the occasions for which they are appropriate. The result is that for any occasion I must select several identities at once, and they must be ones that can be brought together to make a grammatically possible composite identity. In order to avoid confusion I shall reserve the term identity for anything about the self that makes a difference in social relationships, as defined earlier. The composite of several identities selected as appropriate to a given interaction consitutes the selector's social persona in the interaction.

The selection of identities in composing social relationships, then, is not unlike the selection of words in composing sentences in that it must conform to syntactic principles governing (1) the arrangement of social identities with one another in identity relationships, (2) the association of identities with occasions or activities, and (3) the compatibility of identities as features of a coherent social persona.

I would now like to take up referential procedures with respect to Sacks' (1966a:Chapter 2) analysis of *the problem of categorization*. The issue to keep in mind throughout the following abstract discussion is simply this: Is there a systematic basis for the child's selection of what to call others that has to do with the way referential terms for others are relationally organized? Earlier in this chapter I cited Lenneberg's remark that the infant first cognitively categorizes his father as 'daddy' by reference to an open class of possible categories, of which probably 'men' and 'adults' are co-members. Whether or not that is the case (after speech is acquired), the child can quickly come to see that 'daddy' is connected to other categories like itself, such as 'mommy,' and that the two can be co-members in class of categories, 'family.' I want to explore the issue that categories can be organized with respect to how they are used in everyday interactional activities.

Sacks has given the problem of categorization a very detailed treatment, but I will report upon his general discussion only. He says that a child acquires various social categories that members of his culture actually use when they interactionally select identifications for other group members. These categories are taken by members of the culture to go together quite naturally, claims Sacks. They constitute not merely random combinatorial properties but "natural groupings of categories" from the point of view of their users. Sacks terms these natural collections of categories *'membership categorization devices'*. A device (abbreviated MCD) consists of some collection of categories plus rules of application to concrete interactional circumstances.

The selection problem is observed when a device is paired with an actual group or "population" of persons, given that a device must contain *at least* one category and a population *at least* one member. Sacks refers to the referential selection in this pairing operation as the 'problem of categorization' or alternatively, the *'convergence problem of categorization'*. Membership categories are the terms of reference by which *persons* may be classified. Some common examples would be 'female,' 'teacher,' 'husband,' 'child,' 'first baseman,' and 'employer.' The ways in which such categories as these are naturally grouped is an empirical question in every case. Members of the culture organize particular categories in standard ways. For example, 'male' and 'female' are grouped together to form the collection called 'Sex,' 'white' and 'Negro' to form the collection referred to as 'Race,' etc. The MCD consists of these standard groupings plus rules for applying the collection to a given set of persons.

Sacks (1966a:16) poses the selection problem more sharply in his discussion of the relevant competing ways persons can be categorized in interaction, the resolution of the categorization problem being quite central to interactional activity.

> Let us suppose that there is always available more than one device, more than one collection of categories, of which any group of persons, no matter what size, may be categorized. If that is the case, then at all times there will be a choice to be made as to which of the available devices is to be used. Now it is quite clear that there are some devices which are appropriate and useable for only a delimited set of persons. Take the device 'occupation,' for example. In classifying young children that device would not be appropriate, that is, one could not assign a category from among that device's categories to each and every child from among some set of children to be classified. Now if all Devices had this quality—were applicable only to limited collections of people—then the task of categorization might for many occasions be as follows: Select that device which exclusively describes the set of persons at hand, and use that device on them. The issue of correct categorization would be, has the correct category from the device been applied to the person at hand?

H*

As Sacks points out, however, since devices don't have this quality of exclusiveness, the issue of correctness is not as pertinent as the issue of alternative selections—all being possible. If more than one device is appropriate for use in categorizing any set of persons regardless of size, "It would not be a question of simply finding that Device which fits persons at hand, but, more importantly, the problem would 'which of several appropriate devices is to be used'" (Sacks, 1966a:17). Therefore the task would consist of persons using some principled selection procedure to decide which among competing categorizations is relevant to the interactional occasion. From this we see that the main question about categorization activity is not whether the "right" category has been selected for an interactant, but *which out of the possible alternatives is selected* for the relevant purpose of immediate membershipping in interactional circumstances. This distinction is germane to the phenomenon, since it is not the job of an analysis of categorizing activity to list devices and their categories and show independently how particular selections are 'correct' ones irrespective of their actual use. Rather than formulating for 'correctness of use' (in the manner of a "correspondence theory" of categorization terms), the aim is to discover the *procedural basis of 'relevantly correct'* alternative selections of membership categories by interactants engaged in making selections.

In addition to those devices that are not adequate to the task of categorizing *any* set of persons (occupation, for example), there are those that can adequately do that job for *any collection of persons whatsoever;* that is, they are treated by those persons as 'omnirelevant.' The continual problematic character of categorization is due in part to this fact because by virtue of these devices, which Sacks calls Pn-adequate devices (where P stands for population and n for any size), the relevance problem in competing categorizations is always present. For example, there are the Pn-adequate devices called 'Sex,' 'Age,' and 'Race,' to name only a few. They are always available for categorizers' use. The issue of their competing relevance is appreciated by the fact that the categories of a Pn-adequate device belong to that device and to no others, for example, the *Pn*-adequate device 'Sex': 'male' and 'female.' If Pn-adequate devices contained each other's categories, the issue of strict choice between devices would not be posed sharply enough to provide for their competing relevance.

The existence of multiple devices and Pn-adequate devices creates a range of alternative category assignments for interactants' membershipping purposes. When interactants engage in mutual categorizing activity they must decide in a principled way what device or devices to use, such that they both (or all) recognize the categorial selections at hand. Problems they face in treating each other similarly, in terms of the same device, are problems in 'convergence', of categorizations, as Sacks refers to them. To better delineate the problem of convergence let us consider briefly some of the rules of application of MCDs.

The first rule Sacks (1966a:22) calls the 'consistency rule.' It holds only for the use of Pn-adequate devices.

> If, on some occasion, a Pn-adequate Device is appropriate for some portion of a population N, then it may be used as a device to categorize the whole population being categorized.

Thus, if the first member of a population is categorized appropriately as 'female', it then follows that others in the population can be categorized as either 'female' or 'male'. The import of the 'consistency rule' for the general interactional task of categorization is stated by Sacks (1966a:23) in the following passage:

> If any population N consists of at least two members, i.e. requires at least two categorizing 'acts' to complete the job of categorizing, then it is possible that though one device would be 'adequate', that two or more devices can be used. This we have already seen. That is, some members . . . could be categorized by reference to one device's categories, while other member(s) could be categorized by reference to another device. For example, if I see two humans I could call one a 'man' and the other a 'Negro', or one a 'shortstop' and the other a 'baby'. If there are two investigators doing the categorization or two members of the society categorizing some collection of others, then a problem exists as regards the outcome reproduceability of their respective categorizations. Outcome reproduceability of categorization (both from the standpoint of the investigator and the actors) *requires* the use of the 'consistency rule' or some 'combining rules' (e.g. use categories from device I from persons N-1 through N-10 and then use categories from device II for persons N-9 through N( ). This is so even if we are dealing with the production of each categorizer separately, or if there is only one categorizer. That is to say, the problem of 'convergence' . . . must be handled by reference to the 'consistency rule', and, even if only one person . . . is categorizing some population of persons, some form of 'consistency rule' must guide his activity if he is to produce a reproduceable classification, one, for example, that another investigator could later check out and verify. If no such rule were used he might proceed to categorize some persons by using the categories of this device and others by that device's categories, willy-nilly.

In addition to the 'consistency rule' Sacks formulates what he calls the 'economy rule.' This rule is devised to handle the fact that in our culture single categories of single MCDs are often sufficient to the task of referring to a person. They are 'referentially adequate' to achieve categorization in social interaction. The possibility of achieving it by using categories singly from a particular device (that is, that it is referentially adequate to identify someone by saying of him simply that he is a 'doctor' or a 'boy,' etc.) can be stated as an 'economy rule':

> From the member's standpoint it is the case that for any population N, on

some occasions of categorizing its members, the task can be complete if each member of the population has had a single category applied to him (Sacks, 1966a:26).

Sacks suggests the general relevance of this rule for the child's socialization. The child learns appropriate ways to describe his social environment, as evidenced by his acquiring the ability to make utterances like the following:

> The daddy works in the bank. And mommy cooks breakfast. Then we get up and get dressed. And the baby eats breakfast and honey (Sacks, 1966a:26).
>
> The mommy's baby was crying. The baby was eating. Then the baby went to bed. Then the mother was gone. The baby woke up. The mother was home. The baby was playing with the toys. Then her daddy came. Then the mother went to bed. That's all![21]

Recalling the instance of data analyzed in section two, I take it that one of the child's resources for conversing with the mother who answered the door was a categorization procedure for identifying the boy he calls on. To accomplish the purpose of his call he can select from alternative and competing categories and identifier terms. Obviously the categories 'boy', 'kid', 'child', 'eighth-grader', 'joker', etc., are all possibly correct but not relevant. Each would involve the operation of a different MCD than the one used in the data. Noting once again Goodenough's discussion of identity relationships, I now want to raise another key point about categories.

The child's selection of "your son" shows that he has competently performed a referential procedure that takes into account the interactional relevance of his fellow conversationalist. His interlocutor was in fact the boy of the house's mother and he treated her as such. His selection of "your son" involves his assignation of "his (the other boy's) mother" to the voice that answers his summons. That is, he performs a transformation of terms within a given category set, the MCD 'Family.' The availability of referential procedures allowing for such categorial transformations clearly indicates that children use the rules Sacks describes under the problem of category convergence.

Another property of categorization is suggested by this data. Not only are categories multiply organized into collections of MCDs, they are also organized into pairs. These pairs constitute standardized social relationships (Sacks has called them "standardized relational pairs"). There are referential procedures, therefore, that involve the use of category pairs, or what we might call categorial relationships ('Fa-

21. Author's field notes, dictated by a first grader to his teacher who copied it verbatim with typewriter. I wish to thank Kai George for the loan of her collection of stories recorded while teaching at Longfellow School, Berkeley, California. The making of stories was an occasional classroom activity that children were invited to participate in. Family categorizations are uniformly present in them.

ther--son', 'adult-child', 'brother-sister', 'teacher-student', catcher-pitcher', etc.). In the data, the child employs the categorial relationship pair 'mother-son.' Embodied in categorization practices by pairs by categories is what Schutz has called the "reciprocity of perspectives."[22] One crucial aspect of interactional reciprocity pertains to the regulation of social obligations and constraints that hold between respective category pair positions. The pairs align social actors according to the mutually respected rights and obligations attached to the categories and therefore to the incumbents of the categories.

In the data, then, the child's selection of "your son" invokes a structure of obligations and entitlements that are bound to the category pair 'mother-son'. The way in which the child formulates his utterance, which he tenaciously sticks to, is a clue to this structure: "Can your son come out?" He is invoking her right to judge the situation and to grant permission for the occasion (in other words, he is not simply inquiring into the other boy's voluntary availability). The mother's enactment of her categorial entitlements is found in her answer to the boy: she talks for her son and decides his appropriate course of action without conferring with him about it. Consider, for example, had the boy said "Can your brother come out?" whether the kind of analysis he had performed of his interlocutor would have involved very different sorts of categorial procedures.

VI. Selecting an Identification by Means of Personal Names

The second set of referential procedures I will discuss involves the use of naming, in the literal sense of the notion, by means of personal name terms. Beginning with a very simpleminded notion of a personal name, we can recognize that every member of a household has a full version of a personal name, some string of name terms, no less than two, first and last (or abbreviated, FN and LN). Such a full version may be thought of as an "official" name, often used for legal purposes. However, it would be decidedly simpleminded to use a list of official names gathered from bureaus of records to decide what versions of names persons use in everyday household interaction. Some naming practices involve no apparent relation to official name versions. Some versions of each member's name are used regularly by only particular persons in the family, while some versions are used by everybody in it. There are also constraints upon who uses which particular version for a member. As a rule in our culture parents call each other by their first names (FN) and

22. See Schutz (1962:1-47) and in this volume, Cicourel's discussion of the "reciprocity of perspectives" principle.

parents call children by FN too. On the other hand there is a strong constraint against children's calling their parents by FN, although in some families this rule is relaxed.

Name options will also depend upon given interactional circumstances. For example, when outsiders are present, naming rules may differ when various family members with the outsiders. A visiting child may be one of the few outsiders to regularly address a household parent with Title + Last Name (LN), for example, Mrs. Smith. There is no other alternative for the child if a constraint against FN is known to exist. Visiting children may be forced, then, to use referential forms other than names to speak to household adults if they do not select Title + LN. On the other hand, if a constraint against FN address is not presented to a visiting child he may select it and would be regularly using a term that might be proscribed for the children of the house. Nicknames, diminutives, and terms of endearment may be used by parents for their own children, while children and siblings may use nicknames and diminutives among themselves. The family name (LN) may be used to identify the family unit in interaction by either members or outsiders, for example, "We eat nothing but the best in the Smith household," "Smith residence" (on the phone), "Welcome to the Smiths," "We're the Smiths of Scarsdale," "Are you the Smiths?" Children can use FN + LN when referring to a child who is visiting the house; for example, "Can I ask Philip Smith to come over?" These are some of the alternative names that can be found more regularly than others. Highly private or personalized names can often be found among family members, especially for children.

Our concern is not primarily to compile an inventory of name alternatives in given families as findings in themselves, although knowledge of them is necessary for examining what we do in fact want to study about personal name usages. The purpose of an examination of these terms is to detect their interactional properties as referential procedures. Sacks makes the point that naming is misleadingly thought of as "just naming." He suggests that in order to see the interactional power of names one should look to see what else is occurring when a name is used in one of its possible versions. That is, given a particular selection, what does that tell us about social organization and how naming is one aspect of achieving and sustaining that organization? With reference to introductions, Sacks says:

> The question is—forgetting about the fact that first names are used, for now—what is being done with those names. When I talked about 'naming' . . . you might have come to the conclusion that if something other than a correct name is used, then some action may be being done. But, that wouldn't be worried about if what's an obviously correct name is being used. Then

'just naming' is being done. In the case at hand, names used in introductions seem to involve the doing of an instruction to the parties concerned, as to what they may call each other. Now that makes the matter initially interesting, in that we could then ask 'how does A get off telling B and C what they should call each other'. Assuming that it's perfectly plain to you . . . that not anybody has any right to call anybody any particular name they may choose, of the various alternative ways that names are used. I once asked a class to . . . write out, over a day, what version of their name they were called. And they found, first of all, considerable orderliness to that; but by no means that they were called a name. Nor would they figure that the various persons on their list could interchangeably use those names that they were called by somebody. And not only could X not pick up the name by which Y called you, but that you could not insist that X do so if you wanted to. And this is apart from the issues of the way in which what name they call you is informative about what name you should call them. . . .

But then there's the further matter, which in its way in the end might be the most interesting matter, and that is that the doing of naming here is also the doing of an instruction. It is the most interesting because it's two different issues: one of them turns on how you can go about doing instructions; and the other is, is it generic that whenever persons do naming they're also doing something else—perhaps indeed, that they do naming is a procedural rule which says when you find they're doing 'naming', look then for something else that they're also doing. That would have some considerable consequences.[23]

Personal names, then comprise another set of referential resources that a child can draw upon in conversational interaction, and his selection of particular versions for particular interlocutors, including himself, may be informative of social organization, beyond the mere information it conveys about the namer per se. Thus the interesting analytic question Sacks poses is "Given a name use what does it accomplish interactionally?" This sort of question is counterposed to "What names do persons actually use?" In itself the latter is not as analytically productive as the former. In this light I want to briefly consider our instance of data again.

This is a social contact between a child and an adult who is not his parent. He does not select an identification for this adult in a manner appropriate to selecting one for his own mother. What he is interactionally faced with is the task of selecting an identification for an adult who is the parent of another child. We can note that children .regularly confront circumstances in which they must talk to adults who for them fall into the general category of membership 'other children's mothers.' Interacting under the auspices of this class, as contrasted to, say, the category 'babysitters,' the child treats the adult as an incumbent

23. Sacks, Lecture 7, spring quarter, 1967, pp. 8–9.

of a family category that is itself modified by another identification term applied to the child he calls on; for example, the adult is treated as his friend's mother, or Dave's mother, or still, the boy down the block's mother.

The relevance of this point for our discussion of personal names is as follows. I want to suggest that a general analytic principle of some importance has to do with what we might characterize as *the principle of a relevantly absent phenomenon.*[24] I will illustrate this principle with the familiar class of speech acts known as introductions. Suppose a group of known persons are engaged in some mutual interactional focus within an occasion, say a dinner party, and a new member, not known to all the present parties, joins the group. Suppose further that one member, perhaps the host, selects identification terms to introduce the new arrival in the following manner: "Ronald, this is Bill Blake, George Young, James Fuller, and this is Dr. Robinson. This is Ronald Burton." The hose provides everyone with an instruction as to what they can be appropriately called for that and perhaps other occasions. He uses a FN to address the new arrival, which shows their social relationship has been accorded a first-name basis. Only at the end does he instruct the others as to his LN. In the round of introductions we see that he selects FN + LN for all but one person. This interactant is identified by Title + LN. We may say his FN is missing in a round where it was otherwise used for everyone else, in other words, FN is relevantly absent from this introduction sequence. Obviously Dr. R. has a FN, but the host refrains from using it, despite the possibility he might know and use it when he is alone with him. Without going any further into it here, this interactionally accomplishes an honorific identification.

Relevantly absent phenomena can arise in many circumstances, not only in interactional rounds such as introductions, though there they are strikingly visible, perhaps because of sequential organization. In our data I want to argue that the personal names of the caller as well as the called-on are relevantly absent to the participants. The child has four opportunities to provide the door answerer with an identification of himself, and not until the fourth turn at talking does he use a FN to do so, the first three not producing any terms for that purpose at all. I take it that *in this occasion, identification by personal name is crucial to the interactional outcome of the call.* That is, the nature of this whole interactional sequence consists of what we might call an occasion that demands an explicit and spoken identification procedure. Consider by contrast, for example, the initiation of interactions between pedestrian greeters or customers and salesclerks that do not normally call for such

24. I borrow this notion from Sacks.

procedures, because relevant identifications are implicitly made. Activities of calling on others, gaining entry into homes and certain types of establishments, can interactionally *require* such identification procedures. The use of referential resources for identificational work in interactions of this kind enters into the child's communicative competence when moving about his neighborhood and beyond his home territory into the homes of others.

The relevant absence of the caller's personal name and, in fact, the absence of self-identificational speech is paralleled in the data by his omission of the personal name of the one he calls on. Could it be that identifying the boy of the house by means of categorial resources rather than by personal name tells us something about the relationship between identification of self and identifications of others? In the caller's question "Can your son come out?" the called-on's FN may be considered relevantly absent by the mother. It may not be known by the caller, and, reciprocally, the caller's name may not be known by the boy of the house or the mother. In other words, this neighborhood child was attempting to contact another child at his home and found that he had to employ certain referential procedures to do so, but, failing to employ those FN procedures normally used in identificational interactions of this sort, he was unable to complete the contact. Even after he produced his own FN he continued to use the categorial 'son' from the 'Family' MCD to identify the one he was calling on, which categorized the answering adult as 'the boy down the block's mother.'

One clue to this interpretation of the data is the nature of the recognition the mother gives the caller when he uses FN to identify himself. She merely says "Oh," and not something that formulates a recognition of the caller, such as a greeting. If in fact it is the case that the child is unknown to the members of the household and barely acquainted with the child he is calling on, we have a useful finding for the social organization of childhood. Children's culture may not require the same formal procedures for sociability as are found in the adult culture. In children's culture, for one thing, name-exchange may not take place when children engage in everyday activities on the street. Children seeking out others whose names they have not acquired may run into difficulties when adults intervene their contact interactions and are not so ready to permit them to occur on home territories in the same procedural manner with which they regularly take place on the neighborhood streets. More data is needed on these issues. Further, a child who knows these procedural distinctions between the cultures can use other referential resources in conversation to make contact indentifications possible with adult speakers.

VII. Sequential Procedures

I can only allude to the topical importance of studying the child's use of sequential procedures in conversation. Most generally such procedures pertain to coordination of interactions by conversationalists who have as their primary task keeping track of what others say and do as a progressive order of interactional events. If one thinks about it for a moment, to put the matter very simply, it is something short of miraculous that groups of speakers are able to fit their talk together so that it all comes out looking and sounding like a coherent conversation, given the fact that individuals could accomplish this project only by a concerted effort to monitor in the most detailed ways what their cultural fellows are up to at any moment. As automatic as the interaction process looks on the surface, it is always a concerted effort of individuals who perform ongoing analyses of each others' speech and actions. That is the heart of the issue being raised by some of the contributors to this volume—the procedural basis for concerted interactions and activities *necessarily presupposes* a human monitoring apparatus that orients to and skillfully regulates referential and sequential order in the everyday world. Theoretically speaking, this human inferential machinery and its "interpretive procedures," as Cicourel has called them,[25] provide for the practical rationality, or the "properties of practical reasoning," in Garfinkel's sense,[26] found in everyday life activity. Interactants monitor their concerted activities, in part, by means of procedures for interpreting sequential arrangements to ongoing events.

To return to our data, sequential procedures can be exhibited briefly in the interactional development that takes place, as we noted earlier, in the temporal space of about a minute. How can issues in sequencing be explored? We quite naturally begin at the beginning. Events in everyday life are bound to occasions and settings. They are interactions that have recognizable starting points and finishing points, not simply because we say they do but because the participants make them that way. How do interactants go about building interactional events? What procedures do they use to start an interaction? In the case of childhood social organization how do children initiate encounters with others, enter into a state of talk and get a conversation going, sustain and develop it, bring it to a close? I have explored these problems in detail elsewhere (Speier, 1969:154–286) and here I will address myself only to the relation between an occasion of activity, to concerted actions for some practical purpose that have an occasioned character, and conversational resources used to construct the temporal order of that occasion.

The data exhibit one prominent feature of housecalls, be it child or

25. See Chapter 6 in this volume.
26. See especially Garfinkel (1967:262–284).

adult who seeks to call and contact those inside a home territory. This is the feature of announcing one's presence. The announcement needs to be made to gain access to the ecology of the home, but normally only by outsiders. In this case an outsider (or an insider without a key) must announce his presence with a bell provided for that purpose. Thus the interaction is initiated by a ring that is a summons to any member of the household. As Schegloff (1967) has shown in his analysis of telephone conversations, a summoner has obliged himself to speak after his summons is acknowledged (unlike a questioner who has reserved himself a right to speak again, but who is not necessarily obligated to do so).[27] The sequential procedure of summoning in this homecall builds up an initial state of talk from an announcement method that calls for someone's acknowledgment, which is itself normally regarded as a social obligation (though one easily avoided). That acknowledgment is the first spoken action. It is followed by a second spoken action that the caller is obligated to make. This constitutes the opening structure of the occasion and it may be described in Schegloff's (1968:1081) terms as having the property of 'non-terminality,' that is, it is clearly a property of the occasion's opening structure since as a Summons-Answer sequence it could not appropriately occur as a terminal exchange in a conversation. In this obligatory structure generated by the opening procedure, the caller makes himself available for further interaction, just as the answerer has made himself available as the first speaker.

The child wishes to discover the availability of the other child, and his first speech, delivered under an obligation to state the purpose of his call, must employ a procedure that will do the job of discovering that availability. It should be noted immediately that the sequential structure of this occasion can take two distinctive alternations once the Summons-Answer sequence is completed: (1) the caller's first utterance gets him entry through the front gate and from there on through to the front door of the house where the door answerer may await the caller, or (2) the caller's first utterance does not get him entry. The question then is: How is one or the other alternative taken depending upon the concrete particulars of the caller's first speech? Thus the caller's utterance at this point in the sequential development of the interaction must be fashioned to do two things: first, show the status of his own availability for further interaction and, second, discover the availability of the child being called on. As we see from the data, the interaction gets "stalled" on the first item, and makes the second item known only toward the end of the entire sequence.

Now we can see the problem of a relevantly absent phenomenon

27. This point about the structure of questioning and answering has been developed by Sacks, Lecture 2, spring quarter, 1966.

more clearly, because what is absent is the identification being called for in the next slot after the mother's answer to the summons "Who's there?" Unlike telephone S-A structures, house calls of this kind regularly get this query in the A slot. This obligates the summoner to immediately identify himself and/or give the reason for announcing his presence. The slot for identificational work called for by "Who's there?" gets filled with "Can your son come out?" The caller's first utterance, then, does not identify him, but formulates an identification of the one he is relevantly calling on. Because he cannot know in advance who he will be speaking to first, the relevant identification must be made only by an immediate identification of his interlocutor.

The child's utterance does not serve to identify him to the mother. She is unable to make identification by acoustic memory, one possibility that overrides conversational procedures and that would permit a recognized voice immediate entry. Since she does not come down the stairs to make visual identification of the child, the mother must rely entirely on conversational productions. Her second utterance is a request for a repeat from the child and he does repeat exactly what he had initially said to her. The second time around it brings a question from the mother showing her failure to identify the child and to ratify the purpose of his call — why does the child want her son to come out? The nature of the occasion is therefore one of ambiguity about a question that normally is not ambiguous, providing caller identification has been made. That is, "Can your son come out?" normally means by ellipsis "Can your son come out to play?", which in the world of childhood organization is immediately understandable by adults as legitimate grounds for the request. The third speech of the mother shows quite definitely that she requires an identification before the subject of her son's availability can be considered: (pause) "Who is it?"

In utterance 9 the child finally identifies himself and repeats his purpose. Having made an identification, the structural part of the sequence built up around that interaction is completed, despite the fact that the mother apparently doesn't recognize the boy by his FN. In her last speech her answer to the question of her son's availability is "No he can't come right now" and without further consideration she retreats into the house. Not knowing this, the caller speaks again; not getting a reply about the future prospects of making contact with the boy of the house, he figures the mother is no longer available and leaves. Although questions normally bring answers from interactants, an unanswered question can indicate, even in cases of visual contact, a deliberate withdrawal of interactional participation. That is, the child didn't know for certain that his interlocutor was gone, but he didn't wait around too long before he inferred her absence. This is probably due to the nature of the mother's final remark as an utterance that can bring this occasion to a close. It handles the occasion in a way that leave its purpose unaccomplished. It was conceivable to the caller that the mother wasn't interested in providing for a future occasion when the children's contact might be made. It isn't possible to go into it any further here, but this is offered as a clue to the study of the organization of adult–child contacts in the everyday life of the child.

VIII. Conclusion

A new and unexplored question in socialization research asks how children use conversational resources in everyday interactions and activities. To answer it one must construct analyses of their everyday conversational productions as these occur, for instance, in family and household routines. I have addressed myself to only two general classes of such conversational resources. Clearly I have discussed but a few of the referential procedures a child comes to use in interactionally competent ways. A third and highly central class of resources would involve *pronouns*. I barely touched upon procedures involving sequential arrangements of interaction. I have ignored, for example, a direct examination of the central issue of how conversations get concertedly built by participants' orientation to distributing their speech by means of taking turns at talking. Sequential analyses would include detailed investigations on how participants fit their talk together. Where childhood social organization is concerned, the analysis would focus on children's conversational turn-taking and such coordinative phenomena as questions and answers, utterance completion units, interruptions, and jointly produced utterances.[28] How do children manage their methodical participation in these coordinated conversational productions? How do they utilize some of these conversational resources in the performance of routines like house calls, street contacts, greeting and summoning, leave-taking, topically eventful talk, play and game categorization practices, insulting, arguing, introductions, initiating conversation with adults, and so forth?

It has been my intention in this chapter to provide the reader with some basic guidelines for research on the conversational and interactive basis of the social organization of everyday childhood life.

28. I am deeply indebted to Sacks's ongoing analyses of these conversational problems and must credit him for bringing them to light and to my attention. See, for example, his penetrating analysis of the notion of an utterance and how members methodically orient themselves to producing them so as to interrupt or fit their own speech into others' utterances in the sequential development of a conversation without appearing to interrupt. Sacks, Lecture 3, October 12, 1967.

PART THREE

Rules, Situated Meanings, and Organized Activities

The Practicalities of Rule Use*

Introduction

Research interests in formal organizations traditionally have been guided by the basic conception of the employee as a specialized bureaucratic actor. The bureaucratic actor is seen as responsible for the systematic manipulation of an organizationally predefined environment of objects and events by the use of explictly stated policies and procedures designed to advance formally defined goals. A key element of this traditional perspective — however modified to handle intrusive "nonbureaucratic" elements in organizational life — is the view that the process and product of organizational activities is "administratively rational" to the degree that personnel comply with the intent (if not the letter) of formally instituted policies and procedures and commit themselves to the attainment of organizational goals.

This chapter examines certain aspects of the work activities of such bureaucratic actors in a public assistance organization.[1] Drawing on

* This study was inspired by and is heavily indebted to the work and teaching of Harold Garfinkel, as will be evident to those familiar with his seminal thought. The author would also like to acknowledge the many helpful suggestions on the manuscript given him by Aaron V. Cicourel, Thomas Mathiesen, D. Lawrence Wieder, and Thomas P. Wilson. The author alone is responsible for whatever errors or inadequacies may be found in this chapter.

1. Zimmerman (1966). The author was supported during the project by a National Science Foundation Cooperative Graduate Fellowship, which also provided a small research grant that facilitated the completion of the study. Further financial assistance was furnished by the project on "Decision-Making in Common-Sense Situations of Choice" carried on by Drs. Harold Garfinkel, Lindsey Churchill, and Harvey Sachs, sponsored by the Air Force Office of Scientific Research, Office of Aerospace Research, United States Air Force, under A.F.O.S.R. grant number 757–65. Other research funds contributing to this work were provided by the Faculty Research Committee, University of California at Santa Barbara. The author also wishes to express his deep gratitude to personnel at all levels of the Metropolitan County Bureau of Public Assistance and in particular to those with whom he worked in the Lakeside Office.

observational materials collected in the setting,[2] it describes in detail the
work of reception personnel in inducting applicants for public assistance
into the organizational routine. The analysis is concerned particularly
with the judgmental work of receptionists in employing a procedure for
assigning applicants to intake caseworkers.

The study reported here, however, is not concerned with how adequately the formal program of the organization and the structural arrangements whereby it is implemented provide for "rational" goal accomplishment.[3] Nor is it directed to the specification of the conditions
under which personnel comply with or depart from their prescribed
duties as set forth in the formal program, or come to be more or less
partisan to organizational objectives. Its primary concern is to investigate the variety of practices and mundane considerations involved
in determinations of the operational meaning and situational relevance of
policies and procedures for ongoing, everyday organizational activities.
The ways in which this concern contrasts with the traditional viewpoint
may be clarified by reference to the considerations below.

Numerous studies of formal organizations have found that some significant portion of the observed practices of bureaucrats are not easily
reconciled with the investigator's understanding of what the formally
instituted rules and policies dictate.[4] Bureaucrats, in conducting their
ordinary everyday affairs in organizations, have been seen in study after
study to honor a range of "formally, extraneous considerations in making decisions and concerting actions. The asserted contrasts between
theory and practice reported by organizational studies are so commonplace that documentation seems hardly necessary.

It is important to note how such contrasts are obtained.[5] The basic

2. These materials were gathered during a six-month period spent by the investigator in
the organization's Training Division and in one district office (see the description of the
setting below). The investigator was known to the personnel involved as a sociologist
working on his doctoral dissertation. Transcripts made from tape recordings of
work-related verbal interactions between personnel occurring throughout the workday
provided the bulk of the data. All recordings were made with knowledge and at least tacit
consent of the parties concerned. In addition to tape recordings, field notes were taken to
provide records of conversations and events that for one reason or another the investigator
was unable to record. Unstructured interviews were also conducted, usually aimed at
exploring the implications of particular practices or recent events in the setting from the
perspective of personnel. See Zimmerman (1966:Appendix on Method).

3. Bittner (1965:239-255). Bittner's article is concerned with a specification of the
relevance of Garfinkel's work for the study of formal organizations. Bittner's remarks in
this vein have proved to be a valuable resource for the proposals made in this work. The
discussion to follow closely parallels Bittner's article. See in particular Garfinkel
(1967:Chapter 6).

4. See for example: Anonymous (1946:365-370), Bensman and Gerver
(1963:558-598); Blau (1963); H. Cohen (1962); Dalton (1959); Page (1964:88-94); Roy
(1954:255-266); Scheff (1962:208-217); Turner (1947:342-348); and Zawecki (1963).

5. See Bittner (1965:240).

conception referred to above warrants the investigator's use of the formal plan of the given organization as a device for deciding the theoretical status of observed activities (as planned or unplanned, formal or informal). Such a procedure would seem to require, first of all, that the investigator "map out" the alternative possible behavioral dispositions called for by the rules. However, such decisions are typically made on an ad hoc basis. The investigator determines the deviant or conforming status of some activity or event upon encountering it without reference to a set of unambiguous criteria that specify the defining features of situations and the behaviors appropriate to such situations.[6]

By whatever means the investigator accomplishes these crucial decisions, it is typically the case that the issue of what such rules mean to, and how they are used by, personnel on *actual occasions* of bureaucratic work is ignored as an empirical issue. For the investigator to make decisions about rules without clarifying the basis of such decisions—particularly without reference to how personnel make such decisions—invites the treatment of rules as idealizations, possessing stable operational meanings invariant to the exigencies of actual situations of use, and distinct from the practical interests, perspective, and interpretive practices of the rule user. The practices employed by bureaucrats to render such idealizations relevant as prescriptions, justifications, descriptions, or accounts of their activities is lost to analysis by the investigator's unclarified interpretive work in turning the formal plan of the organization into the methodological purpose outlined above.

It is sometimes argued by students of organization that rules and policies are to some degree abstract and general, and hence by their very nature incapable of completely encompassing the perversely contingent features of manifold and changing organizational situations. This conception would seem to speak to the concerns of this chapter.

However, this "defect" of rules is typically dealt with by proposing that informal rules and policies develop in response to this lacuna that warrant modification, redefinition, or circumvention of the formal rule by personnel in light of operating conditions. Invoking one set of rules to account for the interpretation of another set dodges the issue.

In addition, this line of reasoning would propose that whatsoever patterned conduct is observed, it is formulable as conduct in accord with *some* rule. This view slights the question of *what it takes* to warrant the application of any rule—formal or informal—in concrete situations, thus failing to address as a crucial problem the judgmental processes that members must use to employ rules on relevant occasions.

A related issue of interest here is the way in which "departures" from

6. See the discussion by Wilson (1970) of the logical requirements imposed by the social-scientific use of the notion that conduct is rule governed.

the formal organizational plan are dealt with. It has been consistently found that bureaucrats ("governed by" rules and procedures designed to effect rational goal accomplishment) are keenly attuned to a number of practical matters at hand as these are grasped as constraints or facilities, justifications or contra indications, resources or troubles in the course of pursuing bureaucratic work. Indeed, these practical matters often seem to be critical elements informing the bureaucrats' use of the rules, resources, and formal arrangements of the organization.

Investigators typically invoke such features of the bureaucrats' circumstances, and their situationally enforced interests in coming to terms with them, in order to account for the asserted discrepancy between the formally ordained and observed "actual" state of organization affairs. These circumstances are often conceived to be obstacles—or problems to be solved—on the way to rational goal accomplishment. Organization members' ways of dealing with these states of affairs are examined in the interest of deciding whether or not they constitute "functional" or "dysfunctional" detours en route to the ideal of administrative rationality presumably embodied to some degree in the formal plan of the organization.

In contrast, the problem that concerns this chapter is how the formal plan of an organization (or some aspect of it) is used by the organization's members to deal with everyday work activities. What are the features of the sanctioned courses of common-sense judgment that members use to recognize, to interpret, and to instruct others about the operational intent and behavioral implications of such a plan? Thus conceived, the problem dictates, first of all, that the relationship of the formal plan to actual conduct be investigated with specific reference to how members of the organization reconcile the two on a day-to-day basis. This approach also leads to a revision of the theoretical treatment of the range of practical circumstances typically confronted by the bureaucrat. This revision consists in entertaining the possibility that these circumstances may in fact be consulted by bureaucrats in order to decide what the formal plan might reasonably be taken to mean and "what it would take" to implement it in the first instance.

This argument is not to be taken to mean that rule violations do not occur, or that bureaucrats might not respect alternative informal rules in doing their work—although the latter distinction as it is usually drawn would require modification. The point is that the issue of what rules, policies, and goals mean for the bureaucratic actor upon the concrete occasion of their use (for example, to guide, to account for, or to justify action) must be treated as problematic. In accordance with this view, the major assumption guiding the present endeavor is that the relationship of such idealizations to conduct may be found only by investigating the features of the circumstances in which they are deemed relevant and used by members.[7]

Following a brief discussion of the setting of the study, receptionists' use of an intake assignment procedure will be described in detail. This procedure is examined within its organizational context, with close attention paid to the features of actual occasions of its use and the contingencies encountered upon these occasions. Analysis will suggest that the operational import of formal rules and organizational policy (of which the assignment procedure is an instance) is decided by personnel on a case-by-case basis and warranted on "reasonable grounds."

It will be argued that the "reasonableness" of such decisions, from the point of view of personnel, relies upon a taken-for-granted grasp of, and implicit reference to, the situated practical features of task activity (actual task structure).[8] The chapter will suggest an alternative to the compliance model of rule use typically employed in sociological studies of rule-governed behavior: a notion of competent rule use.

The Setting

The study was conducted in one district office of the Metropolitan County Bureau of Public Assistance, located in a large western state. In broad terms, the Bureau — like other public assistance organizations in the country — administers the several programs of federal-state financed assistance (Aid to Families with Dependent Children or AFDC, etc.) as well as a county financed "residual" program (GA, or General Assistance), which provides for those persons not meeting the eligibility criteria of the categoric aids.[9]

Administration of these programs requires an investigation of the applicant's circumstances in order to provide a "factual" basis for determining need and entitlement to assistance under the provisions of the

7. Behind this tack is the assumption that *the* problematic topic of sociological inquiry is the member-of-society's "socially organized common practices" for detecting, describing, warranting, and accounting for the senisble features of everyday activities. Any socially organized setting, precisely in the way it organizes itself, provides an occasion for the study of these practices. The description of the phenomena subsumed under the rubrics of social organization, formal organization, informal organization, and the like is then a description of these practices. Hence, the present study is not a sociology of organizations per se, but an inquiry into the practices members employ in sustaining the "sense" that their own and others' conduct is orderly, understandable, and reasonable — "given the circumstances." See Garfinkel (1967:especially Chapter 1;1966) for the original statement of this view.

8. This notion will be discussed below.

9. Other categories of assistance include OAA (Old Age Assistance), ATD (Aid to the Total Disabled), and MAA (Medical Assistance to the Aged).

several categories. In the Metropolitan County Bureau this responsibility is discharged by the intake division.[10]

Once certified as eligible, the applicant comes under the supervision
of the "approved" division. The routine administration of the case,
including periodic reinvestigation of the applicant's eligibility for assistance, is the responsibility of this division.

Within the "Lakeside Office" of the Bureau (one of several district
offices in the county) the inquiry was focused upon the day-to-day
operation of the intake function. Concentration on the work activities of
intake personnel led as a matter of course to observation of the work
done by reception. Just as the approved worker's caseload is assembled
by virtue of the work of the intake worker in certifying eligibility, so the
intake worker's investigation is preceded by the work of receptionists in
preprocessing new applications for assistance. A discussion of the reception function follows.

The Reception Function

A major responsibility of reception (and a prominent concern of receptionists) is to provide for the orderly and appropriately paced preprocessing of applicants for public assistance and their assignment to an
intake caseworker, who investigates their claim and decides its merit. As
accomplished work, preprocessing and assignment appear to be contingent upon receptionists' performance of a series of related tasks that
may be referred to as the "steps" in the reception process.

These steps involve, but are not exhausted by, screening persons
entering the office (determining the business bringing the person "in"),[11]
categorizing those persons discovered to be new applicants for public
assistance as one or another type of application (as AFDC or GA, etc.),
collecting preliminary information relevant to the subsequent processing
of the application (name, age, residence data, etc.), generating and up-
dating records (providing for the initiation of or search for a previous
dossier on the applicant),[12] and, at the terminus of these activities,

10. A detailed examination of the intake function may be found in Zimmerman (1966).
See also Zimmerman (in Hansen, 1969; and in Wheeler, 1970).

11. Of those coming to the office, some may be seeking employment, others may already
be clients who are in the office to see an approved worker, and a few may be "third
parties" summoned to provide information concerning a case. The bulk of them will be in
to request public assistance.

12. While perhaps obvious, it is worth observing that record-keeping activities such as
these are crucial to the maintenance of an organizational "routine," that is, in the present
case, facilitating the matter-of-course processing of applications. Given what records of
various sorts may be construed to *possibly* report, the generation of records of various
sorts permits, first of all, the identification of the person reported on as one who has been

assigning the applicant to an intake worker, accomplished by use of a procedure operationalizing the maxim, "first come, first served."

Assignment by this procedure is effected by the use of an intake book, a looseleaf binder the pages of which are ruled to form a matrix. One axis of the matrix represents the order in which the panel of intake workers on duty on a given day are to receive assignments; the other axis represents the order of assignments for a given worker (typically six in total). By use of the rule, top to bottom, left to right, in that order (that is, the "next available cell"), applicants are assigned to the cells in the order in which their processing was initiated. The execution of this procedure as described above, invariant to any situational exigencies, may be termed a literal (as opposed to judgmental or interpretive) application of the procedure.[13] This terminal step will be discussed at length later in the chapter.

From the vantage point of an observer not involved in the work process of reception, the execution of these steps has the appearance of a busy but nonetheless orderly round of activities. Applicants (and others) coming into the office appear to be integrated into the reception process in a matter-of-course way.

The routine character of the process will be seen to be one of its most salient features, one to which receptionists orient and, by their management of work activities, seek to preserve. That is, receptionists (and other personnel as well) orient to the management of the day's work so as to provide for the defensible claim that it was accomplished in sufficient-for-all-practical-purposes accord with rule and policy "Sufficient for all practical purposes" may be taken to mean the judgment by competent and entitled persons in the setting that the work was acceptably done, forgiving what may be forgiven, ignoring what may be ignored, allowing for what may be allowed based on both tacit and explicit understandings of such matters *in light of* "what anyone knows" about the practical circumstances of work in general and on particular occasions.

"run through" the usual procedures, and hence as one to whom the typical organizational constraints and opportunities may pertain. Such records may be used to "reconstruct" the person's career in the organizational process in order to argue, according to the circumstances and interests of the reviewer, that the organization has or has not done its job. A much longer list of the uses of records within organizations could undoubtedly be specified. The point to be stressed here is that, whatever the uses to which records may be put, it appears crucial that records of some sort be produced. For however in fact they are generated, the use of records to chronicle (or more likely reconstruct) a given person's fate at the hands of some organizational process seems indispensible for the typical claim of organizations that (at least most of the time) they handle their affairs in a routinized, rational, and responsible fashion. See Zimmerman (1970).

13. See Bittner (1965:241–242) and especially Wilson (1970).

The practical circumstances of work[14] may be encountered in such things as the receptionists' fond hope that applicants _will_ conduct themselves properly, their sure knowledge that _some_ will not, and the often demanding task of dealing with the "oddballs" and "troublemakers" in the context of an ongoing work routine.

That the process is to be kept ongoing is itself a practical feature of the work. To keep things moving requires continual attention to such matters as scheduling and coordinating the activities of applicants, receptionists, and caseworkers. The receptionist must avoid, insofar as possible, marked disruptions or "hitches" in the flow of work and at the same time be able to defend if necessary the sanctionable relationship of her practices on achieving the above to the rules and policies of the organization to which these practices are accountable.[15]

In order to examine how the receptionist, as an everyday accomplishment, achieves the reasonable reconciliation of the formal program of the organization with the practical features of doing work _in_ the organization, it is necessary to examine in more detail what will be called the "actual task structure" of reception. This term refers to the variety of problematic features generated by the attempt to put into practice a programmatically specified task such as that of receptionists outlined above.

ACTUAL TASK STRUCTURE IN RECEPTION

Temporal Features. The temporal-coordinative contingencies of the reception process are inadequately depicted by speaking of the task as a series of steps, or a "first this and then that" matter. From the perspective of a given applicant, the process may perhaps have this appear-

---

14. The description of the "practical circumstances" of receptionists is drawn along the lines suggested by Garfinkel in his discussion of the features of "common-sense situations of choice." These features locate a collection of related, insistent concerns which members appear to attend in generating and deciding among alternatives of fact, sense, and action in socially organized settings. Briefly, these practical concerns are for the temporal coordination of action, the management of the risk of unfavorable outcomes, the persistent fact that performances are subject to evaluation, the problem of "what to do next," the constraint that the decider give evidence by his choice of his competent grasp of "what anyone knows" about the operation of settings in which the choice is made, the problem of determining the socially adequate and effective determination of rules and procedures in dealing with actual concrete situations—given that such rational constructions are merely advisory to action, and the confrontation of these circumstances and the alternatives of choice and action selected by reference to them as together the constituent features of the situation of choice. See Garfinkel (1959a; 1967:96–100) and Garfinkel and Churchill (1964).

15. Even an "excusable mistake" at one point in an ongoing course of activities might in light of subsequent events be later reassessed by others as a "document" of an unfolding pattern of incompetency, that is, as a representation of what "all along" had been the individual's inattention or indifference to duty. See Garfinkel (1967:Chapter 3).

ance (first, the initial contact, then the collection of preliminary information, and so on). For the receptionists, however, these steps are
discontinuous with respect to each applicant. That is, step one of the
process may take place for one applicant at a given time, step two
somewhat later, and so on, with the various steps in the processing of
other applicants intervening.

The steps in the process for receptionists are thus interspersed over
an aggregate of applicants. Reception activities consist in multiple deal-
ings with a set of applicants, imbedded in sequence of varying maturity,
in constant motion, fitted together according to present circumstances
and future prospects, and paced with respect to the ebb and flow of
applicants in and out of the doors.

Viewed in this light, the appearance of the activities (to an observer or
to organization personnel themselves) as a timely and orderly steplike
execution of the various phases of the preprocessing and assignment
routines is provided for by the work of receptionists in attending to and
managing such problems as matching the pace of work to the current
demand (the number of applicants—and others—requesting service at a
given time) in terms of their practical interests in moving applicants
through the process with reasonable speed and a minimum of difficulty.

Troubles and Consequences. Receptionists' practical interests in the
trouble-free development of the workday reflect their knowledge that
things sometimes go awry and that they are accountable to others in the
setting for their efforts to manage the course of work to minimize
disruptions and control departures from routines. As indicated above,
close attention to timing and scheduling are critical features of the
receptionists' task of making the workday "come out right."

Receptionists were seen to monitor the flow of work with the explicit
concern that it be done by a certain time. Accomplishment of the latter
required management of such matters as the timely "closing" of intake,
that is, cutting off the processing of new applications so that no excess of
applicants awaiting interviews over caseworkers available to do interviews occurs at the end of the day.

A consideration adding urgency to concerns about timing and coordination is the proper utilization of the caseworker as a resource. It is the
caseworker's expeditious completion of the intake interview that moves
the applicant out of the office completing the process. On the part of the
receptionists, "proper" utilization requires prompt preparation of each
new applicant for assignment, the promptness gaining its particular temporal specification by reference to the press of demands and available
resources at the time. The dispatch with which caseworkers complete
assigned interviews is a factor over which receptionists apparently have

I

little direct control. The occurrence of an inordinately lengthy interview may be potentially troublesome for receptionists, as will be seen in the following section.

Actual Task Structure and Competent Rule Use

THE INTAKE ASSIGNMENT PROCEDURE

The "literal" application of the intake assignment procedure was defined above as the employment of the "next available cell" rule invariant to any exigencies of the actual situation of use. However, as might be expected, this literal usage was not maintained in every instance of an assignment of an application to an intake worker. If the literal-use model is posited as the "proper" use of the rule, other alternatives would have to be designated as deviations. As was indicated in the introduction, use of such a model would put out of account any exercise of judgment by the rule user, and leave as unproblematic the empirical issue of what the rule intends and how its operational sense is discovered by attempts to employ it in actual situations.

The task taken here will be to examine such "deviations" (dectectable by reference to the literal-use model) as possibly competent "uses" of the rule by personnel employing judgments based upon their understanding of the features of the actual situation of use and the practicalities of action in the setting. Three instances of "deviation" will be analyzed.

Case 1. A third intake was about to be assigned to worker Jones. At this time, Jones was engaged in conducting an interview with her *first* assigned applicant. From the point of view of receptionists, this interview was presumed to have posed unusual problems since it had not been completed at the time a third assignment was contemplated.[16]

A receptionist commented, in connection with the present case:

The biggest problem is keeping these people moving. Jones had her first assignment, well, shortly after 8:00 A.M. [It was 10:30 A.M. at this time.] She hasn't picked up her second and here is a third.

At 11:20 A.M., almost an hour after its assignment, the third intake had yet to be picked up. A receptionist called Jones's unit clerk and informed her that "there's a woman out here who has been waiting a

16. The "unusual" character of the interview thus appears to be formulated by reference to the stacking up of assignments. A prevailing concern of receptionists is to move applicants through the process in a rapid and orderly manner. Effecting this state of affairs assumes the ready availability of the chief resource: the caseworkers. From the point of view of caseworkers, the chief concern is the assembly of information sufficient to insure the rapid processing of the case. Caseworkers were not observed to express or to indicate by their method of conducting an interview any concern that assignments might backlog.

long time." She was told that Jones was conducting an interview (the second assignment). This call had been occasioned by the third applicant's expressed anxiety that she was going to miss a 12:30 doctor's appointment. The receptionist who made the call remarked, "If she has a doctor's appointment at 12:30 she's not going to make it at the rate Jones is going."

The senior receptionist then decided that the third applicant would be switched to another worker. The switch entailed a discussion among receptionists concerning which worker to assign her to, as well as taking the next assignment of the worker receiving Jones's case and assigning it to her. The change also required alternation in the intake book and changes in certain other records.[17] The potential third intake of Jones was in fact assigned to another worker, thereby "suspending" the rule. That the suspension was observable as such may be seen in a receptionist's comment at that time that the "skipped turn" was not "fair."

It is proposed here that this suspension be understood in terms of the actual task structure of the reception function. Reception, as depicted above, is a temporally complex system of activities. The prevailing emphasis is placed upon the rapid accomplishment of the preprocessing on a given case. The concern, aptly expressed by a receptionist, is to "keep people moving."

The case reported here posed a dilemma, since it represented a "snag" upon which several cases were caught. The snag was in part structured into the situation by the intake assignment rule itself, which provided that each case was taken in order under a literal application. The smoothness with which this literal application effects the movement of applicants out of the office is contingent on the dispatch with which intake workers could accomplish the initial interview. Hence, the rule's capacity (literally applied) to achieve the objective of orderly and rapid processing is contingent upon the intake worker's system of relevances in conducting an interview, which are not necessarily congruent with that of reception, hence, disjuncture is guaranteed for *some* portion of the cases, which may lead to situations of the sort documented above.[18]

17. Although such changes are relatively minor in any given instance, it should be kept in mind that they are changes to be accomplished during the continued screening of applicants and during the course of an ongoing assignment procedure. The change reported here also involved a decision as to what cases would be switched, which in terms of the particular instance under review required an estimation of the *dispatch* with which the new worker could handle the case.

18. It should be kept in mind that one of the applicants affected by delay expressed her desire to be dealt with more promptly to the receptionist. It is entirely possible that this, and this alone, was sufficient grounds for the switch. However, it seems reasonable to propose that such a request also appears actionable to receptionists by virtue of their concern for swift and orderly processing. Furthermore, this concern may be reinforced by

I

One solution to such situations, of course, is to maintain the priority of the next available cell rule. Apparently, from the point of view of the receptionist who made the decision, the rule could be suspended and the suspension deemed a "reasonable" solution to the minor dilemma the situation presented.

The critical consideration here is the fact that the literal application of the assignment rule is apparently deemed adequate most of the time to deal with the typical applicant. Processing, from the point of view of receptionists, proceeds in a routine fashion most of the time. This *sense* of routineness provides receptionists a way to recognize the exceptional character of a given event and, thereby, the good grounds for suspending or otherwise modifying the rule as normally applied.[19] That the use of the rule "typically" effects the expected outcome, that, "typically," applicants do not "stack up" in this fashion, and that for most situations only the most commonplace and regular considerations need be entertained, constitutes the receptionists' sense of an organizationally normal state of affairs.

By suspending the rule in light of the exceptional character of the situation, the intent of the rule might be said to be honored — its intent being formulable on a particular occasion by situationally relevant reference to the "usual" course of affairs its routine or precedented use typically reproduces. Through the situated judgmental modification of the routine application of the rule, the "same" business as usual course of affairs may be — for all intents and purposes — reliably reproduced.

In other words, what the rule is intended to provide for is discovered in the course of employing it over a series of actual situations. The use of a procedure, in the way that it is used, generates the state of affairs that, when things go wrong, may be referred to as the end in view "all along." For example, the attempt to use a procedure in a given situation may produce an array of troubles that motivate alterations in the manner in which the rules are put into practice, in turn affecting the state of affairs generated. The modification established, the resultant outcomes

---

the fact that such delays occasion requests of that nature from applicants, that is, the longer the applicant is in the office, the greater the likelihood of her pressing demands against reception that will have to be dealt with. The "reasonable" solution would appear to be: suspend the assignment procedure in such circumstances. It is not implied, however, that receptionists have a *rule* that dictates suspension of the procedure under such conditions. The situation reported here is not, furthermore, among those covered by the institutionalized exceptions to the rule that do exist.

19. Furthermore, the suspension was occasioned by the occurrence of what appeared to be taken by the senior receptionist as a "normal contingency" attendant to the conduct of intake interviews, which "fact" absolved the worker concerned from personal blame. It was "just one of those things," so to speak, out of the control of all parties concerned but susceptible nonetheless to a "reasonable" solution, particularly in light of the applicant's problem of keeping her appointment.

(if less troublesome) might then be invoked or assumed to argue what the rule intended "all along" if an issue subsequently arose around what the rule "really" calls for by way of action.

It may then be argued that the above *kinds* of considerations provide for the receptionist *a* reasonable solution for the dilemma confronted. The present argument, however, is not intended to argue the receptionis's case for her, thereby "justifying" her decisions. The point is rather that receptionists appear to employ such considerations as justifications for the reasonableness of the action. By deciding to suspend the rule in *this* instance of its potential application, the intent of the rule was apparently not seen to be violated. Furthermore, in finding such modifications to be "reasonable," receptionists appear to provide for ways to ensure that the continuing accomplishment of the normal pacing and flow of work may be reconciled with their view of these task activities *as governed by rules,* in this instance, the intake assignment procedure.[20]

If this is generally the case, then it would seem that the notion of action-in-accord-with-a-rule is a matter not of compliance or noncompliance per se but of the various ways in which persons *satisfy* themselves and others concerning what is or is not "reasonable" compliance in particular situations. Reference to rules might then be seen as a common-sense method of accounting for or making available for talk the orderly features of everyday activities, thereby *making out* these activities as orderly in some fashion. Receptionists, in accomplishing a for all practical purposes ordering of their task activities by undertaking the "reasonable" reconciliation of particular actions with "governing rules" may thus sustain their sense of "doing good work" and warrant their further actions on such grounds.

Case 2. The following incident appears anomalous in terms of the preceding discussion. Here, contrary to the implications of the analysis thus far, a suspension of the rule of assignment was apparently allowed for reasons of "personal preference" rather than for practical work considerations.

A GA case was prepared by 10:10 of the same day as the incident reported above. It was assigned to worker Hall at 10:16 A.M. At the same time an OAA case was assigned to worker Kuhn. Several minutes after this, the investigator noted that Hall had taken the OAA case and

20. Unfortunately, the data collected did not clearly establish the *force* of this rule, that is, how much discretionary latitude was formally allowed or informally accepted in its use. However, since the employment of formally granted "discretion" is, as is the case with decisions concerning the employment of *any* rule, an accountable matter within the relevant setting, the question would have to be raised: Through what process was the "discretionary" decision reached, given that the decider might be called to account for the decision? And since considerable discretion appears to be exercised in bureaucratic settings, allowed or not, discretionary and "nondiscretionary" rule use would appear to pose the same problems and be open to the same line of analysis.

Kuhn the GA assignment. What had transpired was the intervention of the OAA applicant who specifically requested that Hall process her case.[21]

Here again the rule was suspended. The same senior receptionist who had permitted the previous suspension on the grounds of exigent circumstances connected with the routine processing of cases allowed the "switch" even though, strictly speaking, a disruption of the normal pacing of work was not immediately at issue. She was considerably more circumspect in permitting the suspension, commenting "We don't do this very often. They're not supposed to get a case just because they want it."

It may first be noted that this suspension has an illegitimate character to it. By this is meant that it was so treated by the receptionist, even though allowed. If this is the case, why did the receptionist not stand by the rule?

In answer to this problem, it is proposed here that single instances of illegitimate suspension *may* be allowed simply in order to avoid confrontation of the issue of procedural correctness, particularly when "making an issue of it" might involve a dispute between the receptionists, the worker, *and* the applicant. Note that in allowing the impropriety it was cast in terms of a "one time only" exception. Further, the switch was occasioned by an applicant's specific request: to deny it "might" have required confrontation of both the applicant and the worker. What is more, the switch was arranged between the two workers, with consent given by both to the change. It is suggested that what is entailed in a circumstance of this sort is a permissiveness in the interest of avoiding difficulties and getting on with the work.

The burden of the preceding argument has been that receptionists orient to a normal course of affairs and seek by their action to guarantee its continuing reproduction. Such an orientation requires judgmental work on the part of receptionists in the use of procedures to effect such results, since contingent circumstance may sometimes render the literal use of such rules inappropriate, that is, the actions that could ordinarily be reconciled with the literal use would lead to "trouble"—potential or actual. One such circumstance is "occasional defiance." By this is meant those instances wherein something recognized as illegitimate in the situations is proposed or encountered, and where such deviance may be permitted to stand by virtue of the explicit provision for its nonprecedential character—simply to sidestep possible resistance (and the troubles it might bring) to enforcement of the "proper" procedure.[22]

21. Apparently, Hall had processed the applicant in a previous application. Further, Hall was openly more favorable to OAA cases as opposed to AFDC and GA cases.
22. The suggestion that receptionists attempt to emphasize the nonprecedential charac-

It is a moot point whether or not the receptionist's insistence on adherence to the procedure would have generated a serious dispute. The fact remains that she did not so insist, even though she gave clear indication of disapproval. At least two alternative accounts are available. The first would be to assign the instance to a defect in the motivation of the receptionist to enforce the "legitimate" ordering of events. The second is to refer the permissiveness to the receptionists' interests in preserving the routine flow of work in the setting. Allowance for occasional deviance would appear to be consistent with this latter interest.

Case 3. An important concern of reception is the management of "difficult" applicants. This is so for several reasons. First, dealing with difficult applicants is a "time out" from attention to the routine processing of cases, requiring a special allocation of effort at the expense of other demands. It may pose problems for these other demands should the applicant make a scene in the office. Second, it represents an instance potentially interpretable as a failure of reception to discharge its responsibilities. Given the concern to manage disruptions of the normal routine, it is not surprising to find that some systematic arrangement exists by which receptionists provide for dealing with potentially difficult applicants.

Operationally, a difficult applicant is one whose demeanor or demands impede the normal processing of cases.[23] Impediment occurs when a receptionist must devote extra effort to the management of one case to the neglect of others; the most dramatic instance is when the applicant creates a scene.

The arrangement for dealing with applicants whose conduct or demeanor suggested difficulties in the above sense involved caseworker Dodd, who was reputed to have a special interest in, and special talent for dealing with, problem cases. The arrangement consisted in the utilization of this worker for applicants perceived by receptionists to either be potentially troublesome or have a "special problem" requiring out of the ordinary treatment. Justification took the form of providing (unofficially) "special services" to particularly distraught applicants. It is to be noted that this arrangement was viable only for that day on which worker Dodd was on the panel of workers available for intake assignments. As the arrangement could not be officially admitted, the administrative

---

ter of the permitted deviance does not imply that the parties involved would not on some future occasion attempt to negotiate further concessions on the basis of the past permissiveness.

23. While it cannot definitely be established here, it may be suggested that "difficult" applicants are recognizable to receptionists from the perspective provided by their grasp of the features of the actual task structure of the reception process. They are, as indicated earlier, concerned with the problems of pacing and coordinating activities, and aware that the success with which they manage such problems is subject to review.

mechanics of the assignment process would not easily permit this arrangement to function five days a week in the absence of at least four other workers deemed able to perform such "special services" and willing to do so.[24]

A note on the character of this arrangement is in order. There attaches to it a clear sense of unofficiality. In contrast to the ad hoc adjustments discussed above, entailed here is a systematic plan providing for the suspension of the intake assignment procedure upon encountering contingencies of a specified kind. The arrangement was explicitly covert. Hence the arrangement may be termed an unofficial or informal arrangement. This labeling is warranted by the fashion in which the arrangement is treated by the participants and not by virtue of its provision for a departure from some idealized version of the officially prescribed rule. That care is exercised to conceal the arrangement suggests that those concerned anticipated official disapproval were the plan to become officially recognized.[25] With this in mind, consider the following. Receptionists, by this arrangement, provide for situations that portend troubles difficult to deal with by activities reconcilable in terms of the "normal routine." The provisions made are to them "unofficial," that is not sufficient as a warrant or justification for their actions outside of the reception process itself. However, in terms of the practical concerns of receptionists with getting their job done and preserving the sense of their accomplishment as a job well done, they by their decision to employ "unofficial" considerations in dealing with the exigent circumstances provide for the possibility of a recognizedly routine processing of cases. By making provision for the occurrence of events not readily accounted for in terms of the "official" procedures, they also provide for the smooth processing of cases that are so treatable.

Hence, while this "understanding" provides for the systematic suspension of the "routine" use of the assignment procedure for a series of potential situations, it also systematically provides for the preservation

24. One product of the reception function is a control list of assigned intakes by file number of the worker which is circulated in the agency. Hence, the assignment process is highly visible and restricts certain kinds of modifications, save by extensive manipulations of records. Such manipulations may have been practiced unknown to the observer.

25. As a consequence, the notion of informal organization achieves its significance only by consulting the viewpoint of organization members. Further, the concept is made relative in that its application would pertain in relationship to *which* elements of a given organization the practices are concealed from which officials. It is conceivable that organizational practice may be unofficial only with respect to its public, there being a uniform understanding that present practices are acceptable as the official solution to organizational problems. Further, the officiality of an act could be a highly contingent affair, depending on time and exigent conditions. Official versus unofficial activities may thus be understood as a contrast in the nature of the warrant for and the audience of *accounts* given of conduct. For a similar view couched in terms of "boundaries of observability" see Wilson (1966).

of an organizational state of affairs which that rule, in part, is understood
to effect, namely, the orderly and rapid movement of applicants through
the process. In recognition of the consequences of troublesome applicants, it provides *a* way of preserving the aggregate effectiveness of the
usual procedures by a willingness to relax the literal application of the
assignment procedure. By concealing the nature of the arrangement, the
freedom to employ this alternative procedure is preserved while at the
same time the aggregate process is permitted to be viewed as presumptively "normal," that is, procedure bound.

It is clearly the case that reciprocities are involved in the arrangements. Dodd could request, and expect that her request be honored, to
be assigned an applicant she might be interested in processing. By
concealing the arrangement, potential claims of other caseworkers for
similiar arrangements is forestalled, permitting the exercise of the receptionists' discretion concerning which workers may be invited to participate.

Summary and Conclusion

From the point of view of receptionists, the steps of the reception
process, including the use of the intake assignment procedure, typically
achieve the desired outcomes. That is, for all practical purposes, and for
most of the time, receptionists are able to coordinate applicants (who
typically cooperate) and bring off the day's work with respect to the
constraints of timing, pacing, and scheduling represented by the described "actual task structure." For receptionists, these outcomes are
typically effected in an acceptable fashion by actions that are describable
by them as in accordance with rules. This provides for the receptionists'
sense of, and way of accounting for, normal everyday routine affairs in
the setting. Further, these routine affairs are looked to by receptionists
to decide what the rule or procedure is "up to" after all.

On a more general level, it appears that the "competent use" of a
given rule or a set of rules is founded upon members' practiced grasp of
what particular actions are necessary on a given occasion to provide for
the regular reproduction of a "normal" state of affairs. A feature of the
member's grasp of his everyday affairs is his knowledge, gained by
experience, of the typical but unpredictable occurrence of situational
exigencies that threaten the production of desired outcomes. Often,
troubles develop over which little control is possible, save to restore the
situation as well as possible. Certain exigencies may be dealt with on an
ad hoc basis and others may be provided for systematically.

The use of formally prescribed procedures viewed from the perspective of the notion of their "competent use" thus become matters not

of compliance or deviance but of judgmental work providing for the reasonableness of viewing particular actions as *essentially* satisfying the provisions of the rule, even though the action may contrast with invocable precedent, with members' idealized versions of what kinds of acts are called for by the rule, or with the sociologists' ideas concerning the behavioral acts prescribed or proscribed by the rule.

CHAPTER TEN

Talking and Becoming: A View of Organizational Socialization

One of the enduring interests of sociologists is the study and analysis of the process by which people become actors upon a social stage. In order to provide a contrast to "socialized man," introductory readers and/or texts in sociology usually include sections on social isolation to manifest the results or effects of the absence or severe restriction of social contacts (see Park and Burgess, 1924:Chapter 4, 226–273). The fields of socialization, human development, and family life are studied by a wide range of social scientists. Adult socialization, although seen for some reason as less problematic, is also receiving more attention of late (Brim and Wheeler, 1966). Works that examine adult socialization are few and suggest that further work can be done.

The specific focus here is the development of means to study adult socialization in the context of organizations. Organizational socialization[1] is the process by which an individual, from both the individual and the organizational perspective, becomes a part of the organization. It begins to take place, we assume, whenever an individual associates with others "under" a common symbolic label referring to that association (Bittner, 1965).[2]

1. Vollmer (1967) uses the concept of organization socialization, but provides no definition of it in the paper. My original conceptualization was made in 1965, and there is little overlap in our foci or method.
2. A distinction is often made between organizations whose stated goals are socialization for future social roles, those whose stated goals are resocialization, and those whose major interest is in some other output. The focus here is a generic one which seeks to

The study of organizational socialization is conventionally assumed to involve at least two dimensions: the social role(s) and the organization as a social structure (the set of "slots" into which persons who play roles in the organization are to fit). However, when these conventions have been closely examined, some suggestive gaps and shortcomings in explanation have appeared. This chapter seeks to identify some of the shortcomings of organizational theory and sociological views of roles in order to address the problem we have called organizational socialization. The first part of the chapter will address the former notions; the second part will address organizational socialization.

Organizational Structure

The sociologist's concern in doing sociology is with making action social, that is, creating tales, stories, reports, accounts, articles, monographs, and essays that make social action reportable, accountable, publishable, and judicable for his purposes and for those of other sociologists. Sociological attempts to understand concerted action among organization members is usually dated from the work of Max Weber.[3]

Weber began by creating a model of social life within bureaucracies that held true whenever, and insofar as, efficiency (formal rationality) was the criterion for action. As a distribution of authority that made the outcome of command predictable, the organization existed for Weber in the pure form as linkage between command and compliance. The literal meaning of the formal rules for which the organization was assembled as a model were taken as describing the actual behavior occurring. Variations from the normatively ordered scheme of behaviors were accounted for by irrational, nonrational, informal, or otherwise foreign behavior deriving from normative conflicts, ignorance, or strains.

Selznick, in *TVA and the Grass Roots* (1966), turns the Weberian theory into a formal theory that is ideally possible but practically unattainable. Formal theories are seen as normative idealizations, as descriptions of organizations based on the assumption that actors follow only the sociological scheme.

Bureaucracy as an administrative system constantly faces external and internal forces that threaten to create tension that will permanently destroy the equilibrium necessary for organizational survival. For Selzn-

---

explore organizational socialization in the context of any organization. It assumes that none of the stated goals or organizations can be achieved without actors' management of the practical problems of organizational life. It is likely that if one could analytically separate the generic from the organizationally specific one would find that the two "processes" are somehow simultaneous, and that adequate accounting for an actor or for one's self means "skill" in both dimensions.

3. The following discussion derives from Bittner (1965).

ick, as for Weber, organizations are seen in the formal sense, but for Selznick, they are additionally seen as adaptive and as schemes. "Schemes" refer here to the notion that an organizational view is always *someone's view*. Selznick locates the source of this scheme in the managerial echelon. It is seen by Selznick as a practical theory in use by managers in their interpretation of the course of organizational events.

Informal or irrational forces in the organization are those that are not included in the managerial view but nonetheless must be dealt with in some day-to-day coping or managing basis; the tension between the ideal and the actual requires somebody's (usually the manager's) constant attention if the organization is to survive.

Organizational socialization is not solely a structural problem. Organizational maps should be distinguished from actual, typical, or "normatively organized" behavior. Some sociologists have concerned themselves with "actors' theories" or perspectives that are rooted in the experience of lower participants rather than in the experience of managers. For example, there are the works of Becker et al (1961), Goffman (1961a), Roth (1963), and others of the "Chicago school." These works suggest that by taking the perspective of the lower participants within an organization one attends to other nonmanagerial practical theories, in this case the problems of work arising out of viewing organizational contingencies through the "worker's eyes."[4]

Bittner argues that the literal meanings of any scheme cannot be attained in practice. Even if schemes for making action social and meaningful are located in the social structure (as Mannheim urged) and assuming that actors are implicated in the scheme (cast by the sociologist in orderly interaction), to ask these actors to act in accord with the lexical meanings of social rules is to ask much of them. Not only are they asked to understand, define, clarify, choose among, compare, and contrast rules, they are asked to understand them as the sociologist would or does (Garfinkel, 1967:Chapter 8).

The actor's operations in concert with the scheme are described as if they met the requirements of rationality without a discussion of rationality itself as a problematic attainment of the theorist and the actor (Garfinkel, 1967:Chapter 8). Instead of giving attention to the requirements of actors in social life that make "rationality" manifest, the sociologist makes use of a scheme that seizes upon actions that are taken as pointing to rational grounds for action, choice, or commitment. That is, sociologists use the scheme to organize actors' behavior within an organization rather than ask how actors defer to, manage, reject, or apply a symbolic framework to the objects that make up their daily environments.

4. See detailed ethnographies of Donald Roy (1953, 1954, 1959–1960).

Rules, the central source of order in organizations according to organizational theorists, are not, indeed cannot be, understood in their literal form. General rules, such as laws pertaining to juveniles that are the ostensive basis for assigning cases to the delinquent or nondelinquent category, are applied to specific cases by juvenile officers, judges, etc., *on the grounds of their situated activity.* In one public defender's office, Sudnow described how cases of child molesting or burglary were assigned to legal categories on the basis of a conception held by the organization's members of what constituted a "normal crime" (Sudnow, 1965). Thus, although general rules may be invoked to explain the assignation of a case, close attention to the working of an organization will reveal devices used to match general rules with specific instances. In effect then, the meaning of the rules resides in the practical procedures by which they are administered (Sudnow, 1967). Rules within organizations, like grammatical rules and rules of logic, take on an indexical quality, that is, they can be understood only contextually, as practical problems that themselves arise out of the association of those people, facing those problems, in those periods of time (Garfinkel, 1967:Chapter 1;Bar-Hillel, 1954).[5]

It is just these contingencies of rule applications that are for members fundamental, normal, taken for granted, and that have been bypassed by theorists constructing organized life from without. Selznick and Weber, as well as many others, draw upon the contextual resources actors have generated *in situ* in order to proceed to their describing and accounting work. Bittner (1965:244–255) has succinctly summarized criticism of this sort.

> When one lifts the mantle of protection from the unstated presupposition surrounding the terms of Weber's theory of bureaucracy, one is confronted with facts of a particular sort. These facts are not sociological data, or even theoretically defensible hypotheses. Instead, one is confronted with the rich and ambiguous body of background information that normally competent members of a society take for granted as commonly known. In its normal functioning this information furnishes the tacit foundation for all that is explicitly known and provides the matrix for all deliberate considerations

5. It is misleading to assume that the situationally based qualities of meanings of organizational procedures or rules do not have systemic or generalizable features. Investigation of a single setting, or culture, or type of organization is an attempt to reveal features of the organization that are likely to occur in many settings. Sudnow's (1967) study of death was an attempt not solely to understand "death work" within the hospital studied but to understand "Death and Dying as Social States of Affairs" (Chapter 4). Our basic assumption is that there is a taken-for-granted basis for everyday life that undergirds all attempts to constrain objects either coming under its jurisdiction or departing from it, and that this is a universal feature in most cultures. Therefore, the manifestation of operations by which this process takes place are taken as indices both of the common-sense realities of organizational life and of the universality of practices by which people handle their everyday organizational affairs.

without being itself deliberately considered. While its content can be raised to the level of analysis, this typically does not occur. Rather, the information enters into that commonplace and practical orientation to reality which members in society regard as 'natural' when attending to their daily affairs. Since the explicit terms of the theory are embedded in this common-sense orientation, they cannot be understood without tacit reference to it. If, however, the theorist must be persuaded about the meaning of the terms in some prior and unexplicated way, then there exists collusion between him and those about whom he theorizes. We call this unexplicated understanding collusive because it is a hidden resource, he use of which cannot be controlled adequately.

These sociologists' views of action contain what Bittner usefully calls a "short-circuiting of social theory." Although he views action from the point of view of the actor, Weber fails to recognize and explicate the underlying common-sense presuppositions of his own theory. That is, he assumes what actors have to create as an everyday task: social order. Or, to formulate the critique in another fashion: theoretical statements are made about X (organizational behavior) at the same time that knowledge of X (how people behave in organizations) is taken as proof that the theoretical statements made about X are adequate. The concept short-circuits theory by building upon what organizationally situated actors assume when they use the concept. To understand what rationality means, one must understand what is taken for granted within organizations in which rationality is said to be found.

To understand organizational behavior, and in this case organizational socialization, one must deal with the relativity of models for making behavior social. Bittner, following Kenneth Burke (1965), suggests some exaggerations (meta-schemes) by which organizations can be studied which are informed by the presumptive mistakes of Weber and his interpreters.

1) The sociologist can proceed to investigate formal organizations assuming that the unexplicated common-sense meanings of the terms used are adequate definitions for the purposes of his investigations. In this case, he uses what he proposes to study as a resource for the study.

2) The sociologist can tag terms with a more or less arbitrary meaning by defining them operationally, what Torgerson (1958) aptly calls measurement by fist. In this case the relationships between the object observed and the terms used to describe it are defined by the procedures used. Interest in the actor's perspective is either abandoned, or some handy version of it is adopted.

3) The sociologist can decide that the meaning of a concept and all the terms and determinations that are subsumed under it must be discovered by studying their use in action by persons who are socially sanctioned as competent to use them. (Listing paraphrased from Bittner, 1965.)

We propose that the construction of organized social action remain in the hands of the actor, while the sociologist seeks to report the way in which the actor manages the problems that face him in organizations. How he manages them is seen in the devices he uses to make them consistent, repetitive, normal, and natural. By means of his linguistic behaviors the actor selects things which through naming become social objects. That is, they have a potential for action when they are named, counted, assessed, and ordered. The fashioning of order takes place as objects at hand become named as part, in the context of, or standing for, order. The primary rule for the study of organizations from a phenomenological point of view is that one must study the ways in which terms of discourse are assigned to real objects and events by normally competent persons in ordinary situations (Bittner, 1965). Garfinkel, and others, suggest the title "ethnomethodology" for this study of stable procedures by which actors relate common-sense constraints to objects in the world. Ethnomethodologists insist that substituting schemes that point out objects as if they had a constitutive meaning is not preferred to studying the ways in which objects come under the control of various schemes.

A study of an organization must then begin with the study of its use by actors. Becoming a socially sanctioned member of an organization, by implication, involves displaying, adhering to, and being sanctioned for use of an ordering scheme or subschemes.

We will assume that this information can be obtained by close attention to the linguistic devices employed by members to discuss their problems. We will also assume that attention should be paid to the setting in which these devices are called upon and to the rules that govern their use. Organization being partially accounted for, our attention shifts to roles, conventionally assumed to be things that must be learned.

Roles and Role Learning

One "traditional" view of role, usually associated with Linton and Parsons, begins with role as a given in a system of social relationships. The aim is typically to proceed to the task of understanding human action by making the assumption that people are people-in-roles. Goffman (1961b) perceptively argues that this formulation, although there is a "dynamic dimension" (role in contrast to status), is based upon an "as if" assumption. Actors' performances are seen as behaviors they would engage in if they were to act solely with reference to the normative demands made of persons occupying their positions in a social system. *Position* is taken to explain behavior, other things being equal. Offenbacher (1967) labels this assumption a " 'black box' type of causal explanation" in which abstractions, that is, rights and duties, are fed at one end only to come out the other end as observed behaviors. Variations from the as if assumption are accounted for with reference to normatively induced strains, stresses, or role conflicts. Abstracted to this level, as Goffman shows: (1) Sociologists are in danger of taking the normatively structured expectations of an abstractly created social system as the reality of human behavior. (2) They may assume that the knowledge about a category (doctor, lawyer, sociologist, or any other structural profile with its attributes) informs us of the nature of interaction in which members of that category engage (Goffman, 1961b).

This traditional conceptualization, in spite of the ostensive actor-relevant nature of it, suffers additionally from short-circuiting. Briefly, as sketched above, short-circuiting takes place whenever an object is described without a separation being made between the description of the action by those implicated in the action and those describing it as a practical, professional task (Bittner, 1965; Sacks, 1963).

This use of "role" draws upon actors' common-sense knowledge as both an object and a resource. To some it appears as a reasonable way to proceed. Many articles are scattered with references that are the scholarly equivalent to "you know what I mean when I say that." A recent monograph on role contains a statement of these assumptions that dismisses them as relatively unimportant problems.

> If one were simply to array all the terms introduced into the literature of role theory, one would confront a sizable glossary of overlapping, vague and imprecise terms. Nevertheless, we have assumed that the central terms of role theory are sufficiently known and communicable among social scientists to overcome whatever obscurities their usage in this report may contain. . . . The priority which ought to be assigned to terminological affairs is contingent upon the stage of theory at which one begins to operate. At this stage in the development of role theory we see this as a low-priority item. We could through rather simple linguistic conventions establish a delimited set of meanings to such central concepts as role, status, expectations, visibility, power, etc. But such a set of definitions independent of a well-delineated theoretical scheme, would shed little light on the crucial problem of the relationships among the constituent terms (Preiss and Ehrlich, 1966: 163–164).

One paragraph later, however, it states:

> From an operational standpoint, establishing hard criteria for the identification of a role is perhaps the most elusive problem of role theory. If we were to exhibit a series of behavior episodes before a group of sociologists and social psychologists, we could probably get rather high agreement in their selection of those episodes which constituted role behavior. But if we asked them to specify the criteria by which they selected some behaviors and excluded others, we would probably discover that their decisions were more

intuitive than specifiable, and that they could achieve little common agreement on criteria. At this level most role theorists have converged, regardless of orientation (Preiss and Ehrlich, 1966:164).

A set of analytic definitions suggested by Preiss and Ehrlich without specified relationships between constituent terms would be relatively undramatic, yet we do not have even that. This lexicon might establish the sociologists' practical usage of the concept "role" as an organizing scheme.[6] It might begin to clarify the meanings of "central terms of role theory [that] are sufficiently known and communicable among social scientists to overcome whatever obscurities their usage . . . may contain." It would move toward clarification of presumptive sociological schemes as symbolic frameworks. The relationships between these schemes (of whatever clarity and logical precision) and the behavior to which they are directed as explication is left in the mores of the profession. That it is a matter of the mores, things assumed but not explained, is perhaps suggested by the statement above that competent observers deal with the relationship between role as a concept and role behavior in an intuitive fashion. The concept is in effect left to spin in the rich vortex of what sociologists assume about what their work points to, stands for, or is a case of.[7]

The study of organizational socialization calls for a modified conception of role that will remain with the actor, avoid measurement by fiat (operationalism), and extricate the concept from some sociological mores. The study of role learning, that is, the use of the concept role to bring order into one's behavior, is based upon a setting (organization)

6. Suggested here is a "workers'-dictionary," which would include definitions of the sociological use of role, examples of its use, mode of "testing," and an assessment of the utility of the concept. The Biddle and Thomas (1966) reader attempts this. The task suggested for consideration at the conclusion of this paper is an "actor's guide to the use of every day role-terms," which would contain the practical use of words referring to role-oriented action within a given organization. If done completely, this would become an organizational or cultural ethnography. See Ladd (1957).

7. One of the finest statements of the importance of distinguishing between the cultural subject (the object to be investigated, in this case role) and the empirical categories created by investigators is supplied by Karl Mannheim (in Kecskemeti, 1952:60).

Accordingly, one would commit the gravest methodological error if one simply equated this cultural subject (which has been defined merely as a counterpart to an objective cultural generalization) with empirical collective subjects defined on the basis of anthropological categories, such as race or class. And for this reason no documentary interpretation of the kind we have in mind can be demolished by proving that the author of a work belongs by descent or in terms of status to a 'race' or 'class' other than the one whose 'spirit' was said to be exemplified by the work. Our formulation shows that we do not object to the investigation of race as a problem of cultural history, or of 'class' as a problem of cultural sociology; surely both topics designate problems which deserve to be solved; all we wanted to do was to point out certain methodological implications which apply to these lines of research. Inquiries of this sort employ two sets of concepts which the investigator must rigorously keep apart; on the one hand, a collective subject will be characterized in terms relating to the documentary interpretation of a cultural product, and on the other, we shall obtain collective subjects that provides the context within which roles are assembled, maintained, or dissembled. The priority list for the sociologists with these aims is headed by the demand for a lexicon of indexical statements (statements that require a social context to provide their meaning) by which actors refer to their behaviors and attitudes. A lexicon of concepts and usages should then be followed with statements of the order of: Given the linguistic tags and descriptions of behavior, what are the situational, objective, and phenomenological factors that make such behavior meaningful and possible?

Social roles can be considered linguistically as situated vocabularies or rhetorics. As Mills (in Manis and Meltzer, 1967) writes, "Motives may be considered as typical vocabularies having ascertainable functions in delimited social situations." They are a shorthand means for the imputation of reasons for conduct. Lofland (1967:9-10) tenders a description of role as a linguistic device. Role can be used in

> designating the set of all those linguistic terms which themselves designate patterns of individual activity or physical characteristics, on the basis of which actors centrally organize the manner in which they organize their own action toward one another.... Roles are *claimed* labels, from behind which people present themselves to others and partially in terms of which they conceive, gauge, and judge their past, current and projected action. And roles are *imputed* labels toward which and partially in terms of which, people likewise conceive, gauge and judge others' past, present and projected action.

A difficulty arising in this definition is that the lexicon of role terms and role imputations that might be built up following Lofland's suggestions would have varying degrees of applicability to the behaviors prescribed to them by actors.[8]

---

of a different sort by using the categories of sciences like anthropology or sociology which form their concepts in an altogether different fashion. (The concept of class, for instance, is defined in terms of an individual's role in this economic process of production, and that of race, in terms of purely biological relationships.) Between these two kinds of subject—the subject of collective spirit, derived from the interpretation of cultural objectifications, and the anthropological or sociological subject—the discrepancy due to their heterogeneous origin is so great that it seems absolutely imperative to interpolate an intermediate field of concepts capable of mediating between these two extremes.

8. For example, roles delineated by respondents in cross-cultural research may have similarity to role concepts in American society but may refer to entirely different activities. The vocabulary of a social group may reference a set of possible behaviors, altered as the group-life situation of the users changes. A study of collegiate subculture or of urban Negroes would probably reveal not only a set of new terms but a set of new behaviors associated with the old terms, e.g., "hip" is now applied to a group in a modified form, "hippies," and connotes retreatism, drug use, hedonism, and a quasiidealism. The root term derives from opium users who lay on their hips: hence, to be on the hip. In the late forties, jazz musicians used it to refer to someone who was sensitive to the latest things and knowledgable. "Hippies" now has a pejorative connotation, and was in all probability generated from without and refers to behaviors having nothing to do with music, knowledge, or sensitivity per se (See Polsky, 1967:Chapter 4). The occupational studies done in Chicago in the twenties might be reinterpreted now within a framework that attends to change in the referent of role terms as well as changes in the terms themselves.

Further, the extent to which the terms themselves could be seen to refer to unseen meanings embedded in a cultural matrix is problematic. The classical works of this sort, begun by Goffman in his dissertation (1953), tend to break down at the point where interactional forms (ploys, collusions, teamwork, etc.) reference a host of meanings that can be understood only by understanding what is at stake or what is being managed. In ôther words, the common-sense features of Anglo- American life, which Goffman admits are a resource in his writings, "fill in" for the reader as he goes along. It may be that the study Goffman made was as successful as it was because he understood the routine bases of action, had the ability to take them as normal and natural and mutually acceptable, and was able to furnish his own credentials as competent in this understanding. These resources allowed him to see through, and see the interactional forms as standing for, other intentions of actors' uses.[9]

We can perhaps bypass the problems we have suggested by making some further distinctions. We have introduced the indexical properties of role terms, noting that their situational properties, and suggesting that the common-sense base of the organization, embeds role terms and role imputations. Furthermore, the process of role imputation, role naming, and role behavior has a common, repetitive, and expected quality. We can assume that the repetitive nature of situated social action leads to typification. Actors derive and use typifications of others' behaviors and motives. In the process they not only organize others' behaviors, they derive meaningful assessments of their own actions. Schutz (1962:60) describes the process.

> The world of everyday life is from the outset also a social and cultural world in which I am interrelated in manifold ways of interaction with fellow-men known to me in varying degreès of intimacy and anonymity.... Yet only on particular situations, and then only fragmentarily, can I experience the other's motives, goals, etc. — briefly, the subjective meanings they bestow upon their actions, in their uniqueness. I can, however, experience them in their typicality. In order to do so, I construct typical patterns of the actors' motives and ends, even of their attitudes and personalities, of which their actual conduct is just an instance or example. These typified patterns of others' behavior become, in turn, motives for my own action, and this leads to the phenomenon of self-typification.

We are led then to understand socialization by attention to the linguistic use of terms referring to organization, organizational life, and to role terms and imputations. The latter, we have suggested, take their meanings from the organizational context in which they have currency. That

9. I would like to thank Paul Ray for suggesting several of the points in this and the two preceding paragraphs.

is, actors order their expectations in settings with reference to vocabularies (especially those referring to typical cases, typical roles, and typical organizational phenomenon, which are themselves features of the settings in which they are found). They cannot be seen simply in the relationship of sign to referent; but as expressions that are known by the style with which they are uttered (ironically, metaphorically, analogically, poetically, prosaically, etc.) (Garfinkel, 1967:31; Garfinkel and Sacks in McKinney and Tiryakian, 1970).

Organizations as Socializing Settings

We have suggested above in our discussions of role and organization that if we could describe and account for socialization as easily as Parsons (1951:205) does ("[Socialization is] the acquisition of the requisite orientations for satisfactory functioning in a role"), there would be no need for concern with either organizational structure or role learning, other than specifying the character of each. That is, specifying the character of role and structure and noting their equivalence. The second step would be to simply classify for the purposes at hand all those actors who were adequate or inadequate for the role statuses outlined. However, features of organizational settings are not exhausted by structural characteristics. To ascribe to this view is analogous to believing that language behavior can be understood by a close study of a dictionary.[10]

Features of organized settings, on the contrary, can never be fully exhausted, because they have a reflexive quality. They are described by competent actors with language terms, nonverbal cues, and behaviors that themselves constitute part of the setting. Words themselves have an indexical quality by virtue of their use within. The qualities of organized and organizational life most at issue are those that are not raised to the conscious level, are assumed, are resources for managing and aligning action, are reciprocal among actors involved, and are characteristic and natural, and are not exhausted by talking about them. In short, they are the common-sense grounds of organizational life.[11]

Characteristics of these grounds have been discussed by Schutz, Garfinkel, and others. An enumeration of them is but a passing bow in

10. Some modern sociology seems to me to be analogous to the Galenic theory of medicine. It was only after actual autopsies began to be done in medicine that it became clear that Galenic theories could not be proven when actual body tissues were examined. In the same way, "structural sociology" has persisted in spite of its obvious glossing of social behavior.

11. This paragraph is based on Chapter 2 in Garfinkel's *Studies in Ethnomethodology* (1967), and additionally draws on Cicourel's work on acquisition of social structure (Chapter 6 in this volume).

the direction of an enormous, yet unfinished, task. (1) These grounds have the character of reciprocity in that *A* assumes that *B* assumes things as he (*A*) does; that, given a change in position, *B* would assume that *A* assumes things as he does, and that the consequence of this would be ordered interaction. (2) They have the character of taking shape from the course of their own development. Things are seen as taking place within a context that orders both "things to come" and things that have passed but takes its own sense from a redefinition of both past and future as the "present" unfolds. A "film of continuity" binds together conversationalists so that "wait and see," "I thought so," and "you didn't mean that" can be employed to discount certain phrases and meanings while waiting for the "real" meaning to "come clear." Events are taken as pointing to the norms in the situation. Yet, these same events cannot be unequivocally assigned that status by nonmembers. (3) An et cetera quality resides in conversational flow. "You know what I mean" is not only a conversational device, it is taken as being literally, for the purposes at hand, true. (4) Normal forms of conversation are employed. That is, if mistakes, misunderstandings, embarrassments, and unclarities in conversation emerge (the features enumerated above vanish or are made to vanish), means for restoration are always present. Goffman (1956a, 1956b, 1957, 1961b) has suggested the existence of these aspects of orderly interaction. (5) Talk in settings is reflexive. "Organizational talk" is talk that is both a feature of the setting and itself descriptive of the setting. Conversation, for example, is a normal part of most work settings.[12] (6) Vocabularies—Cicourel in Chapter 6 in this volume calls them oral lexicons—present in a setting are made up of lists of actors' vocabularies. Cicourel uses Garfinkel's example of a library catalog, in which the titles used to index the books are a part of the things described (books' titles). The role types described in prison research not only organize (presumably) the behavior there, their existence in use is a part of the necessary description of the prison itself (Sykes, 1956). Roles are to be found embedded in the language actors normally use to talk about them. A socialization language for a setting would include the language used to talk about actors' roles, vocabularies, normal usage, etc., as a sign of competence.

Organizations have these features in common, but vary in substance. This is a substance that is practically characteristic (that is, it makes a difference for the things that are done within the organization). Implicit is that these grounds are the fundamental basis for an orderly life. They

---

12. Sociologists' practical work often attends to these features of the work setting, e.g., see the study by Miller and Form (1964:229–231) in which they divide conversations into "sociotechnical" and "social," an example of acceptance of a managerial symbolic framework into which talk is sorted.

cannot be bypassed by the new men, the recruits, because not only are they the basis for life within, they provide grounds for interpretation of the meaning of their behavior.

Susanne Langer (1951:238–239) provides a clear statement of the nature of the assumed taken-for-granted features of life which are problematic to the "newcomer."

> Yet, all these signs and abbreviated symbols have to be supported by a vast intellectual structure in order to function so smoothly that we are almost unaware of them; and this structure is composed of their full articulate forms and all their implicit relationships which may be exhumed from our stock of buried knowledge at any time. Because they do fit so neatly into the frame of our ultimate world picture we can think *with* them and do not have to think *about* them, but our full apprehension about them is really only suppressed. They wear a 'cap of invisibility' when, like good servants, they perform their tasks for our convenience without being *evident* in themselves. Though we ordinarily only see things with the economy of practical vision, we can look at them instead of through them, and then their suppressed forms and their unusual meanings emerge for us. It is just because there is a front of possible meanings in every familiar form, that the picture of reality holds together for us.

This is a well-stated description of the nature of common-sense knowledge: it is that type of experience taken for granted upon which signification, marking, indexing, and symbolization are based. It is an organization of finite meanings. Strangers or new members of an organization are both a part and not a part of the organization. They act within the limits of the system but do not share the common-sense knowledge current among the other members.

How sociologists make these grounds visible to themselves and others should follow "actors' rules" for doing the same thing. How is it that this task can be approached? The final section, prior to a methodological note, addresses itself to the problem of discovering actors' rules as a means to study organizational socialization.

Talking and Becoming

The gathering of an actors' dictionary or oral lexicon is a generally followed practice among anthropological fieldworkers, but in most cases the "deep rules," which allow the linking of the lexicon with the flow of conversation, which underlie continuity and provide clues to others' response, and which allow actors to talk about things not present in the setting, remain as things known to anyone in the society (and perhaps also to the fieldworker himself) (Cicourel, in Chapter 6). The categories chosen, why they were chosen, the sense of closure when words do not provide it, and the use of terms that are normal to the setting, that is, uses of and referrals to role, all provide a context within which the norms (or known standards of behavior) take on significance. Explaining behavior in any organization without reference to the common-sense grounds by which it takes its form is analogous to analyzing a college student's choice of courses and curriculum by means of the college catalog alone.

We have suggested that the ability of speakers and hearers to make sense of conversation — when it is truncated, when "words fail," or when people speak ironically (it isn't really this way, but I am telling you in this way in order to impart some sense of what my tale means to me), or by glossing (hitting the high spots, but you can fill in the rest), by synedoche (using a part to stand for the whole, or vice-versa), or by analogy (something else) — has reference to a source that clarifies the course of events. This source, however, is not equally distributed: sediments of experience in the organization, biographically accumulated knowledge, and situational constraints (can't say what I mean here because of the audience) introduce barriers to socialized, fully acceptable conversational understandings and, hence, to role imputations, typifications, normal events, and the rest. It is not enough to learn the language, as some fieldworkers have suggested (for example, in studies of the poolroom hustler, prisons, drug addicts, etc.), without attention to the rules that make adequate use of it possible. One of the standard suggestions for fieldwork is attention to the oral lexicon and its use, but it may be the very attention to the oral lexicon that allows the listener to absorb the means by which it is used. Some of the very contingencies in understanding (socialization) have been used, inadvertently, by workers to construct prospective schemes of the process. It is assumed by some that the operations by which conversations are maintained of their course — the et cetera clauses, the reflexive nature of talk, the wait and see nature of it — are available to all. In fact, the competent use of such devices is an index of the extent to which one can be considered a competent user, a member of the organization.

Although the ideal study of socialization (organizationally or otherwise) might seek general rules for the implementation of alternative usages, phrases, clauses, bits, or ways of talking, it is more likely initially that a denotative listing (glossary) is needed. Other studies provide some already assembled data on language. For example, Sykes's study of the New Jersey State Prison contains some important descriptions of what he calls argot roles or "a number of distinctive tags for distinctive social roles played by its members in response to the particular problems of imprisonment. It is these patterns of behavior, recognized and labelled by the inmates of the prison, which we have chosen to call argot roles" (Sykes, 1956:86). It is not clear whether these are role terms (self-designations) or role imputations (other designations), or an inductive analysis of the sociologist. There is no mention of the adequate use of these terms in the prison, nor of the relationships between situated usage and rules for their use in the organization. Although this could be done retrospectively, it would only be by way of a hypothesis that would require further information. Glossaries begin the task.

If there is an adequate and competent use of language in accord with some set of actors' rules, then there are logically cases of inadequate use. Cicourel's recent work on socialization of children suggests a method developed by Harvey Sacks (1966). The term contrastive analysis is used to describe the technique. They suggest that, as before, the investigator utilize his own knowledge of the rules implicit in conversational episodes to make those rules explicit. Means by which conversations are maintained are called devices, with two or more categories socially used in a setting by conversationalists to refer to a population of objects. These are describing terms that can be used to link what is being said with some socially relevant categories or referents that are found in the language used. Role, for example, can be used as a device to which categories known within the organization can be referred and can be seen to operate systematically. That is, actors' rules for the assigning of categories to a device are implicit in conversation and writing and can be developed inductively from the study of conversations.[13] Rules are seen to reside in the fact that members are able to describe and make accounts of settings by means of devices to which categories can be referred. Rules are the recognition among members that a device and a category cluster together in some fashion. The way in which the device and the category are linked is itself a source of a rich catalog. Rules, it would seem, refer to the ways in which markings, signifying, indexing, symbolizing, and so on take place.[14] In medical settings, the device patient is used to refer categories such as crock, alcoholic, and malingerer, to certain populations encountered there. The grounds or basis of this referral relationship could be found by investigating the symptoms used to make the transition between categories and the device to which they refer. Sacks offers another example of the use of a device, sex, which can be paired with the two categories male and female.

These categories are recognized by actors as going together, but the difficulty in such a task appears in the construction of these relationships, since the investigator relies in large part on his own com-

13. Further examples of this linguistic analysis are found in the writings of Sacks (mimeo, no date) and of Schegloff (in Garfinkel and Sacks, forthcoming) and other chapters in this volume. The intellectual style of this work is suggestive of the influence of Wittgenstein.

14. See Cicourel's (1964:212–215) discussion of these processes.

mon-sense knowledge of the way actors do describing to make his own
analysis. The way in which contrastive analysis is done is by building up
sets of rules by which these pairings are made, such as the "consistency
rule." The consistency rule reads: if a population is associated with a
category and that category is referred to a device, then other members of
the population can be classified as well by the use of that category or
another. Other rules and their titles seem to be interminable, but the
inductive nature of the work makes the building of categories and devices into rules an interesting pursuit. Uses of categories that are not
linked in the same way to devices (referring to "crock" as to the device
pottery rather than to patient would be in contrast with the normal
association of crock with patient, for example). Categories in sentences
have a continuity that is part of what users rely upon; contravention of
these conventions leads to confusion, clarification, etc. The assumption
that everyone knows the referent of certain categories and the means by
which they are linked to population is the basis for normal use and, by
contrast, abnormal use. Both the hearer and the listener are able to put
together conversations by means of these induced rules of conversation.[15]

We can now return to the problem of indexical expressions. The
discovery of meanings rooted in an organizational context and their
connection with rules of use is a means by which glossaries can be
associated with use of words in the organization. The use of the category
headache, broken leg, or sore throat may or may not be linked to the
device emergency, but understanding of the knowledge that makes this
linkage possible is a sign of knowledge of what members of the emer-
gency-room population mean when they utilize the category to refer to a
person. The meanings that arise and have persistence in any organization have certain "unique" qualities, and these unique and practical
matters give the organization the features that new people must become
aware of. (But see footnote 8 above concerning the generality of the
findings of this sort of work.)

In a sense, the understanding of contrastive analysis as a device
seems to follow upon the doing of ethnographic studies. Some of the
recent work of Sudnow (1967) and Cavan (1966), as well as Garfinkel,
make important use of concepts such as standing patterns of behavior,
conventional usage, normal troubles, and the like to describe the workings of particular organizations or types of organizations. (The use of
types is itself a phenomenological question and probably both follows
and accompanies the gathering of ethnographies.)

The context is in part described by the language used within it. It

15. The preceding paragraphs are based upon Cicourel's description of Sack's (in
Garfinkel and Sacks', forthcoming) technique (See Chapter 6 in this volume).

provides the special meanings that allow the linkage of device and category that is shared by hearer, speaker, and researcher. The researcher's job lies ahead: generating listings or oral lexicons, linking conditions for device, category, and population, and building rules of their use. Presumably this involves gathering information on the conditions under which rules obtain or fail to obtain. Rules should clarify discovered differences in usage among the "new" and "old" members of a group. Cicourel has adopted the use of contrastive analysis to create a developmental model of children's socialization. Contrastive analysis might be utilized also to study how rules develop over a time and how they are maintained as features of the setting over turnovers and change in population. It is the learning of these "members' rules" for the use of language that is the basis for becoming a member of the group. Talking is becoming.

A Recourse, a Method

Socialization again appears, unsolved, as a process in everyday life. Some of the things it is not, and how one should not study it, have been briefly indicated; some of the things it is sociologically have also been suggested. The process involves taking as apparent the matters in daily life that are not apparent; it associates actors with the use of schemes, terms (roles), linguistic labels, and lexicons; it facilitates an indexical understanding of this lexicon, in part by typification and normal usage.

Yet, the learning or acquisition of operative knowledge takes place, by actors' admissions, in the context of generated meanings. These are the objective or limiting factors within which the common-sense base flourishes. An organizational language will contain the information necessary for dealing with the problems of the organization. As these are faced, role terms, role imputations, and typifications arise and have with them sets of acceptable referents. A scheme accounting for the growth of argot roles within a prison could be constructed, but so far we have but the lexicon, not the basis for use (by whom and with what referent in accord with what rules of use).

Acquisition of the common-sense or routine grounds of organizational life is fundamental to the acquisition of the oral lexicon and the surface rules (norms of use, grammar, and syntax) for its use.[16] The base supplies a context in which the vocabularies typical to the organization are embedded. Culture operates in an unseen way, and making it seen is a practice of lay as well as professional recorders of social life.

16. Cicourel has suggested this distinction between "deep rules," which we have called common-sense or routine grounds of organizational life, and "surface rules," referring to specific norms of use that is grammar and syntax. A parallel distinction in regard to rules is found in Rawls (1955).

Let us assume that we wish to examine organizations socially and sociologically. Let us assume that we wish to make it a process that is practical and useful. "Useful" here refers to sociologically useful in the sense of continued reference and cumulative possibilities.

The following are some programmatic suggestions:

1. Learning the natural language of the organization. This would involve fieldwork of a classical anthropological sort based on gathering an oral lexicon or glossary (a listing of words used in the context and with what referent).

   a. Paying special attention to those terms used to designate terms referring to roles.

   b. Listing of the devices and categories and the rules for their use in the setting.

2. Developing a language, or a metalanguage, that would enable the researcher to talk about the language actors use to talk about their roles and the appropriate rules for its use within the setting.

3. Schematically attending to the naming function of members of the organization insofar as this power to order by naming is differentially distributed. In this sense, there is a parallel between studying adults' use of words and the way in which they interpret the meaning of children's use. The power to pass on to subordinates a set of meanings is critical; the way in which this process comes about is a phenomenological question.

4. Doing ethnographic studies of the organization in which socialization is to be studied. That is, how do actors describe to each other the scenes in which they find themselves; what are the ways they use to refer to their own actions and those of others; how are the problems they face on a daily nature handled and managed as a part of the life they lead in the organization?

PART FOUR

Symbolic Interactionism and Ethnomethodology

Symbolic Interactionism and Ethnomethodology*

The problem of developing a consistent theoretical perpsective that would permit the joint analysis of social-psychological and sociological problems has long concerned the sociologist. The development of a methodology that would permit such an analysis has also remained an issue. While various alternatives have been offered, from the borrowing of models from economics and psychology to structural-functionalism, none has proven completely satisfactory. My intent in this chapter is to take two perspectives in contemporary sociology, one old, one relatively new, and to examine their potential for meeting the above issues. Specifically I shall examine symbolic interactions and ethnomethodology. Because both focus in some way on the individual, they provide a view of social organization that may be termed subjective and social-psychological in nature. Analysis of the degree of convergence between the two should permit an expanded treatment of how individuals are linked to, shaped by, and in turn create, social structure. These two

*I am indebted to a number of colleagues and students for their critical reactions to earlier versions of this essay. I am also grateful for the comments and criticisms of Howard S. Becker, Carl J. Couch, Harold Mark, and the students in my 426 seminar on deviance at the University of Illinois.

It is important to note that what follows is my proposed synthesis of interactionism and ethnomethodology. This is not intended as an essay expressing widespread consensus, which, as such is probably not possible at this time.

A much revised and shortened version of this essay appeared in the *American Sociological Review* 34 (December, 1969):922–934.

perspectives are especially relevant to the above problems because they also propose special views of methodology — views that I shall suggest may be combined.

Thus, my intent is to briefly review the basic assumptions of each perspective. Their abilities to stimulate empirical research will be examined with an eye to a synthesis of their respective methods and assumptions.

The Perspectives Defined

Drawing on Garfinkel (1967) and Cicourel (1968), ethnomethodology takes as its basic concern analysis of the routine, taken-for-granted expectations that members of any social order regularly accept. The nature of these expectations and the form they take constitute a central focus of ethnomethodology. Basic to this perspective is the attempt to sharply distinguish scientific from everyday activity. The problems of penetrating everyday perspectives and giving them sociological explanations are repeatedly addressed, and the method of documentary analysis is set forth as a preferred strategy. The abiding concern, however, is with the relationship between everyday, taken-for-granted meanings and the organization of these meanings into routine patterns of interaction.

Symbolic interactionism takes as a fundamental concern the relationship between individual conduct and forms of social organization, most centrally social groups. This perspective grants the human the ability to carry on conversations with himself and asks how selves emerge out of social structure and social situations.

Both perspectives take some variant of the individual and interaction as the unit of sociological analysis. Their methods are similar to the extent that the perspective of the acting person is given primary importance. Fundamentally, then, they posit a link between the person and social structure that rests on the role of symbols and common meanings. To this extent they both share a great deal with what is commonly termed the structural-functional perspective. Both Durkheim and Parsons, for example, have given close attention to how individual perspectives are related to larger collective, or cultural, representations. Locating the unit of analysis in the individual and interaction separates interactionism and ethnomethodology from other points of view, however.

Symbolic Interactionism

The interactionist assumes that humans are capable of making their own thoughts and activities objects of analysis. That is, persons routinely and habitually, manipulate symbols and orient their own actions toward other objects. A great deal of human conduct is assumed to be of this routine nature. Once the meanings of objects have been agreed upon, conduct can flow along lines of custom, tradition, and ritual. In a sense this assumption parallels Weber's concern with the role of ritual and custom in human interaction.

Yet humans possess the ability to self-consciously direct their own activities—to break out of old routines and to construct new lines of action. The interaction process may thus be classified into those behaviors that are routinely organized and those that are actively constructed in a self-conscious and interpretative fashion (Blumer, 1966:537–538). Granted this assumption, a fundamental empirical question becomes the identification of the shifting modes of interpretation that characterize the interaction process. Clearly interaction cannot be so grossly divided into either interpretative or noninterpretative elements. There are many levels and shades of difference between these two extremes, and the extent to which action and objects move between these points remains to be identified. A basic contribution of the ethnomethodologist has been his concern with the routine and less consciously organized forms of interaction and meaning.

Man's environment does not consist of objects that carry intrinsic meaning. Social objects are constructs and not "self-existing entities with intrinsic natures" (Blumer, 1966:539). An object is "anything toward which action can be organized and it may be as physical as a chair or imaginary as a ghost" (Blumer, 1966:539). Objects consist of any event that persons can designate in a unitary fashion and organize action toward. The meaning of an object resides in the meanings that are brought to it and hence must be located in the interaction process. As indicated, the meaning of a class of objects often becomes stabilized and perhaps even written into custom and tradition. Legal codes and etiquette are two examples. Frequently, however, meaning must be worked out and negotiated for organized joint action. At this point the distinctive nature of the human is brought forth and displayed in the interpretative process of self-directed action.

The meanings given to objects typically derive from a group, or organized interactional, perspective. Human life is group life, and concerted action arises out of the ability of persons to be objects of both their own and others' activity. Joint actions, which represent the generic form of all interaction, rest on the ability of the human to grasp the direction of the act of others (Blumer, 1966). Recurrent forms of joint action as seen in social groups, bureaucratic structures, communities, or entire societies rest in a fundamental way on the ability of humans to

join lines of action in a consensual and meaningful manner. For consensual lines of action to emerge there must exist a common community
of symbols. Because the definition of certain objects within a group's
perspective is subject to continual negotiation, at least certain features of
group life are also subject to negotiation and change. As a major hypothesis I suggest that the basic object for all interaction is the self. Because
the self carries a multitude of differing interpretations, it will often be
shifts in these definitions that give group life its changing character.

Stabilities in group structure rest, as suggested above, on standard
meanings and modes of interpretation. To the extent that selves are
consensually defined, stable patterns of action will be observed. At the
heart of group life lie a series of social selves that have been lodged in
that structure. Through the process of *self-lodging,* humans translate
crucial features of their own identity into the selves, memories, and
imaginations of other relevant others. It is in this way that Cooley's
proposition that the other exists in our imaginations of him comes to life.
By lodging the self in interaction, and in the selves of others, a reciprocal
bond is created and the firm foundations for future relationships are
established. Self-lodging thus stands in distinction to what Goffman
(1959) has termed the process of presenting a self. It is certainly the
case that selves have to be presented, but at some point in the cycle of
recurrent interactions the self begins to move out of the presentational
phase and into the lodging phase. Central to self-lodging are certain
variations on Cooley's notion of the lookingglass self, which posited a
three-fold process of presentation, identification, and subjective interpretation. Cooley profoundly noted that upon the presentation of a
self the person took on a sense of pleasure or displeasure according to
his interpretations of the other's reactions. This suggests the hypothesis
that the self is a continually evaluated object, but, most importantly, an
object that rests on affective-emotional reactions and criticisms. It is not
an object that is devastated through criticism, nor is it always calculating
and planning the most fruitful line of action.

This view of the self suggests that one motivational feature of human
conduct is the lodging process. Humans return to those interactional
quarters where the most basic features of their selves have been lodged.
This hypothesis extends Foote's (1951) proposition that identification of
self and other provides the basis of motivation. The self-lodging hypothesis suggests that after the identification process has been negotiated and
settled, a recurrent pattern of identification arises which rests on the
reciprocal definitions given the lodged selves. Once identification has
been established, it ceases to become problematic. The respective selves
now offer their own vocabularies and grounds for identification. In this
way motivation becomes an interactional process subject to finely

graded career phases. The self and its interpretations are grounded in interaction, and, as selves become lodged, the styles of and reasons for interaction become ritualized and subject to the firm rules of tradition and custom.

This conception suggests that human interaction may not be as rational and cognitively directed as some theories suggest. If the person returns to those quarters and settings where crucial aspects of the self have been lodged, his actions cease to be entirely directed on either the most rational or the most effective grounds. That is, self-lodging may place a wedge between the most economical pursuit of a goal or even the rational selection of a goal. The wedge rests on the affective bond between the self and its relevant others, and this bond can justify actions grounded in custom, love, hate, jealousy, or profound respect. This formulation offers one explanation of why certain persons refuse to be promoted within organizations or why some persist in hanging on to the label of deviant. Refusals to move or change may hinge on fondly held conceptions of self that have been lodged and reciprocated by valued others.

By way of slight amplification it is suggested that empirical indicators of the self-lodging process include variations on personal names, styles of speech, modes of dress, and the use of special gestures and body movements. Names (Hughes, 1952:130–144; Stone, in Rose, 1962:86–118) provide convenient clues to the degree of knowledge and involvement each person has with the other. As naming moves from formal titles to variations on either the title or the first name, greater self-lodging may be inferred. This is similarly the case with variations on speech, dress, and gesturing. Each person develops his own style, which belies an attempt to lodge certain portions of the self in the interaction. Another indicator of self-lodging is the degree of involvement, often in terms of time or of topic in conversation. To the extent that any encounter represents verbal communication, each person's involvement in the conversation can be charted by the frequency of his utterances. In this sense dominating or contributing to a conversation becomes akin to getting a portion of the self into that interaction. As an additional hypothesis I suggest that persons judge interactions to be satisfactory or unsatisfactory in terms of their success at self-lodging. If valued portions of the self are not lodged, recognized, and reciprocated, a dissatisfaction concerning the encounter is likely to be sensed.

Because the interactionist lodges social organization in the joint action, I must make clear how joint actions emerge and change over time. Again, following Blumer (1966), it must be noted that joint actions cannot be resolved solely into individual lines of action. When persons come together for the purpose of accomplishing a task, exchanging a

K

greeting, eating a meal, or making love, the behavior observed involves more than the intentions and meanings brought into the situation. The term interaction suggests a central feature of all joint actions — an emergent quality that may not have existed before the parties came together. The fitting together of individual lines of action provides the basic feature of the joint action. Individuals fit lines of action together by identifying the action they are going to engage in and then fitting those definitions around the other's definitions and interpretations. Hence, the joint action becomes more than the mere juggling of definitions — it is the fitting of disparate, conflicting, and often incomplete plans of action into a package of meanings that, at least for the moment of activity, provides the basis of interaction. This feature of the joint action suggests that interaction may have a variable career. That is, observers cannot photograph the beginning phases of an encounter and assume that agreements reached in that phase will remain unchanged until the end. The career of a joint action is contingent on the events that occur during its lifetime. While participants may agree initially on definitions, rules, conduct, and images of self, these definitions may be so vague as to permit conflicting points of view to later emerge that challenge the entire basis of joint action. On other occasions joint actions may be interrupted, as when a child is brought into a marriage. The entry of this new object demands renegotiation, relocation of selves, and perhaps even the adoption of an entirely different perspective so that joint action can continue.

These points should be sufficient to document the point that joint actions have variable careers through time. Because joint actions have careers, a fundamental concern of the interactionist has been with the conditions that give rise to new perspectives, new points of view, and new lines of action. Any social world, Mead (in Brightman, 1927:75–85) suggested, was sustained over time by the formation of a common perspective or symbolic order that expressed the basic forms of thinking and acting common to that world. It was in the face of conflict, or the confrontation of divergent perspectives, that Mead placed the source of change and creative activity on the part of humans. When an old perspective failed to provide answers, new points of view were seen to emerge. This simple point provided Mead (in Dewey, 1917:53–83) with his basic doctrine for the scientific method. Unlike everyday man, who could be satisfied with faulty, incomplete, and contradictory perspectives, the scientist deliberately sought out conditions, events, and activities that challenged previously accepted interpretations. It was in the dialectical process of confrontation, analysis, and resynthesis of perspective that Mead lodged the basic feature of science. Indeed the scientist was the one who sought out negative cases for instances that disproved past theories and hyptheses.

This position led Mead to argue that science was but another type of social process or social order—an order built on explicit rules that valued discovery and negation of past interpretation. This meant that the scientific enterprise as a symbolic order was subject to the same shifts and quirks that other forms of human group life were subject to. This view has since been formulated into the method termed analytic induction, which gives heavy priority to the formation of theories that, until negative cases are located, provide universal explications of the events at hand.

By placing emphasis on conflict and on situations that demanded new interpretation, Mead anticipated subsequent statements concerning the positive functions of conflict (see, for example, Coser, 1956). He also offered a view of social groups that stressed (see Thrasher, 1927) the functions of conflict in the formation of self-conscious group perspectives. Mead hypothesized that unless collectivities met with challenges, distinctive elements of a group structure were unlikely to occur. This was best treated in Thrasher's analysis of playgroups and gangs and of course echoed Simmel's treatment of the positive functions of conflict.

An additional feature of the joint action must be noted. I suggest that all forms of interaction rest on some combination of the following rules. First are civil-legal codes that exist to protect the owners of objects as well as the objects. These would include laws prohibiting violence to the self or property, which are commonly upheld by specific authorities. Second are rules of etiquette or polite interaction, which exist to uphold the ceremonious occasions of interaction (Goffman, 1959, 1963a). These rules find their way into etiquette books and cover problems of dress, introduction, leave-taking rituals, and so on. Last there is a category of rules that display the distinctive nature of enduring social relationships. These are relational rules of conduct that often derive from civil-legal or polite codes, yet they serve to redefine and often make irrelevant other prescriptions. Such would be the case for rules that sanction loud or profane language among coworkers, open states of undress among the married, and theft among certain (white collar) echelons in organizations. Relational rules define how the self is to be presented and display the forms that self-lodging is to take. Agreement to use nicknames, to swear on occasion, to steal behind the boss's back, and to ignore certain clothing rules indicates the ways in which selves have moved beyond the presentational phase into various degrees of reciprocal lodging.

A fully grounded interactional study would include all three categories of rules, and a central concern would be the extent to which persons actively construct their own meanings for standards of conduct that are taken for granted. Thus families from contrasting social strata could be studied in terms of their adherence to one or another of these rules. The distinctive nature of many social relationships is represented in their relational rules that make problematic events that other collectivities assume, and that take for granted rules that others argue over.

THE METHODOLOGICAL ASSUMPTIONS OF INTERACTIONISM

Because human interaction involves behavior of both the covert and overt variety, and because the meanings attached to objects often change during an encounter, the interactionist endeavors to relate covert, symbolic behavior with overt patterns of interaction. This additionally demands a concern for the unfolding meaning objects assume during an interaction sequence. The usual strategy is to work from overt behaviors (Mead, 1934:1–8) back to the meanings attached to those behaviors and objects. This feature of interactionist methodology suggests that behavioral analyses alone (see, for example, Webb et al., 1966) are insufficient to establish valid explanations of human conduct. Similarly, an analysis of the meanings or definitions held by a set of persons and carried into a real or proposed interaction will not supply the needed link between those symbols and interaction. Thus, as a first methodological principle, covert and overt forms of conduct must be examined before an investigation is complete. This resembles Weber's argument that meaning must be attached, often through role-taking, to overt patterns of behavior.

Because this principle suggests analysis of how meaning shifts during interaction, a basic problem becomes the identification of interpretational phases. Studies must be conducted that determine at what point during an encounter objects cease to be negotiated.

A second principle focuses on the self as both an object and a process that must be investigated. The investigator is directed to examine behavior from the perspective of those being studied, and he must indicate the shifting meanings and statuses assigned the self during any interaction. At certain phases in any encounter the self ceases to be a negotiated object and assumes an agreed-upon meaning, and interaction then turns to other concerns. This would be the case in many ritual encounters where the basic activity lies above the self or in the interaction process. Social games, routine work, and even participation in a religious ceremony appear to represent such occasions. By making the self a central object of study, analysis can quickly establish what is taken for granted and what is problematic for the respective interactants. A commitment to this principle permits the researcher to escape the fallacy of objectivism, which is the substitution of the scientist's perspective for that of those studied.

Taking the role of the acting other, or self, leads to a third principle, which states that the researcher must link his subjects' symbols and meanings to the social circles and relationships that furnish those perspectives. Unless meanings can be linked to larger social perspectives, analysis will remain largely psychological in nature. This suggests a two-step process for any study—meanings at both the individual and interactional levels must be identified and related.

The fourth methodological principle of interactionism directs researchers to consider the "situated aspects" of human conduct. If behavior occurs within social situations and if the meaning attached to those situations influences subsequent behavior, the situation must become a variable of analysis. Four components of the situation may be distinguished: the interactants as objects, the concrete setting, the meanings brought into the situation, and the time taken for the interaction. This conception of the situation suggests that variations in behavior can arise from definitions given the respective selves, from the other objects that constitute the situation (for example, furniture or lighting), from the meanings and definitions for action that are held before interaction occurs, and, last, from the temporal sequencing of action itself (see Garfinkel, 1967). All interaction unfolds over time and thus may be seen as having an orderly temporal sequence or career. If meaning shifts during the encounter, then various temporal phases can be identified that parallel those interpretational shifts. For example, encounters between strangers in public behavior settings often begin with the exchange of names or at least the reciprocal recognition of the other through eye contact: next, a task is quickly settled upon, and finally a leave-taking ritual is enacted to release both parties from the interaction (see Goffman, 1963a). Among the acquainted, naming and negotiation of tasks may be bypassed for a more rapid entry into a deep form of interactional involvement such as conversation. The situation as an intrusive variable cannot be ignored. The entry of alien others, the failure of mechanical equipment (Gross and Stone, 1963), and shifts in levels of mutual involvement all relate to interaction as a situated process. In this way concrete situations become both places for interaction and objects of negotiation. It is impossible to separate the two from situational analysis.

I have suggested that the interaction process is characterized by both stability and change. This furnishes a fifth methodological principle—research strategies must be capable of reflecting both aspects of group life. Hypotheses concerning group life must contain, for example, relationships between variables that are interactive in nature. It is insufficient to formulate strictly A-B-type propositions. If interaction represents a significant feature of group life, propositions must be stated in a manner that reflects reciprocal and interdependent effects and causes (Homans, in Faris, 1964:951–977).

Research methods can thus be judged by their ability to yield data of the above order. In this vein methods are seen as ways of acting on the environment. Consequently the act of making observations becomes symbolic and subject to personal fancy, bias, and even ideological preference. Traditionally the interactionist has favored the less rigorous methods of participant-observation and life histories. This has created a restrictive bias with the perspective and has frequently opened practitioners to criticism of poor research.

This criticism overlooks the essential point that the scientific process is built on two features—discovery and verification. The interactionist, properly speaking, will admit into his methodological perspective any research tool that permits the penetration of group life. Hence, a great deal of value can be found in surveys and experiments, as well as in the more favored methods of participant-observation. If priority is given to the discovery process, the issues of verification, reliability, and validity become more than technical in nature. The quality of research is now judged by its public elements and by its authentic representation of central features of human group life. If issues of verification are placed above the discovery process, a wedge is driven between the goals and the methods of sociology. Verification is at issue only after discovery has been accomplished. Of course the two cannot be separated, but I wish to suggest that common criticisms of interactionist research have ignored this feature of the scientific process.

That the interactionist perspective has traditionally given greater attention to the discovery process is seen in the use of concepts. [See Denzin, 1970, Chpts. 1–3] For the interactionist the preferred concepts are sensitizing in nature. This does not mean that operationalization is avoided—it merely suggests that the point of operationalization is delayed until the situated meaning of concepts is discovered. At this point standard methods of observation can be employed. Another feature of this process is the use of multiple methods of observation. Commonly termed triangulation (Webb et al, 1966), this strategy directs the researcher to utilize several different tools in the observational process. The logic for this assumption rests on the fact that no method taken alone can adequately treat all the problems of discovery and verification. Each method has restrictions, and if several different methods are combined in the same study the restrictions of one tool are often the strengths of another. An example of triangulation is seen in the study of socialization in medical school by Becker et al (1961). Here the techniques of direct observation, focused interviewing, unobtrusive behavioral analysis, and quasiexperimentation were combined. Had the study been restricted to only one of these methods, the shifting nature of perspectives and socialization in medical school would probably not have been uncovered.

The triangulation process assumes several elements that can be only indicated at this point. A series of common data bases have to be located, a reliable sampling model that recognizes interaction must be adopted, a series of empirical indicators relevant to each data base and hypothesis must be constructed, and, last, research must progress in a formative manner in which hypotheses and data continually interrelate. An excellent instance of these steps is given in Glaser and Strauss's (1964, 1968) studies of dying in the hospital. Here sampling was progressive and comparative in nature, hypotheses were developed hand in hand with data collection, and multiple methods of observation were utilized. It is important to note that triangulation, as I have spelled it out, involves a synthesis of statistical and theoretical sampling models. The rigorous rules of sampling theory have to be combined with the more theoretically flexible techniques of concept-guided sampling. When natural interactive units are being sampled (such as social relationships, encounters, organizations), it is necessary for the researcher to demonstrate the representativeness of those units in the total population of similar events.

A final methodological principle relates to the type of theory that is formulated. Formal theory (Simmel, 1950) is a common goal of interactionist research. Although historically or situationally specific propositions are recognized, propositions with the greatest universal relevance are sought. This assumes that human affairs, wherever they occur, rest on the same interactional processes. Formal theory, in this sense, builds upon Merton's view of middle-range theory and extends those formulations to a position that calls for soundly grounded empirical propositions of an all-inclusive, universal nature (see Glaser and Strauss, 1967). Properly speaking, the interactionist has not achieved this goal. The perspective remains a perspective, or conceptual framework. It is not a theory in the strict meaning of the term.

Ethnomethodology

As I indicated earlier, the ethnomethodologist directs attention to the question of how a social order is possible. For Garfinkel (1967) the answer merges a Durkheimian concern for large collective representations with an interactionist conception of the rules, norms, and meanings that members of any social order daily take for granted. He states (1967:35):

A society's members encounter and know the moral order as perceivably normal courses of action. . . . They refer to this world as the "natural facts of life" which, for members, are through and through moral facts of life. For members not only are matters so about familiar scenes, but they are so because it is morally right or wrong that they are so. Familiar scenes of everyday activities, treated by members as the "natural facts of life," are massive facts of the members' daily existence both as a real world and as the product of activities in a real world. They furnish the "fix," the "this is it" to which the waking returns one, and are the points of departure and return for every modification of the world of daily life that is achieved in play, dreaming, trance, theater, scientific theorizing, or high ceremony.

These rules, which any bona fide member of a social order is aware of, include the following assumptions concerning face-to-face interaction: (1) interaction flows in a temporal sequence and statements in any encounter cannot be understood without reference to the actual flow of events; (2) persons in any situation will talk about many things that are only tacitly recognized, if at all; (3) normal background affairs and conditions in any situation are taken for granted and typically go unchallenged during any encounter.

The ethnomethodologist hypothesizes that when persons come together for interaction the following assumptions are made. First, they assume that once a situation is defined this definition holds for the duration of the encounter. Second, it is assumed that any object present in the situation is what it is presented as being. Objects will range from selves, to pieces of equipment, to (presumably) such background features as lighting, and so on. Third, it is assumed that the meanings given an object on one occasion will hold for future occasions. This leads to the derivative point that definitions of one set of interactants are assumed to be the same as any other person or persons would develop were they in the same situation. Fifth, persons go through the process of identifying objects and attaching meaning to them by the use of standard terms, symbols, and labels. Thus, participants are assumed to bring with them into any situation a common vocabulary of symbols that permit the smooth flow of interaction.

Because all encounters have careers, the ethnomethodologist posits that persons "make sense out of" their interactions by locating verbal utterances and physical actions in a temporal sequence of ongoing activity. That is, persons in any encounter are unable to interpret their own action without a reference to what has just happened and what is likely to occur in the future. A sixth assumption suggests that, while persons base their definitions of situations on their own biographies and past experiences, any discrepancies that would arise in an encounter because of variations in biography or experience are held in abeyance. In short, situations are defined through the process of interaction. This means, in effect, that persons will often feel a degree of conflict between their public and private definitions. However, that conflict is removed, as much as is possible, from the encounter.

These are assumptions all persons hold and make when they engage in interaction. For the ethnomethodologist they are unstated expectancies or attributions that are part and parcel of the common-sense vocabularies all persons possess by virtue of their membership in a social order.

A basic concern of the ethnomethodologist becomes the penetration of normal situations of interaction to uncover the rules and rituals participants take for granted. This concern is typically phrased as how could one disrupt normal social events so that any person's conception of the normal, real, and ordinary would be challenged. In Garfinkel's studies (1967:54) the common strategy has been to design quasiexperimental fieldstudies in which three conditions are created. First, the situation is structured in such a way that the person being studied could not interpret it as a game, an experiment, a deception, or a play. Second, the person is given insufficient time to reconstruct the situation on his own terms. Third, the person is forced to make whatever new definitions he can by himself (no aid is given by the investigator).

At several points Garfinkel reports experiments that meet the above three conditions. On one occasion students were asked to play boarders in their own homes, on another occasion students were told to overpay and underpay for objects purchased in a store, in another experiment medical students were given discrepent information regarding an application for medical school, and in another study students were told to violate the usual rules of tic-tac-toe.

In all of these studies, which Garfinkel insists are exploratory and illustrative only, it was found that persons who act as "everyday experimenters" find it terribly difficult to challenge the routine rules of interaction. Feelings of distrust, hostility, anger, frustration, and persecution were all reported by his student experimenters. It was reported that the focus of interaction was soon lost when the "experimenter" attitude was assumed, and for all practical purposes the students were unable to carry on normal interaction. Garfinkel explains this inability with the concept of trust, which he defines as the assumption on the part of any person that all others he encounters will share his expectations and definition of the situation. In addition it is assumed that the other person will act on the basis of these assumptions, even in problematic situations.

K*

The use of this concept suggests that when one or more interactants are forced to distrust the other, the normal background features of the situation suddenly become problematic and the organization of joint action soon collapses. Hence these experiments represent small-scale studies concerning the basis of collective behavior. They also offer data on the interpretational phases of encounters.

Another broad concern of the ethnomethodologist has been with the routine productions of persons caught up in ongoing social organizations. On several occasions either Garfinkel or his associates Sudnow (1967), Cicourel (1968), and Douglas (1967) have reported studies concerning the special nature of organizational records. The basic hypothesis guiding these studies, which have ranged from analyses of mental health clinics to those of hospitals, police departments, juvenile courts, and suicide prevention centers, is that members of any social organization develop a special perspective for handling their clients. It is argued that the perspectives of any given organization will be sufficiently different from those of all other similar organizations to make comparisons between such agencies problematic. Borrowed from Garfinkel (1956:181–182), the working definition of social organization employed in these studies is

> the term "an organization" is an abbreviation of the full term "an organization of social actions." The term "organization" does not itself designate a palpable phenomenon. It refers instead to a related set of ideas that a sociologist invokes to aid him in collecting his thoughts about the ways in which patterns of social actions are related. His statements about social organization describe the *territory* within which the actions occur; the *number* or persons who occupy that territory; the character structure. He tells how these persons are *socially related* to each other, for he talks of husbands and wives, of bridge partners, of cops and robbers. He describes their *activities,* and the ways they achieve social *access* to each other. And like the grand theme either explicitly announced or implicitly assumed, he describes the *rules* that specify for the actor the use of the area, the numbers of persons who should be in it, the nature of the activity, purpose, and feeling allowed, the approved and disapproved means of entrance and exit from affiliative relationships with the persons there.

On the basis of this definition, which stresses meanings, vocabularies, and rules of interaction, ethnomethodological studies have suggested that (1) organizations perpetuate themselves through time by generating fictitious records; (2) comparable organizations differ in the meanings they assign to the same events (birth, death, mental illness, cured, etc.); (3) the production of organizational records is basically an interactional process based on rumor, gossip, overheard conversations, discrepent information, and biographically imperfect bookkeeping. Cicourel (1968), for example, noted that agencies created to process juvenile delinquency routinely created delinquents by piecing together long series of conversations between the predelinquent, his parents, the arresting officer, the counselor, and the judge. The sum total of these conversations, which became translated into official reports, became the organizational documentation that a delinquent act had or had not occured. (4) in piecing together these organizational reports it was found that members routinely relied on open-ended categories of meaning and interpretation to classify recalcitrant and ambiguous cases. What Garfinkel (1967:73–75) calls the et cetera clause references this tendency of persons to always fit events into a pattern that complements their ongoing action. Thus one mental health clinic was found to systematically overreport the number of persons processed because such records in effect justified the organization's existence.

It is important to note that these studies amplify the research of interactionists on the labeling process. Becker (1963), for example, has posited the hypothesis that deviance does not reside in social acts but must be traced to definitions that arise during interaction. Cicourel's research suggests that deviance may be as much organizational as interactional in nature and must be traced to the working perspectives of members of social control agencies. Garfinkel's studies additionally propose that disruptions of everyday perspectives can create feelings of distrust that become translated into deviant labels.

In several senses the ethnomethodologist has merged the interactionist's concern with deviance with the study of social organization and social relationships. Their studies crosscut the analysis of civil-legal, polite interactional, and relational rules. The basic interest, however, remains in the taken-for-granted rules that can come from any of the above categories.

These studies of social organization suggest an additional point of convergence with the interactionist perspective. Traditionally interactionists have employed a conception of the organization that stresses work and the interpretations given to positions in a division of labor, noting that the key to an organization lies in its underside, or informal structure. This has led to the proposition (Hughes, 1956) that beside every task division of labor rests a moral hierarchy of positions that dictate how persons are to relate. A typical interactionist study of social organization begins with the formal structure and then details how moral and ideological variations transform that structure into a going concern of social relationships (see, for example, Strauss, et al, 1964). This complements the ethnomethodologist's strategy but suggests that the formal structure cannot be ignored.

Perhaps the most important claim of the ethnomethodologist is the statement that the productions of sociologists are very similar to those in everyday life. This echoes the concern of Mead and others for distinguishing scientific from everyday activities.

The ethnomethodologist's argument involves the following points. First, all sociologists are (or should be) concerned with depicting the taken-for-granted affairs of actors caught up in any social order. To the extent that this concern is taken seriously the sociologist will find that he is forced to make decisions regarding the relationship between his concepts and his observations. In making these decisions it will invariently be the case that unclassifiable instances appear, that coding schemes become too narrow, that statistical tests are inappropriate, or that observations bear little, if any, relationship to central concepts and hypotheses. In the process of deciding when an observation fits or does not fit a conceptual category, Garfinkel (1967:78-79) suggests that the sociologist makes use (even if unconsciously) of the documentary method of analysis. This consists of

> treating an actual appearance as "the document of," as "pointing to," as "standing on behalf of" a presupposed underlying pattern. Not only is the underlying pattern derived from its individual documentary evidences, but the individual documentary evidences, in their turn, are interpreted on the basis of "what is known" about the underlying pattern. Each is used to elaborate the other.

> The method is recognizable for the everyday necessities of recognizing what a person is "talking about" given that he does not say exactly what he means, or in recognizing such common occurrences and objects as mailmen, friendly gestures, and promises. It is recognizable as well in deciding such sociologically analyzed occurrence of events as Goffman's strategies for the management of impressions, Erickson's identity crises, Reisman's types of conformity, Parsons' value systems, Malinowski's magical practices, Bales' interaction counts, Merton's types of deviance, Lazarsfeld's latent structure of attitudes, and the U.S. Census' occupational categories.

The documentary method is used, then, whenever a sociologist claims that an observation fits a conceptual category. In applying this method it will be found that any instance of classifying an observation rests on the earlier discussed assumptions of daily interaction. That is, events will be placed in a temporal sequence, certain statements will be ignored, and common vocabularies of meanings will be assumed. If the method of data collection rests on interviews it is argued that the researcher must give attention to the interaction that occurs between himself and the respondent. In this context Garfinkel and Cicourel suggest that while it is commonly assumed that interviewers and respondents achieve a "rapport" during the interview, this hypothesis is problematic. Cicourel (1967:67) states:

> *The interviewer-respondent "mesh" carries still another assumption:* each

employs linguistic styles and other socially relevant body movements, gestures or facial expressions that communicate a variety of meanings and bits of information about each other's social character, social background, political views, and the like. Such communication may serve to inhibit or to facilitate the interview *per se* as a comfortable social exchange, manage its duration, etc., where each seeks to bargain with the other implicitly about what will be tolerated, how each seeks to convey or blur some image of themselves, their relative interest in each other as persons, and so on.

To handle the problem of interviewer-respondent interaction Cicourel has suggested that sociologists must fall back upon the daily vocabularies of meaning utilized by their subjects. In short, it is unreasonable to assume that the language of the sociologist and the language of the subject mesh or fit in any meaningful degree. Hence data gathered via interviews and questionnaires are viewed by the ethnomethodologist as collaborative products created by the sociologist and his subject. To make sense out of such productions demands a knowledge of the routine meanings held by subjects.

If data are gathered from existing documents the ethnomethodologist suggests that another set of problems may arise. That is, the act of coding a response must be seen as an attempt to make rational and predictable an occurrence that has to be placed within the coder's vocabulary. Thus, Garfinkel points to his studies of coding to show that sociologists themselves rely on et cetera clauses and ad hoc explanations to make sense out of whatever documents they are processing. In this sense the sociologist is again no different from his subject in everyday life.

Cicourel and Garfinkel suggest that there is a way out of the above dilemmas, and this involved a sensitive use of the documentary method wherein the researcher takes as problematic all of his and his subject's behavior. At every step in the research process attention is given to how concepts are linked to observations. In addition the ethnomodologist attempts to make public and observable all of his documentary activities. Thus the background features of situations, the meanings of coders, the dress of respondents, etc., are all treated as pieces of data and potential factors influencing the final sociological production.

At the heart of the ethnomethodologist's solution lie a series of assumptions taken from Schutz (in Natanson, 1963:302–346). For Schutz there existed an inpenetrable barrier between the scientific and the everyday conceptions of reality. The everyday view of reality, for Schutz, was based on a complicated interlocking network of taken-for-granted meanings and assumptions persons held about themselves and, in turn, attributed to all other persons. This view of reality is one that is predicated on the assumption that persons share the same meanings and definitions.

The fundamental conflict between scientific and everyday conceptions arose, argued Schutz (in Natanson, 1963:325–326) from the fact that the scientist could never fully, completely, and accurately enter into the "here and now" world of everyday man. For Schutz the answer was the construction of rational models of action that actors in everyday life would never fully live up to. Schutz's (in Natanson, 1963:340–341) everyday actor becomes a rational construct manipulated by the sociologist. In his system rational models of everyday action were evaluated by the postulate of subjective interpretation, by which he meant that the models must explain the action under analysis, and, last, by the postulate of adequacy, which held that all models of everyday action must be understandable for the actor himself.

The adoption of these assumptions from Schutz can be clearly seen in the recent statements by Garfinkel and Cicourel. At several points Garfinkel (1967:262–283) elaborates in great detail the differences between scientific and everyday rationalities. On other occasions Garfinkel and Cicourel deliberately construct models of everyday man that rest on a social game perspective. This social game model is one attempt to construct a series of rationalities that would permit the analysis of everyday action. While there appears at several points in the recent ethnomethodological literature a departure from the rational constructs of Schutz, it is this perspective that provides a basic assumption for the entire perspective.

Criticism of Both Perspectives

Before attempting a synthesis of ·these perspectives a review of their problematic features is necessary. Interactionism has been criticized on both methodological and theoretical grounds.

Theoretically, critics of certain brands of the perspective have challenged the metaphorical basis of the dramaturgical view. The drama metaphor, they suggest, is alien to the interaction process and gives man an unattractive motivational commitment—that is, to ever win support for a presented self. On other grounds it has been suggested that the theory is so vague on the self as a concept that firm empirical observations cannot be gathered. Indeed, interactionists are vague themselves on the causal status of this concept and Kuhn (1964:61–84) has identified some nine different variants within the perspective on this dimension alone.

This criticism reflects a general dissatisfaction with the perspective because it offers too few concrete hypotheses. Compounded with this issue is the nature of interactionist research. This problem was raised earlier and possible strategies for improving interactionally based research were suggested.

Some critics have suggested that interactionism offers an excellent view of social relationships and social groups but fails to treat larger forms of social organization adequately. In my judgment this criticism is largely misplaced because it ignores the long line of research on the sociology of work and organizational settings stimulated by Hughes. Similarly, the study of collective behavior within interactionism offers a perspective on the problems of mass society (see, for example, Blumer, in Gittler, (1957:127–158; Klapp, 1964; Couch, 1968).

Ethnomethodology has been criticized for its phenomenological bias which on occasion has restricted its practitioners from treating the relationship between individual definitions and larger social units (see Coleman, 1968a:128). Others have suggested that the perspective does not suitably treat the role of the self in interaction and some have noted that there is no clear demonstration of how assumptions taken for granted operate in daily interactions (see, for example, Swanson, 1968:122–124). The failure of the ethnomethodologist to indicate precisely the nature of the documentary method has also raised criticisms (Coleman, 1968a; Hill and Crittendon, 1968). I would criticize both perspectives for their failure to indicate clearly the source of meanings and definitions. In addition they as yet offer no firm strategies for measuring the interaction process.

In the defense of each I would suggest that they offer a view of human conduct that recognizes the complex role of interaction in shaping activity. They point to important distinctions between the interpretative and noninterpretative elements of conduct, and Garfinkel's studies offer experimental strategies for future research. The persistent treatment of scientific and everyday activity within both frameworks offers a fresh perspective on the sociology of knowledge, and this is especially the case with Garfinkel's analysis of scientific rationalities.

A View of Social Organization and the Interaction Process: A Proposed Synthesis

If face-to-face interaction is characterized by shifting modalities of ininterpretation, then a major point of convergence between ethnomethodology and interactionism is the treatment of meaning given social objects.

THE INTERPRETATIONAL PROCESS

One strength of interactionism has been its emphasis on the interpretative process. The special strength of ethnomethodology is its call
for renewed concern with the objects and events that assume noninterpretative statuses in encounters. Clearly the study of interaction must
incorporate both problems. This suggests several hypotheses concerning
the movement of objects from interpretative to noninterpretative roles.
The first prediction suggests that any event that challenges a normal
interpretation creates pressures to bring that event into the normal flow
of interaction. When an object is taken out of its noninterpretative status
and held up for consideration, frustration and groping will be observed at
a rate proportionate to the importance assigned the object. Thus some
objects can be quickly settled upon simply because they occupy a
relatively low position in the interaction. This would be the case with
breakdowns in mechanical equipment at sociable gatherings. They can
either be replaced with other objects or ignored.

A second hypothesis suggests that the fundamental objects for any
interaction involve those that must be negotiated over. In short, objects
taken for granted will not account for the complete variance in behavior
(I am indebted to Herbert Blumer for this observation). Those objects
which are accorded explicit interpretative status will significantly determine the flow of events. On the other hand objects taken for granted
cannot be ignored, and I would hypothesize that objects in this class
receive earliest attention in any encounter. Once their meaning can be
taken for granted they cease to operate as problematic elements.

The nature of the interaction process is such that a complete a priori
classification of objects cannot be given. Earlier I suggested that the self
represents the most significant object for interpretation. To this should
be added the meanings brought into the situation and perhaps the situation as well; although the situation, in a concrete sense, is likely to
contain the greatest proportion of nonproblematic objects. Thus once
persons at a sociable gathering determine that adequate facilities are
available, interaction quickly turns to the problem of negotiating selves.

The problem of meaning still remains vague in both perspectives. As a
point of empirical inquiry I suggest that meaning be treated as an
element of the covert symbolic act and by self-reports be measured in
terms of the expectations for action that are brought into the interaction
(see, for example, McHugh, 1968). Following Garfinkel, such expectations would include assumptions concerning who was going to be
present, the length of time to be spent, the types of selves one was going
to present, the degree of knowledge held about the occasion, and the
types of objects that were going to be encountered. Once the interaction

In this way interaction could be measured by the frequency of joined actions. The emergent effect of interaction would be represented by the frequency of disrupted plans of action; that is, how frequently participants had to alter plans of action they brought into the encounter. Interactions could then be examined in terms of their emergent qualities. Those that flowed basically along noninterpretative lines would be judged less emergent, and so on.

begins, overt activities could then be charted and linked to the shifts in meaning the participants were constructing as they interacted.

DEVIANCE, THE LABELING PROCESS, AND AGENTS OF SOCIAL CONTROL

Because interactionism and ethnomethodology have focused on the deviance and labeling process, an additional series of hypotheses can be offered. If Garfinkel's conception of trust is redefined to specify those situations where two or more actors assume that the other will abide by decisions mutually agreed upon, then violations of trust become violations of these agreements. Examples would include entrusting another with a dark secret about the self, withholding salient information from outsiders, or simply continuing to interact along consensual lines. Breakdowns in joint action could be partly traced to breakdowns in the trust-taking attitude and would be vividly displayed in the betrayal process that characterizes interactions between normals and persons defined as mentally ill (see, for example, Sampson, Messinger, and Towne, 1962:88–96).

As a first hypothesis it could be predicted that continued violations of trust create strains in the relationship that culminate in attributions of deviance directed toward the trust violator. This hypothesis suggests that only certain breakdowns in consensual interaction will produce a deviant label. I would propose that violations of the relational order would lead to a greater proportion of deviant lables then would violations of polite-interactional and civil-legal codes. Thus a failure to abide by rules of deference and demeanor, refusals to act in terms of an agreed-upon division of labor, or leaking of crucial information to outsiders would all represent significant concerns around which trust would have to be sustained.

If the labeling process is lifted to the organizational level I would predict that the readiness of members within social control agencies to validate a deviant label would vary by their perception of the degree of trust-violation attributed to the potential deviant. That is, the extent to which the member of a social relationship can validate a claim of trust violation increases the readiness of members of social control agencies to accept and process the potential deviant.

This hypothesis must be conditioned by the fact that social control agencies continuously monitor their deviant populations in terms of the ability of those populations to meet perceived organizational needs.

As Cicourel (1968) indicates, this monitoring process serves collective organizational needs as well as the concerns of individual members. When these two concerns converge with the attributions of deviance among members of social relationships, greater rates of labeling would be expected. This suggests that members of social control agencies may turn away valid instances of deviance simply because they do not meet the needs of the organization. On the other hand, deviants may be created by such agencies when valid attributions of deviance are not given within the social relationship. This would be the case especially when members of the social relationship are in conflict with the social control agency. Current examples would include police monitoring of ghetto areas and police enforcement of drug abuse laws among college youth. In these instances the labeling process becomes a political and ideological issue, with members of social control agencies responding more to political demands than to socially validated instances of deviance.

SOCIAL RELATIONSHIPS, SOCIALIZATION, AND THE LANGUAGES OF INTERACTION

Returning the discussion to social relationships and trust, I would predict that breakdowns in consensual action often arise because persons hold conflicting definitions of the salient objects in their environment. If a wife persists in directing interaction around objects that a husband regards as taken for granted, consensus may soon collapse and joint action becomes problematic. A sense of dissatisfaction with the interactional partner may be created that soon eventuates in reciprocal alienation, which in turn produces a situation of deviance attribution. The outcome may then be divorce.

Another area of mutual concern for these two perspectives is the language of interaction itself. Ethnomethodology points to elements of the "silent dialogue" that underlies a great deal of face-to-face encounters. Conversely, symbolic interactionism highlights the central aspects of consciously directed and often verbally expressed interaction. It appears that at least two languages, one silent, and one vocal, characterize the interaction process. On the silent level, rules regarding body spacing, the use of gestures, the control of body noises and aromas, and even the ordering of words within spoken conversation can be observed (see Somers, 1968). These often remain unstated and typically represent the "background expectancy set" interactants behave in terms of.

On the overt, or spoken level, prescriptions concerning proper address, naming, tone of voice, and choice of vocabulary are observable. These represent the overt aspects of interaction and their expression often displays the salient features of the silent dialogue (Goffman, 1963a).

If interaction involves both languages, then ethnomethodology and interactionism provide a perspective for analyzing the contingencies of face-to-face encounters. An important line of investigation becomes the problem of socialization. How are persons taught rules that are seldom vocalized? How are sanctions brought to bear upon perceived violations of the silent language? At what point in the socialization process are children assumed to be responsible for their silent behaviors?

These questions are cross-cut by a particular image of socialization implied in these two perspectives. Contrary to some theories, which regard socialization as a discontinuous learning process into well-defined roles, ethnomethodology and symbolic interactionism suggest that socialization is never-ending and often involves more of what is not said than what is stated (see, for example, Whittaker and Oleson, 1968, and Clausen, 1968:130-181). Socialization thus represents one ubiquitous feature of all interactions—the apprehension of another's perspective so that joint action can occur. Indeed if interaction is regarded as a potentially emergent event, socialization is one aspect of the role-taking process. If success at joint action can be measured by the ability of persons to fit lines of action together easily, then this success represents the quality of the ongoing socialization process.

THE STUDY OF SOCIAL ORGANIZATION

Another point of convergence can be suggested. Because both perspectives provide a similar view of the interaction and socialization process, they offer a powerful strategy for organizational analysis. While space prohibits a complete discussion of this convergence, the following points can be indicated. First, organizations become territories of interaction that are focused around complex spoken and unspoken languages. These languages represent the salient organizational concerns, often work related, and they offer prescriptions for action that frequently run counter to formally stated organizational goals. Each organizational role position can be seen as having its own special language, both silent and vocal. This language will communicate special socialization strategies that are daily tested and reaffirmed through interaction. These languages will tend to cluster within, and indeed give focus to, special social orders that exist hand in hand with other social orders. The organization is then conceived in terms of competing perspectives and social orders, each of which rests on its own language and set of meanings. The sum total of these languages represents the organization's collective perspective. The sum total of social or moral orders becomes, the behavioral representation of the organization.

In this way organizations are broken down into interactional units, each of which offer special ways of thinking and acting. It becomes difficult to speak of one organization or one organizational perspective. An organization now becomes a multitude of shifting and competing languages and social orders, a social order that is held together, if at all, by a few very salient symbols such as university X, or mental hospital Y. The name of the organization perhaps represents the only salient symbol all participants would agree upon.

The study of languages, perspectives, and social orders, particularly as these events are viewed by organizational members, represent the special contribution of ethnomethodology and symbolic interactionism to organization analysis. As such they offer a view of organizational life that is social-psychological and subjective in nature.

METHODOLOGY AND THE STUDY OF SCIENTIFIC CONDUCT

Both perspectives offer a series of hypotheses relevant to the analysis of scientific conduct and the development of sociological methodology. Contained within the interactionist perspective is a specific directive for scientific conduct. The scientist is judged by his ability to challenge accepted perspectives—that is, by his ability to be self-consciously interpretative. Developments in science reflect growth stimulated by this challenging stance. In this way Mead partially anticipated Thomas Kuhn's notion of the paradigm model of scientific development. Of equal importance was Mead's ability to separate the rationalities of scientific conduct from the perspectives of everyday life, a point more fully elaborated by Garfinkel in his analysis of the forms of rationality (also see Blumer, 1931).

Thus a hypothesis that runs slightly counter to the Mertonian and Parsonian image of scientific behavior emerges (Kaplan, 1964:855–857). That is, scientific conduct is so imbued with elements from everyday life that unless the scientist self-consciously directs his activity in terms of the norm of discovery, his behavior is unfavorably judged. The norms of the scientific institution parallel those of other enterprises, most notably art, theology, and philosophy (Swanson, 1968:123). Consequently Merton's (1957) four norms of universalism, communism, disinterestedness, and organized scepticism are not unique to science.

In this way Mead and Garfinkel have opened the way for a more open discourse of the value-free problems and scientific behavior. Given their perspectives, it becomes impossible to view science as other than a value-laden enterprise—a position similarly reached by Gouldner (1962) and Becker (1967). It can be no other way if the assumption that science is a human enterprise is granted. Consequently the scientific norms of rationality (Garfinkel), which include (1) official neutrality toward the meaning of objects; (2) an irrelevancy for the real world; (3) an indifference to chronological time; (4) perfect communication; (5) and standards of publicity remain norms that are imperfectly realized (Swanson, 1968:123). This is the thrust of Garfinkel's critique of modern sociology. The sociologist's belief in a perfect system of rationalities has led him further away from the world of social events. The sociologist has pursued his normative system at the expense of concrete behavioral analyses of face-to-face interaction. By forgetting that he is responsive to social demands the sociologist has overlooked the irrational elements of his own conduct—most notably his ability to make sound observations, to reliably code documents, to conduct face-to-face interviews, and so on.

The thrust of ethnomethodology and interactionism becomes clear—the sociologist can never ignore the interactional features of his own conduct. Interactionism and ethnomethodology offer some recipes for corrective action. They may be standard hypotheses.

If the scientific observer is subject to interactional demands, and hence less than perfect as a recorder of social events, then multiple observers and multiple methods, which overcome one another's restrictive biases, become the most valid and reliable strategies of observation. Concretely this suggests that any observation based on the triangulation principle will yield data that are more reliable and valid than an investigation that is not so based.

Because the scientist brings unique interpretations to bear upon his own conduct, a major source of variance in any investigation becomes the nature of these interpretations. Specifically, this predicts that two experimenters, for example, will produce different findings to the extent that they conceive their role differently (see Friedman, 1967). This would also hold for interviewers, coders, and unobtrusive observers.

Third, the interaction process between an observer and a subject must be examined for its effect on the quality of data. To the degree that the interaction is emergent, and hence conducive to the production of new meanings or the alterations of existing attitudes and definitions, observational encounters become noncomparable events for any form of collective analysis. If an encounter proceeds along taken-for-granted lines, which is a measure of the degree of emergence, similar observational encounters could be pooled for collective analysis. This proposition directs investigators to carefully record the nature of the interaction process with a special eye to events that they judge to be unique within each encounter.

Additional hypotheses could be offered, but space restricts their elaboration. The basic point is that both interactionism and ethnomethodology direct scientific interest in the scientific process itself.

In concluding this proposed synthesis, I would offer as a final point the convergence of ethnomethodology's interest in the study of face-to-face interaction with the methodological principles of symbolic interactionism discussed earlier. The documentary method, as a strategy of point to empirical instances of theoretical concepts, can be easily merged with the use of analytic induction, sensitizing concepts, the method of role-taking, and the strategies of linking individual perspectives with larger social units.

Similarly, Garfinkel's use of the quasi-experiment in natural field settings can become a model for more rigorous studies of face-to-face encounters. This is especially so if recent findings on experimenter effect and subject perceptions are incorporated into the experimental design (see, for example, Friedman, 1967).

Summary

I have proposed a synthesis of two comtemporary social-psychological perspectives that offer strategies of analysis for such basic sociological problems as deviance, socialization, and organizational behavior. The basic assumptions of these perspectives were reviewed, as were certain criticisms of each. Their respective methodological positions were stated and a series of hypotheses were set forth as a means of bringing the two closer to concrete empirical analysis. Hopefully this discussion will stimulate greater attention to the common problems treated by both perspectives.

CHAPTER TWELVE

DON H. ZIMMERMAN AND
D. LAWRENCE WIEDER

Ethnomethodology and the Problem of Order: Comment on Denzin

The emergence within sociology of something called ethnomethodology is undoubtedly puzzling to many practitioners in the field. To be sure, sociology is accustomed to the development of new "subfields" of interest, but ethnomethodologists generally reject such a classification. Published works are few, and those that are available appear to pose considerable difficulty for sympathizers and critics alike. Since ethnomethodology has developed within sociology, the resistance of the enterprise to assimilation in terms of received sociological theory, research, and general perspective must frustrate those seeking answers to such questions as: What *is* ethnomethodology? How does it relate to recognized positions within the field? Just what is the basis for its radical claims?

It is in this (presumed) context of general puzzlement that Denzin's attempt to compare and contrast ethnomethodology and symbolic interactionism is at once a welcome display of sympathetic interest and an occasion to repair certain misconceptions that stand in the way of finding answers to the kinds of questions noted above. Denzin is explicitly aware of certain hazards of the task he undertakes. He states his biases at the outset, declaring his commitment to the symbolic interactionist view, and acknowledges that "a large body of literature recurrently cited by ethonomethodologists is as yet unpublished (in Douglas, 1971:3).

Inspecting Denzin's remarks, it seems that his avowed commitment to symbolic interactionism has led him to misconstrue systematically a number of critical issues. While Denzin has fallen short in his attempt to provide an adequate depiction of ethnomethodology for the purposes of comparison with symbolic interactionism, the effort has the positive merit that a framework for discussion of the issues raised has been provided.

The remarks that follow focus on the underlying structure of Denzin's discussion of ethnomethodology, and in particular on his assertion that both ethnomethodology and symbolic interactionism are fundamentally concerned with the same problems. No attempt will be made to provide a point-for-point commentary. Instead, we answer what we take to be Denzin's misunderstanding of ethnomethodology by providing a positive characterization of it. Such an approach, we believe, is in keeping with the spirit of Denzin's paper, namely, to add more light and less heat to the discussion of what must for many be the enigma of ethnomethodology.

The Problem of Order

Denzin (in Douglas, 1971:3) tells us that his analysis will be couched "in terms of the biases that reside in the interactionist point of view." Unfortunately though understandably, he goes on to propose that both symbolic interactionists and ethnomethodologists take as their "basic concern the question of how it is that social order is possible" (p. 4). In his discussion of symbolic interactionism it is relatively clear what he means by the problem of social order. His conception parallels that of Parsons's problem of social order and Weber's problem of adequate causal analysis.

In brief, the problem of order is posed by the problematic relationship of the factual order on the one hand, and the normative order, on the other. The factual order refers to what can be seen from the perspective of the scientific observer, who, by means of his science, makes observable the orderly (that is, regular, repetitive) actions characteristic of the society in question. These regularities are observable without reference to the point of view of the actor. The notion of normative order involves essential reference to the point of view of the actor and includes his categories for classifying the social and physical environment, value elements that order such categories in terms of preference, duty, affect, etc., and the rules or norms that specify the particular kinds of actions appropriate to situations thus categorized and evaluated. In such terms, actors develop conceptions of themselves, the objects of their actions, other persons in their situation, and the developing character of the situation of action, which are the bases of "causes" of their action and which are observable to the scientist. It is the analyst's task to discover how members' conceptions are related so as to produce the orderly patterns of behavior that he observed without respect for the actor's point of view.

Let us make clear that we recognize that the solution to the problem of order posed by the symbolic interactionists is different in its particulars from that of the structural functionalists. Denzin points out in much detail that "objects, selves, situations, definitions and meanings are continually being defined, negotiated, and acted towards" (pp. 6–7). He specifies that any sharing of actors' conceptions is an emergent process (pp. 7–8) that occurs over the contingencies of interaction and may well be characterized by conflict and interruption (pp. 8–9). Moreover, the course of emergent definitions may vary with the particular dynamics of the situation under study (p. 13).

Yet, the goal of the analysis remains parallel to that in other formulations of the problem of social order. He suggests that "the interactionist endeavors to demonstrate the relationships between definitions of situations and views of self and the varieties of non-verbal, yet behavioral acts that persons engage in during any interactional sequence (p. 10). Denzin also notes that interactionists maintain "a distinction between the everyday and scientific conception of reality" (p. 11). While he is concerned with "learn[ing] his subject's view of reality" (p. 12), the interactionist treats the point of view of the actor as only one aspect of the problem of order. "The interactionist strives to move beyond his knowledge of the subject['s] world to scientifically valid descriptions and explanations of that world" (p. 12).

Denzin's conception of the analyst's task as the discovery of the source of objective patterns of behavior by examining the actor's point of view is further elaborated by his remark that "the interactionist asks how shifting definitions of self are reflected in on-going patterns of behavior" (p. 11). As a summary of the symbolic interactionist position he says, "[h]is answer to the question of how social order is possible lies in the assumption that society is possible because interacting selves share the same basic symbolic order of meanings, definitions, and situations" (pp. 15–16).

According to Denzin, ethnomethodology, in apparent contrast to the interactionist "solution" of the problem of order, looks to "the rules, norms, definitions and meanings that members of any moral order daily take for granted" (p. 16). Denzin's characterization misrepresents the

actual concerns of ethnomethodology. Indeed, his assertion that ethnomethodologists seeks a solution to the problem of order in terms of
"rules, norms, definitions and meanings" severely delimits our central
phenomenon, at the same time turning it into an essentially unquestioned
resource for analysis. We are, to be sure, concerned with rules and other
normative constructions, but by no means exclusively, and not in the
way Denzin suggests.

What is implied by the proposal that "rules, norms, definitions and
meanings" are but one set of phenomena or topics for ethnomethodology
rather than resources? It is not simply that such normative constructions
are problematic, if what is meant is that the determination of their
content awaits detailed investigations. (In the context of this discussion,
"content" refers to the prescriptions for or prescriptions of particular
actions that actors presumably employ as guides for their conduct.) Nor
are we recommending a focus on the "negotiated" or "processual"
character of such constructions (as would an interactionist on Denzin's
portrayal) if the implication of those terms is that special concepts or
methodologies are required to understand how stable contents are
achieved by members over the course of interaction. Whether "problematic," "negotiated," or "processual," whether couched in the language
of norms, as in the case of structural functionalists, or shared emergent
meanings, as in the case of interactionists, the end result is the same:
stable social action is the product of the actor's orientation to and
compliance with shared, stable (if only within a particular interaction)
norms or meanings. Norms, or meanings, presumably govern, guide,
direct, and, for the analyst, account for action. To assume that these
subjective but intersubjectively shared constructions perform such functions is to make them available as a resource for social-scientific analysis
and explanation of regularities in social life. That is, the description of
such shared norms or meanings presumably provides the analyst with
the resources for predicting and explaining actual events in the society.

How can norms or symbols become *topics* of study? The first step is
to suspend the assumption that social conduct is rule governed, or based
in and mounted from shared meanings or systems of symbols shared in
common. The second step is to observe that the regular, coherent,
connected patterns of social life are *described* and *explained* in just such
terms, or close relatives of them, by laymen and professional sociologists alike. The third step is to treat the appearances of described and
explained patterns of orderly social activities as *appearances* produced,
for example, by and through such procedures as analyzing an event as
an instance of compliance (or noncompliance) with a rule. To take these

three "steps" is to leave the problem of order altogether as the analyst's problem. These steps describe; albeit in adumbrated terms, the ethnomethodological interest in "rules, norms, definitions and meanings." The ethnomethodologist is *not* concerned with providing causal explanations of observably regular, patterned, repetitive actions by some kind of analysis of the actor's point of view. He *is* concerned with how members of society go about the task of *seeing, describing,* and *explaining* order in the world in which they live.[1]

The ethnomethodologist treats the fact that he lives and acts within the same social world that he investigates in quite a different way than do the varieties of traditional sociologists. For one who lives within the social world it appears orderly and regular in a variety of ways. These varieties of orderly appearance of the world can be enhanced and expanded by the application of sociological methods of description. The population can be enumerated and classified. Rates of crime, patterns of housing segregation and occupational mobility, and the like, can be described. These types of patterns are analyzed as larger manifestations of the same patterns of orderly activity that we experience and describe

---

1. Denzin apparently reached his conclusion that ethnomethodology was concerned with taken-for-granted, shared rules from his reading of Garfinkel's "Studies of the Routine Grounds of Everyday Activities" (1967:35–75). This paper does indeed focus sharply on the notion of rule, but the properties of rules and other normative constructions developed in this paper should lead the reader to a far different conclusion. Garfinkel's (1967:68) discussion of the "cultural" or "judgmental" dope, for example, should alert the reader to the fact that something more than the standard interest in rules or norms as explanations of conduct lies behind the argument, for example,

> By "cultural dope" I refer to the man-in-the-sociologist's-society who produces the stable features of the society by acting in compliance with pre-established and legitimate alternatives of action that the common culture provides. . . . The common feature in the use of [models of the social actor] is the fact that courses of common sense rationalities of judgment which involve the person's use of common sense knowledge of social structures over the temporal "succession" of here and now situations are treated as epiphenomenal (1967:68).

A careful reading of "What is Ethnomethodology" (1967:1–34), a more recent paper reflecting the development of Garfinkel's thought since the "Routine Grounds" paper, would have focused attention on such statements as

> A leading policy of ethnomethodological studies is to *refuse serious consideration* to the prevailing proposal that efficiency, efficacy, effectiveness, intelligibility, consistency, planfulness, typicality, uniformity, reproducibility of activities — i.e., that rational properties of practical activities — be assessed, recognized, categorized, described by using a rule or standard obtained outside actual settings within which such properties are used, produced, and talked about by settings' members. All procedures whereby logical and methodological properties of the practices and results of inquiries are assessed in their general characteristics by rule are of interest as *phenomena* for ethnomethodological study *but not otherwise* (1967:33; emphasis added).

to each other, however partially, in the actual scenes in which we live. Sociologists treat these patterns as facts and seek to give causal explanations of them. Ethnomethodologists, in direct contrast, ask a different order of question about the apparent orderliness or patterned nature of the social world as it appears in daily life and in sociological accounts.

We notice that the apparent orderliness and coherency of the scenes of daily life are matters that members are continually and unavoidably engaged in recognizing and making recognizable to each other. We notice that over the course of interaction members persuade and otherwise make evident to each other that events and actions directed toward them are coherent, consistent, planful, connected, and the like. We notice that any setting can be examined for the ways in which its visibly organized features are accomplished by members party to that setting through their efforts at detecting, counting, recording, analyzing, and reporting on events in that setting (Garfinkel, 1967:33–34). In light of these matters we ask such questions as: How are members going about the task of investigating the scenes of their actions so that they see and report patterning and structure in those scenes? How are events being analyzed so that they appear as connected? By what procedures are descriptions being done so that they portray order? How is the factual character of such accounts established? and How is the sense or appearance of a world in common and common understanding concerning its shared features accomplished?

To give substance to these general remarks, we next examine one topic of ethnomethodological interest in some detail. Since the preceding argument has claimed that ethnomethodologists' conception of, and concern with, rules it is quite different from that implied in a traditional statement of the problem of order, we select as the topic for consideration ethnomethodological studies of rules.

Ethnomethodological Interests in Rules

A study of how coders treated coding rules in dealing with the contents of records of a psychiatric clinic illustrates some of these interests. Garfinkel (1967:18–24) found that no matter how elaborately a set of instructions was developed for coders, coders found, nevertheless, that they had no choice but to employ ad hoc practices for deciding the definite sense of the instructions when they encountered actual notations in the clinic files. In order to see what a notation in these files meant, coders found that they had to acquire and adopt the standpoint of a socially competent member of the clinic staff. In so doing they continually interpreted notations in terms of what those notations had to mean when understood in terms of what the coders took to be the "actual" ways of clinic operations. In turn, they elaborated the sense of both the notations and the coding rules to see what the notation could mean "in this specific case" vis-à-vis the alternatives provided by the coding rules. Coders continually saw and described to each other further provisions of the rules that were not stated as such. In the course of coding they discovered and employed qualifying conditions for the proper use of the rules. They further found that on many matters no clear decisions could be made, although in order to get the work done they nevertheless had to opt for categorizing the noted event one way or another.

These practices of ad hocing, which Garfinkel calls "et cetera," "unless," and "let it pass," were found to be essential to following the coding rules; that is, coders found that they could not proceed in the work of coding and still recognize that they were coding actual events in the round of clinic affairs if they suppressed the use of these practices. Yet, the use of these practices means that in no clear sense do the coding rules that the coders use describe what they were doing and what they were looking for when they coded. It does mean that coders could argue that they had coded the contents of the clinic folders in accordance with the rules, but that in doing so they would have to appeal to the same ad hoc grounds that they employed in doing the coding in the first place.

The same kind of ad hoc elaboration of rules in use has been studied in other settings. In his study of the work of receptionists in a public welfare agency Zimmerman examined the use of rules for assigning applicants to intake workers (see Chapter 9 in this volume). By following their work step by step he watched the assignment of applicants to intake workers by a rule that treated applicants on a first come, first served basis to be assigned to intake workers in a repeating serial order. He observed that from the point of view of the intake workers, the receptionist, and himself as witness to the scene from within it, the use of the rule routinely produced a moving, coordinated, sequenced, orderly flow of cases. That is, from within that scene and to interested parties of that scene, the assignment produced what they described as a coherent, orderly flow.

He further found that the receptionists were attentive to the appearance of that orderly flow *as* the intended product of the use of the rule. They understood the rule in that way. This means that the set of ideas involved in the problem of order were matters of explicit recognition and description by parties to the setting. When it appeared to the receptionists and other officials that what they observed and described as the orderly flow of applicants and interviews was becoming disrupted, they altered the presumtively legitimate sequence of assignments to keep the scene moving in its routine way. These alterations of the rule in the course of using it were nevertheless counted as compliance with the rule.

In Chapter 9 in this volume Zimmerman writes:

> It would seem that the notion of action in accord with a rule is a matter not of compliance or noncompliance per se but of the various ways in which persons *satisfy* themselves and others concerning what is or is not "reasonable" compliance in particular situations. Reference to rules might then be seen as a common-sense method of accounting for or making available for talk the orderly features of everyday activities, thereby *making out* these activities as orderly in some fashion. Receptionists, in accomplishing a for all practical purposes ordering of their task activities by undertaking the "reasonable" reconciliation of particular actions with "governing rules" may thus sustain their sense of "doing good work" and warrant their further actions on such grounds.

Both of the above mentioned studies indicate that the actual practices of using rules do not permit an analyst to account for regular patterns of behavior by invoking the notion that these patterns occur because members of a society or some organization are following rules. Instead, these studies show that the ways that members employ rules requires that they continually develop what a rule means when they come to treat actual cases and when they find that they must defend the rationality of their choices. By invoking rules and elaborating their sense for specific cases, members are able to describe their own courses of action as rational, coherent, precedented, and the like, "for all practical purposes." The work of making and accepting such descriptions of conduct makes social settings appear as orderly for the participants, and it is this *sense and appearance* of order that rules in use, in fact, provide and that ethnomethodologists, in fact, study.

Further, it has been suggested by Wieder (1969), in his study of a deviant subculture in a halfway house for paroled narcotic addicts, that rules are used in this way when persons come to describe and explain the actions of others. He finds that parolees, staff, and he, as a participant-observer, not only invoked the notion of a convict code to find the good sense of some particular parolee act, but also that, by continually elaborating the sense of the convict code, the appearance of parolee conduct as regular, repetitive, and patterned was located and described.

Wieder found in his own ethnographic formulations (treated as events in that setting) and in the formulations of staff members that accounts of a set of rules that halfway house residents were seen to follow were obtained by taking fragments of resident talk and elaborating those fragments by hearing them as rules. Hearing talk as rules involved the search for resident behavior that would have been produced if that talk was a statement of a rule. In the process of searching for behaviors that would fulfill the possible rule, diverse behaviors obtained their sense as the same kind of behavior. That is, a variety of different kinds of acts were seen by the observer and the halfway house staff as instances of a single pattern. Diverse behavioral events were seen as the "documents of" or "pointing to" the same underlying motivational source and were thereby seeable and describable as parts of the same pattern.

Through the development of accounts of parolee behavior as rule governed by employing the documentary method of interpretation (which ethnomethodologists study as a member's method of making sense of events, not as a method that we advocate, as Denzin suggests) as a way of finding connections between the various things that parolees said and between what they said and what they did, the staff and the observer were able to see and describe the conduct of parolees as coherent, more or less rationally and acceptably motivated, regular, and more or less the same as it had been in the past regardless of specifically which parolees were in residence in the halfway house at the time.

These three studies point to the fact that for ethnomethodologists the various aspects of the problem of order (the existence of observable patterns of behavior, the coherence and stability of patterns of motivation, the linkages between patterns of motivation and patterns of behavior) are made visible for societal members and social scientists alike through members' practices of investigating and reporting on their own affairs. Our concern with "order" is specifically and only with *how* it is being made visible, hence "created" for practical action, through these practices.

Thus, the program of inquiry sketched by the preceding remarks does not treat the accounts of patterned action achieved by laymen or professional sociologists as revealing a pattern of events having an existence independent of the accounting practices employed in its "discovery." Indeed, that such accounts display the property that they are accounts of independent events is a feature of the phenomenon of members' accounting practices of critical interest to ethnomethodology. The distinction between the account or description and the thing accounted for or described is an essentially unexamined resource for laymen and sociologists, for on this distinction rests the "orderly structure" of the social world. Once brought under scrutiny, the "orderly structure" of the social world is no longer available as a topic in its own right (that is, as something to be described and explained) but instead becomes an *accomplishment* of the accounting practices through and by which it is described and explained. It is in this decision to bring such accounting practices under investigation as phenomena in their own right without presupposing the independence of the domain made observable via their use that constitutes the radical character of the ethnomethodological enterprise.[2]

By not recognizing that this was the kind of concern with and conception of order that ethnomethodologists have, it is easy to see how Denzin understood many aspects of ethnomethodology as the exact opposite of the way they are understood by ethnomethodologists. Our interest in rationality, for example, is not in how we can develop rational constructs of the actor to explain regularities in human behavior, as Denzin suggests.[3] Instead, we are concerned with such matters as how members of organizations use the ideas and language of rationality in finding and describing the more or less orderly character of those organizational settings in which they act (Bittner, 1964). Our interest in the "documentary method of interpretation" is not in it as our method, but as a method that members use in discovering and portraying orderly and connected events. Our concern is not "the penetration of normal situations of interaction to uncover the rules and rituals participants take for granted" (Denzin in Douglas, 1971:19) but is instead the ways that members assert that there are rules that have been, are, and will control their action in locating their action as a coherent part of the present scene. Our interest in the practices of ad hocing that occur in coding is not their sense as a critique of standard sociological methods and our grounds for rejecting those methods (Denzin, in Douglas, 1971:30); instead our interest is in the ways that a study of coding can reveal the type of ad hocing that goes on in any effort to describe by rule. We do not take it that persons share the same meanings and definitions (Denzin, in Douglas, 1971). Instead we attempt to show that members continuously rely on, and if pressed insist upon, the capacities of others to find a presumptively shared sense in what they are saying. Finally, we are not concerned with How are situations defined? How do interactional rules emerge? and How is stable social action possible? (Denzin, in Douglas, 1971:36). Instead we are concerned with How do persons go about seeing, describing, and proposing a definition of the

2. See Zimmerman and Pollner (in Douglas, 1970) for a perspective on the ethnomethodological program.

3. Denzin consistently fails to distinguish between the *description* of a procedure and its advocacy. Schutz's discussion (1962:40–46) of the rational type is directed toward the methodological problems of a social science committed to the problem of order as traditionally defined. He was not writing about his own procedures. Similarly, Denzin's quotation of Garfinkel's discussion of the concept of organization is misleading inasmuch as Garfinkel was describing the idea of organization as it is used by sociologists.

situation? How do persons make a rule emergent and how do they use it? (the practice of et cetera); and How do persons see and describe social action as stable?

In conclusion, we suggest that the problems encountered with Denzin's discussion of ethnomethodology stem from the failure to consider seriously the claims to a radical departure from traditional sociological thinking advanced by advocates of this approach. Whatever the gains or losses of this "radical departure" might subsequently prove to be, proper understanding of what ethnomethodologists are trying to do cannot be achieved without explicit recognition of the fundamental break with the sociological tradition discussed above.

Symbolic Interactionism and Ethnomethodology: A Comment on Zimmerman and Wieder

by Norman K. Denzin

In replying to the remarks of Professors Zimmerman and Weider, I will restrict my remarks to a single point: their claim that ethnomethodology proposes a radically different view of the problem of social order and its analysis. I will grant their point concerning my misconstruing the ethnomethodologists' use of rational models of human action and of the documentary method, although I submit that their sources for justification are sufficiently ambiguous to furnish the grounds for alternative explanations.

My aim in the essay under consideration was to indicate how symbolic interactionism encompasses a large number of the problems and peculiarities now taken as the special province of ethnomethodology — namely, that the study of human conduct, within any type of social order, demands consideration of how interacting selves cooperate in the construction of a routine, and for the moment a taken-for-granted set of meanings necessary for joint action. For the interactionist any social order emerges through the process of interaction in a situation where selves take the point of view of one another. The foundation of such orders is to be found in the meaning interacting selves bring to the objects and acts at hand. Meanings arises out of interaction, and not the other way around. The task of the interactionist is to discover how interacting selves come to agree upon certain meanings and definitions for coordinated action. The central role of the self in shaping such definitions is of paramount importance. Space restricts additional amplification of these features of the interactionist approach. It is necessary to note only that such a conception of the interaction process demands a special view of empirical research. My essay touched on these points, but a cardinal feature of interactionist research is the casting of the researcher's self into the position of those he is studying.

The radical claim of the ethnomethodologist is the decision to abandon the assumption that order exists. He proceeds instead, if I understand Professors Zimmerman and Weider correctly, to ask how members in any situation construct order by making certain rules appear to be operative. They suggest, for example, that coders persist in bringing their own interpretations to bear upon the complex instructions contained in coding manuals. When pressed, such persons explain their actions by evoking the perspective of their agency or some set of significant others. The radical claim thus emerges and is embodied in the doctrine which directs the sociologist to bring everyday accounting practices under investigation as phenomena in their own right.

This, I suggest, is neither radical nor new. It represents a fundamental feature of interactionist research. This I indicated earlier. What is radical is the assumption that such investigations can be conducted in the absence of any consistent conception of the human as an active, self-directing organism. In no publication of the contemporary ethnomethodologist do I grasp any sense of how they conceive the human organism. Nor am I told how rules are constructed and brought into being. I am as yet unclear how one knows when he has penetrated the foundations of a social order. How does the analyst know he is not being duped by those he is observing? If the documentary method is not taken as a method of analysis, what method is employed in such studies?

A basic proposition appears to underlie this line of thought. The meaning of an object arises out of the interaction process. This suggests the related proposition that such meanings are taken for granted, seldom publicly enunciated, and more often than not remain as unstated elements in the interaction process. The assumption of a rule-governed social order thus suspended, analysis proceeds to examine how order is made to appear through the interaction process.

These assumptions display a remarkable similarity with the interactionist perspective wherein the source of any social order, be it a social relationship or a complex organization, is lodged in the interaction process—a process, to cite Simmel, that is crystallized, made normal, and often ritualized through daily contact. Yet this view leaves unanswered such questions as where and how meaning arises, how it is organized, under what conditions it is stabilized, and most centrally how one goes about studying such fabrics and conditions of the human experience.

I suggest that the ethnomethodologist leaves these basic questions answered; that his radical claim echoes a long concern of the interactionist. Yet the position rests on unfirm empirical grounds because no solid methodological principles are set forth to guide such inquiry. Missing also is any sense of how the self enters into this constructing and making order apparent process.

Lest these remarks be taken as too critical, I wish to conclude with what I regard as the special contributions of ethomethodology. This is a perspective that calls for renewed interest in the dynamics of face-to-face interaction, an interest that has been noticeably absent in recent theories and research. An important implication of this line of thought is to suggest that the foundations of any social order are to be found in what interacting selves bring into concrete situations. Social order becomes an interactional enterprise and not a monolithic system that settles down and around persons, ever giving them directions for action.

This suggests a related point that is the concern of the ethnomethodologist for the silent aspects of language that persons employ in their daily encounters. This merges the symbolic interactionist's focus on verbal utterances with a broadened view of the linguistic structures that shape the interaction process. The potential for bringing a theoretical perspective to bear upon the study of language is increased with this interest.

A profound, and in my judgment radical, contribution of the ethnomethodologist is his analysis of the no ns and rituals that underlie scientific conduct. It is no longer possible to view the scientist as free from the pressures of norms, values, and idiosyncratic preferences. The scientist is an interactional animal. Garfinkel's work demands an analysis of these norms and rituals. Procedures of coding, interviewing, constructing hypotheses, and putting theories to test must now be examined from an interactionist-ethomethodological perspective. A failure to begin such studies only heightens the wall that currently exists between the enterprise of sociology and the study of everyday life.

By calling for the study of the taken-for-granted meanings that persons shape into rationales for action, the ethnomethodologist opens the way for a more systematic analysis of the functions of ritual and tradition in the social order. Man ceases to be an ever-rational organism seeking the maximum rewards for his actions. He is an organism who will engage in whatever actions he deems necessary to justify his own conduct. The taken-for-granted constructs of everyday life emplify this point—when pressed, man will explain his actions with rationales that are uninterpretable from another's perspective. Thus, from the view of the person, his actions can be interpreted only as being rational. That

L

they may be rational only within his belief and linguistic system is irrelevant.

Additional contributions of the ethnomethodologist could be cited. Risking the charge that I have again misunderstood this perspective I must conclude with a point that may only be resolved through empirical research. Namely, that I see a great deal of similarity between these two approaches because of their mutual focus on the interacting human as he actively constructs his own meanings and interpretations for everyday action.

PART FIVE

Sociological Theory and Truth

Theorizing*

All versions of theorizing convey as an essential part of their meaning a tacit stipulation concerning the adequacy of a favored method of analysis, of a preferred solution to the problem of "seeing sociologically." At certain points, different proponents of different versions of theorizing find it impossible to talk together because they differentially decide where to stop doubting. Such decisions are expressions of the form of life of the theorist, which he seeks to persuade others to accept, and which he argues for as a condition of his existence as a theorist. As arguments per se such exercises are uninteresting, but as displays of the form of life of a theorist or of the possible forms of life that theorizing produces they are interesting and worth examination.

In this chapter, I want to display one version of theorizing and to describe this version against the background of other possibilities. Thus, I want to suggest some of the possibilities for theorizing that I find exciting, certain grounds for finding other possibilities less exciting, and some ideas for proceeding with the work. My main thrust will be directed to proposing that an understanding of theorizing is an understanding of a form of life, and that this form of life constitutes a particular method for treating and reconstructing one's biography as a prac-

---

*This chapter collects bits and pieces of the fourth chapter of my manuscript "The Grounds of Theorizing: Rules, Grammar, and Tradition." These ideas have been nourished through a continuous collaboration with Peter McHugh over the past few years, though he is not responsible for the present statement. Many of these ideas crystallized more intelligibly for me under the cross-questioning of my colleague Irwin W. Goffman over the past year and in an informal bimonthly seminar in which we have jointly participated with a small group of graduate students in the New York area.

tically conceived corpus of knowledge. We often call the results of such a reconstruction theoretic knowledge, but I prefer to conceive of the methods that enter into such an achievement as the methods of theorizing. I shall try to show how the methods of theorizing are essentially methods for creating a theoretic actor or, methods for producing a possible society.

Introduction

Most discussions of theory proceed as if the term could be isolated from the analytic tradition (language) in which it normally functions. When Homans, Levy, and Merton inform us as to what a theory *is*, they are generally talking from within a linguistic framework whose deep structure they have already assimilated into their definition and which they assume without question as the necessary condition(s) of an adequate response. The question in this sense is not whether they are correct or incorrect but whether we want to speak their languages, whether we want to live sociologically in the terms they create for us. The question should be: Do we want to speak their language?

Much of the uneasiness experienced by sociologists with hypothetico-deductive models of theorizing has been dumbly attributed to facts like these: that they gloss what we desire to explicate, that they fail to comprehend the "normative" character of action, that they are unable to grasp the "indexical" character of our subject matter, etc., as if we (the reputable ones) never gloss, and as if our descriptions of indexical performance are not indexically tied to the conditions of *their* occurrence. Holding the deductive model of theorizing to our requirements is to treat it concretely, for an analytic grasp of such a method would see it within the terms of its language and would bring into question the language itself.[1]

I take it that the trouble we have with the deductive model stems from none of these concrete sorts of considerations but from the existential fact that we cannot live with it as sociologists, we cannot see with it, it chokes us rather than liberates us; we just do not find it compelling. I want to spend part of this chapter trying to show why it is that as sociologists we often do not feel at home with this language and, in doing so, to explicate another possibility for living as a sociologist.

1. The analytic character of criticism is a common theory in the later philosophy of Wittgenstein, and one can see it most clearly in Hegel's *Preface to the Phenomenology*, wherein he says: "To judge that which has contents and workmanship is the easiest thing; to grasp it is more difficult; and what is most difficult is to combine both by producing an account of it." In Wittgenstein's language, this is to grasp the *form of life* which makes the work possible.

Let me note, in a preliminary way, one trouble with the language of deductive theorizing. Generally, adequate theorizing is identified with deductive explanation through the device of natural science: this is only to say that those who promote the priority of deductive theorizing tend to do so on the grounds that it respects the procedures of scientific practice. Adequate theorizing is then used as a synonym for adequate *scientific* theorizing. I do not want to argue – as many have – over sociology's scientific status or even over the historic correctness of this formulation. I merely want to point out that in its historic senses, theorizing as an idea does not necessarily entail any conception of scientific procedure as we currently understand it. Not only does theoria supercede our various practical conceptions of science, there is an honorable analytic tradition that asserts that the scientific impulse actually *denies* the possibility of theorizing (knowledge versus opinion in Plato, fact versus essence in Husserl, usage versus form of life in Wittgenstein)[2] in the sense that the so-called natural attitude describes a necessary condition of failure for theorizing.

Aristotle used theoria as that kind of mental activity in which we engage for its own sake, as contemplative: to theorize meant to inspect or to keep one's gaze fixed on. To theorize was to turn one's mind in a certain direction, or to look at the world under the auspices of a certain interest. Such a look has been variously captured in Husserl's notion of reflexiveness and in Heidegger's idea of astonishment.

Originally, theoria meant spectator at games, so it could be identified with whatever such a spectator does (watching, for example), but this is too concrete, for it might suggest the mob of spectators dumbly looking on. Even before this usage, however, theoria referred to the envoy sent to consult an oracle and was the title of the collection of state ambassadors that a city-state delegated to the sacral festivals of another city-state. According to some sources, since these festivals were usually connected with games, theory came to mean spectator and, more particularly, a traveler who visits foreign places to learn something about their customs and laws (Lobkowicz, 1967:6–9). Because the witnessed events were usually connected with divine things, theory came to be seen as a particularly sublime way of life (in Pythagoras, for example, we have the idea of the spectator as a truly free man because he contemplates the transcendental).

Theoretical life meant more than science because it was not conceived as arising from mere curiosity or from practical necessity, but out

2. In fact, the competence-performance distinction in the work of Chomsky is this kind of idea, though he tends to treat competence concretely as the problem of the native speaker rather than as the *investigator's method* of formulating the native speaker.

of wonder, as an attempt to escape from ignorance. If we begin with
the Greeks in order to locate the primordial deep grammar of the usage,
we find that theorizing was a more inclusive and powerful notion than
science and that it encapsulated as parameters the ideas of spectator,
search, and self, with the process originating in wonder and culminating
in a transcendental realization.[3]

What I am saying, then, is that to understand the idea of theorizing by
grasping the form of life it expresses is to recover part of our history. It
is then that we can see how an identification of theory with "scientific
theory" is a degenerate usage. To equate theorizing with scientific theorizing I repeat, is not a matter of correctness. Instead, the trouble we
often experience in adapting to such usage perhaps derives from our
inarticulate feeling that it is not responsive to the very basic and primordial human possibilities which the idea of theorizing locates.

These preliminary comments enable me to establish certain limits to
my discussion of theorizing. The ideas of wonder, astonishment, spectator, search, and self help to locate such limits, but there are more
contemporary expressions that perhaps serve to convey something of
the character of the activity of theorizing—as I conceive it—in terms
that are more palatable.

We are so accustomed to thinking of theories as reports or descriptions of states of affairs external to the theorist that we assume without
question one particular family of uses of theory—to refer, to describe.
Conceive, for the moment, of Austin's (1965) notion of a performative,
that is, that in uttering an expression we are doing an activity. If we
conceive of theories as performatives, we ask, what activity is being
done in the statement of the theory? Is it describing? Is it reporting the
facts? Is it making predictions? Let us *see* the theory as doing none of
these things, and, instead, let us treat it as expressing self, or as doing a
display of mind.[4] Through theorizing the theorist searches for his self,
and his achievement in theorizing is a recovering of this self. Note in
passing that the different sorts of questions that are asked of theorizing
in this game (Is it correct? Does it work?) become senseless, for how do
you speak of reacting to a display of mind? It's beautiful one might say
that, and that he wants the method (or one might treat it aesthetically).

When we grasp the character of theorizing in this way we can understand at once the sense of Wittgenstein's claim that he was not engaged

3. This idea of returning to the Greeks is used in the work of Heidegger (see, for
example, *What Is Philosophy?* and *Introduction to Metaphysics*) where he emphasizes the
importance of grasping the form of life in which our contemporary problems originated for
the Greeks, since that primordial situation shows all of the possibilities in the posing of the
problem. Stephen Karatheordoris encouraged me to take Heidegger more seriously.

4. Stanley Raffel's (1970) paper was a crucial resource in my presentation of this idea.

in producing "theories." His entire enterprise was devoted to showing how any concrete and degenerate version of theory always *necessarily* glossed the form of life which made it all possible, and that to show such a form of life is simultaneoudly to find one's self. As one of Wittgenstein's interpreters says:

> If it is accepted that "a language" (a natural language) is what native speakers of a language speak, and that speaking a language is a matter of practical mastery, then such questions as "What should we say if . . . ?" or "In what circumstances would we call . . . ?" asked of someone who has mastered the language (for example, oneself) is a request for the person to say something about himself, describe what he does. So the different methods are methods for acquiring self knowledge (Cavell, 1969:66).

Or again,

> Instead of accumulating new facts, or capturing the essence of the world in definitions, or perfecting and completing our language, we need to arrange the facts we already know or can come to realize merely by *calling to mind* something we know. Wittgenstein says that these perspicuous representations are "the way we look at things" (Cavell, 1964:964).

This "calling to mind" is a way of recovering what one has all along, it is a way of seeing and as such it is inextricably tied to a way of living. More than this, it is to reconstitute or re-create out of one's life and history of a society another possibility for seeing. To theorize is to re-formulate one's self.[5]

Since formulate means to express in a form, or to create a form, to re-formulate means to create or express in another form. The re-creation of a form is essentially (analytically intelligible as) a method: it is a theorist's method for re-forming society (his method for showing society in one of its many possible forms). Seen in this way, his method is a procedure for showing the form in which the world has meaning for him. The method analytically locates the meaning of the world for the theorist and, in a sense, it is through the method that the actor lives as a theorist. Thus, the theory means the method and the method shows the meaning of the concrete actor as a theorist.

The possible society that is an achievement of theorizing consists in and of the methods for its production. Analytically, the possible society is a method for re-forming society, and the author of such a doing can be conceived as a theoretic actor. A theoretic actor is one who can be seen as acting under the auspices of an interest in methodically re-forming society and, in so doing, is revising his own meaning as a theorist (self-clarification).

5. Of course this notion does not originate with Wittgenstein; it can be found as well in the Greek philosophers. For a very nice statement from within another tradition, see Collingwood (1933:Chapter 8).

L*

Before entering in further detail into a description of the production of a possible society, we would do well to reconsider certain features of the deductive model of theorizing. Since it could be argued that deductive theories culminate in the production of possible societies, various senses of "possible" must be explicated.

Theory as Correct Form

Take the following typical definition of adequate theory by Homans (1964:809): "A theory of a phenomena is an explanation of it, showing how it follows as a general conclusion from general propositions in a deductive system." Most definitions are like this, but whether or not they agree with Homans's to the letter, they each participate in a common conception of theory. In all of these versions theories are identified with a form in which statements are made and are treated as congeries of elements and of relationships between elements, which are — in some sense — normatively stipulated.

The question I then want to consider is: How is it possible (this is not an ironic question) for "theory" to mean the organizational format of some collection of assertions? Or, better, How is a version of "theory" as *correct form* possible? It should be noted that I am at this point concerned not with criticizing such a conception (for my purposes Wittgenstein has done this), but with understanding such a version of theory as itself a display of a form of life.

I want to begin to grasp the language that sanctions the identification of theory with correct form by explicating the understandings and conventions that a user is required to "know without question" as a condition of his activity. For example, if I asked Homans why he subscribes to such a notion, he would undoubtedly refer me to his papers wherein he tacitly alludes to the following grounds: that when all is said and done, his usage is grounded upon his conception of the history and precedents of the natural sciences, which he elects to use as grounds for his notion of "adequate theory" as correct form. Again, I do not want to argue this election, for that would be like arguing about the life he lives; rather, I want to submit it to analysis, to make it a topic, to understand it.

What if we forgot everything we conventionally know about theory (all the concrete this-and-thats) and ask How is it possible to entertain a notion of correct form as a preferred achievement of theorizing? The following possibilities come to mind:

1) Correct form is beautiful, it is an end in itself, one just likes it.

2) Correct form leads to correct statements about the world (usually, historically), it leads to true statements.

3) Correct form is compelling to an audience; it is persuasive, etc.

4) Correct form achieves a certain precision in talking about the world because it standardizes our vocabularies.

Looking at (1) we can see that the user who offers such ground is telling us that correct form is its own justification, that he just likes it, that, in a way, he "finds himself" through correct form. This is an honorable, interesting tradition (think of someone like Tarski), and in sociology we do not often find it congenial only because we do not need to live that way.

The other grounds offer more grist for our mill: correct form leads to truth; correct form leads to the induction of belief; correct form is precise and standard. Note how each is concerned with the "world" or with their effects upon others—with consequences. Note also how they are each concerned with inducing order or with producing some concerted effect. Thus, in one case (2) correct form will lead to "truth," which will unify disparate observers (will make a community), here think of Descartes, for example. In another case (3) correct form will be persuasive (will create belief), think of the Sophists here; and, in another case (4) correct form will create a standard language (common norms), think of Carnap here. Note the difference between these three versions and version (1)—he is merely saying that correct form will keep him alive, will keep him sane; each of the others justifies theorizing on the grounds that it will (could, should) lead to the production of a collective.

What we see is that the notion of theory as correct form justifies itself as a method for the production of a collective. Analytically, such a collective should be understood as concerted agreement; so these particular instances of positivistic theory rest in the last analysis on this particular form of life (this is their game). Theory is identified with correct form because in this game correct form is a condition for the production of agreement. From whom is such agreement solicited? From the collective of colleagues (scientists). Then theory is designed to produce agreement (consensus?) in one's colleagues. What kind of life would make intelligible this rock-bottom fact of needing to theorize in order to produce agreement?

In this version, theorizing is designed to remove doubt, to be persuasive: as in all cases, when theorizing justifies itself or lives in terms of its convincingness to an audience, such approval is a condition of its adequacy (its existence). Thus, a persuasive character is essential to such theories, for in the end (as Wittgenstein says so well) they seek to transform an audience's way of looking at the world.

But do not all theories reduce to such persuasive grounds? Conceive of an alternative—of not taking the audience seriously. Thus, the theorist uses the audience only as a concrete occasion to undress his language, to exhibit his form of life, or to show another possibility for seeing. In this case, the audience is analytically irrelevant, for they are more like spectators that colleagues: if they want to see this way they can follow by example and seek to learn the methods, but they are not indespensible. The theorist—in this case—does not depend upon his audience, for he is not seeking to integrate with them.

Let me suggest, as against all of the works written on positivism, that this characterization of the relation between theorist and audience serves to capture the analytic character of positivism; it begins to locate the form of life from which positivisms (in all their forms) derive. One might also note parenthetically why it is so difficult for substantive radicals (like leftist sociologists) to escape from positivism, for they all share this essential human condition of wanting to unite with their audience.

Again, I am not making ironic comparisons but am rather trying to show another version of theorizing. To theorize in my language is not to try to overcome the multiplicity of stipulations that locate different colleagues in their divergent perspectives; it is instead to explicate one stipulation and to show the form of life that makes it a sensible existential condition for the theorist. Rather than eliminate "bias," we celebrate it, refashion it, carry it to its limits, and provide methods for its production.

One question we might begin to pose is: How is it possible (what is the grammar) to see theory construction as the production of a collective? Is there a difference between theorizing in order to produce a collective, that is, to justify theory because it leads to the production of a collective, and theorizing as the search for the collective that it presupposes (that makes possible theorizing itself)? That is, in my version of theorizing, theorizing is the methodic search for the collective that it presupposes (the form of life).

From my perspective, any other conception of theorizing is degenerate, concrete, and practical, since it locates its own justification in terms of the services it renders, its contributions to other concrete selves, its effects upon an audience; to formulate one's self as an achievement of theorizing is to render one's common-sense audience irrelevant; it is to destroy the audience for one's theory.

The possible society can then be seen as the analytically conceived conditions of living together which the theorist elects to explicate when these conditions include this election itself and its grounds. As a user of language and a follower of rules, the theorist is simultaneously addressing self and community, for the self is essentially public and the community is part of his self (part of his history, his biography, his corpus of knowledge).

Perhaps we can now appreciate another problem of deductive theorizing in that it does not permit us to recover our form of life and by making this need superfluous it diminishes (by making impractical or comical) the impulse to theorize. Let me attempt to explicate more specifically the source of this tension.

The Concrete Notion of Possible Society. Let me attempt to state my point in a different way: what hypothetico-deductive forms of theorizing appear to destroy under all concrete occasions of their use is sociology as a form of life. That is, the theoretic impulse in sociology is an achievement in explicating and showing a sociological conception of the world: the possible society is not merely a method for reconstituting a form of life as self, but, in so doing, it shows a sociological conception of the world. The possible society is a method for producing a theoretic actor, and it is the grammar of such a theoretic actor that imparts to the method its sociological character.

The proponents of deductive theorizing themselves state that conditions of adequacy for the construction of such theories are conditions not for all theories but for their sort of (deductive) theories in particular. While sociologists are generally too concrete to understand the implications of such a distinction, some philosophers are not.

For example, Morgenbesser's (in Kyburg and Nagel, 1963) proposed reading of the controversy over deductive explanation suggests that the model describes necessary and sufficient conditions not for the use of "explanation" but rather for the use of "deductive explanation." Whether we accept this reading or not (and I suspect that it is quite suspicious in that it provides a surface rather than a deep description of the grammar of "deductive explanation"), it serves to reorient our attention to another problem. For given that the deductive model supplies a description *only* of the conditions for its application, the question then becomes: Why do we want to use this method? I am suggesting that its use deprives us of our impulse to theorize (to see sociologically) in one of its strongest senses.

Thus, in arguing against some opponents of the deductive model who claim that it does not adequately apply to the study of human actions, Morgenbesser seeks to demonstrate how (in practice and in principle) we can rearrange our language in order to realize such an application. This is certainly correct, and, in the example he uses, Morgenbesser (in Kyburg and Hagel, 1963:175–176) shows how the description of Bill's taking and eating chicken from the refrigerator can be subsumed under "general laws that make it probable that Bill, when hungry and in the house, etc., will eat something which he will first have to remove from the place where the food is kept." In other words, Bill's eating chicken is *explained* under the description of his eating edible food from the refrigerator.

We must note though that "edible food" is not "chicken" and that the proposed explanation does not preserve what we might take to be the grammar of the action for Bill (his action of eating *chicken*). The particular situation has meaning for Bill in his disposal of the chicken, and the description of his action as "eating edible food" seems like a limp reproduction of this action. The point of all of this is that while the deductive model *can* be applied to the field of human actions, it is only accomplished through a transformation of the meaning of the action. The deductive model changes (we won't say "distorts") the description of the action to meet its own requirements, and while in principle there is nothing wrong with this and all description does it, it is still an election that does not have to be made. All I am arguing is that one cost of this election is that it prevents us from comprehending a version of a possible society, that it results in a description that is too concrete. Note again that this is a trouble only for me, since others might appreciate concrete descriptions for their purposes.

The argument over deductive theorizing has often crystallized in the example of William the Conqueror's failure to invade Scotland, with Scriven arguing, for example, that an explanation need not invoke general laws, and Homans (in Fakis, 1964:968) arguing that it *could*. Now of course such an explanation as Homans suggests can be constructed, but the question is, are such exercises accomplished only at the expense of what appears to be most distinctive of our subject matter? I would argue that we are not interested in saving a form of explanation at the expense of all that is distinctive of sociologizing; my interest lies in showing on each and every occasion of concern the distinctiveness of a way of sociologizing.

Thus, our task might be reformulated not as one of "explaining" the failure of William to invade Scotland, for in any strong sense this is an impossible task but as one of showing what is possible in the conception of his failure to invade as a phenomenon of interest. Thus, instead of asking "Why did William fail to invade Scotland?" (who knows, who cares?), we ask how the question itself becomes interesting as an intelligible and orderly request for an account. We would then be involved in explicating some version of the circumstances and context of William the Conqueror as a recognizable social object, some notion of the expectations that hold for one in such a context, some idea of how absent events (his failure to invade . . .) become interestingly absent (inasmuch as William failed to do many things in his life besides invade Scotland). In these cases we would be treating the question (explicandum) grammatically, not by searching for new information (factual answers to a "why" question) but by reformulating the conditions that make the mere posing of the question sensible to the theorist.

We can appreciate the sense of Wittgenstein's attack upon reductionism: if every sentence is in order as it is, reductionism does not leave language alone, it does an excavation. The possible society is part of the unformulated environment of the theorist which he methodically "brings to mind": it is not a "new" society which he carefully discovers through "empirical research." In fact, as I have said, it is not a society at all but consists of the *methods* of bringing some society to mind. The notion of possibility that I am trying to explicate cannot be adequately serviced through the use of a deductive model of theorizing because such a version does not (in practice) explicate the unformulated environment that is "before our eyes all along" but creates a "probable" society. As I am using it, the possible society describes a version of what the explicandum means to the theorist who produces it and how it is constituted by and for him as a recognizable object. It is not a series of factual answers to questions posed by the explicandum as a "datum" awaiting "explanation." Furthermore, the explicans that deductive theorists produce as their version of a possible society do not explicate the explicandum but, rather, produce an environment that *could have* contingently preceded it. Though in principle the explicans could explicate the explicandum, in practice they do not, largely because the success of the deductive model tends to be defined in terms of its explantory capacity, which is in turn defined by its ability to locate "causes." As long as such concrete, practical purposes are adhered to, the achievement of the sort of analytic status described in this chapter will not be possible. As I am using the idea of a possible society, it is intended to describe a method of explicating features that are available in the observer's intial formulation of the event (the event to be explained); thus, it should be treated more as a redescription than as an explanation.[6]

For our purposes, then, whether or not some description of an event can be converted into premises containing lawlike statements, etc., is irrelevant, for it can certainly be accomplished. The point is, rather, why we, as sociologists, should elect to proceed in such a way. What compelling reasons could possibly be offered that could induce us to abandon our worlds and our history?

6. See Melden (1956) for a somewhat similar statement of this position.

An Analytic Notion of Possible Society

So far, we have been more negative than constructive. That is, we have alluded to the idea of theorizing as methods for constructing (what we have called) a possible society, but we have devoted most of our time to discussing the deductive version of theorizing as an expression of a form of life. However, the advantage of such a procedure is that it permits us to specify, in many cases, examples of what a possible society is not (some concrete notions of possibility?).

We have attempted to show how the possible society produced through theorizing is not equivalent to the achievement of a causal-reductive description because such descriptions show no interest in explicating the constitutive properties (the analytic possibilities implicit in) of the concrete society (object) which first engages the sociologist's attention. That is, we could say with Urmson (1967:Chapter 10) and Kovesi (1967) that the analytic notion of the theorist is not reproduced through a deductive analysis. To put it bluntly, the analytic notion of the theorist is his application of competence (not performance) and is a product of his methods of knowing (reason?). Consequently, descriptions of experience or of performance are just not to the point, for they themselves become intelligible only through the theorist's analytic notion. *What we want are the theorist's methods for the creation of his idea, for it is in his production of the idea that his activity acquires its analytic status as an instance of theorizing.*[7]

What I am attempting to say has been said by Kovesi (1967:19) in another way:

> I am not saying that there are two sorts of objects, objects of sense and objects of reason. . . . I am simply saying that knowing is different from perceiving, and we do not perceive something called murder; we know that certain acts are acts of murder in the same way as we know that certain objects are tables. We do not perceive something called 'table' over and above the material elements that have to be present in order that something should be a table. In an important sense, in the world there *is* no value and there are no murders, tables, houses. But our language is not about *that* world in which there is no value or no tables, houses. . . . That world, the world of raw data, cannot be described for the sense of that world also lies outside it and the very description of it, likewise, lies outside it. Thereof one really cannot speak.

Analytically, we have methods for making sense of the materials of the world, where out methods for making sense are not entailed by descriptions of these materials. The possible society is a procedure for imposing a sense upon the materials available to us; the "possible"

---

7. And these methods are available in his corpus of knowledge – this is what "possible" suggests – and are not to be discovered through "empirical research" as new facts.

character of the society consists in the fact that it is the product of a sense-transforming operation.

Theorizing consists of the methods for producing a possible society. A possible society is the theorist's methods for re-forming his knowledge of society. Since the theorist is engaged in re-forming *his knowledge* of society, he can be seen as re-forming his knowledge. One who is re-forming his knowledge is re-forming his self: theorizing is then best described not as a sense-transforming operation but as a self-transforming operation, where what one operates upon is one's knowledge of the society as part of one's history, biography, and form of life. The question we want to consider is how this transformation is done.

Methods

As I am using "possible," it serves to provide one version of "analytic" in this sense: that it formulates one of the horizon of possibilities generated through a conception of the object. The possible society is the theorist's method for transforming an object into a horizon of possibilities, and this into one possible possibility. The possible possibility that is achieved is the analytic meaning of the society to (and for) the theorist.

The conditions for constructing a possible society are then conditions of formulating one sense of a society as an intentional object for the theorist. The possible society is what society means to him, and should then be understood as a method for creating an environment, a possible world: the "truth" of such a method resides in its intelligibility and sensibility and, in this way, the methods describe the conditions of sensibility in this world, that is, the language that members of such a world are required to speak (the rules and auspices under which members of this world are required to act).

If to theorize is to employ rules for constructing a sensible and intelligible environment, then theorizing describes the conditions of sensibility and intelligibility for some typical actor (rules and grammar). Such a construction acquires its authority (its reality) from its methodic, public character, and it "exists" only insofar as it is accomplished.

The result of the construction is a world-for-some-actor (the theorist), and such a world is described in terms of the items of its production. These items are the theorist's methods for constituting a rule-guided, relevant, and sensible environment. We describe the environment *analytically*, not in terms of the concrete characteristics it shows or its particular substantive contents but as methods for creating such characteristics and contents. The possible society is then an intentional object for the theorist which is constituted by his methods for producing it.

If the possible society is a method for uncovering a tacit and unformulated "possibility-for-seeing" which is available in the theorist's corpus of knowledge, all of the materials for theorizing are already present in the corpus, and theorizing becomes a transformation of the corpus or a reconstitution of its character. We must then ask how one acts upon himself and his corpus in such a way as to be counted as theorizing.

Shwayder (1965:12–13) presents a paradigmatic solution of sorts to this question. We can begin with it and then proceed to complete the details which he fails to supply.

> In this work we bring under systematic review our ordinary ways of thinking about animal behavior. Behavior, therefore, is indirectly the subject matter of investigation.... We shall always be considering the observer's view of behavior. The conceptualization of the behavior we investigate will always be strictly and even ruthlessly third-person. Even when we consider how we think about our own behavior, we must do so as an outside observer would....
>
> I take all our common ways of thought, hence our common ways of talking about behavior as fundamental data.... I assume that the imagined observer's characterizations of behavior are given in consideration of what he sees in the movements and the circumstances of the animal observed.... What must an (outside) observer see in the movements constituting the behavior and in the circumstances of the animal in order that he should meaningfully ... be able to say ... the observed conditions warranting the characterization in question will always be ones taken to be open to the view of an imagined observer....
>
> My theory represents an attempt to explain and understand what it is to *see* certain things *in* the movements of animate creatures.... They are phenomena which we see as residing in the movements only because we have these ways of thinking about the movements....
>
> What must the conceptualizing observer of animal movements see in and around these movements that will license him to characterize the movements in a certain way.

Shwayder elects the convention of calling A the animal imagined to be moving in certain ways, O an imagined conceptualizing observer of A, and We a theoretical commentator on the reported observations of O. We is supposed to have available the apparatus of the ensuing theory, and he applies that by drawing out the implications of O's report.

As I have been proceeding, the one who is engaged in the activity of theorizing is both We and O in this scheme, that is, he is one (We) who draws out the implications and formulates the conditions for his own conceptualized observations (O) of behavior. In this view, theorizing is (analytically) third-person in the sense that the theorist treats himself (his corpus of knowledge, O) as the topic of inquiry. The idea of theorizing speaks to this point: that whatever he (We) conceives of

himself-as-observer as having to see "in the movements and circumstances of the animals involved"—these particular conditions for an
"adequate application" of the characterization—are only possible
through a method of seeing that is itself supplied by an analytic notion.
Analytically, we should not understand *We* and *O* as two concrete
persons (though they could be), or even as two ways of conceptualizing
one concrete person (*We* as theoretic, *O* as practical). Rather, once *We*
assimilates *O* to his purposes, *O* is best seen as parameters (rules,
grammar, constitutive condtions) and *We* as an election.

The parameters or conditions of an analytic characterization of an
event which *O* generates becomes possible only through an analytic
stipulation which *We* supplies and through which the conditions themselves become analytically intelligible. Many modern philsophers and
sociologists proceed as if a formulation of the conditions of recognition
for an object (such as rules) served to depict the analytic character of
theorizing, but note this: no matter which conditions one locates as
necessary to the recognition that an animal is *X*ing (no matter what "a
conceptualizing observer of animal movements" *must* be formulated as
having to see), the imperative feature of such a recognition is sensible
only in terms of s stipulation to which it is responsive. Theorizing
consists of the methods employed by a *We* to see in the conditions
supplied by himself as *O*, their analytic sense.

The essential point here is that the reflexive character of theorizing is
not furnished by *We*'s inspection of his own behavior as *O* (as in the
cliche, *We* "explicates his common-sense-knowledge" or *We* "makes
himself a stranger to the situation"), but through *We*'s grasp of "*We*'s
inspection of his own behavior as *O*." To theorize is not to act as a *We*
but is to formulate the entire *We–O–A* scheme as an instance of what
one is doing. One who shows such a grasp is a theoretic actor.

Husserl's notion of reflexiveness captures this moment. The reflexive
turn which essentially characterizes theorizing treats the ordinary formulation of objects in the world as concrete insofar as the method of
formulating is itself unheeded in the formulation of the object. The
concrete grasp of the world does not include itself (its act of grasping) as
a topic of inquiry. Thus, reflexiveness is not a mere suspension of the
natural attitude; rather, it constitutes an expansion of the possibilities
inherent in ordinary looking in order to include such ordinary looking
within its purview. This reflexive feature of reflectiveness, then, includes
reflectiveness and its achievements and grounds as objects of reflection.

To say that theorizing "expands the possibilities inherent in ordinary
looking" locates the crux of our problem: we wish to understand the
methods for doing such an expansion. So, also, when Shwayder speaks

of the "imagined observer's characterizations of behavior" he is speaking of the possible ways in which the theorist as a member can see in the movements and circumstances of the animal that it is Xing. Whether one decides to *see* what an animal is doing as Xing presupposes some notion on Xing. Such a notion is selected from the theorist's conception of the possibilities for conceiving of Xing, and even within the terms of his particular conception there are a variety of possible methods for seeing it in the movements and circumstances of the animal.

As a method, then, the possible society describes the reflexive movement of the theorist from his original conception of the object as a horizon of possibilities to his particular possibility, and the conditions that the theorist as O formulates serve to encapsulate the steps of this transformation. To say it more concretely, the conditions formulated by the theorist (for group, society, bureaucracy, capitalism, motive, social action, interruptions, etc.) are necessary transforms of a horizon of possibilities, and each set of conditions concretely supresses but analytically shows the character of such a transformation.

I want to suggest that such an achievement, such a transformation, is accomplished through a method of creating examples for the purpose of deciding whether or not they are true in all possible worlds. The theorist's method can then be seen as one of inventing, collating, and excluding possibilities. Now we can return to Wittgenstein (1967:7,2e).

> From its seeming to me — or to everyone — to be so, it doesn't follow that it is so. What we can ask is whether it can make sense to doubt it.

To be certain is to conceive of grounds for doubt as lacking; in a particular case we are just unable to imagine what doubt here would look like. Conceive of the cases in which what we conceive as a condition for the recognition of Xing would be sensible to doubt (for example, is assigning "purpose" a required condition for recognizing an event as an "action" — imagine what doubt might look like here; could we imagine a world in which we speak of "action" without requiring the assignment of "purpose"? The condition is not beyond doubt, for no condition is, but as a rule we decide to stop doubting, we cannot imagine what doubting would look like).

A universe of possible conditions is generated and addressed in this way: for each condition we imagine what a mistake would look like; we ask ourselves what it would be like to be counted wrong, or whether or not we have a clear idea of a mistake. The ability to conceptualize a doubt is a parameter of our form of life in the sense that such a life carries with it its conditions for intelligible doubt.

In constructing a possible society, the theorist achieves analytic conditions as those conditions that he cannot conceive of doubting. The achievement is a function of the ways in which he can imagine conditions to be doubtable (the ways in which he can imagine a mistake). Thus, analytically we deepen the notion of possible society in the sense that it appears as the set of conditions about which the theorist relaxes doubt in that he regards as unintelligible the contemplation of other possibilities.

> What sort of proposition is: "What could a mistake here be like"? It would have to be a logic proposition. But it is a logic that is not used, because what it tells us is not learned through propositions — It is a logical proposition; for it does describe the conceptual (linguistic) situation (Wittgenstein, 1969:57,9e).

To conceptualize a mistake is to deepen one's grasp of the situation in this way: that it is the situation as a form of life which makes possible the conceptualization of doubt. To be certain is to feel that doubt loses its sense (it is senseless to speak of contemplating doubt), and this senselessness is always embedded in a way of looking at the world. Why, then, does doubt lose its sense? *Our game is just like that, this is the way we live;* and since the unintelligibility of doubt describes our situation, to speak of knowing or of being certain is to describe the way we live.

There is deeper sense to doubt, however, than the ability to imagine a mistake, and this sense resides in Wittgenstein's frequent admonitions to "imagine the facts as other than they are." Take as a "fact" some description of an event that a sociologist decides to warrant as not requiring further doubt. If we wish to formulate this event analytically, we want to locate its "essense" or the necessary conditions that a sensible recognition of the event requires. But for whom is any list of necessary conditions necessary? Other worlds can always be located to show that one man's necessary (analytic) conditions are merely contingent or conventional conditions. When Wittgenstein says that no proposition is beyond doubt while at the same time every description ultimately presupposes some proposition that is not doubted he is saying that every theory rests upon a stipulation that can be distrusted from the perspective of another theory.

To put it otherwise, the notion of "analytic" is relative to a language, resting ultimately upon a stipulation that is doubtable in terms of another language. To formulate analytic conditions is to formulate conditions of recognition for a notion over as many possible worlds (languages) as one commands, while there is always another language that could deny the invariance of the claim. This we know, but here is the fascination of the idea: in our conceptual explorations we are not stripping the events of the world down to their bare essenses; rather, we are using these events-of-the-world to show our version of language and life. The analytic formulation of the world can never contain all of its possible possibilities, and, consequently, all it can do is show the organized conditions of stipulating sensibility which pervade the language of the theorist.

When we formulate the parameters, conditions, or rules for the production (recognition) of an X, we are describing the X from within one particular language: *the X itself is irrelevant* since we never hope to exhaust the possibilities for its description (that is, its relevance does not lie in its status as an object to be described); rather, we use it as an occasion to display our language. In this way, each and every occasion of a description is a demonstration of the *use of a theoretic language*.

To imagine facts as other than they are is a methodic bit of counsel since it implores us to construct our conceptions of the world by imagining the possible conditions of their failure. To imagine facts as other than they are is decidedly not to imagine many possible, different interpretations of the facts as they are; it is to imagine different worlds for these same facts. In the sense that to imagine facts otherwise is to imagine other worlds, the sorts of mistakes or alternatives or possibilities we are conjuring up are ways of living and seeing the world. To imagine the facts otherwise, to imagine different usage, is to invent a form of life (a possible society). And how does our final possible society relate to all of the other possible possibilities which we have progressively invented, discarded, and assimilated in order to achieve our final product? They relate in the same way that our language related to all other possible languages; some we incorporate and transform into items-in-our-life, while others we identify as outside of *our* bounds of sense. And finally, what does our possible society show but whatever we regard as the parameters and rules of sensibility-in-our-language, our boundaries for talking sense.

We might now begin to put some flesh of the age-old idea of theorizing an issuing out of an impulse to "make problematic." To theorize is to methodically doubt, but the analytic character of doubting is conveyed as the conditions under which the contemplation of possibilities becomes intelligible *and* as a conjuring up of other-world possibilities. Doubt is essential to theorizing because the contemplation of other possibilities is the method of formulating the necessary conditons of sensibility in one's language: the construction of possible societies is a way of discovering the conditions of sensibility for one's own language.[8] In a way, then, it is through such methods that the theorist comes to constantly re-cover and articulate his logos.

8. "The mere awareness of other possibilities is, philosophically, of the utmost importance: it makes us see in a flash other ways of world interpretation of which we are unaware, and thus drives home what is conventional in our outlook" (Waismann, 1952:13).

The theorist finds his self by re-formulating the deep structure of his theoretic language, and he accomplishes this by discarding what is concrete and conventional from what is bedrock in his language. The fact is, as theorist one continually returns to this bedrock through theorizing itself.

Conclusion

In conclusion let me note certain practical implications of the point of view presented here. First, it will probably be recognized that I have nowhere provided rules for theorizing and, of course, it is an essential feature of my description of theorizing that this be impossible. For how would one provide rules for inventing and collating the possible possibilities that a problem generates for a theorist? The sorts of possibilities that a problem generates are just not formulable in advance by list or in a calculus that a theorist could follow as determinate rules; such possibilities are generated through the activity of theorizing itself and cannot be anticipated in advance of the activity. How, then, does one learn theorizing? I would say that one "gets the hang of it" by watching someone theorize (or re-cover his theoretic language) on a variety of particular examples.

This chapter suggests implications for the conducts of work in sociology. Baldly, the position states that any concern with the contingent features of *performance* (in Chomsky's sense) presupposes a degenerate version of analysis. This includes all of those concerned with the "facts," with true results, probably true results, invariances in performance, and the like. However, it also includes those who attempt to formulate *competence* (again, in Chomsky's sense) concretely. So, for example, Chomsky's own idea of formulating the knowledge (competence) of the native speaker is (from this perspective) analytically misdirected because he should be formulating his own investigative knowledge (competence) which makes possible "the formulation of the competence of the native speaker" (that Chomsky *should* do this is of course presumptuous on my part and I intend such a remark analytically, that is, that *his* mind would have to be explicated before I could count his work as an instance of theorizing in my language). For example, while I suspect that most positivists would regard Chomsky's latest work as analytically degenerate vis-à-vis his early materials, in my terms it is the latest work in which he seeks to explicate the character of his form of life (seventeenth-century rationalism) and which I find to be the most powerful analytic contribution. Of course these implications hold also for the various revisionist "schools" of positivism represented in this volume.

On the Failure of Positivism*

I shall attempt in this chapter to describe how seeking truth might actually be done. Emphasis will be on the *behavior* of seeking truth, on the institutional and essentially public character of truth, in contrast to the usual psychological and semantic descriptions that depict private disembodiments of that behavior. Positivism, ostensibly a behaviorist epistemology and the most influential program for the conduct of science, nevertheless has been permitted to develop without much attention to whether or not it is capable of being followed in behavior, whether or not it can be done. I hope to indicate that, limited as it is to perceptions by the individual observer, the world of positivism is a romantic one, for it leads us to expect that truth can be found in the private senses of some man. But this is a demonstrably inadequate picture of the social institution where the actual ascriptions of scientific truth take place.

Our inquiry will thus assess the sheer asocial logic of conventional epistemology against the active possibility of its realization in the ongoing practices of a social institution. By such ideas as social institution, ongoing practices, and behavioral achievement I mean to make reference to a canon of rules that members use and the observing analyst formulates in describing some social activity, and that transforms what would otherwise be private individual performance into public social understanding. When as sociologists we describe, theorize, and so forth, we do not do so simply by citing the concrete practice itself—this holds no interest whatever. We are instead engaged in the analytic observation

*This paper was an early contribution to a series of informal seminars and investigations conducted with colleagues in the New York area. For more recent work, see a paper co-authored with Alan F. Blum, "The Social Ascription of Motive."

or conception of a concrete practice according to some rule or grammar, and it is this latter that permits us to distinguish between, say, the description of a mathematical notation and schizophrenic babble. The notation and the babble could be concretely identical; an ordinary member will understand the two depending upon what canon of rules he applies, and a sociologist describes the two by having formulated these canons. To be recognizable as a behavioral production, in other words, truth or a method or whatever requires that some grammar by which this canon and not that one can formulate for us the concrete activities for which that very formulation itself provides. Another way of saying this is: to analytically describe an activity we must formulate whatever a member must know to do the activity. What we shall be engaged with here, then, are the various formulations of scientific procedure insofar as they can be understood to be self-descriptive or methodic in themselves.

Truth of whatever kind, whether metaphysical, interactional, or scientific, thus cannot be sociologically conceived except as just this kind of behavioral production. It has no status apart from the ways it can be achieved by being intelligible according to some rule-guided way of looking, so the possibilities for ways of looking will be our concern. We shall not, therefore, be engaged in "just philosophy," if by that is meant the analysis of ideals irrespective of their self-descriptive adequacy as members could use them in socially organized courses of human action. Our interest is in their adequacy as canonical formulations of the rule-guided practices we call the institution of science.

Such an aim will require a brief analysis of the several epistemologies of positivism with regard to their formulability as actual behavioral practices and possibilities. Whatever their content as ideals, we shall ask whether correspondence and positivist theories of truth could ever describe institutionalized scientific and thus social canons of action. It will be suggested that they cannot, largely because of their exclusive reliance upon physical objects and the private sense data of observers. That is, positivism is concrete and cannot formulate for us how we could observe positivism to have been done. We shall investigate whether these conventional precepts of scientific work are behavioral possibilities or not—whether or not, however sleek their verbal manifestations, they are glosses of actual scientific practice insofar as they cannot be seen *in* ostensibly scientific activities. To the degree that such ideals are impossible to conceive or formulate in that way, they will confabulate the construction of theories, the development of methods, and the making of observations, matters which are the very identity of a discipline. It is best to know about them.

We shall thus take up four matters, not necessarily in order: (1) the adequacy of positivist ideals as formulations of truth-seeking practices;

(2) the failure of positivist ideals as formulations of truth-seeking practices; (3) an examination of institutionalized public truth as an alternative formulation; and (4) how public truth reorganizes certain traditional premises of procedure.

Positivist Formulations

The two fundamental epistemologies of truth have traditionally been called the correspondence theory and the coherence theory. Generally, a correspondence theory asserts that a proposition is true if there is an object corresponding to the proposition, and it is this position that embraces positivism. A coherence theory asserts that a proposition is true if it is consistent with experience. The history of philosophy has been fraught with arguments about these theories, arguments that are reflected in the conduct of sociology. They are probably familiar to us, but are easily available in any case, so we shall be brief and direct in examination of them.[1]

There is no need now to labor over lexical definitions of truth. Because the adequacy of various formulations is the central issue, to begin with a definition would presuppose the subject. More deeply, lexical definitions shut off our understanding of practices because they do not tell us how they could be used or done as behavioral accomplishments, something we have already concerned ourselves with briefly and shall return to throughout the chapter. A single sentence, for example, is used in behavior in various ways, sometimes this way, sometimes that way — "The president of the United States is a Republican" can be a threat, a factual assertion, an irony, and so on — and to stipulate one kind of true usage or another at this juncture would restrict us to some lexicon that could have no more than a coincidental connection to behavior.

We can say that truth has been asserted to have something to do with fact, both pure and applied (Northrop, 1959); with events, both seen and unseen (Russell, 1927, 1929); with ideas, both testable and untestable (Woozley, 1949); and with language, both verbal and nonverbal (J. L. Austin, 1964). And we can indicate the history of what correspondence and coherence "are about" by enlarging on the phenomena with which they deal: experience and thought, life and mind, practice and theory, objects and language — all united by concepts, which are a means for describing these things. Whether concepts are asserted to be more ex-

1. For a summary of these philosophical positions, see Nagel and Brandt (1965: especially 121–177). See also J. L. Austin, in Caton (1963); Tarski (1944); and Wittgenstein (1953).

perience than thought, more life than mind, more practice than theory, more objects than language, has traditionally been thought to mark one's commitment to the way truth is to be achieved.

Positivist theories assert that a proposition is true if there is an object corresponding to the proposition. There must always be a relation between a belief and an object, according to this view: between a sentence and a world of objects, between a proposition and the objects to which it makes reference, or, by extension, between a statement about a statement and the latter's world of objects. In this scheme we have a language that makes assertions about independent objects and that can be truly or falsely connected to those objects. Truth requires a special kind of connection. Schools within positivism have developed out of differences in the kind of relationship that is thought to be required.

1. TRUTH IS A COPY

One version that can be quickly rejected is that correspondence is a "copy" relation, a mental reflection of reality.[2] In this instance truth exists when a statement reflects, as a picture, some substance in the real world. When asked how words can contain meaning, the proponent of this view would state that the names of things resemble pictures of things, that statements are pictures of objects or states of affairs.

The question here is just how a statement can be a picture, since metaphor is inadequate as a description of the behavior required by an epistemology, and our first interest is in behavior. Does a word, concept, or sentence have the same relation to objects that a picture has to what it depicts? What objects in the world correspond to conditionals like "if" and "perhaps"? What is "if" a picture of? What is the difference between "that is deviant" and "that is not deviant," that is, what element in the world corresponds to "not?" A picture relies entirely upon material objects, but the phenomena incorporated in sentences are not always material. What materially corresponds to "someone" in the sentence "Someone loves Mary?" What sort of photograph could picture this for us? Pictures show things, sentences state things. Showing is representing and arranging; stating is referring and describing. The great advantage of words and concepts is that they needn't simulate the spatial properties of the objects they describe—they are not part of the furniture of the world—and in this respect the copy theory fails.

2. TRUTH IS AN IMAGE

Another theory is the one that suggests that words can become concepts

2. Langer (1948). This was also Wittgenstein's (1961) early position. He later took up a very different position, of course.

because they are associated with mental images (Hume, 1927; Locke, 1894). According to Locke, images are unilaterally created by the impingement of physical objects upon the mind. But Vygotsky (1962: Chapters 5, 7) and Bruner et al (1956: 35–41, 268–275) have shown that we can conceptualize before we have images in many cases, and that we can therefore sort images according to some expectation rather than the other way around. Further, our language often incorporates nonmaterial abstractions like "function" and "virtue," abstractions that cannot be dealt with by imagists. And it is these concepts that form the very heart of social order. Because imagists make such concepts impossible, so do they make social order impossible. Sociology would not be permitted to even entertain the truthful possibility of statements like "The family in society X functions to socialize the child," or "In society X large numbers of children are considered a virtue," or "In society X economy and family are institutionally segregated." More, since a family or an economy is not a thing-in-the-world but a set of rule-guided activities, the very existence of families and economies themselves would be impossible, not to mention their relations — we would have to say that they cannot truthfully be said to exist and that their relations cannot exist either. Similarly, the institution of science — the canon of ideas and procedures — could have nothing to do with truth. To treat concepts as if they are only as good as objects in the world is to eliminate innumerable kinds of perfectly acceptable truth statements, and in this the image theory would reduce us to something like the practice of eidetics — imagine a visible display that could literally and completely reproduce the sociological concepts of function, society, rule.

3. TRUTH IS A REFLEX

A more recent formulation is the one that asserts that general words and statements are the names of properties that exist in particular objects and situations in the world (Woozley, 1949; J. L. Austin, in Nagel and Brandt, 1965: 161–176). It asserts that there is a single property that appears at different instances, say the yellow pencil and egg yolk and coward. Everything that is not a particular, that can appear in more than one place at one time, is a universal. The pencil and yolk are examples of the single universal "yellowness."

This theory, depending on the form it takes, cannot account for two matters. First, words as properties of particular objects makes it impossible to use relational or comparative statements. How does it account for "This pencil is yellower than that egg yolk," or "This group is more cohesive than that group?" Being "yellower" or "more cohesive" is not the name of a universal property, because other objects cannot have them, for they are relations between two particular objects. Yet yellower and more cohesive are certainly concepts and contain propositions of fact as people use them in both ordinary life and in science.

The second of the reflex formulations is that a statement refers to (a) general types of situations, ones that conventionally *may* occur; and (b) to actual history, in which these types of situations do or do not occur. Truth here resides in the correlation between these two aspects of a statement, given that the situation is a "standard" one. Well, at least we are here finally brought to language, which is an *"Absolutely and purely conventional"* human matter (J. L. Austin, 1964: 171). That is, the words we use need not be connected to the world in any *necessary* way. They are man's arbitrary appointments and no longer require a pictorial or intrinsic connection to objects. But they are saddled with a flawed connection, however sophisticated, by having to "correlate" with actual history under standard conditions.

The notion of standard conditions does, of course, implicate the possible existence of nonstandard conditions, and so a decision will have to be made in each case as to whether conditions are standard or not. How? What are the criteria for this decision? Some other set of arbitrary linguistic appointments? If so, and it is difficult to see how it could be otherwise, we are forced to conclude that these conventions too would be subject to the test of standard conditions: we would have to construct standard conditions for deciding on the standardness of conditions, which is circular. If instead we are to look to the world so that it might itself inform us, we are back to objects as determinants and nothing new has been offered us. Either way, a solution disappears.

4. TRUTH IS A TEST

The pragmatists tried to discover what distinguishes true ideas from those that are false and from those that are neither true nor false.[3] They concluded that true ideas are those we can verify, false ideas those we cannot; that all true ideas are useful and all useful ideas are true; and that an idea is true so long as it is profitable to our lives.

But can we verify all our true ideas? Can we verify dreams, for example? Not if no one believes our description. Can we settle a claim over who made the last move in a chess game? Not if it went unrecorded. We cannot verify all true ideas. Epistemological truth consists in analytic verifiability rather than verifiedness. James seems to have con-

3. James (1949) and Peirce (1960). Pragmatism is not positivism. But it does rest on certain versions of correspondence, and so I include it here should it be thought to provide an alternative to positivism.

fused a question like "What does the truth of a belief consist of?" for one like "How can we test the claim of a belief to be true?"

With regard to utility, perhaps all true ideas are useful, but false ones can also be useful. The man who closes his windows at night because he thinks the air will make him sick may also close out malaria-carrying mosquitoes. The fear is erroneous, but it is useful to him. Utility does not distinguish between true ideas and false ideas.

Turning to profitability, it is difficult to distinguish from usefulness. How can something be unprofitable and useful, profitable and useless? Yet even if we ignore this question we can ask if an idea loses its truth when profitability ceases. Such an assumption implies that all statements can be true at one time and false at another. Can all propositions be true today and false tomorrow? It seems that a particular one cannot. "On August 30, 1969, the American Sociological Association held its annual meeting in San Francisco, California" will never be false in the future if it is true on August 30, 1969. A particular statement does not lose truth, and in the latter sense pragmatism's emphasis on profitability is inadequate.

In summary, the nature of truth as correspondence is still unreported. The positivist theories we have addressed so far, which assume that correspondence is unidirectional, that material objects determine the accuracy of correspondence, are fallible by their own logic. Common to all these theories is a referential dictum: language and conception must comply with independent objects. The truth practices of men, comprised by their use of an institutional canon in language, are in positivism limited to conforming to a determinant world of objects and only those objects. Language is given no purchase of its own. This is a behavioral impossibility, however, since it is a circular and contradictory directive that presupposes knowledge of the object in the first place, that is, we must know before conceiving it the object of reference which is to be the test of that conception. We are expected to find out if the exchange is an economic one by consulting the exchange, while at the same time we are to suspend any conception of it as economic. This formulation entails that the character of an object or state of affairs is self-evident and sending out its own particular self-identifying signals, our task being to devise some mechanism for getting on its beam. Here is the proverbial paradigm of sociological method: ask and you will hear, look and you will see. Differences and similarities between wars in the Pelopennesus and wars in Vietnam, between male and female roles, between industrial society and developing society, could be "discovered" only by lining up so that these unconceived objects could imprint themselves upon us in the way coins are minted.

In sociology the minting procedure is supposed to be accomplished by sampling: be sure that all units (objects) have a chance to be asked the question, and then they will tell you what they are. We are expected to select objects (to know about them) and then to wait until they tell us what they are (not to know about them). How we could justify a claim to proper alignment remains unstated, and that we should distinguish objects while suspending knowledge of them is a behavioral contradiction.

Positivism is a plan that can be only tautological, stipulative, contradictory, and elliptical. We want to consult the world, naturally, but to be ordered to consult the world by looking at it is to provide no description of the way it might be done. Of course we look, but how? The object-determined standard requires of shared or common truth that each observer be located in precisely the same position—physically, psychologically, socially—vis-à-vis the object. Otherwise, observers would have a different line on the object and, therefore, would be receiving different signals. But this isn't the way science, not to mention the everyday social order, works. Many observers, in various positions in the world, talk of truth and falsehood in shared and concerted ways. We have before us the phenomenon that some things are said to be true, and are enforced to be true, across whole groups whose members occupy grossly different positions. This is only to say that the world is socially organized. Imagine the pristine positivist: A, well, concretin, as it were, a concretin who is only *encumbered* by language and canon, not oriented by them, whose task is to absorb and record as a litmus some world of objects that has a life of its own. Besides its self-contradictoriness, then, positivism disregards social organization by making it impossible to think of any kind of socially organized conduct as truth-producing conduct.

We shall turn next to coherence theories of truth, which have been construed as alternatives to correspondence theories but have the same flaws.

Coherence Theories

Generally, coherence theories are attempts to offset two elements in positivist theories: (1) that truth and meaning exist in a relationship between statements and objects, and (2) that the object determines the relationship. Now the world comes to be produced in the mind rather than reflected in the mind. (Impure coherence adds as a condition of truth that a proposition must also be consistent with "experience," but this begs the question because experience is either a product of the material world, in which case coherence is really correspondence, or a total mental construction, which would be tautological.)

According to Bradley (1914) and Blanshard (in Nagel and Brandt,

1965), coherence concepts differ from correspondence concepts in that they are words and thoughts, not images or pictures. "Yellow" and "cohesion" are a result of the mind's comparing yellow or cohesion until a certain concept arises that exists in that mind. The cohesion is not out in the world but rather is a result of one's thinking about it. It is the concepts themselves that are universals, not any cohesion in the world.

The logical objection here is the view's contradiction of itself. If cohesion is a result of minds' comparing cohesion until a certain concept arises, what is it that has been compared? An independent source of conceptualization is proposed (comparison with something) while at the same time concepts are supposed to be entirely mental. A program of coherence would require behavior in violation of its premise.

As with positivism, the behavioral problem with coherence is its difficulty in accounting for social order, for if concepts are entirely personal how do we explain the phenomenon of concept shareability? And if we admit shareability we contradict the notion of the concept as purely mental, because sharing entails communication and the existence of others with whom the concept "corresponds." This is the argument that often sullies the purity of the coherence advocate. It makes him admit that truth is no longer dependent solely upon internal mental consistency but on consistency with experience as well. He hopes by doing this to maintain his original point, because it enables him to say that shareability results from the similarity in experience of those who share—that those with similar experiences will have similar concepts, and so coherence can still be an epistemology of truth.

This adaptation has two faults, however, depending on what the advocate means by "similar." First, if by similar he means "grossly similar," say of the kind between members of a whole society, he obscures so much of importance that he is merely asking us to search for new terms to solve the same old problem. We need to distinguish differences within a society—roles and institutions, for example—that are importantly dissimilar. The second fault is the obverse of the first: if he wants similar to mean the specific biography and location of particular individuals, we must invoke the empirical phenomenon of those with different biographies and in different locations who nevertheless agree that they are seeing the same things, whose concepts cohere. Coherence fails to describe how we could do in behavior the kinds of things it demands we do.

Thus, neither correspondence nor coherence is useful to us, on either formulative, analytic, or concrete behavioral grounds. They are self-contradictory as formulations and fail to amount for behavioral usage besides. Starting from radically opposite premises, they each result in a singular kind of failure: there can be no "truth" (a) to differences in behavior by persons in the same location, or (b) to the same behavior by those in different locations. In each case the institutionalization of a canon of truth procedures is ignored, life being instead the impoverished result of its two competing sources, material objects versus individual mind. Correspondence posits a single, despotic reality so unmalleable that it does not permit us to talk of the truth of differences in communication and action by persons in the same location in the system, because, being in the same location, unilateral determination from the single location in the world to conceptualization would obviate that as a possibility. Coherence reverses the behavioral inadequacy of correspondence. It posits so many realities that one cannot talk of the truth of the same communication and action by persons in different locations. Both of these theories design a world consisting solely of physical objects and private minds, and where they differ is in which side they place their trust: if correspondence suffers from misplaced concreteness, coherence is afflicted by misplaced fancy.

Analytic Truth

Neither of these views of truth can do for us what they claim, and the fact that so many men have labored fruitlessly for so many years recommends that we abandon the search. That truth might reside in some thing, universally and eternally there for the discovery, is to formulate an insoluble problem. We must accept that there are no adequate grounds for establishing criteria of truth except the grounds that are employed to grant or concede it — truth is conceivable only as a socially organized upshot of contingent courses of linguistic, conceptual, and social courses of behavior. The truth of a statement is not independent of the conditions of its utterance, and so to study truth is to study the ways truth can be methodically conferred. It is an ascription, and little could be done for the study of truth by describing Galileo's incline or Weber's attitudes or the values of puritanism and the motives of scientists, for this would be to presuppose that Galileo and Weber and so on are acceptable. To study truth we needn't study the per se theories of Galileo and Weber, for this would be to study the object as if it could somehow tell us what criteria had been applied to it. Rather, we need study the ascription (or not) of truth to those theories insofar as those ascriptions are warranted by socially organized criteria. Actually, this principle applies to any phenomenon of social order. In the field of deviance, for example, it is wholly inadequate to say that deviance resides in the pristine act — deviance, as with truth, is socially defined

M

and treated. Nothing becomes a violation, nor a truth, until it is so treated. The phenomenon of truth is one phenomenon of social order, its "criteria" therefore no more or less than the way it is socially done.

As a matter of fact, A. J. Ayer, a positivist, comes finally to this. Instead of asking what is really real, he asks what is real as opposed to illusory. Let us adapt an example he uses (Ayer, undated):

> Suppose that someone claims to have discovered a lost Titian, and hires a set of experts in order to find out if the painting is a Titian. There is a definite procedure for finding out if it was painted by Titian, for the experts examine the grain, give the radiation test for age, consult the records to see if the painting exists someplace else, and so on. In the end, different experts may disagree, but they know the evidence which tends to support or refute their opinions. Suppose that these men maintain the position that the picture exists solely in the observer's mind, others of them that it is objectively real. What possible experience could any of them have which would be relevant to this argument one way or the other? In the ordinary sense of the term "real," in which it is opposed to the term "illusory," they must all agree that the picture is "real" without doubt. The two sides have satisfied themselves that the picture is real in this sense because they have obtained a set of correlated sense-impressions that lead them to discover that the picture is real, in the sense that real is opposed to illusory? It seems clear that there is none. If there is no other method for solving whether the picture is really real or really mental, we might as well assume that the question cannot be answered, and so proceed on whatever evidence is at hand and all the evidence that is potentially available to us, which leads us to conclude that the picture is real.

Ayer believes that he rescues correspondence, but only because he stops too soon. For, while the individuals involved may receive sense impressions and make sense observations, the validation of these observations—that is, support for the assertion that the observations are not illusory—comes from *agreement among the whole group* of those concerned with the painting. In fact, Ayer suggests that each expert may very well *disagree,* that is, have different sense impressions or make different inferences from them; he resolves such variation by asserting that the two sides can satisfy themselves only by acting collectively. It comes to be a "satisfaction" by acting in concert, and to act in concert is to vitiate any differences in the sense observations of individuals:

> Beneath the uniformity that unites us in communication there is a chaotic personal diversity of connections, and, for each of us, the connections continue to evolve. No two of us learn a language alike, nor, in a sense, does any finish learning it while he lives (Quine, 1960: 13).

Validation by agreement is produced not by the chaotic personal diversity of individual sense data but by a methodic group process. Sense observation in its strict meaning can never itself be a collective property, whereas validation can never be an individual property. Thus, what we call "sensing" is more nearly like the individual observer, and "knowing" (truth) more nearly like the concession of validation by agreement. And don't these distinctions depict the individual scientist in the first case, and the institution of science in the second?

The difference between sensing and knowing is the one between private psychological perception (or misperception) and collective public truth. Sensing something is partly a matter of using objects in experience. Alas, if this were an important characteristic of truth, positivism and correspondence might suffice. But knowing something is a collective act, requiring some public enabling rule which can generate validation from others who are engaged in the endeavor. The scientist as individual is a senser, but science as enterprise is knowing. Consequently the collective activity called science cannot use the scripture of sense impressions, for two different people cannot have the same ones. Instead, it needs perforce an institutional epistemology in the sense that a finding, as discovered or invented by an individual perceiver, does not become a truth (or error) until the collective of science agrees that it is, until the collectively enforced procedural canon produces admission to the collective body of knowledge. It is a version of psychological reductionism to equate science — and therefore truth — with the activity of one observer. This is what makes truth a behavioral accomplishment in the social sense of the phrase, and furnishes another good reason for abandoning positivism.

A second parallel reason, one that can be distinguished from the first for explication's sake, is that the expressions of "facts," "truths," and the like are linguistic. Whether one accepts that language is the instrumental vehicle of a conception of truth, or that language and conception are synonymous, sentences are the things we use in making claims to truth. As the ultimate ground of a sense-datum theory, private individual perception requires that an entirely private language be capable of expressing perception and hence truth. But this is ridiculous, since one consequence of a private language would be that no one *could* know what is being talked about; not that it is merely difficult to know, or that another strange though learnable language is being spoken, but that it would be impossible to know the claim *under any condition*. Now could there be a language of truth in which no one could know what is being said?

If people could not be brought to use a word in any regular way, if one who had been taught as we have should go on to give the name (red) to what we should call the complementary colour, if another used it as we do on Monday but in a different way on Tuesday, and if others did not even show these degrees of regularity — then . . . there would be no distinction between mistakenly or correctly. Unless the words had a regular use I should not know it was red, and I should not know what colour it was, because there would be nothing to know (Rhees, in Pitcher, 1966: 269–270).

Imagine what sociology would be like if terms like social organization, socialization, and ecology were private, if they were used in no regular and public way. It certainly couldn't be a discipline, or methodic, or even sensible. It takes on its sense, and thus the possibility of truth, by ascending from sense data to language, from privacy to the public social order. In so doing, the conditions, emergence, and admission of truth become forms of public language. Consequently, truth resides in the rule-guided institutional procedures for conceding it.

So what are we to make of the conclusion that something comes to be called true, not because it corresponds to reality but because it has been formulated in terms of some institutional canon? If something cannot be a valid truth in the same way it can be privately perceived, how are we to describe the activity called science, which deals in valid truths?

We can begin by citing a fundamental consequence of the failure of positivism: nothing—no object, event, or circumstance—determines its own status as truth, either to the scientist or to science. No sign automatically attaches a referent, no fact speaks for itself, no proposition for its value. A nude proposition is without any immanent status, because its truth value cannot be assessed by observing its relation to a datum. We have just done away with this view. Rather, just as an event comes to be intelligible to the scientist only after applying to it some rule of grammar[4]—a proposition comes to be knowledge only after conceiving it in terms of some rule of the canon that depicts the linguistic procedure by which the proposition is given life as a course of institutional action. That a finding is "true" (or false or ambiguous) comes to be so only after applying to it the analytic formulation of a method by which that finding could be understood to have been produced. Having discovered that collectively developed and enforced grammars of agreement and method are a determining and not merely tangential characteristic of science, we can summarize by saying that an event is transformed into the truth only by the application of a canon of procedure, a canon that truth-seekers use and analysts must formulate as providing the possibility of agreement. By grammar I mean the way in which a statement can be understood to have been made. Thus, *any claim to truth is successful if the claimant can analytically describe his method* for us.

4. By grammar I do not mean technical forms of usage but rather the rule(s) of transformation from private to public, the way we analytically "see" social competence in concrete individual performance. See, for example, Chomsky (1968). His distinction between competence and performance is comparable to ours between analytic and concrete.

Method is of course the "how" rather than the "what," the use rather than the substance, in conventional terminology. In detail this requires that whatever the substantive object of attention, we are expected in assessing truth to consider the *way attention was given,* namely that attention can be described rather than presupposed. This is the particular sort of method that makes science distinctive and another reason for abandoning the object-limited theories of positivism, for they can deal with only what is known not how it is known. Thus, again, objects have nothing at all to do with truth. Truth is completely and deeply a procedural affair, and that is the way claims to truth are conceded. What can be done, for example, with the Tumin-Davis and Moore argument except to look at how each part of it—each idea, test, or observation—could be the product of some rule-guided procedure? A debutante finding depends not upon itself but upon its institutional construal. This has important consequences for our suppositions about reality, objectivity, and the relation between theory and method.

With regard to reality, and if we equate it with truth, we must admit that there are as many realities as there are describable procedures. Because there are in principle many rules of construal, so can there be many realities, all with equivalent status as truths.

It might be objected here that this is a return to the worst feature of coherence, namely, that any idea at all is now permitted to be called true, because individuals could adopt and abandon distinct and incompatible rules of procedure at will, whereas by science we mean something that holds across individuals. This is a just objection so far as it goes—people *could* take any procedure at all as adequate, and each of them could take some different procedure. But they do not. They do some things together, that is, institutions are an ineluctable form of collective life. And the fruits of what they do separately can be collectively enjoyed, in the sense that what one did others would have done, because the same rules are made institutionally available as resources in behavior. That is, we needn't abandon the idea of objectivity so long as we recognize that objectivity is made possible by having met a *generally accepted rule of procedure* within the collectivity (Kaufmann, 1958: 237), not that something could hold independently of the procedures we use together in order to decide that it holds. This is just another way of describing validation by public method. To be known to have met a rule of procedure is to have described one's method by formulating its public institutional character. It is to transform the mere individual sense datum "performance" into methodic "competence" by making publicly available an analytic description of one's method. This description is at once the formulation of a method and the transformation of its surface content. Subjectivity, if we want to stay with these terms, now comes to be the experience of the issue at hand to the individual, and note the proximity of this to sense data as a possession of the individual scientist. By default, we are forced to include that canonical validation by description is *more* objective than the sense perceptions of the scientist. Abject relativism is here personified by the ubiquitous notion of sense data, because sense data are incapable of objectification by public formulation.

A further implication concerns the idea of successive approximations. If they can be said to occur at all, successive approximations are to the formulability of method rather than to the properties of objects. And since methodic formulation is understood in terms of the institutional canon, it is not eternal. Kuhn (1962), for example, is on to this when he argues that anomalies, or discoveries, can be so only because the canon we have been following prepares us *not* to see the stuff of anomaly (see also Polanyi, 1955–1956).

Finally, we should address the conventional separation of theory from method, a cleavage that parallels the fruitless physical-mental dualism of correspondence-coherence and that has misled us into the belief that truth is substantive, when instead truth is an institutional grammar. If there is no tenable epistemology for a single world of real objects, theory is right off transformed from an acquiescent handmaiden of correspondence into the sovereign of reality by agreement. Yet sociology can be distinct from other endeavors not by having theories—they are equally common among men on the street—but by having special procedures for invoking these theories; and we want to maintain the possibility of this distinction. We have theories, which are substantive descriptions of realities and are incorporated into the body of truth; and procedures, which are empty of substance yet essential to the distinctive character of the enterprise, and which are the means for incorporation of theory. There is thus nothing to either theory or method alone, for theory is not distinctive and procedures are without content. The consequence of this is not merely that they are unable to stand apart—they cannot even be conceived as separate practices. Neither can be adequately conceived except as an integral part of the practice of the other: theory is method, method is theory.

Thus, any distinction between sociology and the man on the street can be grounded only if the sociologist's theories-procedures are themselves taken as topics of inquiry. This is what it means to publicly formulate one's method. The man on the street gets there however he may, without any attention to theories-procedures except as they help to get him there. His theories-procedures have no problematic status insofar as he is not constrained to describe them. Sociology could be distinctive only by treating itself as the phenomenon for investigation. Sociology is not a program for saying that "In society X children are considered a virtue"—the member can do that, and the tourist too. It is instead a program for describing the theoretic-procedural rule(s) by which it can be said that "In society X children are considered a virtue," the rules by which it can be said commonsensically and the rules by which it can be said sociologically. Members can give many reasons for having children, and I suppose sociologists might parrot these reasons. This wouldn't be news, however, unless the member's reason were news, and even then the sociologist remains the member's mouthpiece. The news comes only when it can be shown that the member's reason can be studied, with emphasis on studied—that is, when a reason can be given to study the reason for children, or suicide, or whatever—a reason that provides a way of giving attention to these phenomena.

A (distinctive) discipline can be achieved only by having created the (distinctive) possibility of itself. This is, for example, represented by the self-correcting rule in science, which produces a pervasive pre-occupation with the structural possibilities for its own corpus and character. Another topic is the rule of doubt. How the principle of doubt can be publicly formulated is the kind of procedural behavior that needs sociological description. These are the grounds for rejection of the positivist picture of behavior, since it cannot account for institutional rules, yet it is according to these rules that we proceed to truth.

In sum, the failure of positivism necessarily turns us to what people do collectively. In what they do it is the publicly available method that constitutes the truth. Truth is not constituted by particular faces, attached to proper names, observing concrete objects. It is necessary to remove the province of truth from the physical object world to the social world. No canon, no collective, no institution can go outside itself to a world of independent objects for criteria of knowledge, since there is no other way except by its own rules to describe what's being done with regard to knowledge. Sociology, then, is responsible not just for its substantive discoveries but for having created the very possibility of them, because it has created itself. Sociological truth, as with any other kind, exists only because sociology has generated its own ways of conceding truth. It is not an aggregation of private people sensing individual objects, but a public, rule-guided, and institutionalized canon of social procedure.

References

Adams, Bert N.
  1966 Coercion and Consensus Theories: Some Unresolved Issues. *American Journal of Sociology* 71 (May): 714–717.
American Ethnological Society
  1967 *Proceedings of 1967 Spring Meeting.*
Anonymous
  1946 Informal Social Organization in the Army. *American Journal of Sociology* 51 (March).
Austin, J. L.
  1961 *Philosophical Papers.* Edited by J. O. Urmson and G. L. Warnock. New York: Oxford Univer   Press.
  1964 *Sense and Sensibilia.* New York: Oxford University Press.
  1965 *How To Do Things with Words.* Edited by J. O. Urmson. New York: Oxford University Press.
Ayer, J. J.
      Language, Truth and Logic. New York: Dover.
Baldwin, John
  1967 The Economics of Peace and War: A Simulation. *Journal of Conflict Resolution* 11 (December): 383–397.
Bales, Robert F.
  1951 *Interaction Process Analysis.* Cambridge: Addison-Wesley.
  1966 Comment on Herbert Blumer's Paper. *American Journal of Sociology* 71 (March): 545–547.
Banton, M., ed.
  1965 *The Relevance of Models for Social Anthropology.* London: Tavistock.
Bar-Hillel, Yehoshua
  1954 Indexical Expressions. *Mind* 63: 359–379.
Barron, Margaret, ed.
  1964 *Contemporary Sociology.* New York: Dodd, Mead and Co.
Becker, Howard S.
  1963 *Outsiders: Studies in the Sociology of Deviance.* New York: Free Press.
  1967 Whose Side Are We On? *Social Problems* 14 (Winter).

Becker, Howard S., et al
  1961 *Boys in White*. Chicago: University of Chicago Press.
Becker, Howard S., ed.
  1964 *The Other Side: Perspectives on Deviance*. New York: Free Press.
Bell, N., and Vogel, E., eds.
  1960 *A Modern Introduction to the Family*. New York: Free Press.
Bellugi, U., and Brown, R., eds.
  1964 *The Acquisition of Language*. Monograph. Social Research in Child Development 29.
Bensman, Joseph, and Gerver, Israel
  1963 Crime and Punishment in the Factory: The Function of Deviance in Maintaining the Social System. *American Sociological Review* 28 (August).
Berger, Peter, and Luckmann, Thomas
  1966 *The Social Construction of Reality*. Garden City: Doubleday.
Biddle, B. J., and Thomas, E., eds.
  1966 *Role Theory*. New York: Wiley.
Bierstedt, R.
  1957 *The Social Order*. New York: McGraw-Hill.
Bittner, Egon
  1961 Popular Interests in Psychiatric Remedies: A Study in Social Control. Unpublished doctoral dissertation, Department of Sociology, University of California at Los Angeles.
  1963 Radicalism and the Organization of Radical Movements. *American Sociological Review* 28: 928–940.
  1965 The Concept of Organization. *Social Research* 32:·230–255.
  1967a Police Discretion in Emergency Apprehension of Mentally Ill Persons. *Social Problems* 14: 278–292.
  1967b The Police on Skid-Row: A Study of Peace Keeping. *American Sociological Review* 32: 699–715.
Black, Mary B.
  1963 On Formal Ethnographic Procedures. *American Anthropologist* 65: 1347–1350.
Blalock, Hubert M.
  1969 *Theory Construction: From Verbal to Mathematical Formulations*. Englewood Cliffs, New Jersey: Prentice-Hall.
Blau, Peter M.
  1960 Orientations Towards Clients in a Public Welfare Agency. *Administrative Science Quarterly* 5 (December).
  1963 *The Dynamic of Bureaucracy*. Chicago: University of Chicago Press.
  1964 *Power and Exchange in Social Life*. New York: Wiley.
Blumer, Herbert
  1931 Science Without Concepts. *American Journal of Sociology* 36 (January): 515–531.
  1954 What Is Wrong with Social Theory? *American Sociological Review* 19 (February): 3–10.
  1956 Sociological Analysis and the "Variable." *American Sociological Review* 21 (December): 683–690.
  1966 Sociological Implications of the Thought of George Herbert Mead. *American Journal of Sociology* 71 (March): 535–544.
Bogue, D. J., and Murphy, M. M.

1964 The Effect of Classification Errors upon Statistical Inference: A Case Analysis with Census Data. *Demography* 1: 42–55.

Bossard, J., and Ball, E.
1948 *The Sociology of Child Development*. New York: Harper and Brothers.

Bradley, F. H.
1914 *Essays on Truth and Reality*. Oxford: Clarendon.

Bridgeman, Percy W.
1927 *The Logic of Modern Phisics*. New York: Macmillan.
1936 *The Nature of Physical Theory*. New York: Wiley.
1950 *Reflections of a Physicist*. New York: Philosophical Library.
1951 The Nature of Some of Our Physical Concepts. *British Journal of the Philosophy of Science* 1 (February).

Brightman, Edgar Sheffield, ed.
1927 *Proceedings of the Sixth International Conference of Philosophy*. New York: Longmans, Green.

Brim, O. G.
1959 *Education for Child Rearing*. New York: Russell Sage Foundation.

Brim, O., and Wheeler, S.
1966 *Socialization After Childhood*. New York: Wiley.

Broom, L., and Selznick, P., eds.
1963 *Sociology: A Text with Adapted Readings*. New York: Harper and Row.

Brown, Roger
1958 *Words and Things*. Glencoe, Illinois: The Free Press.
1965 *Social Psychology*. New York: Free Press.

Brown, Roger, et al
1962 *New Directions in Psychology I*. New York: Holt, Rinehart and Winston.

Bruner, Jerome S.; Goodnow, Jacqueline J.; and Austin, George A.
1956 *A Study of Thinking*. New York: Wiley.

Bryson, L.; Finkelstein, L.; Hoagland, H.; and MacIver, R. M., eds.
1955 *Symbols and Society*. New York: Harper.

Bucher, J.
1961 *The Concept of Method*. New York: Columbia University Press.

Buckley, Walter
1967 *Sociology and Modern Systems Theory*. Englewood Cliffs, New Jersey: Prentice-Hall.

Burke, K.
1965 *Permanence and Change*. Second revised edition. Indianapolis: Bobbs-Merrill.

Burling, Robbins
1963 Garo Kinship Terms and the Analysis of Meaning. *Ethnology* 2: 70–85.
1964 Cognition and Componential Analysis: God's Truth or Hocus-Pocus. *American Anthropologist* 66: 20–28.

Campbell, D., and Walker, D. E.
1966 Ostensive Instances and Entitativity in Language Learning. Unpublished manuscript.

Campbell, Norman
1920 *Physics: The Elements*. Cambridge: Cambridge University Press.
1921 *What Is Science?* New York: Dover.
1928 *Measurement and Calculation*. New York: Longmans, Green.
1935 *Action, Perception, and Measurement*. London: Harrison.

Carnap, Rudolph
  1937 *The Logical Syntax of Language*. London: Routledge and Kegan Paul.
Caton,   ed.
  1963 *Philosophy and Ordinary Language*. Urbana: University of Illinois Press.
Cavan, S.
  1965 *Liquor License*. Chicago: Aldine.
Cavell, S.
  1964 Existentialism and Analytic Philosophy. *Daedalus* (Summer).
  1969 The Availability of Wittgenstein's Later Philosophy, in *Must We Mean What We Say?* New York: Charles Scribner and Sons.
Chappel, V. C., ed.
  1964 *Ordinary Language*. Englewood Cliffs, New Jersey: Prentice-Hall.
Chomsky, N.
  1965 *Aspects of a Theory of Syntax*. Cambridge, Massachusetts: M.I.T. Press.
  1968 *Language and Mind*. New York: Harcourt, Brace and World.
Chomsky, N., and Halle, M.
  1965 Some Controversial Questions in Phonological Theory. *Journal of Linguistics* 1: 97-138.
Church, J., ed.
  1966 *Three Babies: Biographies of Cognitive Development*. New York: Random House.
Churchill, L.
  1966 On Everyday Quantitative Practices. Unpublished paper presented at the annual meeting of the American Sociological Association.
Cicourel, Aaron V.
  1964 *Method and Measurement in Sociology*. New York: Free Press.
  1967 Fertility, Family Planning and the Social Organization of Family Life: Some Methodological Issues. *The Journal of Social Issues* 23 (October): 57-81.
  1968 *The Social Organization of Juvenile Justice*. New York: Wiley.
Claussen, J., ed.
  1968 *Socialization and Society*. Boston: Little, Brown, and Co.
Cloward, Richard A.
  1959 Illegitimate Means, Anomie and Deviant Behavior. *American Sociological Review* 24 (April): 164-176.
Cloward, Richard A., and Ohlin, Lloyd E.
  1960 *Delinquency and Opportunity*. New York: Free Press.
Cofer, C. N., and Musgrave, B. S., eds.
  1963 *Verbal Behavior and Learning*. New York: McGraw-Hill.
Cohen, Albert K.
  1955 *Delinquent Boys*. New York: Free Press.
  1966 *Deviance and Control*. Englewood Cliffs, New Jersey: Prentice-Hall.
Cohen, Harry
  1962 *The Demonics of Bureaucracy: A Study of a Government Employment Agency*. Unpublished doctoral dissertation, University of Illinois.
Coleman, James S.
  1964 Collective Decisions. *Sociological Inquiry* 34 (Spring): 166-181.
  1968a Review Symposium of Harold Garfinkel, Studies in Ethnomethodology. *American Sociological Review* 33.

1968b Games as Vehicles for Social Theory. Paper presented at the annual meeting of the American Sociological Association.

Collingwood, R.
1933 *Essays in Philosophical Method.* New York: Oxford University Press.

Conklin, H.
1955 Hanunoo Color Categories. *Southwestern Journal of Anthropology* 11: 399–344.
1959 Linguistic Play in Its Cultural Context. *Language* 35: 631–636.

Coser, Lewis A.
1956 *The Social Functions of Conflict.* Glencoe, Illinois: The Free Press.
1967 *Continuities in the Study of Social Conflict.* New York: Free Press.

Couch, Carl J.
1968 Collective Behavior: An Examination of Some Stereotypes. *Social Problems* 15 (Winter): 310–322.

Dalton, Melville
1959 *Men Who Manage.* New York: Wiley.

Demerath, N. J. III, and Peterson, Richard H., eds.
1967 *System, Change, and Conflict.* New York: Free Press.

Denzin, Norman K.
1969 Symbolic Interactionism and Ethnomethodology: A Proposed Synthesis. *American Sociological Review* 34 (December): 922–934.
1970 *The Research Act.* Chicago: Aldine.

Dewey, John, ed.
1917 *Creative Intelligence: Essays in the Pragmatic Attitude.* New York: Henry Holt and Co.

Douglas, Jack D.
1967 *The Social Meaning of Suicide.* Princeton: Princeton University Press.
1970a *The Relevance of Sociology.* New York: Appleton-Century Crofts.
1970b *Youth in Turmoil.* Washington, D.C.: United States Government Printing Office.
1970c *Crime and Justice in America.* New York: Bobbs-Merrill.
1970d *Deviance and Respectability: The Social Construction of Moral Meanings.* New York: Basic Books.
1970e *Freedom and Tyranny: Social Problems in a Technological Society.* New York: Random House.
1971a *American Social Order: Social Rules In A Pluralistic Society.* New York: Free Press.
Forthcoming *Existential Sociology* New York: Appleton-Century Crofts.
Observing Deviance. New York: Random House

Dubin, Robert
1969 *Theory Building.* New York: Free Press.

Durkheim, Emile
1938 *The Rules of Sociological Method.* Translated by S. A. Solovay and John H. Mueller. Chicago: University of Chicago Press.
1951 *Suicide.* New York: Free Press.

Edie, James M., ed.
1967 *Phenomenology in America.* Chicago: Quadrangle.

Elkin, F.
1966 *The Child and Society: The Process of Socialization.* New York: Random House.

Emerson, Joan P.
    1969 Negotiating the Serious Import of Humor. *Sociometry* 32 (June): 169–181.
Erickson, Eric
    1950 *Childhood and Society*. New York: Norton.
Erwin-Tripp, S., and Slobin, D.
    1966 Psycholinguistics. *Annual Review of Psychology* 17: 435–474.
Faris, Robert E. L., ed.
    1964 *Handbook of Modern Sociology*. Chicago: Rand McNally.
Festinger, Leon
    1957 *A Theory of Cognitive Dissonance*. New York: Row, Peterson.
Fodor, J. A., and Katz, J. J., eds.
    1964 *The Structure of Language*. Englewood Cliffs, New Jersey: Prentice-Hall.
Foote, Nelson N.
    1951 Identification as a Basis for a Theory of Motivation. *American Sociological Review* 16 (February): 14–21.
Frake, Charles O.
    1961 The Diagnosis of Disease Among the Subanun of Mindanao. *American Anthropologist* 63: 113–132.
    1964 Comment to Burling. *American Anthropologist* 66: 119.
Freeman, Howard D., and Simmons, Ozzie G.
    1963 *The Mental Patient Comes Home*. New York: Wiley.
Friedman, Neil J.
    1967 *The Social Nature of Psychological Research*. New York: Basic Books.
Garfinkel, Harold
    1952 The Perception of the Other: A Study in Social Order. Unpublished doctoral dissertation, Department of Sociology, Harvard University.
    1956 Some Sociological Concepts and Methods for Psychiatrists. *Psychiatric Research Reports* 6: 181–195.
    1959a Aspects of the Problem of Common-Sense Knowledge of Social Structure. *Transactions of the Fourth World Congress of Sociology, IV*. Milan and Stresa.
    1959b Parson's Primer. An unpublished draft of a manuscript based on notes from Garfinkel's course Sociology 251. University of California at Los Angeles. Spring.
    1960 The Rational Properties of Scientific and Common Sense Activities. *Behavioral Science* 5 (January): 72–83.
    1961 Reflections on the Clinical Method in Psychiatry from the Point of View of Ethnomethodology. Prepared for the seminar on ethnoscience, Stanford University. April.
    1964 Studies of the Routine Grounds of Everyday Activities. *Social Problems* 11 (Winter): 225–250.
    1965 Sign Functions: Organized Activities as Methods for Making an Invisible World Observable. Paper delivered at the annual meeting of the American Sociological Association.
    1966 Dittoed transcriptions of lectures.
    1967 *Studies in Ethnomethodology*. Englewood Cliffs, New Jersey: Prentice-Hall.
Garfinkel, Harold, and Churchill, Lindsey

1964 Some Features of Decision Making in Common-Sense Situations of Choice. Unpublished research proposal, Department of Sociology, University of California at Los Angeles.

Garfinkel, Harold, and Sacks, Harvey
1967 On "Setting" in Conversation. Unpublished paper presented to the American Sociological Society, San Francisco.

Garfinkel, Harold, and Sacks, Harvey, eds.
Forthcoming *Contributions to Ethnomethodology*. Bloomington: Indiana University Press.

Geertz, H.
1961 *The Javanese Family: A Study of Kinship and Socialization*. New York: Free Press.

Gibbs, Jack P.
1966 The Sociology of Law and Normative Phenomena. *American Sociological Review* 31: 315–325.
1968 The Issue in Sociology. *Pacific Sociological Review* 11 (Fall): 65–74.

Gittler, Joseph B., ed.
1957 *Review of Sociology*. New York: Wiley.

Gladwin, Thomas, and Sturtevant, William C., eds.
1962 *Anthropology and Human Behavior*. Washington, D.C.: Anthropological Society of Washington.

Glaser, Barney G., and Strauss, Anselm L.
1964 *Awareness of Dying*. Chicago: Aldine.
1967 *The Discovery of Grounded Theory*. Chicago: Aldine.
1968 *Time for Dying*. Chicago: Aldine.

Goffman, Erving
1953 Communication and Conduct in an Island Community. Unpublished doctoral dissertation, Department of Sociology, The University of Chicago.
1956a Embarrassment and Social Organization. *American Journal of Sociology* 62: 264–271.
1956b The Nature of Deference and Demeanor. *American Anthropologist* 58 (June): 473–502.
1957 Alienation from Interaction. *Human Relations* 10: 47–60.
1959 *The Presentation of Self in Everyday Life*. Garden City: Doubleday.
1961a *Asylums*. Garden City: Doubleday-Anchor.
1961b Role Distance, in *Encounters*. Indianapolis: Bobbs-Merrill.
1963a *Behavior in Public Places*. New York: Free Press.
1963b *Stigma: Notes on and Management of Spoiled Identity*. Englewood Cliffs, New Jersey: Prentice-Hall.
1967 *Interaction Ritual*. New York: Doubleday.

Goode, W.J., AND Hatt, P.K.
1952 *Methods in Social Research*. New York: McGraw-Hill.

Goodenough, Ward H.
1956 Componential Analysis and the Study of Meaning. *Language*.

Gouldner, Alvin W.
1955 *Patterns of Industrial Bureaucracy*. London: Reutledge and Kegan Paul.
1962 The Myth of a Value-Free Sociology. *Social Problems* 9 (Winter): 199–213.

1968 The Sociologist as Partisan: Sociology and the Welfare State. *The American Sociologist* 3 (May): 103-116.

Greer, Scott
1969 *The Logic of Social Inquiry.* Chicago: Aldine.

Gross, Edward, and Stone, Gregory P.
1963 Embarrassment and the Analysis of Role Requirements. *American Journal of Sociology* 70 (July): 1-15.

Gross, Neal; Mason, Ward S.; and McEachern, Alexander W.
1958 *Explorations in Role Analysis.* New York: Wiley.

Gumperz, J. J.
1966 Linguistic Repertoires, Grammars and Second Language Instruction, in *Report of the Sixteenth Round Table Meeting on Linguistics and Language Teaching.* Georgetown University, Monograph No. 18.

Gumperz, J., and Hymes, D., eds.
1964 The Ethnography of Communication. *American Anthropologist* 66: 127-132.

Gurwitsch, Aron
1964 *The Field of Consciousness.* Pittsburgh: Duquesne University Press.

Habermas, Jürgen
1966 Knowledge and Interest. *Inquiry* 9 (Winter): 285-300.

Handel, Warren
1968 Campbell and Bridgeman on Measurement. Dittoed paper. Department of Sociology, University of California at Santa Barbara.

Hansen, Donald A., ed.
1969 *Explorations in Sociology and Counseling.* Boston: Houghton Mifflin.

Harvey, O. J., ed.
1963 *Motivation and Social Interaction.* New York: Ronald Press.

Hempel, Carl G., and Oppenheim, Paul
1948 Studies in the Logic of Explanation. *Philosophy of Science* 15: 135-178.

Hill, Richard J., and Crittenden, Kathleen Stones, eds.
1968 *Proceedings of the Purdue Symposium on Ethnomethodology.* Layfayete, Indiana: Purdue Research Foundation.

Hix, H.
1954 Kotarbinski's Praxeology. *Philosophy and Phenomenological Research:* 238-243.

Hockett, S. F., and Ascher, R.
1964 The Human Revolution. *Current Anthropologist* 5: 135-147.

Hoffman, L. W., and Hoffman, M. L.
1966 *Review of Child Development Research, II.* New York: Russell Sage Foundation.

Holt, John
1969 *How Children Learn.* New York: Petman Publishing Corporation.

Holton, Gerald, ed.
1967 *Science and Culture.* Boston: Beacon Press.

Holzner, Burkhart
1968 *Reality Construction in Society.* Cambridge, Massachusetts: Schenkman Publishing Co.

Homans, George C.
1961 *Social Behavior: Its Elementary Forms.* New York: Harcourt, Brace and World.

1964 Bringing Men Back In. *American Sociological Review* 29 (December): 809–818.

1967 *The Nature of Social Science.* New York: Harcourt, Brace and World.

Horton, John
1966 Order and Conflict Theories of Social Problems as Competing Ideologies. *American Sociological Review* 71 (May): 701–713.

Householder, Fred, and Saporta, Sol, eds.
1962 Problems in Lexicography. Supplement to *International Journal of American Linguistics* 28: Indiana University Research Center in Anthropology, Folklore and Linguistics, Publication 21.

Hsu, F., ed.
1961 *Psychological Anthropology.* Homewood, Illinois: Dorsey.

Hughes, Everett C.
1956 *Men and Their Work.* Glencoe, Illinois: The Free Press.

Hughes, Everett C., and Hughes, Helen MacGill
1952 *Where Peoples Meet.* Clencoe, Illinois: The Free Press.

Hume, David
1927 *Selections.* Edited by C. W. Hendel, Jr. New York: Scribners.

Husserl, E.
1962 *Ideas: General Introduction to Pure Phenomenology.* Translated by W. R. Boyce Gibson. New York: Collier Books.

Hyman, H.
1955 *Survey Design and Analysis: Principles, Cases and Procedures.* Glencoe, Illinois: The Free Press.

Hymes, D., ed.
1964 *Language Culture and Society.* New York: Harper and Row.

Israel, Marvin
1969 Comment on James Coleman's Review of Harold Garfinkel's Studies in Ethnomethodology. *The American Sociologist* 4 (November): 333–334.

Jacobs, Jerry
1967 A Phenomenological Study of Suicide Notes. *Social Problems* 15 (Summer): 60–72.

James, William
1949 *Pragmatism: A New Name for Some Old Ways of Thinking.* New York: Longmans, Green.

Kaplan, Abraham
1964 *The Conduct of Inquiry.* San Francisco: Chandler.

Katz, Jerrold J.
1966 *The Philosophy of Language.* New York: Harper and Row.

Katz, Jerrold J., and Postal, P. M.
1964 *An Integrated Theory of Linguistic Descriptions.* Cambridge, Massachusetts: M.I.T. Press.

Kaufmann, Felix
1944 *Methodology of the Social Sciences.* New York: Oxford University Press.

1958 *The Methodology of the Social Sciences.* New York: Humanities Press.

Kecskemeti, Paul, ed.
1952 *Essays in the Sociology of Knowledge.* New York: Oxford University Press.

Kluckhohn, C., and Murray, H. L.
  1948 *Personality in Nature, Society and Culture.* New York: Knopf.
Kockelmans, Joseph J., ed.
  1967 *Phenomenology.* Garden City: Doubleday-Anchor.
Kuhn, Thomas
  1961 The Function of Measurement in Modern Physical Science. *Isis* 52: 161–193.
  1962 *The Structure of Scientific Revolutions.* Chicago: University of Chicago Press.
Kyburg, H. E., and Nagel, E., eds.
  1963 *Induction: Some Current Issues.* Middletown, Connecticut: Wesleyan University Press.
Lacombe, Roger
  1926 *La Methode Sociologique de Durkheim: Etude Critique.* Paris: Felix Alcan.
Ladd, John
  1957 *The Structure of a Moral Code.* Cambridge-Harvard University Press.
Langer, Susanne
  1951 *Philosophy in a New Key.* Second edition. New York: New American Library.
Lazarsfeld, Paul F.
  1949 The American Soldier: An Expository Review. *Public Opinion Quarterly* 13: 377–404.
Lazarsfeld, Paul F., and Rosenberg, M., eds.
  1955 *The Language of Social Research: A Reader in the Methodology of Social Research,* The Free Press.
Leiter, Kenneth C.
  1969 "Getting It Done:" An Ethnography of Coding. Unpublished master's thesis, University of California at Santa Barbara.
Lemert, Edwin M.
  1951 *Sociopathic Behavior.* New York: McGraw-Hill.
Lenneberg, E., ed.
  1964 *New Directions in the Study of Language.* Cambridge: M.I.T. Press.
Levy, Marion J.
  1952 *Social Action and Social Structure.* Princeton: Princeton University Press.
Lewis, David K.
  1969 *Convention.*
Lindesmith, Alfred
  1947 *Opiate Addiction.* Bloomington, Indiana: Principia Press.
Lindzey, Gardner, ed.
  1954 *The Handbook of Social Psychology.* Cambridge: Addison-Wesley.
Linton, Ralph
  1936 *The Study of Man.* New York: Appleton-Century Crofts.
Lobkowica, N.
  1967 *Theory and Practice: History of a Concept from Aristotle to Marx.* Notre Dame, Indiana: University of Notre Dame Press.
Locke, John
  1894 *Essay Concerning Human Understanding.* Edited by A. C. Fraeser. Oxford: Clarendon.

Lofland, John
1967 Role Management: A Programmatic Statement. Mimeographed paper No. 30 of the Center for Research in Social Organization, University of Michigan. June.
1969 *Deviance and Identity*. Englewood Cliffs, New Jersey: Prentice-Hall.

Louch, A. H.
1966 *Explanation and Human Action*. Berkeley: University of California Press.

Lounsbury, Floyd G.
1956 A Semantic Analysis of Pawnee Kinship Usage. *Language* 32: 158-194.

Lyons, J., and Wales, R. J., eds.
1966 *Psycholinguistic Papers*. Edinburgh: Edinburgh University Press.

Maccoby, E.
1961 The Choice of Variables in and Study of Socialization. *Sociometry:* 357-371.

McHugh, Peter
1968 *Defining the Situation*. Indianapolis: Bobbs-Merrill.

McKinney, John C., and Tiryakian, Edward, eds.
1970 *Theoretical Sociology: Perspectives and Developments*. New York: Appleton-Century Crofts.

Manis, Jerome, and Meltzer, Bernard, eds.
1967 *Symbolic Interaction: A Reader in Social Psychology*. Boston: Allyn and Bacon.

Matza, David
1969 *Becoming Deviant*. Englewood Cliffs, New Jersey: Prentice-Hall.

Mead, George Herbert
1932 *The Philosophy of the Present*. Edited by Arthur E. Murphy, with prefatory remarks by John Dewey. Lectures of the Paul Carus Foundation, third series. Chicago: Open Court.
1934 *Mind, Self and Society: From the Standpoint of a Social Behaviorist*. Edited by Charles W. Morris. Chicago: University of Chicago Press.

Mead, Margaret
1930 *Six Cultures: Studies of Child Rearing*. New York: Wiley.

Melden, A.
1956 *Free Action*. London: Routledge and Kegan Paul.

Merleau-Ponty, M.
1962 *Phenomenology of Perception*. Translated by C. Smith. London: Routledge and Kegan Paul.

Merton, Robert K.
1957 *Social Theory and Social Structure*. Revised edition. Glencoe, Illinois: The Free Press.
1968 *Social Theory and Social Structure*. Enlarged edition. New York: Free Press.

Merton, Robert K.; Broom, Leonard: and Cottrell, Leonard S. Jr., eds.
1959 *Sociology Today*. New York: Basic Books.

Miller, D., and Form. W. H.
1964 *Industrial Sociology*. Second edition. New York: Harper.

Miller, D. R., and Swanson, G.
1958 *The Changing American Parent*. New York: Wiley.

Mills, C. Wright
  1940 Situated Actions and Vocabularies of Motive. *American Sociological Review* 5: 904–913.
Moerman, M.
  1969 Analysis of Lue Conversation: Providing Accounts, Finding Breaches, and Taking Sides. Unpublished paper.
Moore, Merritt H., ed.
  1936 *Movements of Thought in the Nineteenth Century.* Chicago: University of Chicago Press.
Morris, Charles W.
  1946 *Signs, Language, and Behavior.* New York: Prentice-Hall.
Morris, R. T.
  1956 A Typology of Norms. *American Sociological Review* 7: 610–613.
Murchison, C., ed.
  1931 *Handbook of Child Psychology.* Worchester, Massachusetts: Clark University Press.
Nagel, Ernest
  1961 *The Structure of Science: Problems in the Logic of Scientific Explanation.* New York: Harcourt, Brace and World.
Nagel, Ernest, and Brandt, R. B., eds.
  1965 *Meaning and Knowledge.* New York: Harcourt, Brace and World.
Nagel, E.; Suppes, P.; and Tarski, A., eds.
  1962 *Logic, Methodology and Philosophy of Science.* Stanford: Stanford University Press.
Natanson, Maurice
  1956 *The Social Dynamics of George Herbert Mead.* Washington, D. C.: Public Affairs Press.
  1962 *Literature, Philosophy, and the Social Sciences.* The Hague: Martinus Nijhoff.
Natanson, Maurice, ed.
  1963 *Philosophy of the Social Sciences.* New York: Random House.
Nicholson, Robert F.
  1969 Sociological Homuneuli: Professional Dilemmas in Taking Alfred Schutz Seriously. Unpublished paper presented at the Second West Coast Conference on Existentialism in the Human Sciences, San Jose State College.
Northrop, F. S. C.
  1959 *The Logic of Sciences and Humanities.* New York: Meridian.
Oeser, O. A., and Harary, Frank
  1962 A Mathematical Model for Structural Role Theory I. *Human Relations* 51 (May): 89–110.
  1964 A Mathematical Model for Structural Role Theory II. *Human Relations* 17 (February): 3–17.
Offenbacher, D.
  1967 Roles, Norms and Typifications in Contemporary American Society. Unpublished paper presented at the annual meeting of the American Sociological Association, San Francisco.
Oleson, Virginia, and Whittaker, Elv
  1968 *The Silent Dialogue.* San Francisco: Jossey-Boss.
Page, Charles H.
  1964 Bureaucracy's Other Face. *Social Forces* 25 (October).
Park, R. E., and Burgess, E. W.

1924 *An Introduction to Sociology.* Second edition. Chicago: University of Chicago Press.

Parsons, Talcott
1937 *The Structure of Social Action.* New York: McGraw-Hill.
1951 *The Social System.* New York: Free Press.
1960 Pattern Variables Revisited: A Response to Robert Dubin. *American Sociological Review* 25 (August): 467–483.

Parsons, Talcott, and Bales, R.
1955 *Family, Socialization and Interaction Process.* Glencoe, Illinois: The Free Press.

Parsons, Talcott, and Shils, Edward, eds.
1951 *Toward a General Theory of Action.* Cambridge: Harvard University Press.

Pepinsky, Harold, ed.
1970 *People and Information.* New York: Pergamon Press.

Piaget, J.
1960 *The Child's Concept of the World.* Paterson, New Jersey: Littlefield, Adams, and Co.
1965 *The Language and Thought of the Child.* Cleveland: World Publishing Co.

Pierce, C.
1960 *Collected Papers, V.* Edited by C. Hartshorne and Paul Weiss. Cambridge: Belknap.

Pike, K. L.
1954 *Language in Relation to a Unified Theory of the Structure of Human Behavior.* Glendale: Summer Institute of Linguistics.

Pitcher, George, ed.
1966 *Wittgenstein.* New York: Doubleday.

Polanyi, Michael
1955–1956 The Stability of Scientific Beliefs. *British Journal of the Philosophy of Science.*
1958 *Personal Knowledge: Towards a Post-Critical Philosophy.* Chicago: Uinversity of Chicago Press.

Pollner, M.
Forthcoming Tell it to the Judge: A Study of Practical Sociological Reasoning in a Municipal Court. Unpublished doctoral dissertation, Department of Sociology, University of California at Santa Barbara.

Polsky, Norman
1967 *Hustlers, Beats and Others.* Chicago: Aldine.

Preiss, J., and Ehrlich, H.
1966 *An Examination of Role Theory.* Lincoln: University of Nebraska Press.

Quine, Willard Van Orman
1960 *Word and Object.* Cambridge: M.I.T. Press
1961 *From a Logical Point of View.* Second edition, revised. New York: Harper and Row.
1965 *Elementary Logic.* Revised edition. New York: Harper Torchbooks.

Raffel, Stanley
1970 Notes on Authorship. Unpublished paper.

Rawls, J.
1955 Two Concepts of Rules. *Philosophical Review* 64: 3–32.

Rose, Arnold M., ed.
  1962 *Human Behavior and Social Processes: An Interactionist Approach.* Boston: Houghton Mifflin.
Roth, J.
  1963 *Timetables.* Indianapolis: Bobbs-Merrill.
Roy, Donald F.
  1953 Work Satisfaction and Social Reward in Quota Achievement. *American Sociological Review* 18: 507-514.
  1954 Efficiency and "The Fix," Informal Intergroup Relations in a Piecework Machine Shop. *American Journal of Sociology* 60 (November): 255-266.
  1959-1960 "Banana Time"—Job Satisfaction and Informal Interaction. *Human Organization* 18 (Winter): 158-168.
Rudner, Richard S.
  1966 *Philosophy of Social Science.* Englewood Cliffs, New Jersey: Prentice-Hall.
Russell, Bertrand
  1927 *Philosophy.* New York: Norton.
  1929 *On Knowledge of the External World.* New York: Norton.
Sacks, Harvey
  1963 Sociological Secription. *Berkeley Journal of Sociology* 8: 1-16.
  1966a The Search for Help: No One To Turn To. Unpublished doctoral dissertation. Department of Sociology, University of California at Berkeley.
  1966b Unpublished lectures and research notebooks.
  1967 Unpublished lectures and research notebooks.
  n.d. An Introduction to the Study of Conversation. First draft of an unpublished mimeographed paper.
Sampson, Harold; Messinger, Sheldon L.; and Towne, Robert D.
  1962 Family Processes and Becoming a Mental Patient. *American Journal of Sociology* 62 (July): 88-96.
Saporta, S., ed.
  1966 *Psycholinguistics.* New York: Holt, Rinehart and Winston.
Scheff, Thomas J.
  1962 Differential Displacement of Treatment Goals in a Mental Hospital. *Administrative Science Quarterly* 7 (September).
  1966 *Being Mentally Ill: A Sociological Theory.* Chicago: Aldine.
  1968 Negotiating Reality: Notes on Power in the Assessment of Responsibility. *Social Problems* 16 (Summer): 3-17.
Schegloff, Emanuel A.
  1967 The First Five Seconds: The Order of Conversational Openings. Unpublished doctoral dissertation, Department of Sociology, University of California at Berkeley.
  1968 Sequencing in Conversational Openings. *American Anthropologist* 70 (December): 1075-1095.
Schneider, D.
  1968 *American Kinship: A Cultural Account.* Englewood Cliffs, New Jersey: Prentice-Hall.
Schutz, Alfred J.
  1962 *Collected Papers I: The Problem of Social Reality.* Edited by Maurice Natanson. The Hague: Martinus Nijhoff.

1966 *Collected Papers III: Studies in Phenomenological Philosophy*. Edited by I. Schutz. The Hague: Martinus Nijhoff.

Sears, R.; Maccoby, E.; and Levin, H.
1957 *Patterns of Child Rearing*. Evanston: Row, Peterson, and Co.

Selznick, P.
1966 *TVA and the Grass Roots*. (Originally published in 1949.) New York: Harper Torchbooks.

Shils, Edward A., and Finch, Henry A., eds.
1949 *Max Weber on the Methodology of the Social Sciences*. New York: Free Press.

Shneidman, Edwin S., ed.
1967 *Essays in Self-destruction*. New York: Science House, Inc.

Short, James F., Jr., and Strodtbeck, Fred
1965 *Group Process and Gang Delinquency*. Chicago: University of Chicago Press.

Shwayder, D. S.
1965 *The Stratification of Behavior*. New York: Humanities Press.

Simmel, Georg
1950 *The Sociology of Georg Simmel*. Translated and edited by Kurt H. Wolff. Glencoe, Illinois: The Free Press.

Skinner, B. F.
1953 *Science and Human Behavior*. New York: Macmillan.
1957 *Verbal Behavior*. New York: Appleton-Century Crofts.

Smelser, Neil J.
1968 *Essays in Sociological Explanation*. Englewood Cliffs, New Jersey: Prentice-Hall.

Smith, Dorothy E.
1969 A Sub-version of Mental Illness. Unpublished mimeographed paper.

Smith, F., and Miller, G. A., eds.
1966 *The Genesis of Language: A Psycholinguistic Approach*. Cambridge: M.I.T. Press.

Sommers, Robert
1968 *Personal Space*. Englewood Cliffs, New Jersey: Prentice-Hall.

Speier, Matthew
1968a Procedures for Speaking and Hearing. Unpublished mimeographed paper.
1968b Some Conversational Sequencing Problems for Interactional Analysis: Findings on the Child's Methods for Opening and Carrying on Conversational Interaction. Unpublished mimeographed paper.
1969 Socialization and Social Process in Children's Conversations. Unpublished doctoral dissertation, Department of Sociology, University of California at Berkeley.

Speièr, Matthew, and Turner, Roy
Forthcoming *Socialization: The Acquisition of Membership*. New York: Basic Books.

Spuhler, J. N., ed.
1959 *The Evolution of Man's Capacity for Culture*. Detroit: Wayne State University Press.

Stinchcombe, Arthur L.
1968 *Constructing Social Theories*. New York: Harcourt, Brace and World.

Strauss, Anselm L.

1959 *Mirrors and Masks: The Search for Identity.* Glencoe, Illinois: The
        Free Press.
Strauss, Anselm L., et al
    1964 *Psychiatric Ideologies and Institutions.* New York: Free Press.
Sudnow, David
    1965 Normal Crimes: Sociological Features of the Penal Code in a Public
        Defender's Office. *Social Problems* 12 (Winter): 255–272.
    1967 *Passing On: The Social Organization of Dying.* Englewood Cliffs, New
        Jersey: Prentice-Hall.
Sudnow, David, ed.
    1969 *Studies in Interaction.* New York: Free Press.
Suppes, Patrick
    1957 *Introduction to Logic.* Princeton: Van Nostrand.
Swanson, Guy E.
    1968 Review Symposium of Harold Garfinkel, Studies in Ethnomethodology.
        American Sociological Review 33 (February): 122–124.
Sykes, G.
    1956 *The Society of Captives.* Princeton: Princeton University press.
Tarski, A.
    1944 The Semantic Theory of Truth and the Foundation of Semantics.
        Philosophy and Phenomenological Research (March): 341–375.
Thrasher, Frederick M.
    1927 *The Gang.* Chicago: University of Chicago Press.
Tiryakian, Edward, ed.
    1970 *The Phenomenon of Sociology.* New York: Appleton-Century Crofts.
Torgerson, W.
    1958 *Theory and Method of Scaling.* New York: Wiley.
Turner, R.
    1958 Talk and Troubles: Contact Problems of Former Mental Patients. Un-
        published doctoral dissertation, Department of Sociology, University
        of California at Berkeley.
Turner, Ralph H.
    1947 The Navy Disbursing Officer as a Bureaucrat. *American Sociological
        Review* 12 (June).
Urmson, J. O.
    1967 *Philosophical Analysis.* New York: Oxford University Press.
Vollner, H.
    1967 Organizational Socialization Among Scientists. Unpublished paper
        presented at the annual meeting of the American Sociological Associ-
        ation, San Francisco.
Vygotsby, L. S.
    1962 *Thought and Language.* Cambridge: M.I.T. Press.
Waismann, F. W.
    1952 Analytic-Synthetic Variables. *Analysis* 13 (October).
Wallace, Anthony F. C., and Atkins, John
    1960 The Meaning of Kinship Terms. *American Anthropologist* 62 (Febru-
        ary): 58–80.
Wallace, Walter L., ed.
    1969 *Sociological Theory.* Chicago: Aldine.

Warriner, Charles K.
  1969 Social Action, Behavior, and *Verstehen*. *Sociological Quarterly* 10 (Fall): 501−511.

Webb, Eugene J., et al
  1966 *Unobtrusive Measures: Nonreactive Research in the Social Sciences.* Chicago: Rand McNally.

Weber, Max
  1947 *The Theory of Social and Economic Organization.* New York: Oxford University Press.

Weir, R.
  1962 *Language in the Crib.* The Hague: Mouton.

Wheeler, Stanton, ed.
  1970 *On Record: Files and Dossiers in American Society.* New York: Russel Sage Foundation.

Whiting, B., ed.
  1963 *Six Cultures: Studies of Child Rearing.* New York: Wiley.

Whyte, William Foote
  1955 *Street Corner Society.* Chicago: University of Chicago Press.

Wieder, D. Lawrence
  1964 The Concept of Role and the Problem of Order. Unpublished dittoed paper.
  1969 The Convict Code: A Study of a Moral Order as a Persuasive Activity. Unpublished doctoral dissertation, Department of Sociology, University of California at Los Angeles.

Williams, Robin M.
  1960 *American Society.* Revised edition. New York: Knopf.
  1966 Some Further Comments on Chronic Controversies. *American Journal of Sociology* 71 (May): 717−712.

Wilson, Thomas P.
  1966 Small Groups and Social Organization. Unpublished paper delivered at the annual meeting of the American Sociological Association, Miami.
  1968 Sociology and the Normative Paradigm. Department of Sociology, University of California at Santa Barbara.
  1970 Conceptions of Interaction and Forms of Sociological Explanation. *American Sociological Review.*

Winch, Peter
  1958 *The Idea of a Social Science.* London: Routledge and Kegan Paul.

Wittgenstein, Ludwig
  1953 *Philosophical Investigations.* New York: Macmillan.
  1958 *The Blue and the Brown Books.* New York: Harper and Row.
  1961 *Viz Tractatus Logico-Philosophicus.* Translated by Pears and McGuinness. London: Routledge and Kegan Paul.
  1969 *On Certainty.* Edited by G. E. M. Anscombe and G. H. von Wright. New York: J. J. Harper.

Woozley, A. D.
  1949 *Theory of Knowledge.* New York: Hutchinson.

Zawecki, John Stanley
  1963 The System of Unofficial Rules of a Bureaucracy: A Study of Hospitals. Unpublished doctoral dissertation, University of Pittsburg.

Zetterberg, Hans L.
  1965 *On Theory and Verification*. Third and enlarged edition. Totowa, New
       Jersey: Bedminster Press.
Zimmerman, Don H.
  1966 Paper Work and People Work: A Study of a Public Assistance Agency.
       Unpublished doctoral dissertation, Department of Sociology, Univer-
       sity of California at Los Angeles.

Index

355

The International Library of
Sociology
and Social Reconstruction

Edited by W. J. H. SPROTT
Founded by KARL MANNHEIM

ROUTLEDGE & KEGAN PAUL
BROADWAY HOUSE, CARTER LANE, LONDON, E.C.4

CONTENTS

PRINTED IN GREAT BRITAIN BY HEADLEY BROTHERS LTD
109 KINGSWAY LONDON W C 2 AND ASHFORD KENT

GENERAL SOCIOLOGY

Brown, Robert. Explanation in Social Science. *208 pp. 1963. (2nd Impression 1964.) 25s.*

Gibson, Quentin. The Logic of Social Enquiry. *240 pp. 1960. (3rd Impression 1968.) 24s.*

Homans, George C. Sentiments and Activities: Essays in Social Science. *336 pp. 1962. 32s.*

Isajiw, Wsevelod W. Causation and Functionalism in Sociology. *165 pp. 1968. 25s.*

Johnson, Harry M. Sociology: a Systematic Introduction. *Foreword by Robert K. Merton. 710 pp. 1961. (5th Impression 1968.) 42s.*

Mannheim, Karl. Essays on Sociology and Social Psychology. *Edited by Paul Keckskemeti. With Editorial Note by Adolph Lowe. 344 pp. 1953. (2nd Impression 1966.) 32s.*

 Systematic Sociology: An Introduction to the Study of Society. *Edited by J. S. Erös and Professor W. A. C. Stewart. 220 pp. 1957. (3rd Impression 1967.) 24s.*

Martindale, Don. The Nature and Types of Sociological Theory. *292 pp. 1961. (3rd Impression 1967.) 35s.*

Maus, Heinz. A Short History of Sociology. *234 pp. 1962. (2nd Impression 1965.) 28s.*

Myrdal, Gunnar. Value in Social Theory: A Collection of Essays on Methodology. *Edited by Paul Streeten. 332 pp. 1958. (3rd Impression 1968.) 35s.*

Ogburn, William F., and **Nimkoff, Meyer F.** A Handbook of Sociology. *Preface by Karl Mannheim. 656 pp. 46 figures. 35 tables. 5th edition (revised) 1964. 45s.*

Parsons, Talcott, and **Smelser, Neil J.** Economy and Society: A Study in the Integration of Economic and Social Theory. *362 pp. 1956. (4th Impression 1967.) 35s.*

Rex, John. Key Problems of Sociological Theory. *220 pp. 1961. (4th Impression 1968.) 25s.*

Stark, Werner. The Fundamental Forms of Social Thought. *280 pp. 1962. 32s.*

FOREIGN CLASSICS OF SOCIOLOGY

Durkheim, Emile. Suicide. A Study in Sociology. *Edited and with an Introduction by George Simpson. 404 pp. 1952. (4th Impression 1968.) 35s.*

 Professional Ethics and Civic Morals. *Translated by Cornelia Brookfield. 288 pp. 1957. 30s.*

Gerth, H. H., and **Mills, C. Wright.** From Max Weber: Essays in Sociology. *502 pp. 1948. (6th Impression 1967.) 35s.*

Tönnies, Ferdinand. Community and Association. *(Gemeinschaft und Gesellschaft.) Translated and Supplemented by Charles P. Loomis. Foreword by Pitirim A. Sorokin. 334 pp. 1955. 28s.*

SOCIAL STRUCTURE

Andreski, Stanislav. Military Organization and Society. *Foreword by Professor A. R. Radcliffe-Brown. 226 pp. 1 folder. 1954. Revised Edition 1968. 35s.*

Cole, G. D. H. Studies in Class Structure. *220 pp. 1955. (3rd Impression 1964.) 21s. Paper 10s. 6d.*

Coontz, Sydney H. Population Theories and the Economic Interpretation. *202 pp. 1957. (3rd Impression 1968.) 28s.*

Coser, Lewis. The Functions of Social Conflict. *204 pp. 1956. (3rd Impression 1968.) 25s.*

Dickie-Clark, H. F. Marginal Situation: A Sociological Study of a Coloured Group. *240 pp. 11 tables. 1966. 40s.*

Glass, D. V. (Ed.). Social Mobility in Britain. *Contributions by J. Berent, T. Bottomore, R. C. Chambers, J. Floud, D. V. Glass, J. R. Hall, H. T. Himmelweit, R. K. Kelsall, F. M. Martin, C. A. Moser, R. Mukherjee, and W. Ziegel. 420 pp. 1954. (4th Impression 1967.) 45s.*

Jones, Garth N. Planned Organizational Change: An Exploratory Study Using an Empirical Approach. *About 268 pp. 1969. 40s.*

Kelsall, R. K. Higher Civil Servants in Britain: From 1870 to the Present Day. *268 pp. 31 tables. 1955. (2nd Impression 1966.) 25s.*

König, René. The Community. *232 pp. Illustrated. 1968. 35s.*

Lawton, Denis. Social Class, Language and Education. *192 pp. 1968. (2nd Impression 1968.) 25s.*

McLeish, John. The Theory of Social Change: Four Views Considered. *About 128 pp. 1969. 21s.*

Marsh, David C. The Changing Social Structure in England and Wales, 1871-1961. *1958. 272 pp. 2nd edition (revised) 1966. (2nd Impression 1967.) 35s.*

Mouzelis, Nicos. Organization and Bureaucracy. An Analysis of Modern Theories. *240 pp. 1967. (2nd Impression 1968.) 28s.*

Ossowski, Stanislaw. Class Structure in the Social Consciousness. *210 pp. 1963. (2nd Impression 1967.) 25s.*

SOCIOLOGY AND POLITICS

Barbu, Zevedei. Democracy and Dictatorship: Their Psychology and Patterns of Life. *300 pp. 1956. 28s.*

Crick, Bernard. The American Science of Politics: Its Origins and Conditions. *284 pp. 1959. 32s.*

Hertz, Frederick. Nationality in History and Politics: A Psychology and Sociology of National Sentiment and Nationalism. *432 pp. 1944. (5th Impression 1966.) 42s.*

Kornhauser, William. The Politics of Mass Society. *272 pp. 20 tables. 1960. (3rd Impression 1968.) 28s.*

Laidler, Harry W. History of Socialism. Social-Economic Movements: An Historical and Comparative Survey of Socialism, Communism, Co-operation, Utopianism; and other Systems of Reform and Reconstruction. *New edition. 992 pp. 1968. 90s.*

Lasswell, Harold D. Analysis of Political Behaviour. An Empirical Approach. *324 pp. 1947. (4th Impression 1966.) 35s.*

Mannheim, Karl. Freedom, Power and Democratic Planning. *Edited by Hans Gerth and Ernest K. Bramstedt. 424 pp. 1951. (3rd Impression 1968.) 42s.*

Mansur, Fatma. Process of Independence. *Foreword by A. H. Hanson. 208 pp. 1962. 25s.*

Martin, David A. Pacificism: an Historical and Sociological Study. *262 pp. 1965. 30s.*

Myrdal, Gunnar. The Political Element in the Development of Economic Theory. *Translated from the German by Paul Streeten. 282 pp. 1953. (4th Impression 1965.) 25s.*

Polanyi, Michael. F.R.S. The Logic of Liberty: Reflections and Rejoinders. *228 pp. 1951. 18s.*

Verney, Douglas V. The Analysis of Political Systems. *264 pp. 1959. (3rd Impression 1966.) 28s.*

Wootton, Graham. The Politics of Influence: British Ex-Servicemen, Cabinet Decisions and Cultural Changes, 1917 to 1957. *316 pp. 1963. 30s.*
Workers, Unions and the State. *188 pp. 1966. (2nd Impression 1967.) 25s.*

FOREIGN AFFAIRS: THEIR SOCIAL, POLITICAL AND ECONOMIC FOUNDATIONS

Baer, Gabriel. Population and Society in the Arab East. *Translated by Hanna Szöke. 288 pp. 10 maps. 1964. 40s.*

Bonné, Alfred. State and Economics in the Middle East: A Society in Transition. *482 pp. 2nd (revised) edition 1955. (2nd Impression 1960.) 40s.*
Studies in Economic Development: with special reference to Conditions in the Under-developed Areas of Western Asia and India. *322 pp. 84 tables. 2nd edition 1960. 32s.*

Mayer, J. P. Political Thought in France from the Revolution to the Fifth Republic. *164 pp. 3rd edition (revised) 1961. 16s.*

CRIMINOLOGY

Ancel, Marc. Social Defence: A Modern Approach to Criminal Problems. *Foreword by Leon Radzinowicz. 240 pp. 1965. 32s.*

Cloward, Richard A., and **Ohlin, Lloyd E.** Delinquency and Opportunity: A Theory of Delinquent Gangs. *248 pp. 1961. 25s.*

Downes, David M. The Delinquent Solution. A Study in Subcultural Theory. *296 pp. 1966. 42s.*

Dunlop, A. B., and **McCabe, S.** Young Men in Detention Centres. *192 pp. 1965. 28s.*

Friedländer, Kate. The Psycho-Analytical Approach to Juvenile Delinquency: Theory, Case Studies, Treatment. *320 pp. 1947. (6th Impression 1967). 40s.*

Glueck, Sheldon and **Eleanor.** Family Environment and Delinquency. *With the statistical assistance of Rose W. Kneznek. 340 pp. 1962. (2nd Impression 1966.) 40s.*

Mannheim, Hermann. Comparative Criminology: a Text Book. *Two volumes. 442 pp. and 380 pp. 1965. (2nd Impression with corrections 1966.) 42s. a volume.*

Morris, Terence. The Criminal Area: A Study in Social Ecology. *Foreword by Hermann Mannheim. 232 pp. 25 tables. 4 maps. 1957. (2nd Impression 1966.) 28s.*

Morris, Terence and **Pauline,** assisted by **Barbara Barer.** Pentonville: A Sociological Study of an English Prison. *416 pp. 16 plates. 1963. 50s.*

Spencer, John C. Crime and the Services. *Foreword by Hermann Mannheim. 336 pp. 1954. 28s.*

Trasler, Gordon. The Explanation of Criminality. *144 pp. 1962. (2nd Impression 1967.) 20s.*

SOCIAL PSYCHOLOGY

Barbu, Zevedei. Problems of Historical Psychology. *248 pp. 1960. 25s.*

Blackburn, Julian. Psychology and the Social Pattern. *184 pp. 1945. (7th Impression 1964.) 16s.*

Fleming, C. M. Adolescence: Its Social Psychology: With an Introduction to recent findings from the fields of Anthropology, Physiology, Medicine, Psychometrics and Sociometry. *288 pp. 2nd edition (revised) 1963. (3rd Impression 1967.) 25s. Paper 12s. 6d.*

The Social Psychology of Education: An Introduction and Guide to Its Study. *136 pp. 2nd edition (revised) 1959. (4th Impression 1967.) 14s. Paper 7s. 6d.*

Homans, George C. The Human Group. *Foreword by Bernard DeVoto. Introduction by Robert K. Merton. 526 pp. 1951. (7th Impression 1968.) 35s.*

Social Behaviour: its Elementary Forms. *416 pp. 1961. (3rd Impression 1968.) 35s.*

Klein, Josephine. The Study of Groups. *226 pp. 31 figures. 5 tables. 1956. (5th Impression 1967.) 21s. Paper 9s. 6d.*

Linton, Ralph. The Cultural Background of Personality. *132 pp. 1947. (7th Impression 1968.) 18s.*

Mayo, Elton. The Social Problems of an Industrial Civilization. With an appendix on the Political Problem. *180 pp. 1949. (5th Impression 1966.) 25s.*

Ottaway, A. K. C. Learning Through Group Experience. *176 pp. 1966. (2nd Impression 1968.) 25s.*

Ridder, J. C. de. The Personality of the Urban African in South Africa. A Thematic Apperception Test Study. *196 pp. 12 plates. 1961. 25s.*

Rose, Arnold M. (Ed.). Human Behaviour and Social Processes: an Interactionist Approach. *Contributions by Arnold M. Rose, Ralph H. Turner, Anselm Strauss, Everett C. Hughes, E. Franklin Frazier, Howard S. Becker, et al. 696 pp. 1962. (2nd Impression 1968.) 70s.*

Smelser, Neil J. Theory of Collective Behaviour. *448 pp. 1962. (2nd Impression 1967.) 45s.*

Stephenson, Geoffrey M. The Development of Conscience. *128 pp. 1966. 25s.*

Young, Kimball. Handbook of Social Psychology. *658 pp. 16 figures. 10 tables. 2nd edition (revised) 1957. (3rd Impression 1963.) 40s.*

SOCIOLOGY OF THE FAMILY

Banks, J. A. Prosperity and Parenthood: A study of Family Planning among The Victorian Middle Classes. *262 pp. 1954. (3rd Impression 1968.) 28s.*

Bell, Colin R. Middle Class Families: Social and Geographical Mobility. *224 pp. 1969. 35s.*

Burton, Lindy. Vulnerable Children. *272 pp. 1968. 35s.*

Gavron, Hannah. The Captive Wife: Conflicts of Housebound Mothers. *190 pp. 1966. (2nd Impression 1966.) 25s.*

Klein, Josephine. Samples from English Cultures. *1965. (2nd Impression 1967.)*
1. Three Preliminary Studies and Aspects of Adult Life in England. *447 pp. 50s.*
2. Child-Rearing Practices and Index. *247 pp. 35s.*

Klein, Viola. Britain's Married Women Workers. *180 pp. 1965. (2nd Impression 1968.) 28s.*

McWhinnie, Alexina M. Adopted Children. How They Grow Up. *304 pp. 1967. (2nd Impression 1968.) 42s.*

Myrdal, Alva and **Klein, Viola.** Women's Two Roles: Home and Work. *238 pp. 27 tables. 1956. Revised Edition 1967. 30s. Paper 15s.*

Parsons, Talcott and **Bales, Robert F.** Family: Socialization and Interaction Process. *In collaboration with James Olds, Morris Zelditch and Philip E. Slater. 456 pp. 50 figures and tables. 1956. (3rd Impression 1968.) 45s.*

Schücking, L. L. The Puritan Family. *Translated from the German by Brian Battershaw. 212 pp. 1969. About 42s.*

THE SOCIAL SERVICES

Forder, R. A. (Ed.). Penelope Hall's Social Services of Modern England. *288 pp. 1969. 35s.*

George, Victor. Social Security: Beveridge and After. *258 pp. 1968. 35s.*

Goetschius, George W. Working with Community Groups. *256 pp. 1969. 35s.*

Goetschius, George W. and **Tash, Joan.** Working with Unattached Youth. *416 pp. 1967. (2nd Impression 1968.) 40s.*

Hall, M. P., and **Howes, I. V.** The Church in Social Work. A Study of Moral Welfare Work undertaken by the Church of England. *320 pp. 1965. 35s.*

Heywood, Jean S. Children in Care: the Development of the Service for the Deprived Child. *264 pp. 2nd edition (revised) 1965. (2nd Impression 1966.) 32s.*

An Introduction to Teaching Casework Skills. *190 pp. 1964. 28s.*

Jones, Kathleen. Lunacy, Law and Conscience, 1744-1845: the Social History of the Care of the Insane. *268 pp. 1955. 25s.*

Mental Health and Social Policy, 1845-1959. *264 pp. 1960. (2nd Impression 1967.) 32s.*

Jones, Kathleen and **Sidebotham, Roy.** Mental Hospitals at Work. *220 pp. 1962. 30s.*

Kastell, Jean. Casework in Child Care. *Foreword by M. Brooke Willis. 320 pp. 1962. 35s.*

Morris, Pauline. Put Away: A Sociological Study of Institutions for the Mentally Retarded. *Approx. 288 pp. 1969. About 50s.*

Nokes, P. L. The Professional Task in Welfare Practice. *152 pp. 1967. 28s.*

Rooff, Madeline. Voluntary Societies and Social Policy. *350 pp. 15 tables. 1957. 35s.*

Timms, Noel. Psychiatric Social Work in Great Britain (1939-1962). *280 pp. 1964. 32s.*

Social Casework: Principles and Practice. *256 pp. 1964. (2nd Impression 1966.) 25s. Paper 15s.*

Trasler, Gordon. In Place of Parents: A Study in Foster Care. *272 pp. 1960. (2nd Impression 1966.) 30s.*

Young, A. F., and **Ashton, E. T.** British Social Work in the Nineteenth Century. *288 pp. 1956. (2nd Impression 1963.) 28s.*

Young, A. F. Social Services in British Industry. *272 pp. 1968. 40s.*

SOCIOLOGY OF EDUCATION

Banks, Olive. Parity and Prestige in English Secondary Education: a Study in Educational Sociology. *272 pp. 1955. (2nd Impression 1963.) 32s.*

Bentwich, Joseph. Education in Israel. *224 pp. 8 pp. plates. 1965. 24s.*

Blyth, W. A. L. English Primary Education. A Sociological Description. *1965. Revised edition 1967.*

1. Schools. *232 pp. 30s. Paper 12s. 6d.*
2. Background. *168 pp. 25s. Paper 10s. 6d.*

Collier, K. G. The Social Purposes of Education: Personal and Social Values in Education. *268 pp. 1959. (3rd Impression 1965.) 21s.*

Dale, R. R., and **Griffith, S.** Down Stream: Failure in the Grammar School. *108 pp. 1965. 20s.*

Dore, R. P. Education in Tokugawa Japan. *356 pp. 9 pp. plates. 1965. 35s.*

Edmonds, E. L. The School Inspector. *Foreword by Sir William Alexander. 214 pp. 1962. 28s.*

Evans, K. M. Sociometry and Education. *158 pp. 1962. (2nd Impression 1966.) 18s.*

Foster, P. J. Education and Social Change in Ghana. *336 pp. 3 maps. 1965. (2nd Impression 1967.) 36s.*

Fraser, W. R. Education and Society in Modern France. *150 pp. 1963. (2nd Impression 1968.) 25s.*

Hans, Nicholas. New Trends in Education in the Eighteenth Century. *278 pp. 19 tables. 1951. (2nd Impression 1966.) 30s.*
Comparative Education: A Study of Educational Factors and Traditions. *360 pp. 3rd (revised) edition 1958. (4th Impression 1967.) 25s. Paper 12s. 6d.*

Hargreaves, David. Social Relations in a Secondary School. *240 pp. 1967. (2nd Impression 1968.) 32s.*

Holmes, Brian. Problems in Education. A Comparative Approach. *336 pp. 1965. (2nd Impression 1967.) 32s.*

Mannheim, Karl and **Stewart, W. A. C.** An Introduction to the Sociology of Education. *206 pp. 1962. (2nd Impression 1965.) 21s.*

Morris, Raymond N. The Sixth Form and College Entrance. *231 pp. 1969. 40s.*

Musgrove, F. Youth and the Social Order. *176 pp. 1964. (2nd Impression 1968.) 25s. Paper 12s.*

Ortega y Gasset, José. Mission of the University. *Translated with an Introduction by Howard Lee Nostrand. 86 pp. 1946. (3rd Impression 1963.) 15s.*

Ottaway, A. K. C. Education and Society: An Introduction to the Sociology of Education. *With an Introduction by W. O. Lester Smith. 212 pp. Second edition (revised). 1962. (5th Impression 1968.) 18s. Paper 10s. 6d.*

Peers, Robert. Adult Education: A Comparative Study. *398 pp. 2nd edition 1959. (2nd Impression 1966.) 42s.*

Pritchard, D. G. Education and the Handicapped: 1760 to 1960. *258 pp. 1963. (2nd Impression 1966.) 35s.*

Richardson, Helen. Adolescent Girls in Approved Schools. *Approx. 360 pp. 1969. About 42s.*

Simon, Brian and **Joan** (Eds.). Educational Psychology in the U.S.S.R. *Introduction by Brian and Joan Simon. Translation by Joan Simon. Papers by D. N. Bogoiavlenski and N. A. Menchinskaia, D. B. Elkonin, E. A. Fleshner, Z. I. Kalmykova, G. S. Kostiuk, V. A. Krutetski, A. N. Leontiev, A. R. Luria, E. A. Milerian, R. G. Natadze, B. M. Teplov, L. S. Vygotski, L. V. Zankov. 296 pp. 1963. 40s.*

9

SOCIOLOGY OF CULTURE

Eppel, E. M., and M. Adolescents and Morality: A Study of some Moral Values and Dilemmas of Working Adolescents in the Context of a changing Climate of Opinion. *Foreword by W. J. H. Sprott. 268 pp. 39 tables. 1966. 30s.*

Fromm, Erich. The Fear of Freedom. *286 pp. 1942. (8th Impression 1960.) 25s. Paper 10s.*
The Sane Society. *400 pp. 1956. (4th Impression 1968.) 28s. Paper 14s.*

Mannheim, Karl. Diagnosis of Our Time: Wartime Essays of a Sociologist. *208 pp. 1943. (8th Impression 1966.) 21s.*
Essays on the Sociology of Culture. *Edited by Ernst Mannheim in co-operation with Paul Kecskemeti. Editorial Note by Adolph Lowe. 280 pp. 1956. (3rd Impression 1967.) 28s.*

Weber, Alfred. Farewell to European History: or The Conquest of Nihilism. *Translated from the German by R. F. C. Hull. 224 pp. 1947. 18s.*

SOCIOLOGY OF RELIGION

Argyle, Michael. Religious Behaviour. *224 pp. 8 figures. 41 tables. 1958. (4th Impression 1968.) 25s.*

Nelson, G. K. Spiritualism and Society. *313 pp. 1969. 42s.*

Stark, Werner. The Sociology of Religion. A Study of Christendom.
Volume I. Established Religion. *248 pp. 1966. 35s.*
Volume II. Sectarian Religion. *368 pp. 1967. 40s.*
Volume III. The Universal Church. *464 pp. 1967. 45s.*

Watt, W. Montgomery. Islam and the Integration of Society. *320 pp. 1961. (3rd Impression 1966.) 35s.*

SOCIOLOGY OF ART AND LITERATURE

Beljame, Alexandre. Men of Letters and the English Public in the Eighteenth Century: 1660-1744, Dryden, Addison, Pope. *Edited with an Introduction and Notes by Bonamy Dobrée. Translated by E. O. Lorimer. 532 pp. 1948. 32s.*

Misch, Georg. A History of Autobiography in Antiquity. *Translated by E. W. Dickes. 2 Volumes. Vol. 1, 364 pp., Vol. 2, 372 pp. 1950. 45s. the set.*

Schücking, L. L. The Sociology of Literary Taste. *112 pp. 2nd (revised) edition 1966. 18s.*

Silbermann, Alphons. The Sociology of Music. *Translated from the German by Corbet Stewart. 222 pp. 1963. 32s.*

SOCIOLOGY OF KNOWLEDGE

Mannheim, Karl. Essays on the Sociology of Knowledge. *Edited by Paul Kecskemeti. Editorial note by Adolph Lowe. 352 pp. 1952. (4th Impression 1967.) 35s.*

Stark, W. America: Ideal and Reality. The United States of 1776 in Contemporary Philosophy. *136 pp. 1947. 12s.*
  The Sociology of Knowledge: An Essay in Aid of a Deeper Understanding of the History of Ideas. *384 pp. 1958. (3rd Impression 1967.) 36s.*
  Montesquieu: Pioneer of the Sociology of Knowledge. *244 pp. 1960. 25s.*

URBAN SOCIOLOGY

Anderson, Nels. The Urban Community: A World Perspective. *532 pp. 1960. 35s.*

Ashworth, William. The Genesis of Modern British Town Planning: A Study in Economic and Social History of the Nineteenth and Twentieth Centuries. *288 pp. 1954. (3rd Impression 1968.) 32s.*

Bracey, Howard. Neighbours: On New Estates and Subdivisions in England and U.S.A. *220 pp. 1964. 28s.*

Cullingworth, J. B. Housing Needs and Planning Policy: A Restatement of the Problems of Housing Need and "Overspill" in England and Wales. *232 pp. 44 tables. 8 maps. 1960. (2nd Impression 1966.) 28s.*

Dickinson, Robert E. City and Region: A Geographical Interpretation. *608 pp. 125 figures. 1964. (5th Impression 1967.) 60s.*
  The West European City: A Geographical Interpretation. *600 pp. 129 maps. 29 plates. 2nd edition 1962. (3rd Impression 1968.) 55s.*
  The City Region in Western Europe. *320 pp. Maps. 1967. 30s. Paper 14s.*

Jackson, Brian. Working Class Community: Some General Notions raised by a Series of Studies in Northern England. *192 pp. 1968. (2nd Impression 1968.) 25s.*

Jennings, Hilda. Societies in the Making: a Study of Development and Redevelopment within a County Borough. *Foreword by D. A. Clark. 286 pp. 1962. (2nd Impression 1967.) 32s.*

Kerr, Madeline. The People of Ship Street. *240 pp. 1958. 28s.*

Mann, P. H. An Approach to Urban Sociology. *240 pp. 1965. (2nd Impression 1968.) 30s.*

Morris, R. N., and Mogey, J. The Sociology of Housing. Studies at Berinsfield. *232 pp. 4 pp. plates. 1965. 42s.*

Rosser, C., and Harris, C. The Family and Social Change. A Study of Family and Kinship in a South Wales Town. *352 pp. 8 maps. 1965. (2nd Impression 1968.) 45s.*

RURAL SOCIOLOGY

Chambers, R. J. H. Settlement Schemes in Africa: A Selective Study. *Approx. 268 pp. 1969. About 50s.*

Haswell, M. R. The Economics of Development in Village India. *120 pp. 1967. 21s.*

11

Littlejohn, James. Westrigg: the Sociology of a Cheviot Parish. *172 pp. 5 figures. 1963. 25s.*

Williams, W. M. The Country Craftsman: A Study of Some Rural Crafts and the Rural Industries Organization in England. *248 pp. 9 figures. 1958. 25s. (Dartington Hall Studies in Rural Sociology.)*
The Sociology of an English Village: Gosforth. *272 pp. 12 figures. 13 tables. 1956. (3rd Impression 1964.) 25s.*

SOCIOLOGY OF MIGRATION

Humphreys, Alexander J. New Dubliners: Urbanization and the Irish Family. *Foreword by George C. Homans. 304 pp. 1966. 40s.*

SOCIOLOGY OF INDUSTRY AND DISTRIBUTION

Anderson, Nels. Work and Leisure. *280 pp. 1961. 28s.*

Blau, Peter M., and **Scott, W. Richard.** Formal Organizations: a Comparative approach. *Introduction and Additional Bibliography by J. H. Smith. 326 pp. 1963. (4th Impression 1969.) 35s. Paper 15s.*

Eldridge, J. E. T. Industrial Disputes. Essays in the Sociology of Industrial Relations. *288 pp. 1968. 40s.*

Hollowell, Peter G. The Lorry Driver. *272 pp. 1968. 42s.*

Jefferys, Margot, with the assistance of Winifred Moss. Mobility in the Labour Market: Employment Changes in Battersea and Dagenham. *Preface by Barbara Wootton. 186 pp. 51 tables. 1954. 15s.*

Levy, A. B. Private Corporations and Their Control. *Two Volumes. Vol. 1, 464 pp., Vol. 2, 432 pp. 1950. 80s. the set.*

Liepmann, Kate. Apprenticeship: An Enquiry into its Adequacy under Modern Conditions. *Foreword by H. D. Dickinson. 232 pp. 6 tables. 1960. (2nd Impression 1960.) 23s.*

Millerson, Geoffrey. The Qualifying Associations: a Study in Professionalization. *320 pp. 1964. 42s.*

Smelser, Neil J. Social Change in the Industrial Revolution: An Application of Theory to the Lancashire Cotton Industry, 1770-1840. *468 pp. 12 figures. 14 tables. 1959. (2nd Impression 1960.) 50s.*

Williams, Gertrude. Recruitment to Skilled Trades. *240 pp. 1957. 23s.*

Young, A. F. Industrial Injuries Insurance: an Examination of British Policy. *192 pp. 1964. 30s.*

ANTHROPOLOGY

Ammar, Hamed. Growing up in an Egyptian Village: Silwa, Province of Aswan. *336 pp. 1954. (2nd Impression 1966.) 35s.*

Crook, David and **Isabel.** Revolution in a Chinese Village: Ten Mile Inn. *230 pp. 8 plates. 1 map. 1959. (2nd Impression 1968.) 21s.*
The First Years of Yangyi Commune. *302 pp. 12 plates. 1966. 42s.*

Dickie-Clark, H. F. The Marginal Situation. A Sociological Study of a Coloured Group. *236 pp. 1966. 40s.*

Dube, S. C. Indian Village. *Foreword by Morris Edward Opler. 276 pp. 4 plates. 1955. (5th Impression 1965.) 25s.*
India's Changing Villages: Human Factors in Community Development. *260 pp. 8 plates. 1 map. 1958. (3rd Impression 1963.) 25s.*

Firth, Raymond. Malay Fishermen. Their Peasant Economy. *420 pp. 17 pp. plates. 2nd edition revised and enlarged 1966. (2nd Impression 1968.) 55s.*

Gulliver, P. H. The Family Herds. A Study of two Pastoral Tribes in East Africa, The Jie and Turkana. *304 pp. 4 plates. 19 figures. 1955. (2nd Impression with new preface and bibliography 1966.) 35s.*
Social Control in an African Society: a Study of the Arusha, Agricultural Masai of Northern Tanganyika. *320 pp. 8 plates. 10 figures. 1963. (2nd Impression 1968.) 42s.*

Ishwaran, K. Shivapur. A South Indian Village. *216 pp. 1968. 35s.*
Tradition and Economy in Village India: An Interactionist Approach. *Foreword by Conrad Arensburg. 176 pp. 1966. (2nd Impression 1968.) 25s.*

Jarvie, Ian C. The Revolution in Anthropology. *268 pp. 1964. (2nd Impression 1967.) 40s.*

Jarvie, Ian C. and Agassi, Joseph. Hong Kong. A Society in Transition. *396 pp. Illustrated with plates and maps. 1968. 56s.*

Little, Kenneth L. Mende of Sierra Leone. *308 pp. and folder. 1951. Revised edition 1967. 63s.*

Lowie, Professor Robert H. Social Organization. *494 pp. 1950. (4th Impression 1966.) 50s.*

Mayer, Adrian C. Caste and Kinship in Central India: A Village and its Region. *328 pp. 16 plates. 15 figures. 16 tables. 1960. (2nd Impression 1965.) 35s.*
Peasants in the Pacific: A Study of Fiji Indian Rural Society. *232 pp. 16 plates. 10 figures. 14 tables. 1961. 35s.*

Smith, Raymond T. The Negro Family in British Guiana: Family Structure and Social Status in the Villages. *With a Foreword by Meyer Fortes. 314 pp. 8 plates. 1 figure. 4 maps. 1956. (2nd Impression 1965.) 35s.*

DOCUMENTARY

Meek, Dorothea L. (Ed.). Soviet Youth: Some Achievements and Problems. *Excerpts from the Soviet Press, translated by the editor. 280 pp. 1957. 28s.*

Schlesinger, Rudolf (Ed.). Changing Attitudes in Soviet Russia.
2. The Nationalities Problem and Soviet Administration. Selected Readings on the Development of Soviet Nationalities Policies. *Introduced by the editor. Translated by W. W. Gottlieb. 324 pp. 1956. 30s.*

Reports of the Institute of Community Studies

(*Demy 8vo.*)

Cartwright, Ann. Human Relations and Hospital Care. *272 pp. 1964. 30s.*

Patients and their Doctors. A Study of General Practice. *304 pp. 1967. 40s.*

Jackson, Brian. Streaming: an Education System in Miniature. *168 pp. 1964.* (*2nd Impression 1966.*) *21s. Paper 10s.*

Jackson, Brian and **Marsden, Dennis.** Education and the Working Class: Some General Themes raised by a Study of 88 Working-class Children in a Northern Industrial City. *268 pp. 2 folders. 1962.* (*4th Impression 1968.*) *32s.*

Marris, Peter. Widows and their Families. *Foreword by Dr. John Bowlby. 184 pp. 18 tables. Statistical Summary. 1958. 18s.*

Family and Social Change in an African City. A Study of Rehousing in Lagos. *196 pp. 1 map. 4 plates. 53 tables. 1961.* (*2nd Impression 1966.*) *30s.*

The Experience of Higher Education. *232 pp. 27 tables. 1964. 25s.*

Marris, Peter and **Rein, Martin.** Dilemmas of Social Reform. Poverty and Community Action in the United States. *256 pp. 1967. 35s.*

Mills, Enid. Living with Mental Illness: a Study in East London. *Foreword by Morris Carstairs. 196 pp. 1962. 28s.*

Runciman, W. G. Relative Deprivation and Social Justice. A Study of Attitudes to Social Inequality in Twentieth Century England. *352 pp. 1966.* (*2nd Impression 1967.*) *40s.*

Townsend, Peter. The Family Life of Old People: An Inquiry in East London. *Foreword by J. H. Sheldon. 300 pp. 3 figures. 63 tables. 1957.* (*3rd Impression 1967.*) *30s.*

Willmott, Peter. Adolescent Boys in East London. *230 pp. 1966. 30s.*

The Evolution of a Community: a study of Dagenham after forty years. *168 pp. 2 maps. 1963. 21s.*

Willmott, Peter and **Young, Michael.** Family and Class in a London Suburb. *202 pp. 47 tables. 1960.* (*4th Impression 1968.*) *25s.*

Young, Michael. Innovation and Research in Education. *192 pp. 1965. 25s. Paper 12s. 6d.*

Young, Michael and **McGeeney, Patrick.** Learning Begins at Home. A Study of a Junior School and its Parents. *About 128 pp. 1968. 21s. Paper 14s.*

Young, Michael and **Willmott, Peter.** Family and Kinship in East London. *Foreword by Richard M. Titmuss. 252 pp. 39 tables. 1957.* (*3rd Impression 1965.*) *28s.*

14

The British Journal of Sociology. *Edited by Terence P. Morris. Vol. 1, No. 1,*
March 1950 and Quarterly. Roy. 8vo., £3 annually, 15s. a number, post
free. (Vols. 1-18, £8 each. Individual parts £2 10s.

All prices are net and subject to alteration without notice

1268 H.B.